STUART

A History of the American Light Tank

Volume 1

by
R.P. Hunnicutt

Line Drawings
by
D.P. Dyer

Color Drawing
by
Uwe Feist

Foreword
by
Colonel James H. Leach DSC, U.S. Army (Retired)

PRESIDIO

Published by Presidio Press
Novato, California 94947

Library of Congress Cataloging-in-Publication Data

Hunnicutt, R.P., 1926-
   A history of the American light tank / by R.P. Hunnicutt.
   p. cm.
   Includes bibliographical references and index.
   Contents: v. 1. Stuart
   ISBN 0-89141-462-2
   1. Tanks (Military science) I. Title.
UG446.5.H847 1992
358'. 1883—dc20

Printed in the United States of America

CONTENTS

ACKNOWLEDGEMENTS

The research for this book has extended over the past thirty years parallel with the study of the medium and main battle tank development. As with the earlier books in this series, the collection of the late Colonel Robert J. Icks was a valuable source of material, particularly for the tanks prior to World War II. His collection is now in the library of the Patton Museum at Fort Knox, Kentucky. John Purdy, David Holt, and Charles Lemons of the Patton Museum were particularly helpful in locating both data and photographs from the Museum's collection. Some sections of this book could not have been written without their assistance. Major Patrick J. Cooney and Jon T. Clemens of Armor Magazine also were helpful in obtaining photographs of some of the early tanks.

I also would like to express my thanks to Colonel James Leach who agreed to write the foreword for this volume. His comments on his early service with the M2A2 and M3 light tanks were extremely useful. Dr. Norris Perkins was the source of many photographs of the early vehicles. His service as a tank officer during the formation and training of the Second Armored Division provided the basis for his excellent book "Roll Again Second Armored". This book is undoubtedly the best source on the early training with the M2A4 and M3 light tanks in the U.S. Army.

Technical details of the six-ton tank M1917 and its production background came from Hayes Otoupalik who has done extensive research on this vehicle. He also provided the photographs showing the tank in production. Dale Wilson also described many of the problems that had to be overcome before the tank reached production. These were included in his superb history of the World War I Tank Corps "Treat 'Em Rough".

Roy Hamilton and Jacques Littlefield tracked down details of the M3 and M5 light tank series to complete the data sheets on these vehicles. Leon Burg of the Technical Library at the Tank Automotive Command (TACOM) located numerous reports on the development program during World War II. The Ordnance Museum at Aberdeen Proving Ground also was a valuable source of information. Dr. William Atwater, Armando Framarini, and Alan Killinger provided material essential to the completion of this book.

Obtaining color photographs of the early light tanks presented a difficult problem. Fred Pernell at the National Archives in Washington, D.C. was extremely helpful in locating the color photographs included in this book.

In England, David Fletcher and George Forty of the Tank Museum at Bovington Camp found numerous photographs and documents pertaining to the American light tanks in British service. Additional valuable information came from Mike Willis at the Imperial War Museum in London.

As usual, the four view drawings were prepared by Phil Dyer and the dust jacket painting was the work of Uwe Feist. Alan Millar and HMS Typography were a great help in the final assembly of the text and photo captions.

Other contributors included: Bill Beasley and The First Armored Division Association, James D. Berry, Henry Gardiner, Lieutenant Colonel Elmer Gray, Michael Green, Colonel H.D. Heiberg, Colonel G.B. Jarrett, Robert Lessels, Donald J. Loughlin, Jim Mesko, Brigadier General Paul McD. Robinett, Michael Rogers, Brigadier G. MacLeod Ross, William Wagner, General I.D. White, Lieutenant Colonel George Witheridge, Randall Withrow, Charles Yust, and Steven Zaloga.

FOREWORD

by
Colonel James H. Leach DSC U.S. Army (Retired)

Those advocates and veterans of "light armor", soldiers—marines, engineers—designers, and historians will rejoice as they pore through these pages of Dick Hunnicutt's most recent contribution to the historical annals of the American Armored Forces.

His testimonial to the Stuart tank and related systems is one of his most comprehensive and difficult to date, because of the wide variance of combat and combat support vehicles studied, developed, or fielded since World War I. Thousands of hours of research and study of hundreds of photographs, documentation, drawings and interviews with many older and rapidly passing pioneers in the endeavor, has obviously been a challenging task.

My own exposure to light tanks began in the period 19 June 1938 through December 1941. I served as BOG-bow gunner, machine gunner and tank commander on the M2A2 "Mae West" light tank, which mounted one caliber .50 and two Browning caliber .30 machine guns. My unit, the 193rd Tank Battalion stationed at Fort Benning, Georgia, was equipped with these tanks, as was the 11th Tank Company at Schofield Barracks, Hawaii, when the Japanese attacked on 7 December 1941.

Nine days later, the 193rd tankers, reequipped with maneuver worn M3 light tanks repossessed from the 2nd Armored Division, were on a troop train headed west to San Francisco's Angel Island. The 2nd Armored Division's ordnance personnel, in order to improve the combat readiness of these tanks, established an assembly line to replace some of the engines and tracks on the M3s.

Ready for combat we were not! For example, two other non-commissioned officers and myself, plus a Private First Class volunteer from the 2nd Armored Division, were the only tankers in our company who had ever fired the tank's 37mm gun, much less trained on it. This situation foremost in mind, we set up an "on tank" training program while on the rolling trains. We moved our crews over the flat cars to our tanks for a crash familiarization course on the tank and the 37mm gun.

Ten days or so later, while our S.S. President Taylor plowed westward toward the Philippines, to reinforce our sister units the 192nd and the 194th Light Tank Battalions (as the scuttlebutt went), we were able to test fire the 37mm guns on some of the tanks positioned on the ship's open deck. We discovered to our dismay that several of the 37s would not return to battery for a second shot. When the gun went into recoil, the gun shield dropped just enough to bind the tube, preventing its return to battery—and to think we were enroute to war. Later, we enlarged the hole in the gun shield, but this was an ordnance job. Perhaps God was with us for we were to land "peacefully" at Honolulu harbor on 7 January 1942, exactly one month

following the surprise attack. We were to reinforce the Hawaiian defense forces along with the 11th Tank Company.

Subsequently, lessons of the Philippine and North African campaigns wisely resulted in the reorganization of our light tank battalions into medium battalions. These were equipped with three M4-Sherman tank companies and one company of light tanks using M3, M5, or M24 tanks. Their role as a fighting vehicle was changed to that of reconnaissance, scout, flank and advance guard, economy of force and escort where they made major contributions to the success of our world-wide armor operations.

Former tankers, Army Chief of Staff Gordon Sullivan and Colonel Harry Summers both noted the near tragedy with the employment of light infantry and light tanks during the Korean War. Task Force Smith of the 24th Infantry Division rushed from Japan along with light M24 Chaffee tanks from the 78 Heavy (in name only) Tank Battalion and the 24th Reconnaissance Company were no match for the North Koreans equipped with Russian made T34 tanks. The T34 had successfully stood against the famous German Panther during World War II. According to Colonel Summers, the rapid arrival of our M4 Shermans, M26 Pershings and M46 Pattons, along with the 3.5 inch antitank rocket, soon rectified the situation.

One of the underlying themes of this book highlights the continuing effort and study by our Army's branch boards, laboratories and industry from World War I to the present. Their unrelenting goal is, and has been, to design and develop for the future, as they improve upon existing vehicles and weapon systems for the safety and success of the user.

Certainly, the diversity of our industrial base has met and continues to meet this challenge. Who would have dreamed, for example, that the United Shoe Machinery Corporation would develop and produce Quad-50 anti-aircraft guns, that the Standard Oil Development and C.F. Braun Companies would take the lead in flame thrower development, or that Firestone would attempt to upgun the M3 light tank to mount a 75mm howitzer, or that J. Walter Christie, forever the innovator in combat vehicles, would remain a groomsman and never the groom.

Dozens of little known and now unknown companies participated in a myriad of programs in their overall effort to give our troops the best systems current technology could deliver. They still do.

In this publication, Dick Hunnicutt once again has assembled a superb book that the user, designer, developer, producer and historian can use in our continuing effort to provide weapons and support systems worthy of our courageous "Men of Steel"—those who serve in the American Armored Forces—the Combined Arms Team.

INTRODUCTION

The first American manned tanks to go into battle were the light tanks of the 1st Tank Brigade (later the 304th Tank Brigade) commanded by Lieutenant Colonel George S. Patton, Jr. during World War I. These tanks which attacked at St. Mihiel on 12 September 1918, were French built Renault M1917s, since the United States Army at that time had no tanks of its own. At home, a crash program was underway to produce an American version of the Renault. However, the lack of preparedness in the United States delayed the program and none were available prior to the end of hostilities, despite a massive expenditure of time and money. After the war, 952 of the American built Renaults were completed and designated first as the six-ton special tractor and later as the six-ton tank M1917. It continued to serve in the United States Army until the mid 1930s.

The objective of this volume is to trace the development history of the American light tank from the production and modification of the French Renault until the end of World War II. The greatest emphasis is on the wartime development of the M3, M5, and M24 series of light tanks and the other vehicles using these chassis. Some coverage also is included on postwar modifications and service of

the vehicles developed during World War II. In addition, the development of the 76mm gun motor carriage M18 and its various derivatives is described. Although the M18 was not a light tank, it had many of the same characteristics and seems appropriate for inclusion in this volume. The same consideration also applies to some of the tracked landing vehicles. In particular, the LVT(A)(1) and the LVT(A)(4) were classified by the United States Army as amphibian tanks despite their extremely light armor. Thus, they are also included.

No attempt has been made to provide a complete combat history of these vehicles. Some actions are briefly described to show when the various tanks were first committed to battle and to illustrate their characteristics, good and bad. The story of the tank in action is better left to those who fought in them and to the histories of the units that used them. Some of these histories have been briefly quoted to illustrate the performance of the tanks and the tactics they used against a frequently more powerful adversary.

As usual in a research project of this kind, many gaps remain to be filled. The author would be grateful for any information that would help to complete the early light tank history.

R.P. Hunnicutt
Belmont, California
April 1992

PART I

EARLY DEVELOPMENT OF THE LIGHT TANK

Above, a Renault FT17 is moving up with American troops. This version of the tank is armed with the Hotchkiss 8mm machine gun.

WORLD WAR I AND POSTWAR MODIFICATIONS

On 13 June 1917, General John J. Pershing arrived in France with the leading elements of the American Expeditionary Forces. Since the United States Army had no experience with tanks, a board was appointed in July to study their employment and to define the Army's requirements. The recommendations of this board proposed the use of both light and heavy tanks. The heavy tank selected was the Anglo-American Mark VIII design which was to be assembled in France using components manufactured in the United States and Great Britain. To meet the light tank requirement, arrangements were made to manufacture the French Renault FT17 in the United States. Initially, it was estimated that production quantities of both the light and heavy tanks would be available by April 1918. Unfortunately, these estimates proved to be wildly optimistic and no American built tanks reached the troops prior to the Armistice in November. Mark V and Mark V Star heavy tanks were obtained from Britain to equip one battalion and French built Renault FT17s were purchased for the light tank units.

Renault FT17s of the 1st/304th Tank Brigade go into action with the 35th Division near Boureuilles, France on 26 September 1918. The front tank is fitted with a machine gun and the second is armed with a 37mm cannon.

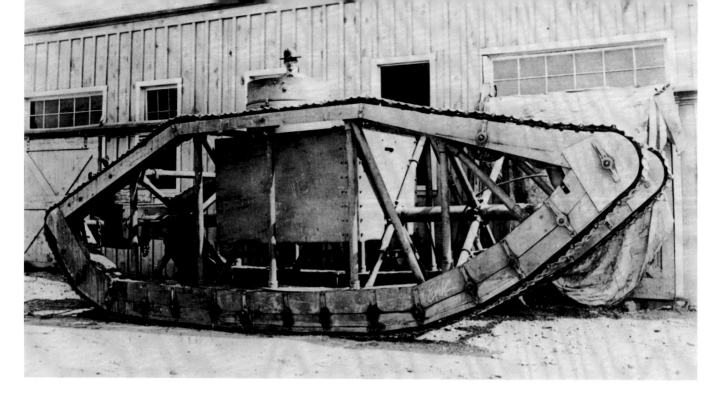

The skeleton tank is illustrated above. The armored box enclosing the two man crew and the power plant can be seen with a vision slot for the driver.

Considering the unprepared state of the country at the beginning of the war, the slow start of tank production is not surprising, despite the overconfident statements made by people who should have known better. In addition, the problem of adapting foreign equipment to American production methods also created difficulties. For example, the Renault tank design used metric measurements and the drawings had to be converted to the English system for production in American plants. Also, although the major assemblies in the French tank were interchangeable, many of the individual components were not. In French practice, skilled craftsman were used to hand fit these items into a complete assembly. Redesign of these components was required to adapt them to the American system of mass production. These factors, plus pride in their own engineering capabilities, were strong incentives for American

companies to propose their own tank designs rather than manufacture a foreign vehicle.

One interesting homegrown concept was proposed by the Pioneer Tractor Company of Winona, Minnesota. Referred to as the skeleton tank, it was an attempt to duplicate the trench crossing ability of the large rhomboidal British heavy tanks using a lightweight vehicle. Although it was 300 inches long, 101 inches wide, and 114 inches high, its weight was only about nine tons. The 12 inch wide, 11 inch pitch tracks were carried on rigidly mounted rollers installed on a tubular frame sheathed with wood. The complete structure was assembled using iron pipe and standard plumbing fittings. The two man crew rode in a ½ inch thick armored box in the center of the vehicle with the driver in the front and the gunner in the rear under a turret. A single .30 caliber machine gun was proposed

The front (left) and rear (right) views below clearly show the pipes and fittings used to assemble the skeleton tank. Details of the tracks also are visible.

The open top hull and dummy turret of the skeleton tank appear at the right. Note the cramped position for the driver between the two engines.

as armament. Two liquid-cooled Beaver four cylinder engines with a combined output of 100 horsepower were installed with radiators and transmissions. One power train was located on each side of the armored compartment. The transmission provided two speeds forward and one reverse with a maximum speed of five miles/hour. Only one pilot vehicle was assembled and it was fitted with a dummy turret and armament.

A more successful American design was the Ford three-ton tank or to use its offical designation, the three-ton special tractor M1918. Intended to take advantage of the Ford Motor Company's huge production capacity, it utilized as many standard Ford automobile parts as possible. Although referred to as a three ton vehicle, it actually had an empty weight of about 6200 pounds. There was no turret and the two man crew rode in the front hull with the driver on the right and the gunner on the left. The armor ranged in thickness from ½ inch on the front vertical surface to ¼ inch on the floor. The armament consisted of a single .30 caliber machine gun in the front hull. The gun mount selected for production was similar to that on the American version of the Renault FT17. This mount was intended for the Marlin tank machine gun. However, the new Browning .30 caliber tank machine gun was originally

installed in a ball mount similar to that adopted later for both the six-ton tank and the heavy tank Mark VIII. At one time, the 37mm gun also was considered as alternate armament, similar to the arrangement on the Renault FT17. The vehicle measured 160 inches long, 64 inches wide, 64 inches high and was powered by two Ford Model T engines with planetary transmissions mounted in the rear hull. The transmissions provided two speeds forward and one reverse. The two engines were geared together and the combination was equipped with a self-starter. The twin engine power plant developed a total of 34 horsepower at 1700 rpm and propelled the tank through a worm gear final drive to each track sprocket. At that time, its power to weight ratio of 9.4 horsepower/ton was considered very high providing a maximum speed of 8 miles/hour. Like many other tanks of the period, the little vehicle was cramped

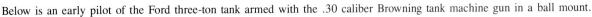

Below is an early pilot of the Ford three-ton tank armed with the .30 caliber Browning tank machine gun in a ball mount.

Above, the early Ford three-ton tank on the left is compared with the later version on the right. Note that the ball mount for the Browning tank machine gun has been replaced by the mount for the Marlin tank machine gun. Additional details of the later vehicle can be seen below.

and hot inside, but it handled easily with one lever controlling each transmission. The neutral position was in the center of the lever arc with the low gear to the rear and the high gear in the forward position. Turns were achieved by putting one lever in neutral and the other in high. Use of the foot brake on the neutral side served to tighten the turn. A 17 gallon fuel tank gave the vehicle a range of about 34 miles. Two bogies, each with three rollers, supported each side of the tank through a leaf spring suspension. The upper track run was carried on two rollers per side mounted on leaf springs. The single pin steel tracks were seven inches wide with a seven inch pitch. There were 40 shoes per track with a ground contact length of 56 inches at zero penetration. This resulted in a ground pressure of 9.2 psi, but this rapidly decreased as the track penetration increased.

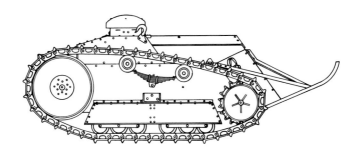

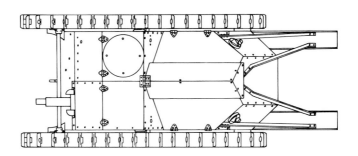

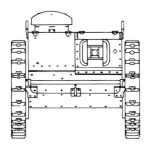

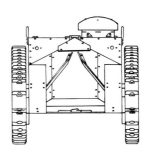

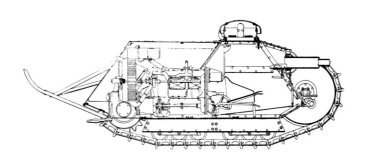

Scale 1:48

Three-Ton Special Tractor M1918

The spaced out panel on the rear hull plate was a much later addition to aid the flow of cooling air. The original production vehicles had a single piece rear hull plate. The exhaust pipes also have been relocated.

The Ordnance Department was highly impressed by the Ford vehicle's low cost and ease of production. As a result, they enthusiastically recommended its adoption to General Pershing. One of the initial run of 15 tanks was completed by Ford and shipped to France for evaluation by the Tank Corps. After tests in early November 1918, the Tank Corps reported that it was inadequate for use as a light tank and recommended that it be procured as a light artillery tractor. They considered that only the Renault FT17 met the minimum requirements for a light tank. A contract had been awarded to Ford for 15,000 of the three ton vehicles and a production rate of 100 per day was expected by early 1919. In these quantities, the cost was estimated to be $4000/vehicle. However, the contract was cancelled after the Armistice and only the original 15 vehicles were produced.

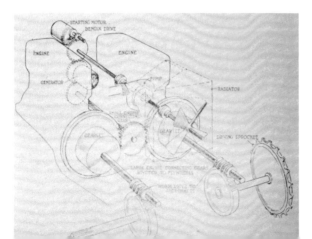

Details of the Ford power train are shown above and at the left. The method of springing the suspension bogies is sketched below.

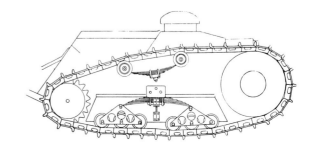

Above, the three-ton Ford tank is fitted with towing gear and, at the left below, it is towing a 75mm gun and caisson. Note the solid rear hull plate on this vehicle and the original exhaust pipes.

At the right above, the Ford three-ton tank is under test during May 1919. Below, two of the little vehicles are fitted with an unknown special attachment after the removal of the tail piece. Again, note the original solid rear hull plate and the exhaust arrangement.

The Ford Mark I is shown above. The armament was not installed. Note the similarity of the suspension bogies to those on the Ford three-ton tank.

Another Ford project was the three man tank referred to as the Mark I. This design was armed with a 37mm gun in a turret and a .30 caliber machine gun in the right front hull. The driver was located in the left front hull. The vehicle measured 198 inches long, 78 inches wide, 93 inches high and it weighed about 15,000 pounds with a maximum armor thickness of ½ inch. A 60 horsepower, six cylinder, liquid-cooled Hudson engine gave it a power to weight ratio of 8 horsepower/ton and a maximum speed of 9 miles/hour. Like the smaller Ford vehicle, the Mark I utilized a separate planetary transmission for each track. Leaf springs supported the tank through three bogies, each with three rollers, on each side of the vehicle. The steel single pin track was 12 inches wide with a pitch of seven inches. A contract for 1000 Mark I tanks was awarded to Ford, but it was cancelled after the Armistice and only the single pilot was completed. Tests of this vehicle revealed that the center of gravity was located too far to the rear limiting the tank's ability to negotiate obstacles. Also, the track adjustment method was unsatisfactory since the idlers could not be moved independently.

Front and rear views of the Mark I in its original configuration appear below. At the right, the track support rollers have been removed. This latter photograph was dated 18 March 1925.

Another light tank, designated as the Mark II, was identical to the American version of the Renault, except that it was powered by the 60 horsepower Hudson engine used in the Mark I. Only one pilot of this vehicle was approved for assembly and further work was cancelled with the end of the war.

Above is the general assembly area at the Van Dorn Iron Works, Cleveland, Ohio. The photographs on this and the next four pages were provided through the courtesy of the Van Dorn Plastic Machinery Company, Strongsville, Ohio, by way of Mark L. Beveridge and Hayes Otoupalik.

By October 1918, most of the problems had been resolved and production of the American version of the Renault FT17 was finally underway. Contracts for 4440 of these tanks had been awarded to the Van Dorn Iron Works of Cleveland, Ohio; the Maxwell Motor Company of Dayton, Ohio; and the C. L. Best Company of Dayton, Ohio. By the Armistice on 11 November 1918, 64 tanks had been completed and a total of 209 were finished by the end of December with another 289 being assembled. Two of the new tanks arrived at Bourg, France on 20 November 1918 and eight more were received in early December. A total of 952 American Renaults were completed by the time

production was ended. They consisted of two soft steel pilot tanks, 374 tanks armed with the 37mm gun, 526 machine gun tanks, and 50 unarmed signal tanks equipped with a radio in a fixed superstructure. The Van Dorn Iron Works built 400 of the 950 production tanks and C. L. Best and the Maxwell Motor Company produced 325 and 225 tanks respectively.

The Renault FT17 pioneered the configuration that was to dominate future tank design. With the armament mounted in a fully rotating turret, the driver in the front hull, and the power plant in the rear, it was widely copied and produced throughout the world.

Below is the turret assembly area at the Van Dorn Iron Works.

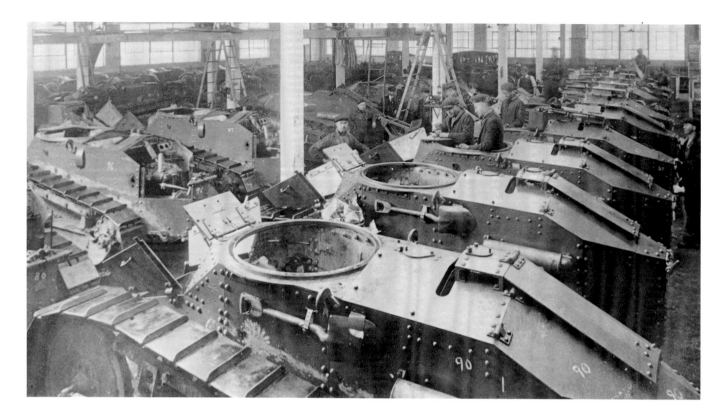

The hull and chassis of the M1917 tanks are undergoing final testing and inspection at the Van Dorn Iron Works prior to the turret installation.

The American built Renault differed in several features from the original French tank. Initially, the American vehicle was designated as the six-ton special tractor model 1917, but this was soon changed to the six-ton tank M1917. The large steel rimmed wooden idlers on the French vehicle were replaced by all steel idlers on the American model and a fire screen bulkhead was installed separating the crew from the engine compartment. Experiments were successfully conducted using replaceable laminated glass plates behind the vision slots to prevent the penetration of bullet splash. However, this feature was not adopted for the production tanks.

Below, the front of the completed six-ton tank M1917 is shown with the hatches open and closed.

18

The completed M1917 tank appears above. This version is fitted with the mount for the .30 caliber Marlin tank machine gun.

Below are rear views of the completed M1917 tank with the engine compartment doors open and closed.

The two types of armament are illustrated here. Above is the 37mm gun M1916 in the original production mount. Below, the .30 caliber Marlin tank machine gun is installed in its mount.

Above, the M1917 tanks are operating during a test run at the Van Dorn Iron Works prior to the turret installation. Below, the completed tanks are ready for shipment. As mentioned earlier, the photographs on this and the previous four pages were provided through the courtesy of the Van Dorn Plastic Machinery Company, Strongsville, Ohio, by way of Mark L. Beveridge and Hayes Otoupalik.

The three views above show the six-ton tank M1917 as originally designed and built. This version has the mount for the 37mm gun fitted, but the gun itself has not been installed.

The tank hull was a bolted assembly of flat, face-hardened, steel armor plates connected by commercial angle iron. The thickness varied from $\frac{6}{10}$ inches on the vertical plates to ¼ inch on the floor. A riveted steel tail-piece assembly was attached to the rear of the hull to improve the trench crossing ability. Access to the driver's station was through three doors in the front hull. Two of these were hinged at the hull sides and were latched together at the center. The third door was hinged at the top of the driver's cupola and could be raised to permit an unobstructed view in the forward direction. A slot in this door provided forward vision when it was closed. Four additional vision slots were located in the armor plates on each

side of the driver. The armor configuration around the driver's compartment differed from that on the French built tank which had only two additional vision slots. The driver was seated about six inches above the hull floor and his instrument panel was mounted just below eye level at his right. Webbing stretched between the hull side walls formed a back rest for the driver.

The hull construction of the M1917 is illustrated in these three photographs. The numbers in the view at the lower right indicate the rear armor plate (1), side armor plate (2, 3), track frame (4), and the track support bracket (5).

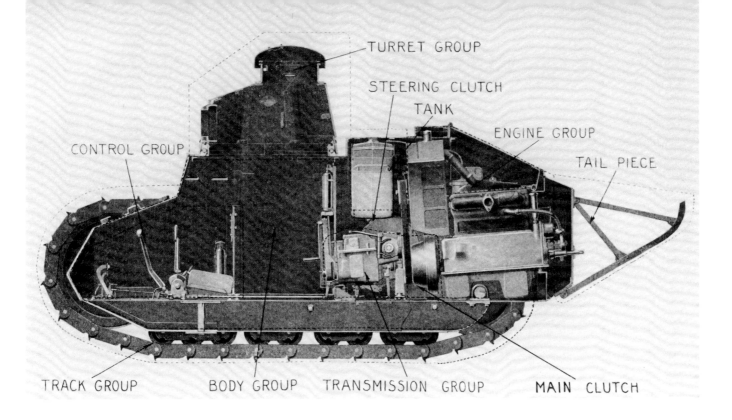

TURRET GROUP

STEERING CLUTCH
TANK

ENGINE GROUP

TAIL PIECE

CONTROL GROUP

TRACK GROUP   BODY GROUP   TRANSMISSION GROUP   MAIN CLUTCH

The sectional view above and the lubrication chart below at the right reveal the internal arrangement of the M1917.

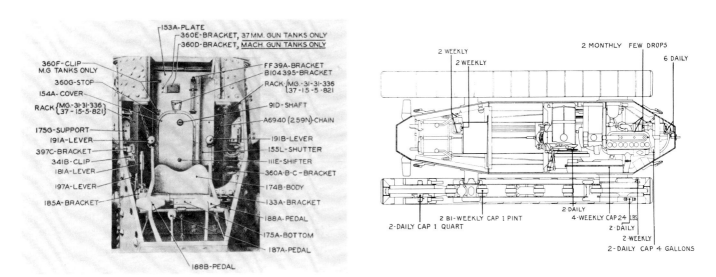

The driver's compartment is above at the left and his instruments and controls are shown below. The numbers in the left view indicate the gear shift (1), spark lever (2), throttle (3), steering clutch levers (4), clutch (5), accelerator pedal (6), and brake (7). The right-hand view shows the magneto (1), speedometer (2), oil pressure gage (3), ignition switch (4), odometer (5), wire conduit (6), and spark plug leads (7).

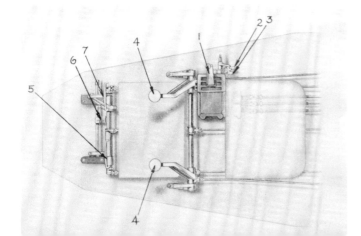

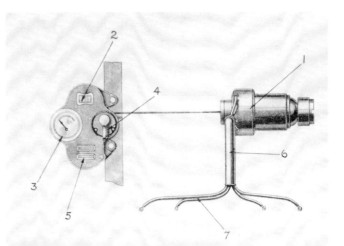

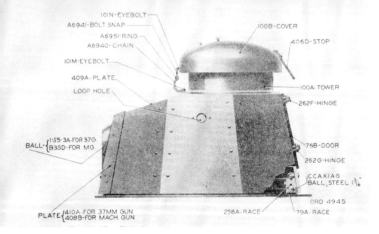

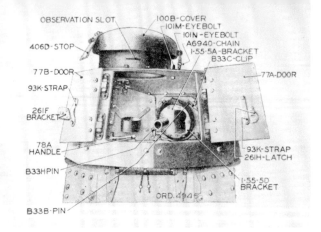

The side and interior of the M1917 turret are shown above. The interior view includes the mount for the 37mm gun. The fully stowed late version of the 37mm gun tank M1917 can be seen below from the front and side. The sectional drawing is a round of 37mm ammunition.

An octagonal turret was installed on a bearing race in the hull roof above and behind the driver's station. This turret was assembled from eight flat $\frac{6}{10}$ inches thick armor plates bolted together with angle iron. It was free to rotate 360 degrees, but it could be locked in any position by the turret brake. Two pistol ports, referred to at that time as loop holes, were provided, one in each side wall of the turret. A round cupola, called a tower, was mounted on the turret roof. Its dome shaped cover was hinged and could be partially raised for ventilation. This movement was limited by a stop on the rear of the cover. The tower contained three vision slots and a hole was later added to the dome for the use of signal flags. All of the American built tanks were fitted with this octagonal turret assembled from flat steel plates. However, many of the French built vehicles featured a rounded steel turret. Access to the gunner's station was through doors in the rear and right rear turret walls. The gunner stood at the rear of the driver or he could be suspended from the turret in a sling type seat. Armament consisted of either a 37mm gun or a .30 caliber machine gun. On tanks equipped with the cannon, 238 rounds of 37mm ammunition were stowed in two 100 round hull side racks, one 13 round side rack, and one 25 round tray in the turret. Originally, the 13 round rack was intended for smoke ammunition. The final stowage arrangement for

tanks armed with a machine gun specified 4200 rounds of .30 caliber ammunition in 84 belts containing 50 rounds each. Forty-two belts were stowed on each side of the hull.

Below are two views of the French Renault FT17 used by American troops. The early turret at the left could only mount the 8mm Hotchkiss machine gun. The later turret at the right could be fitted with either the machine gun or the 37mm cannon. Note that the muffler is located on the right side of the French built tanks.

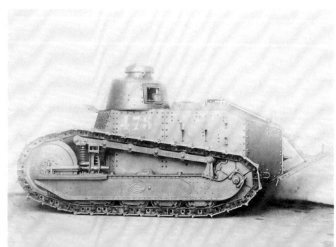

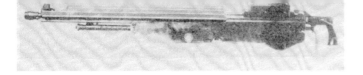

Above are the Marlin tank machine gun (left) and the Browning tank machine gun (right). Below are two versions of the early Marlin mount modified to carry the Browning tank machine gun. The design in the two right-hand photographs was adopted as an interim installation pending the availability of the the new ball mount.

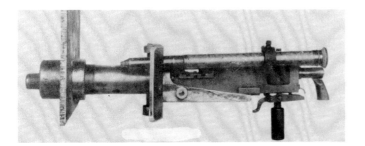

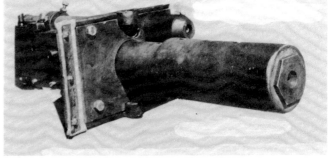

Although all of the production tanks were designed for the use of the Marlin tank machine gun, tests of the new Browning gun indicated that it was a much superior weapon. Thus, in September 1919, the Tank Corps representative to the Ordnance Technical Board recommended that the Marlin gun be replaced by the Browning in all of the tanks armed with a machine gun. This resulted in a number of interim designs, some of which were intended to fit the Browning gun into the original Marlin mount.

Some of these utilized a telescopic sight. However, the final design standardized a 9.1 inch diameter ball mount with open sights for the Browning now designated as the .30 caliber tank machine gun M1919. The ball mount movement was limited to 30 degrees and 48 degrees in the horizontal and vertical directions respectively. Except for the front plate assembly and ammunition stowage, the cannon and machine gun turrets with the ball mounts were identical.

One version of the ball mount is illustrated in the sketch at the right and in the photograph at the lower right. A telescopic sight could be installed on this mount, but it was not included on the M1917. The machine gun version of the late six-ton tank M1917 appears below. Note that the exhaust muffler is located on the left side.

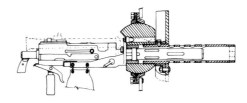

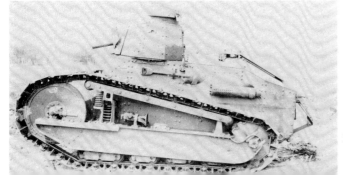

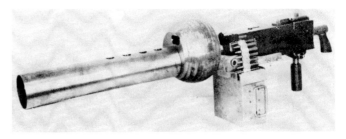

Above, the late (left) and early (right) versions of the 37mm gun tank M1917 can be compared. At the left is a French manufactured 37mm gun installed in the M1917 using an early version of the ball mount. The shield and part of the turret armor have been removed to reveal the weapon.

Originally, it had been intended to arm the cannon tanks with the 37mm French Puteaux gun. However, an early decision replaced this weapon with the 37mm gun M1916. This gun was identical to the infantry cannon with a modified cradle. The mount underwent several design changes before it was standardized during the postwar period as an 11⅞ inch diameter ball in the turret front plate. The ball mount permitted a movement of 30 degrees horizontally by 56 degrees vertically and a telescopic sight was located on the left side of the cannon.

Below, the French FT17 (right) can be compared with the U.S. M1917 (left). The latter shows that it was possible for a large man to drive the six-ton tank. In this photograph dated 1927, 2nd Lieutenant Robert J. Icks has folded his 6 feet 4 inches into the driver's compartment. Note the differences in the front armor configuration between the two tanks. Fake vision slots have been painted on the hull and turret of the French tank.

26

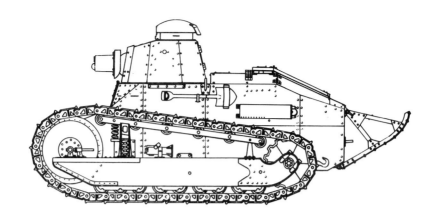

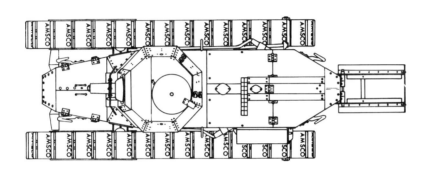

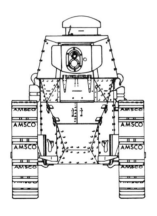 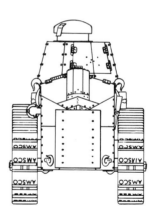

THE TURRETS BELOW ARE ARMED WITH THE MARLIN TANK MACHINE GUN (LEFT) AND THE BROWNING TANK MACHINE GUN (RIGHT)

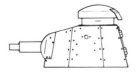 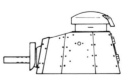

Scale 1:48

©D.P. Dyer

Six-Ton Tank M1917

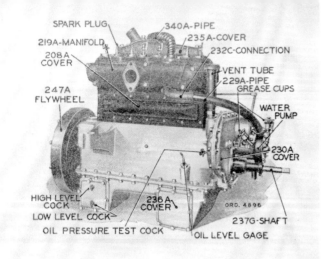

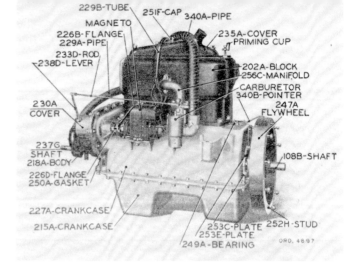

The exhaust side (left) and intake side (right) of the Buda engine that powered the M1917 are shown above. Below, the fuel system is at the right and the mounting arrangement for the exhaust muffler appears at the left. The numbers indicate the exhaust manifold (1), exhaust extension (2), muffler header (3), and the muffler (4). Again, note that the latter was mounted on the left side of the American built tanks.

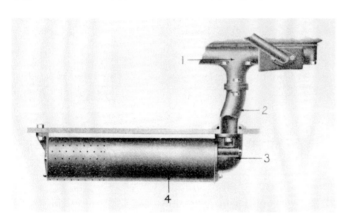

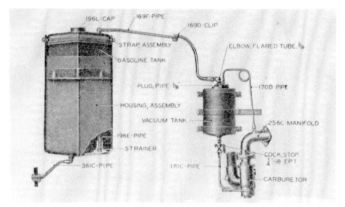

The four cylinder Buda HU gasoline engine was adapted to replace the Renault power plant in the American built vehicle. Mounted in the rear hull engine compartment, it developed 42 horsepower at 1460 rpm and drove the tank at a maximum road speed of about 5½ miles/hour through a selective sliding gear transmission. The latter provided four speeds forward and one reverse.

The power train for the M1917 is illustrated in the drawing below. At the right is the inside crank arrangement for starting the tank engine under emergency conditions. The numbers indicate the handle (1), sprocket (2), chain (3), lower sprocket (4), pinion and gear (5, 6), engaging plunger (7), and the jaw clutch (8).

Two steering clutches, one installed on each side of the transmission, controlled the distribution of power to the tracks. The two steering clutch hand levers enabled the driver to maneuver the tank using clutch-brake steering. Pulling back either lever released the clutch on that side causing the tank to turn in that direction. Further movement of the lever applied the brake on that side and the tank would pivot around that track. Power was transmitted from the steering clutches through the reduction gears on each side of the tank to the track sprockets.

A 30 gallon fuel tank was installed in the engine compartment above the transmission. The double walls of this

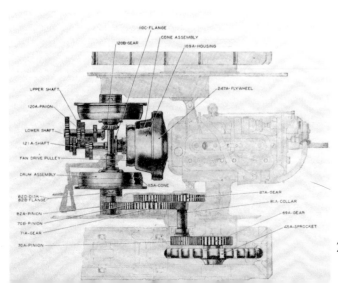

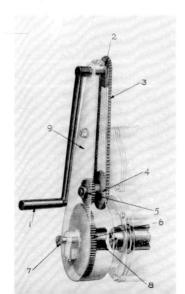

28

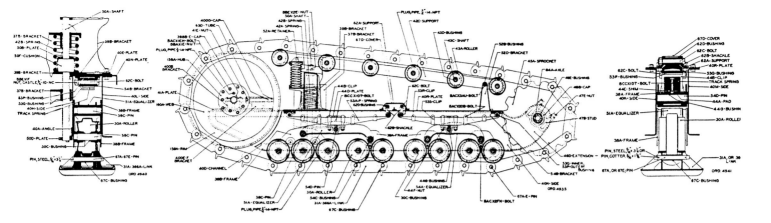

Details of the M1917's suspension can be seen in the drawings above. The sectional view at the left was taken through the suspension shaft and large coil spring. The right-hand section is through the mount for the bogie leaf spring. At the right is a photograph of the hull with the tracks installed. The numbers indicate the idler (1), hull armor (2), track frame (3), rollers (4), roller frame (5), upper roller frame (6), sprocket (7), track frame extension (8), track tension spring (9), support spring (10), track (11), leaf spring support (12), an pivot bracket (13).

tank were separated by a layer of felt to absorb fuel leakage if the fuel tank was penetrated. When the felt was saturated, a tube connected to the outer shell drained the excess fuel to the outside of the vehicle.

The tank was supported by a combination coil and leaf spring suspension. Two bogies, referred to as trucks, were installed inside an inverted U beam track frame on each side of the vehicle. The front and rear bogies were fitted with five and four track rollers respectively and were attached to the track frame by leaf springs. The track frame itself was pivoted at the rear around the rear axle and attached at the front to a hull bracket through a large coil spring. The track tension was maintained by pressure from six track support rollers mounted on a support frame. This frame was pivoted to the track frame at the rear and supported by the hull bracket at the front through a small coil spring. Track tension was adjusted by shifting the large steel idler at the front of each track. The 13⅜ inch wide, cast steel, single pin track with integral grousers had a pitch of 9.842 inches and was assembled with 32 shoes per track.

For severe conditions, 16 additional separate grousers (8 per track) were provided later for installation spaced equally around the track.

The six-ton tank was not equipped with a self-starter and had to be hand cranked. This required the tail piece to be disconnected and lowered to the ground to permit the use of the crank. For emergencies, an inside cranking device was installed extending through the fire screen bulkhead into the crew compartment. Needless to say, it was difficult to use in the limited space available.

In late 1919, a self-starter was installed experimentally in one tank by the North East Electric Company. It proved to be satisfactory during tests and the Tank Corps recommended the same installation for all of the American built six-ton tanks. However, this recommendation was rejected because of costs.

Below, the mechanism for adjusting the track tension by moving the idler appears at the left and a separate track link and grouser can be seen at the right.

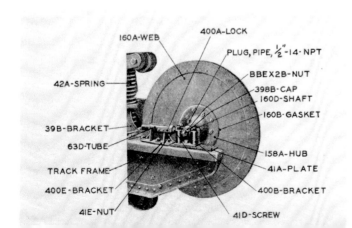

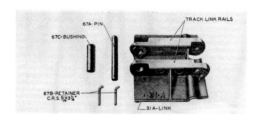

29

The photographs above show the installation of the Kegresse-Hinstin suspension and track on the six-ton tank. Apparently the cupola was removed in the left-hand view. Note that this is a French FT17 with the muffler on the right side and the different front armor configuration.

Despite the limited funds available, several other projects were proposed to upgrade the six-ton tank. Captain S. H. Clapp, an officer stationed at the Camp Meade, Maryland Tank School, designed a new spring suspension for the vehicle.

In January 1922, Item 4415 of the Ordnance Committee Minutes (OCMs) authorized the procurement of the Kegresse-Hinstin rubber track adapter kit for one six-ton tank. Although it was originally intended for installation on an American built tank, the adapter kit was designed to fit the French Renault and it was necessary to obtain one of these from the Tank School for the test program. The new suspension and tracks were installed during August 1925 under the supervision of an engineer from the factory. The tests revealed that the track life was limited to about 400 miles by the failure of the drive fins and the rubber grousers. However, the rubber tracks provided a good ride and the system was much quieter than the original steel tracks and suspension. The road damage also was greatly reduced.

At that time, all funds for tank development and operation were extremely scarce and policy required that all available resources be directed toward the development of a new light tank rather than the modification of a vehicle already obsolete. Despite these restrictions, one last effort was made to improve the six-ton tank. During 1929, a single vehicle was modified at the Holabird Quartermaster Depot. The hull was lengthened to permit the installation of a new power plant. This was a six cylinder Franklin air-cooled engine that developed 67 horsepower. The original transmission was used with a reinforced case. The tank was equipped with a self-starter and the idlers were modified to reduce noise. After tests, six additional tanks were modified in the Ordnance Department shops during 1930 and 1931. These vehicles were fitted with the Franklin series 145 air-cooled engine which developed 100 horsepower at 3100 rpm and the engine, transmission, and clutches were mounted on a frame which allowed them to be removed from the vehicle as a unit. A twelve volt electrical system also was installed to permit the use of a radio. Later, the original pilot tank was modified to the same standard bringing the total production of the improved tank up to seven. The empty weight of the modified vehicle increased to about 14,200 pounds and the engine was governed down to 2500 rpm to minimize the failure of other components in the system. This limited the maximum road speed to

The pilot installation of the Franklin engine in the M1917 can be seen below. This vehicle served as the prototype for the M1917A1 and it was later brought up to that standard. Note the differences between the original pilot and the M1917A1 on the following page.

The standardized M1917A1 is above with its power train at the right. Note that the latter was mounted on a single frame for easy removal. Although the tank was equipped with a self-starter, it retained the inside crank which can be seen at the left side of the photograph.

about 9 miles/hour. Standardized as the six-ton tank M1917A1, all seven vehicles were used by the new Mechanized Force formed at Fort Eustis, Virginia in 1930. Another design study by Captain George H. Rarey showed the M1917A1 fitted with a Christie independent suspension and a modified transmission. It also was armed with a 37mm gun and a coaxial .30 caliber machine gun.

Below is a concept study prepared by Captain George H. Rarey adapting a Christie type suspension to the M1917A1.

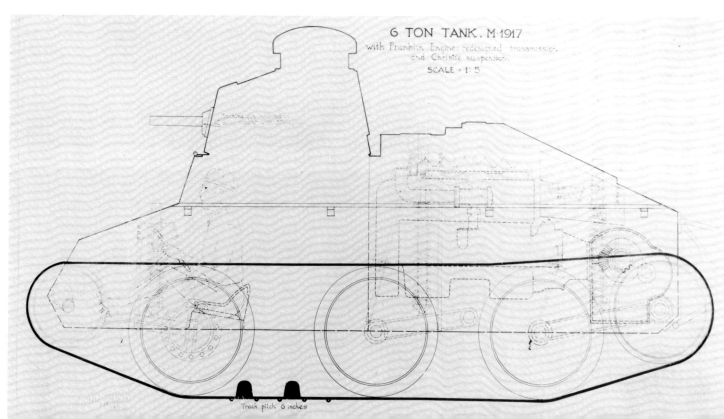

6 TON TANK. M·1917
with Franklin Engine, redesigned transmission
and Christie suspension.
SCALE = 1:5

Track pitch 6 inches

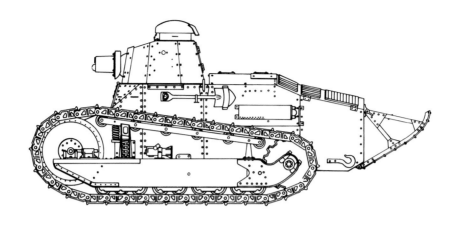

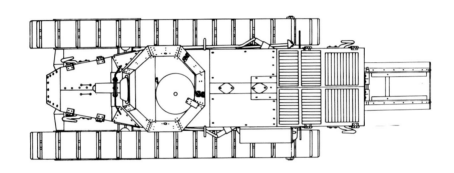

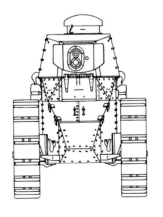 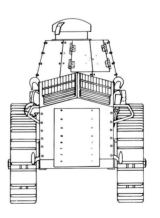

Scale 1:48

Six-Ton Tank M1917A1

The American built M1917 signal tank is shown above and at the left. Note the lack of armament and the large armored superstructure required to house the radios of that period.

The original French FT17 tank production included an unarmed version on which the turret was replaced by a large fixed superstructure housing a radio and its operator. As mentioned earlier, this signal tank also was included in the American production run. However, on 14 November 1924, the requirement for a signal tank was eliminated from the organization of the light tank battalion and OCM 4369, dated 6 January 1925, recommended that all such tanks be placed in storage. At that time, there were 45 signal tanks on hand. Work continued on the development of radio equipment suitable for installation in the limited space available in the standard fighting tank. One such set was the SCR 189 which incorporated both sending and receiving equipment. The SCR 190 receiver also was installed in the six-ton tank for test purposes.

At the left, a signal tank is in operation during a training exercise. Below is a signal tank based upon the M1917A1 tank. Note that the antenna has been shifted from the superstructure roof to the cupola cover.

33

The M1917 at the left is equipped with a radio and the antenna is installed on the cupola cover. The SCR 190 radio receiver is shown above and, at the left below, it is installed in the M1917. The SCR 189 (receiver and transmitter) appears at the right below.

Below are three M1917s from the 66th Infantry (Tanks) equipped with radios and the cupola mounted antennas. Two are machine gun tanks and the center vehicle is armed with the 37mm gun.

These radio equipped M1917s are participating in training exercises.

The six-ton tank provided the basic vehicle for a number of experiments. One of these was the development of smoke screen equipment for use during armored operations. Initial experiments used white phosphorus in cylinders attached to the sides of the vehicle. The bulk of this arrangement, combined with the hazards involved in

handling the white phosphorus, ended this phase of the program. The work then shifted to the use of titanium tetrachloride in three experimental arrangements. The first used two cylinders of titanium tetrachloride and one small cylinder of carbon dioxide to supply pressure for ejecting the titanium tetrachloride. The cylinders were mounted on top of a six-ton tank. Tests with this apparatus indicated that a titanium tetrachloride smoke screen was practical, but the arrangement was much too bulky. The second experiment placed all three cylinders inside the tank, but they occupied too much of the limited space inside the fighting compartment. A third configuration was similar to the second, except that the titanium tetrachloride cylinders were mounted at the rear of the tank outside of the armor. However, they were controlled from inside the vehicle. Tests at Edgewood Arsenal during 1926 indicated that a two mile long screen approximately 50 feet high could be maintained for 15 to 18 minutes under moderate breeze conditions. The cloud produced was dense and effective.

The photographs above and below show the M1917 fitted with the two rear mounted tanks for producing smoke screens.

The M1917s in these two photographs are armed with the Browning tank machine gun in the interim mount adapted from that for the original Marlin tank machine gun. More details of this mount can be seen on page 25.

The original intention was to transport the M1917 on a trailer towed by a truck (top left). However, this method was dropped after numerous accidents. Heavy trucks were then adapted as tank carriers (top right and below). Note that the tail piece was frequently removed when the tank was being transported.

At the left, an M1917 has just climbed onto its carrier.

Below, the M1917s from the 66th Infantry (Tanks) prepare to mount their carriers.

37

The Marine Corps M1917 (top left) is part of the Expeditionary Force to Shanghai, China in 1927. Compare the final ball type machine gun mount on this tank with the original Marlin machine gun mount on the M1917 at Fort Knox (top right). Below, the M1917s are engaged in training operations. The grill over the engine cooling air exhaust port also was a postwar modification.

No further tanks were modified to the M1917A1 standard, but they, along with the M1917s, remained in use for training purposes, particularly for National Guard units, until the late 1930s. With the outbreak of World War II, many of these old tanks were transferred to Britain and Canada for use in their training program.

Below, an M1917A1 (left) is being used for instruction. At the right, an early unarmed six-ton tank serves as a tractor to tow a 155mm howitzer.

Above and at the left, the M1917s are loaded onto railway cars for transfer to Canada in 1940. Note that the signal tanks (above) also were included.

Below are three M1917s during training at Camp Borden, Canada in October 1940.

NEW LIGHT TANK DESIGNS

During the year following the Armistice in November 1918, the Ordnance Department reviewed the entire tank situation to determine the best course for future development. These studies concluded that the highest priority should be given to the development of a fast medium tank. Thus most of the limited resources available were assigned to the medium tank program with, as previously described, some effort being made to upgrade the existing stock of six-ton light tanks. However, on 24 May 1922, the Chief of Ordnance requested the Chief of Infantry to provide specifications and general requirements for a new light tank. The reply, dated 6 June 1922, called for a two man vehicle armed with a 37mm gun and a .30 caliber machine gun, both of which could be operated by one man in the same position. It was to be armored against .30 caliber armor piercing ammunition on the front and was to be protected from the same rounds on the sides at impact angles greater than 45 degrees. Cross-country speeds of two to twelve miles/hour were required with a cruising range of 50 miles. The tank was not to exceed five tons in weight and would be transportable on a heavy truck.

The priority of the medium tank program continued to have an effect and nothing really happened until June 1924 when the Chief of Ordnance directed Rock Island Arsenal to make studies of a light tank weighing approximately five tons. The attitude of the user did not help the situation as is indicated in the following quotation from an official letter dated 18 September 1924.

> "The Tank Corps appears to hold the view that a single type of tank of medium weight will prove the most effective armament for the Tank Corps and that a light tank of five tons weight will not be necessary."

Further correspondence continued until OCM 5165, dated 28 January 1926, recommended that the Manufacturing Service be authorized to proceed with the development of the light tank. On 5 February, the Chief of Ordnance ordered Rock Island Arsenal to proceed with the light tank design. The work began, but on 1 September, the Automotive Design Section was transferred from Rock Island to the Office of the Chief of Ordnance to facilitate cooperation between the designers, the Office of the Chief of Infantry, and the Tank Board at Fort Meade, Maryland. At that time, the earlier designs produced at Rock Island placed the engine in the rear of the tank. The studies at the Office of the Chief of Ordnance located the engine in the front.

Another group that influenced the design of the new tank was the Ordnance Advisory Committee of the Society of Automotive Engineers. This committee reviewed all of the proposed designs during its meeting at Aberdeen Proving Ground on 15 September 1926. The committee concluded that the front engine arrangement was superior resulting in a better location for the center of gravity. As a result, work was now concentrated on the front engine layout and the chassis was designed to be used as the basis for either a light tank or a cargo carrier. The front engine location was particularly important for the latter application. By 15 March 1927, the design had reached a stage where bids could be requested for the manufacture of a pilot tank. The winning bid was received from the James Cunningham, Son & Company of Rochester, New York and they were awarded the contract on 12 April 1927 to build one pilot tank to be delivered in 120 days.

The pilot chassis, designated as the T1, was completed on 1 August 1927 and demonstrated on 1 September at Rochester. At that time, a wooden mock-up of the turret and superstructure was installed to give the chassis the appearance of a complete tank. The shop tests at Rochester and the later evaluation at Aberdeen Proving Ground showed that the new T1 was far superior to the old six-ton tank.

The front mounted power plant was an eight cylinder, V type, liquid-cooled engine developing 110 horsepower at 2700 rpm. It drove the tank through a Cotta type sliding gear transmission with three speeds forward and one

The light tank T1 pilot appears in these photographs. A dummy turret and hull superstructure have been installed. On this pilot vehicle, the hull front extends forward of the tracks. Note the short exhaust pipe and large muffler.

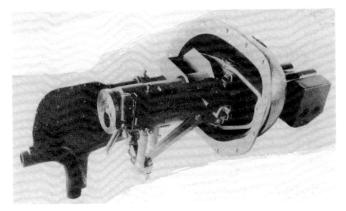

Above is the combination gun mount T1 fitted with the 37mm gun M1916 and the .30 caliber M1919 Browning machine gun. A telescopic sight is installed on the left side of the mount which was balanced by the large counterweight attached to the front of the gun shield.

reverse. Clutch-brake steering was used and the final drives and track sprockets were located at the rear of the tank. The driver rode in the center of the vehicle behind the engine and in front of the gunner's station in the turret mounted at the rear. In the turret, a 37mm gun M1916 was installed alongside a .30 caliber machine gun in the same ball mount. Doors on the rear of the hull provided access for the two man crew. The maximum armor plate thickness was ⅜ inches on the vertical surfaces. An unsprung link type suspension supported the vehicle which rode on 12 inch wide, 6.5 inch pitch, tracks. The suspension consisted of four bogies with two rollers each installed on each side of the tank. The bogies were connected by links in an attempt to equalize the shocks. Following tests at Aberdeen, the light tank T1 was converted to the light cargo carrier T1 by replacing the turret and superstructure with a wooden cargo body. A later modification converted the same chassis into an artillery wire reel carrier.

After the approval of the T1 by the Chief of Infantry, the manufacture of six additional vehicles was authorized. These consisted of four light tanks and two light cargo carriers. Incorporating minor modifications from the test program, they were designated as the light tank T1E1 and the light cargo carrier T1E1. One of the cargo carriers was later converted into the 4.2 inch mortar motor carriage T1. The new tanks could be identified by two obvious changes. The front of the hull did not extend in front of the tracks as

on the T1 and the fuel tanks were relocated to each side of the vehicle above the tracks. The circulation of the engine cooling air also was modified on the new tanks. Like the T1, the T1E1s were manufactured by James Cunningham, Son and Company and the new vehicles were running by April 1928. Because of the enthusiastic response by the Chief of Infantry, the Ordnance Committee approved the standardization of the T1E1 as the light tank M1 on 24 January 1928. However, this standardization was withdrawn by order of the Secretary of War on 30 March 1928. The new tank had a loaded weight of 15,515 pounds giving a power to weight ratio of 14.2 horsepower/ton. It reached a maximum road speed of 17.5 miles/hour and a 50 gallon fuel capacity provided a range of about 75 miles.

A view of the light tank T1E1 is at the upper right. Note the external fuel tanks over the tracks on each side of the vehicle and the long exhaust pipe without the large muffler. Details of the unsprung link type suspension can be seen below and at the lower right.

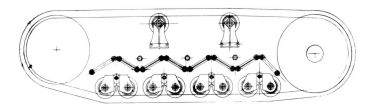

41

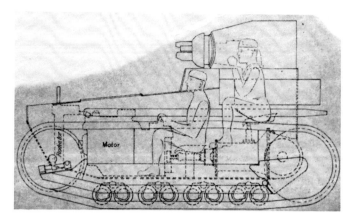

The internal arrangement of the light tank T1E1 appears in the sketch above. Note that fenders have been added over the tracks on the T1E1 in the photographs at the left.

On 20 June 1928, the four T1E1 tanks were received at Fort Meade, Maryland for issue to the 4th Tank Company. This was a unit of the first Experimental Mechanized Force organized on 1 July 1928 to evaluate equipment and tactics for mechanization. Operations of the 4th Light Tank Company emphasized the great superiority in performance and reliability of the new vehicles over the old six-ton tank. During October 1928, five T1E1s (three tanks and two cargo carriers) made a road march from Fort Meade to Gettysburg, Pennsylvania and return under their own power. The total distance of 144 miles was covered at an average running speed of over ten miles/hour. This compared to an average running speed of about nine miles/hour for a wheeled convoy over the same route earlier in the Summer.

One of the T1E1 tanks had been detached from the 4th Light Tank Company on 16 August 1928 and sent to Aberdeen Proving Ground for tests. This tank operated for 2020 miles over a period of 57 days at an average speed of over 12 miles/hour without any serious problems. This can be compared to the six-ton tank which required a major overhaul after about 80 miles.

A front view of the T1E1 is at the left. Below, the tank is climbing a 35 degree slope during tests at Aberdeen Proving Ground. Note that the gun shield and counterweight have been removed from this vehicle.

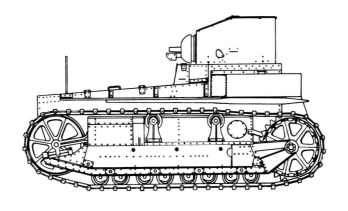

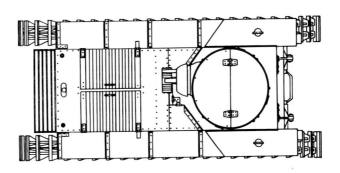

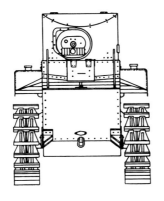 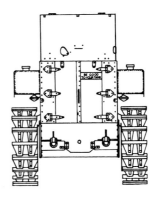

Scale 1:48

Light Tank T1E1

Above, the T1E1 is operating with the troops during training exercises. At the left below, the tank demonstrates its performance at Aberdeen. Note that the fenders have not yet been installed.

Above at the right, the T1E1 is loaded on one of the Mack trucks that served as a carrier for these tanks. Below, the T1E1 is climbing aboard its carrier during training operations.

The light tank T1E2 is shown in these photographs. Note the modified suspension with the three track support rollers and the changes in the fender installation.

During the evaluation of the T1E1, it was noted that the maximum armor thickness was only $\frac{3}{8}$ inches compared to the $\frac{6}{10}$ inch armor on the six-ton tank. This was considered inadequate and thicker armor was recommended. Other improvements were proposed as a result of the test program and on 30 November 1928, OCM 7346 approved the manufacture of an additional pilot vehicle designated as the light tank T1E2. This vehicle was to include the recommended modifications that could be incorporated without changing the basic design. Once again, the low bidder was James Cunningham, Son and Company and the contract for the new tank was awarded on 8 December 1928. The T1E2 was completed on 3 June 1929 and subsequently shipped to Aberdeen Proving Ground for tests.

The new turret on the T1E2 is armed with the high velocity, semiautomatic, 37mm gun and a .30 caliber machine gun in the combination gun mount T3.

The light tank T1E2 differed from the earlier T1E1 in several respects. A more powerful Cunningham liquid-cooled V-8 engine was installed developing 132 horsepower at 2600 rpm. The armor plate thickness was increased to a maximum of ⅝ inches and the turret was redesigned. The low velocity 37mm gun M1916 was replaced by a long barreled Browning semiautomatic 37mm gun with a muzzle velocity of 2000 feet/second. These changes raised the loaded weight of the tank to 17,790 pounds, but the more powerful engine still slightly increased the power to weight ratio to 14.8 horsepower/ton. The overall dimensions of the T1E2 were slightly larger than the T1E1, the link type suspension was modified, and the track width was increased from 12 to 13 inches.

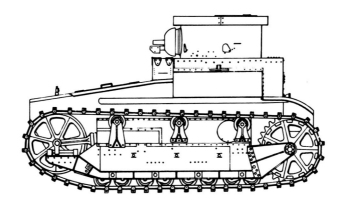

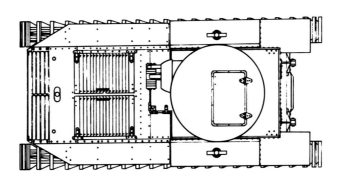

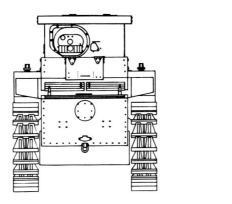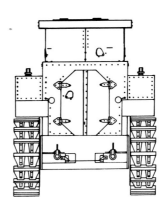

THE DRAWING SHOWS THE LIGHT TANK T1E2 FITTED WITH THE COMBINATION GUN MOUNT T1 ARMED WITH THE 37mm GUN M1916

Scale 1:48

©D.P. Dyer

Light Tank T1E2

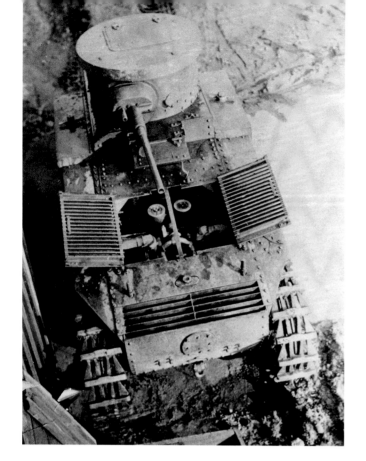

The hatches providing access to the crew and engine compartments can be seen in the top and rear views. Below is the interior of the tank looking forward with the driver's front armor and the engine compartment hatches open. The driver's seat is shown, but the gunner's sling type seat has been removed.

The machine gun has not been installed in the front view at the left. Below at the left, the T1E2 is crossing a trench during test operations. At the lower right, the T3 combination gun mount has been replaced by the earlier T1 mount with the low velocity 37mm gun.

The light tank T1E3 appears in these two photographs. The T3E1 combination gun mount installed in the original T1E1 turret was a modified version of the T3 that included a flat inner shield. Note that the T1E3 retained the T1E1 fenders with the new suspension.

The rough ride of the unsprung link type suspension on the T1E1 and the T1E2 resulted in another modification. T1E1 number two was fitted with a spring-hydraulic suspension which featured coil springs inside hydraulic shock absorbers on the three rear bogies and a coil spring suspension on the front bogie. The original T1E1 power plant was replaced by the more powerful engine used in the T1E2 and the higher velocity semiautomatic cannon from the latter vehicle was installed in the T1E1 turret. A 12 volt electrical system replaced the T1E1's original 6 volt equipment and an Eclipse combination hand and electric inertia starter was installed in place of the Delco starter. The modified vehicle was redesignated as the light tank T1E3. Tested at Aberdeen during April 1931, its riding quality was considered far superior to the earlier vehicles.

The new spring-hydraulic suspension used on the T1E3 is illustrated in the drawing below.

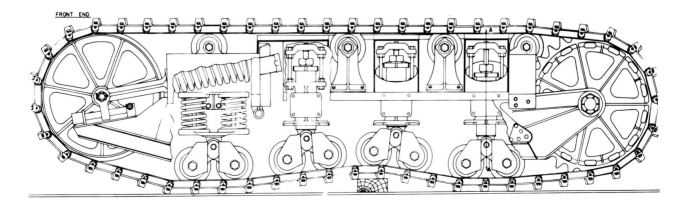

The reversed configuration of the light tank T1E4 with the driver in front and the engine in the rear is obvious in the photographs on this page. Note the new tracks and suspension installed on this tank. The short 37mm gun M1924 required a long counterweight for balance in the T2 combination gun mount.

Operations with the T1E1 revealed several disadvantages of the front mounted engine. Among these were the limited forward vision of the driver from his position behind the engine and the exposure of the crew to the engine heat and exhaust fumes which tended to blow back into the crew compartment. To correct these problems, one of the T1E1 pilots was rebuilt reversing the chassis so that the engine was in the rear and the final drives and the track sprockets were in the front. The link type suspension of the T1E1 was replaced by a semi-elliptic leaf spring design with two articulating bogies on each side of the tank. This suspension was similar to that of the British Vickers Armstrong light tank previously tested at Aberdeen. A lighter track using drop forged steel shoes 13¼ inches wide with a four inch pitch was installed. Designated as the light tank T1E4, the converted vehicle was armed with the semiautomatic 37mm gun M1924 and a coaxial .30 caliber machine gun. The cannon had a muzzle velocity of 1350 feet/second. The maximum armor plate thickness was increased to ⅝ inches and the loaded weight was raised to 17,270 pounds. Powered by the original 110 horsepower engine, the T1E4 was underpowered and tended to stall during turns because of the power loss associated with the clutch-brake steering. To correct this problem, a more powerful Cunningham V-8 engine was installed which developed 140 horsepower at 2600 rpm.

Above are interior views of the driver's station (left) and the rear of the fighting compartment (right) in the T1E4. Details of the semi-elliptic spring suspension are clearly visible in the photograph at the right.

The fourth T1E1 after its conversion to the T1E5 appears above and at the right. It retained the turret and armament of the T1E1.

To avoid the power loss inherent in the clutch-brake steering system and to improve the handling characteristics, a controlled differential steering unit supplied by the Cleveland Tractor Company was installed in T1E1 number four. The more powerful 140 horsepower engine also replaced the original power plant. Redesignated as the light tank T1E5, the vehicle showed greatly improved performance during tests at Aberdeen and the controlled differential steering system was recommended for installation in all tracked vehicles which operated faster than six miles/hour.

Compare the rear hull configuration of the light tank T1E6 shown here with that of the T1E4 on page 50.

A further modification of the light tank T1E4 replaced the V-8 Cunningham power plant with a liquid-cooled V-12 engine manufactured by the American LaFrance and Foamite Corporation. This new engine developed 244 horsepower at 2800 rpm. The tank weight increased to 19,900 pounds, but the more powerful engine brought the power to weight ratio up to 24.5 horsepower/ton. Redesignated as the light tank T1E6, the modified vehicle showed improved performance with a maximum road speed of 20 miles/hour. However, the installation of the larger engine was extremely crowded and difficult to service.

The light tank T1E6 retained the turret and armament of the T1E4. Above, the tank is operating during its test program at Aberdeen Proving Ground in 1934. The rear hull configuration and the exhaust pipes are obvious identification features for this vehicle.

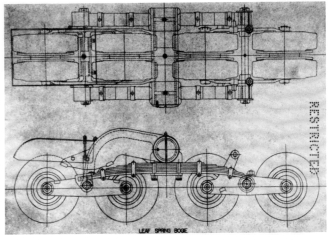

Above, the track and suspension bogie on the T1E6 can be seen at the left and at the right is a drawing of the bogie assembly used on both the T1E4 and the T1E6. Below, the crowded installation of the V-12 engine in the T1E6 is obvious.

Above are two photographs of the track development chassis T1 with its single .30 caliber machine gun installed. Note the different tracks in the two views.

During this period, two additional vehicles were used for the development of tracks and suspensions. The first of these was the track development chassis T1. It had the appearance of a small one man tank and was armed with a single .30 caliber machine gun in the front plate. However, the armor plate was only ⅛ inch thick and could have been easily penetrated by .30 caliber ammunition. The empty weight of the T1 was about 3000 pounds and it was powered by a 42 horsepower Ford Model A engine. The second vehicle was the track development chassis T2 constructed of ⅜ inch armor, but without armament. It was powered by an 87 horsepower V-8 LaSalle engine and was fitted with a leaf spring suspension. Later, it provided the basis for the 75mm howitzer motor carriage T1.

The track development chassis T2 appears below in these photographs dated 25 April 1930. It is fitted with the same tracks as the light tank T1.

At the right is the Cunningham Scout proposed in 1934.

Above, the Christie M1928 kicks up dust during a test run with the tracks installed. An aircraft type gun mount is provided in addition to the bow machine gun.

LIGHT TANKS AND COMBAT CARS

With the National Defense Act of 1920, Congress abolished the World War I Tank Corps and assigned all tanks to the Infantry. Thus the postwar development programs reflected Infantry requirements which emphasized good tactical mobility at the expense of long range strategic mobility. Since the Infantry expected the tanks to operate with the foot soldiers, there was no need for high speed and the light tanks would be transported on wheeled carriers to the area of operations. With the mechanization of the army beginning in 1928, the Cavalry required a combat vehicle to perform its mission of reconnaisance and to act as a covering force. Armored cars partially filled these requirements, but their limited cross-country capability restricted their use in many situations. What the Cavalry needed was a combat vehicle that could move rapidly for long distances on roads and still operate cross-country like a tank. One solution to the problem was the combination wheel or track vehicle which had been under development since 1919 by J. Walter Christie. By 1928, this work had produced a highly mobile chassis with an independently sprung, eight wheel, suspension system capable of operating with or without tracks. A later model, the Christie M1931, was a slightly modified version of the M1928 vehicle with a maximum

armor thickness of $\frac{5}{8}$ inches and a loaded weight of 22,220 pounds. Seven of the M1931s were ordered as the convertible medium tank T3. When operating without tracks, the rear pair of wheels on six of the tanks were chain driven from the sprocket. The seventh was gear driven. Four of the new vehicles were transferred to the Cavalry at Fort Knox, Kentucky and were redesignated as the combat car T1 to comply with the law assigning all tanks to the Infantry. One of these vehicles was modified at Fort Knox and redesignated as the combat car T1E1. In addition to other changes on the T1E1, the chain drive was replaced by a gear drive. Another proposed version was to be powered by a six cylinder Cummins diesel engine which developed 120 horsepower. It was hoped that the torque characteristics of the diesel would reduce the amount of gear shifting

At the right is one of the T1 combat cars fitted with a .50 caliber machine gun in a new mount replacing the 37mm gun in the combination gun mount T1.

The crossed sabers of the Cavalry are visible on the turret of this T1 combat car at Fort Knox. This vehicle still retains the T1 combination gun mount used on the medium tank T3.

required with the gasoline engine. This vehicle was assigned the designation combat car T1E2, but it was never completed.

The T1 combat cars differed from the T3 medium tanks only in the armament. In the combat cars, the tank's 37mm gun M1916 was replaced by a .50 caliber machine gun in a new mount. In both vehicles, a 338 horsepower V-12 Liberty engine provided a power to weight ratio of 30.4 horsepower/ton. The coil springs for each of the eight dual road wheels were installed inside of the ⅝ inch thick side armor and were separated from the interior of the vehicle by a 0.188 inch thick nickel steel side wall. The 14 inch

The suspension spring arrangement can be seen in the lubrication chart below. Note the space required inside the hull for this type of suspension.

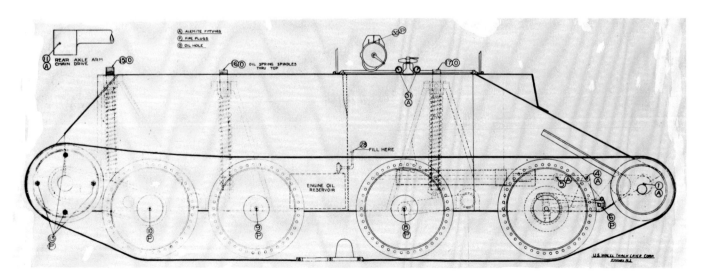

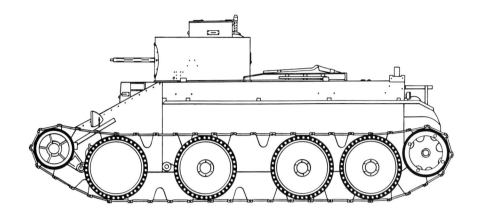

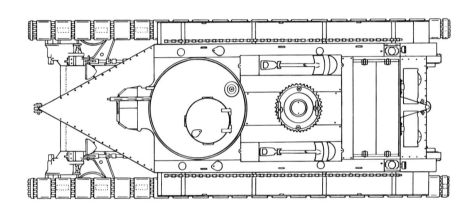

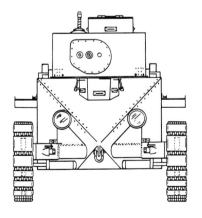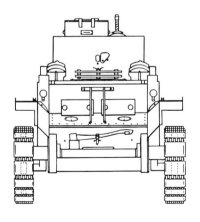

Scale 1:48

© D.P. Dyer

Combat Car T1

The recovery of a T1 combat car after an accident is shown in this series of photographs. Details of the tracks and front hull bottom are visible in the top view.

vertical wheel travel of the independently sprung road wheels provided an excellent ride over rough terrain. The track shoes consisted of forged steel plates 10¼ inches wide with a 10 inch pitch. A combination driving lug and center guide was located on the inner surface of every other track shoe. When running on wheels, the tracks were stowed on shelves on each side of the hull. The two man crew consisted of the driver in the front hull and the gunner in the turret. A steering wheel was provided for use when driving on wheels. It was removable and clutch-brake steering was used for operation on tracks. With maximum road speeds of about 47 miles/hour on wheels and approximately 27 miles/hour on tracks, the T1 easily met the Cavalry's requirement for long range strategic mobility. At the same time, the independently sprung eight wheel suspension gave it excellent cross-country capability.

At that time, a light tank was classified as a two man vehicle that could be transported on a carrier. A medium tank was specified as one too heavy for a carrier with a maximum weight of 25 tons. The Christie M1931, with a weight of about 11 tons, was considered too heavy for a carrier and thus was classified by the Infantry as a medium tank. However, it really did not need a carrier since its performance on roads greatly exceeded that of any transport vehicle then available. With its two man crew, light armor and armament, it would have been better classified as a light tank.

During the Summer of 1932, a 246 horsepower V-12 engine manufactured by the American LaFrance and Foamite Corporation was installed in a T1. Tested at Aberdeen Proving Ground, the vehicle was further modified by the installation of a new cooling system, clutch, and a universal joint between the engine and transmission. Designated as the combat car T1E3, it was shipped to Fort Knox for additional tests. Although the vehicle was much quieter than the original T1, its performance with the lower power engine was unsatisfactory. The Liberty engine was reinstalled and the designation was changed back to the combat car T1.

The T1s continued to be used in various experiments. A Browning .50 caliber aircraft machine gun was fitted

Above is a combat car T1 retaining the combination gun mount T1 with the 37mm gun and .30 caliber machine gun. It has been fitted with a radio antenna, but otherwise it is identical to the medium tank T3 below.

for test replacing the heavy barrel .50 caliber weapon in the turret. A governor was considered for installation, but it was rejected because of space requirements. A tachometer was authorized with an indicator on the driver's instrument panel. By May 1936, the maintenance costs on the T1 combat cars and the T3 medium tanks were becoming excessive. Newer vehicles were now available and as the T1s and T3s became unservicable they were condemned and used as targets. One example remains on display today by the Ordnance Museum at Aberdeen Proving Ground.

Below, the original Liberty engine (left) can be compared with the American LaFrance V-12 (right) installed in the combat car T1E3.

Above is the convertible armored car T5 on 1 September 1931. Later, it was redesignated as the combat car T2. Note the armor plate installed on the rear suspension bogie which was later removed.

Following the demonstration of the Christie M1928, the War Department directed the Chief of Ordnance, in cooperation with the Chief of Cavalry, to procure an armored car based on the convertible wheel/track concept. The Chief of Cavalry prepared specifications for such a vehicle, but an agreement could not be reached with J. Walter Christie, President of the U. S. Wheel Tracklayer Corporation. He objected to the specification requirements for minimum dimensions of the crew compartment. The funds were then allocated to the Ordnance Department to design and build a convertible armored car for use by the Cavalry. Built at Rock Island Arsenal during 1931, the new vehicle was originally designated as the armored car T5. This was changed with the introduction of the new nomenclature to the combat car T2.

The T2 was manned by a crew of three. The driver and one gunner rode in the front hull and the other gunner occupied the cylindrical turret mounted on the center of the car. Armament consisted of one .50 caliber machine gun and one .30 caliber machine gun in the turret combination mount. Another .30 caliber machine gun was carried for use either from the front hull position or from an

Below is the combat car T2 after the suspension armor was eliminated. Straps have been added to retain the tracks in the stowed position on the fenders when running on wheels.

This later photograph, dated 5 February 1932, shows the combat car T2 after the removal of the front idler.

antiaircraft mount on the turret. The T2 was powered by an air-cooled Continental A70 radial engine which developed 156 horsepower at 2000 rpm. This engine drove the vehicle through a modified Cotta transmission and clutch-brake steering was used when running on tracks. The front two wheels of the six wheel suspension were steerable when the tracks were removed. The four rear wheels were installed in two bogies suspended by leaf springs. The cen-

ter guide steel tracks were 10 inches wide with a pitch of 4½ inches. The tracks were driven by sprockets mounted at the rear of the vehicle and they were carried over the three road wheels on each side and around an idler at the front. Later, this idler was removed and the tracks passed directly around the front road wheels. Shelves on each side of the hull were used to stow the tracks when operating on wheels. Armor on the T2 varied from ⅜ inches to one

Below, the combat car T2 is ready for operation on wheels after the temporary installation of a water-cooled engine. The rear end also has been raised 7½ inches. This photograph was dated 30 March 1932.

Above is the combat car T2E1 on 25 November 1932 after its arrival at Aberdeen Proving Ground. Note the brace installed on the suspension bogie.

inch in thickness. As originally assembled, a plate of armor was installed on the outside of each rear suspension bogie. Later, this plate was eliminated.

Proving ground tests indicated that the T2 was underpowered and that the weight was badly distributed. A conference during April 1932 outlined changes that were required to make the vehicle suitable for use by the Mechanized Cavalry. A Continental R-670 air-cooled radial engine was installed providing about 200 horsepower at 2000 rpm. The fighting compartment was enlarged and the vehicle was shortened, improving the weight distribution. The second .30 caliber machine gun was eliminated leaving only the two coaxial turret weapons. These

modifications were made at Rock Island Arsenal and the vehicle was shipped to Aberdeen for test under the new designation of combat car T2E1. However, the proving ground evaluation indicated that the performance was still inadequate and the project was dropped.

The designation combat car T3 originally was applied to a modified light tank T1E1 intended for use by the Mechanized Cavalry. However, that vehicle could not meet the Cavalry strategic mobility requirements and the designation was cancelled. Later, the T3 designation was assigned to a proposed improved version of the combat car T2. However, with the cancellation of that vehicle, the T3 also was dropped.

Below, another view of the combat car T2E1 appears at the left. The bogie brace has been removed in this photograph. At the right, the T2E1 appears in the half-track configuration on the right side. Note that the drive chain, normally used only for wheel operation, is installed. On the left side, the track is carried around the front idler for full-track operation.

Above, the combat car T4 is rigged for running on wheels with the tracks in the stowed position. Below, the tracks are installed during the tests at Aberdeen Proving Ground. These views show the original hull and turret configuration of the T4.

Following the construction and test of combat cars T1 and T2, conferences were held during February 1932 to define the characteristics of a new combat car. The proposed vehicle was to be convertible for operation on either wheels or tracks. The weight limit was set at nine tons with maximum speeds of 40 miles/hour on wheels and 22 miles/hour on tracks. Manned by a crew of four, the new combat car was to be armed with one .50 caliber machine gun and one .30 caliber machine gun in a turret combination mount. An additional .30 caliber machine gun was located in the right front hull. Although he found the general characteristics satisfactory, the Chief of Cavalry suggested that the weight be reduced to 8½ tons and that the maximum speed on tracks be increased to 30 miles/hour. The Ordnance Department pointed out that the two changes were incompatible since the higher speed would require a larger, more powerful engine which would increase the weight above even the nine tons originally proposed. After further discussion, the War Department approved the development program, but limited the weight to 8½ tons even if this resulted in a lower maximum speed than originally specified. Designated as the combat car T4, a pilot vehicle was completed at Rock Island and delivered to Aberdeen Proving Ground in September 1933.

Above, the complete power train is being removed as a unit from the combat car T4.

After initial tests, the T4 was demonstrated at Aberdeen in April 1934 and the Chief of Infantry proposed the procurement of a medium tank similar to the combat car, but with heavier armor. This vehicle appeared as the convertible medium tank T4 and it was eventually standardized as the convertible medium tank M1. On 7 June 1934, OCM 11531 approved the combat car T4 as a limited procurement type. However, tests conducted by the Cavalry Board on combat cars T4 and T5 resulted in recommendations for a series of changes. These included a redesign of the front hull replacing the half-hexagon head covers of the driver and bow gunner with a flat front plate similar to that on the combat car T5. A new turret was required with

the inside diameter increased from 44 inches to about 56 inches. The combination gun mount was dropped and the .30 caliber and .50 caliber machine guns were installed in separate mounts in a flat front turret plate inclined 20 degrees toward the rear. The rear part of the turret was

At the right is a mock-up of a turret configuration proposed for the combat car T4 by the 1st Cavalry (Mechanized). Below, the combat car T4E1 shows the turret and hull design finally selected and proposed for production.

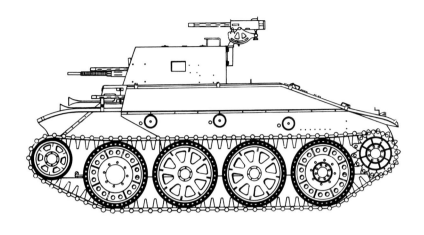

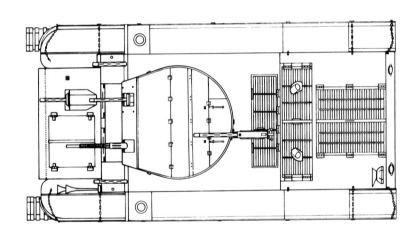

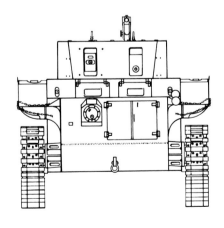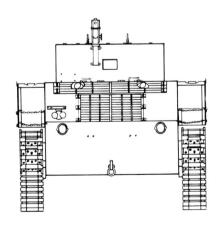

Scale 1:48

©D.P. Dyer

Combat Car T4E1

Front and rear views of the combat car T4E1 appear above. Note the short pitch track compared to the Christie tracks on the combat car T1.

circular resulting in a D shape plan form. The turret was rotated manually with a gear release for operation as a free turret.

The original T4 pilot was modified to the new specification. The changes increased the unloaded weight of the combat car to about 10 tons resulting in a power to weight ratio of approximately 24 horsepower/ton with the 235 net horsepower air-cooled Continental R-670 radial engine. As on the earlier convertible vehicles, a removable steering wheel was used when driving on wheels. Controlled differential steering was provided for operation on tracks.

As on the light tank T1E5, the performance with the controlled differential steering was far superior to the earlier clutch-brake arrangement. When operating on wheels, the tracks were stowed, half on top and half suspended below the hull side shelves. Designated first as the convertible combat car T4, 10 tons, the nomenclature was later changed to the combat car T4E1. The Cavalry Board strongly recommended the procurement of the T4E1, but they were overruled by higher authority in favor of the lighter weight combat car T5 which could be produced at approximately half the cost.

Below is the combat car T4E1 with the full armament proposed for the production vehicles. This consisted of five .30 caliber machine guns and one .50 caliber machine gun. A new type of short pitch track has been installed.

The combat car T4E2 appears in these photographs from Rock Island Arsenal dated 27 June 1935. The numbers in the upper view indicate the removable machine gun barrel guard (1) and the suspension spring adjustment points (2, 3, and 4).

The T4E1 pilot was later modified again by removing the turret and installing a barbette superstructure. The armament in this configuration consisted of one .50 caliber machine gun and three .30 caliber machine guns in the barbette structure and one .30 caliber machine gun in the hull bow mount. Designated as the combat car T4E2, the weight increased to over 13 tons and the vehicle was used to develop components for the medium tank T4E1.

Above is the combat car T5. Removable windshields have been provided for the driver and bow gunner and canvas covers have been fitted over the open top turrets.

In the Spring of 1933, the Secretary of War directed that the development of future light tanks and combat cars be aimed at producing a vehicle with a maximum weight of 7½ tons. In response to this directive, a new project was initiated on 3 June 1933 and the characteristics of a proposed design were forwarded to the Ordnance Committee on 10 July. They called for a combat car weighing 14,000 pounds, armed with one .50 caliber machine gun and two .30 caliber machine guns. Armor protection was to be provided against .30 caliber ammunition at all ranges. The new vehicle was expected to have a maximum road speed of at least 30 miles/hour and a cruising range of 100 miles. Provision was to be made for the installation of radio equipment. The new car was to incorporate controlled differential steering and a volute spring suspension. Since it was intended to operate only on tracks, it was not convertible. Recommended by the Ordnance Committee, the characteristics were approved by the War Department on 9 August 1933. The construction of one pilot was authorized and the vehicle was designated as the combat car T5, 7½ ton. In October, the armament arrangement was approved locating the .50 caliber machine gun and one .30

Below, note the chrome plated horn and headlights on the combat car T5 in the left view dated 24 March 1934. They had not yet been installed in the earlier photograph at the right dated 2 March 1934.

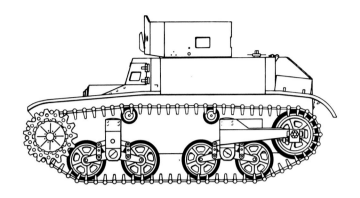

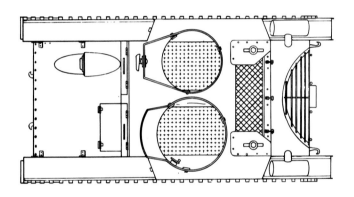

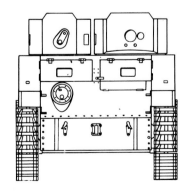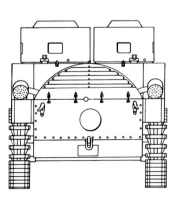

Scale 1:48

Combat Car T5

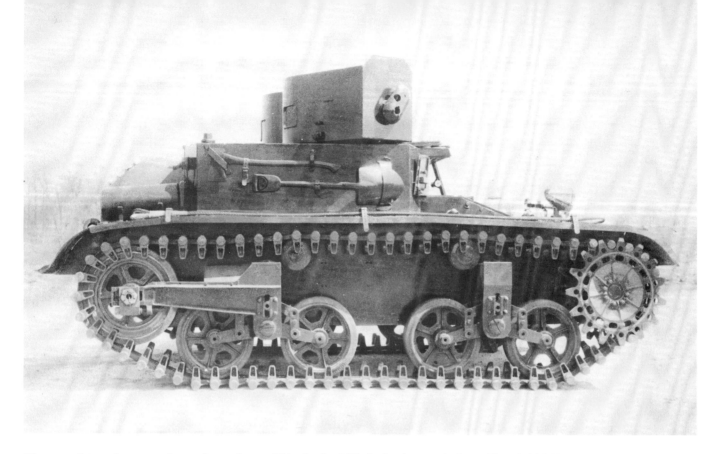

The new volute spring suspension on the combat car T5 is clearly visible in the photograph above. The windshields and turret covers have been removed in this view dated 3 April 1934.

caliber machine gun in separate turrets. The remaining .30 caliber machine gun was to be installed in a ball mount in the right front hull.

The pilot combat car T5 was built at Rock Island Arsenal and demonstrated with the light tank T2 at Aberdeen Proving Ground on 23 April 1934. The vehicle weighed 12,580 pounds without guns or ammunition, but with a driver and a full tank of fuel. It was powered by the air-cooled Continental R-670 radial engine which developed about 235 net horsepower at 2400 rpm. After preliminary tests, the T5 pilot was shipped to Fort Benning,

Georgia in August 1934 for evaluation by the Infantry. In March 1935, it was proposed that the T5 pilot be rebuilt to replace the two turrets with a barbette superstructure. This was to assist the Infantry in selecting the configuration for the light tank T2 intended for production during the fiscal year 1936. The T5 was returned to Rock Island Arsenal for the conversion. The new superstructure mounted a .50 caliber machine gun and one .30 caliber machine gun in the front plate and one .30 caliber machine gun in each side and the rear. A fifth .30 caliber machine gun was installed in the hull bow mount. Designated as

No armament has been installed in the T5 at the left. A machine gun has been mounted in the later view at the right. The little vehicle was nicknamed "Susie".

70

the combat car T5E1, the vehicle was returned to Aberdeen for test during June and July of 1935. It was considered comparable to the T5 except for excessive engine temperatures resulting from the presence of the new superstructure.

The combat car T5E1 with the barbette superstructure is illustrated in these photographs.

Combat car M1, serial number 45, appears above at Aberdeen Proving Ground on 19 February 1937. The .30 and .50 caliber machine guns have been mounted in the turret and the .30 caliber machine gun has been installed for the bow gunner. M1 combat cars with serial numbers 42-60 used the 6½ inch diameter ball mount M10 for the bow gunner.

After further testing, a single turret configuration was selected for the production version of the new combat car. Originally designated as the T5E2, it was standardized for production as the combat car M1. The turret designed for the combat car T4E1 with the flat front plate and the D shape plan form was installed armed with a .50 caliber machine gun and a .30 caliber machine gun in separate mounts. This turret was mounted on M1 combat cars with serial numbers 2 through 58. On combat cars 59 through 90, the turret was assembled from eight flat armor plates. Such a configuration had been recommended to simplify production during time of war. Neither turret was fitted with a cupola and the roof consisted of a triple sectioned hinged cover which could be folded to provide a forward shield with vision slots. The later production M1 combat cars also replaced the early round top engine compartment cover with an angular flat sided cover. The .30 caliber bow machine gun was retained and an additional .30 caliber machine gun was provided for use on the turret anti-aircraft mount. The modified suspension eliminated the connection between the rear bogie bracket and the idler. A 14 tooth sprocket replaced the original 15 tooth design and new 5½ inch pitch, double pin, rubber block tracks replaced the 4¾ inch pitch steel tracks on the earlier

vehicle. The track width remained at 11½ inches. The production vehicle had a combat weight of 18,790 pounds with a maximum armor thickness of ⅝ inches. It had a maximum road speed of about 45 miles/hour and was capable of 15 to 20 miles/hour cross-country. Manufactured at Rock Island Arsenal, 38 M1 combat cars were produced during fiscal year 1935, 19 in fiscal year 1936, and 32 in fiscal year 1937 for a total of 89. However, other sources assign combat car M1 serial numbers 1-41 for the model 1935, 42-60 for the model 1936, and 61-90 for the model 1937 giving a total of 90. This is explained by the fact that serial number 1 was assigned to the original T5 pilot vehicle and it did not appear in the production figures. Overlap sometimes occurred in the annual production which might account for the discrepancy between the serial numbers assigned annually and the yearly production figures.

Combat car M1, serial number 32, is shown at the right. This vehicle is fitted with the 6½ inch diameter ball mount M8 for the bow gunner.

Above, combat car M1, serial number 22, can be seen with the turret open and all weapons mounted. Note how the folded turret roof provides a shield with vision slots. The interior arrangement of the combat car M1 appears in the cutaway drawing below.

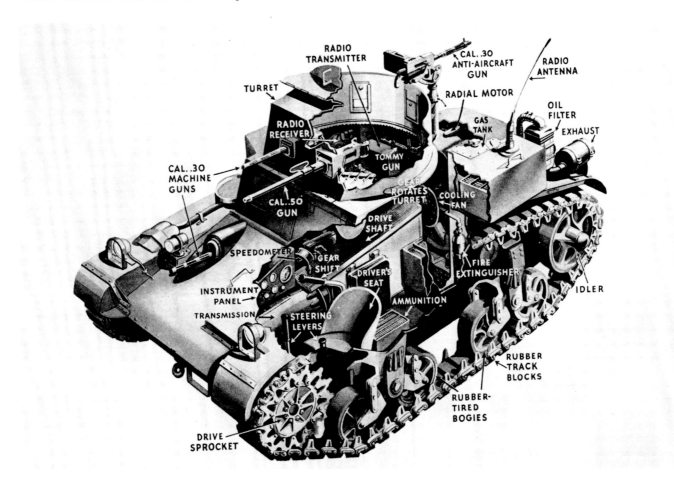

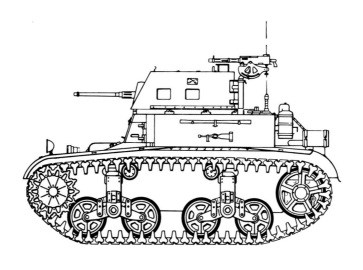

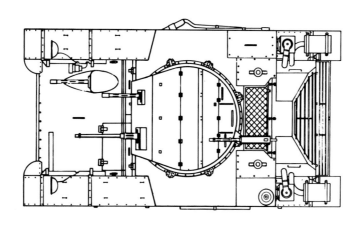

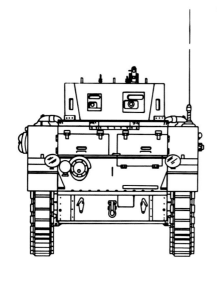

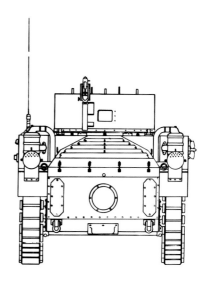

©D.P. Dyer

Combat Car M1

Above is the 6½ inch diameter ball mount M8 which was installed in the hull of M1 combat cars with serial numbers 2-41. At the right is the 3½ inch diameter ball mount M13 provided in M1 combat cars 61-90 and all M1A1 and M2 combat cars. The sighting arrangement shown in this photograph was not standard. Below, the M15 and M16 turret mounts are shown at the left and right respectively.

The M15 and M16 mounts above could be used in the left side of the combat car M1 turret, but only the M15 was installed in the combat cars M1A1 and M2. Below, two views of the M18 mount appear at the left. This mount was used in the right side of the turret on the M1, M1A1, and M2 combat cars. The antiaircraft bracket mount is shown below at the right.

75

Features of the M1 combat car in service with the Cavalry are illustrated above and below. At the top right, note the angular configuration of the engine compartment cover on the production vehicle compared to the round cover on the T5 pilot.

Below, the driver's station is at the left with the front and side armor doors open. The small size of the M1 combat car is emphasized by the crew in the open turret at the lower right.

Above, General Chaffee's Mechanized Cavalry Brigade visits the 1939 New York Worlds Fair as they return from maneuvers at Plattsburg, New York. Below are two views of the late model M1 combat car with the angular flat side turret.

Above, maintenance is being performed on an M1 combat car of the 13th Cavalry. Note the angular engine compartment cover parked behind the turret.

In early 1936, the original T5 pilot was modified once again. This time the major change was replacement of the Continental gasoline engine by a Guiberson radial diesel. Designated as the model T-1020, this air-cooled power plant developed about 220 net horsepower at 2200 rpm. The vehicle designation now became the combat car T5E3 and it was under test at Aberdeen Proving Ground from May to September 1936. When received at Aberdeen, the engine was fitted with an inertia starter. However, it was almost impossible to start the vehicle with this unit and it was replaced by a Coffman cartridge starter which was used during the remainder of the test program. Later, three production M1 combat cars were fitted with the Guiberson diesel and redesignated as combat cars M1E1. These three vehicles were delivered to Fort Knox in February 1937.

Below are two views of the Guiberson T-1020 diesel engine, serial number 1.

78

Above is the combat car M1E2 showing the greater space between the suspension bogies.

During the Summer of 1937, an M1 combat car was modified by reworking the rear hull to improve access to the engine and to increase the fuel capacity. The idler was shifted to the rear and the rear bogie was moved back 11 inches. Since these were experimental modifications, the hull changes were made with soft steel not armor plate. The modified vehicle was designated as the combat car M1E2 and it was evaluated at Aberdeen from 3 August to 5 October 1937. With its longer ground contact length, the quality of ride and firing platform stability were superior to the standard M1, but a slightly greater steering effort was required. The new hull arrangement did improve access to the power plant. After completion of the tests, the M1E2 was restored to the standard M1 configuration and reissued to the troops. As a result of this test program, it was directed that all combat cars manufactured during fiscal

year 1938 would incorporate the features of the M1E2 and would be designated as combat cars M1A1. They retained the same angular turret design as the late M1 combat cars with eight flat sides. Twentyfour of these were completed during the fiscal year, seven of which were powered by the Guiberson diesel engine and designated as combat cars M1A1E1. These production vehicles also were equipped with constant mesh transmissions. The M1A1 combat cars were assigned serial numbers 91-114.

Below is the fully armed combat car M1A1. At the right is a lineup of combat cars with an M1A1 first in line. An early M1 combat car is second.

Above, an M1A1 combat car is fording a stream. Note the 3½ inch diameter M13 mount for the bow gunner's .30 caliber machine gun. Other details of the M1A1 combat car can be seen in the photographs at the left and below.

Above is the combat car T5E4 powered by the Guiberson five cylinder T-570-1 engine and fitted with the rubber torsion rear bogies and trailing idler. Below is a closeup view of the rear bogie and the trailing idler.

The original T5 pilot, now the T5E3, was subjected to still another modification in late 1937. Now designated as the combat car T5E4, it was fitted with a trailing idler which extended the ground contact length of the tracks reducing the ground pressure. Rubber torsion units were installed to replace the volute springs in the rear bogies and in the trailing idler. Tests starting in January 1938 at Aberdeen Proving Ground and later at Fort Knox indicated that the use of the trailing idler improved both the ride quality and the stability of the vehicle as a firing platform. The rubber torsion units performed well, but their durability was very low. As a result, they were not recommended for use in production vehicles. During part of the test program, the model T-1020 engine was replaced by another Guiberson diesel. This was the five cylinder, 150 horsepower, model T-570-1. The turret was removed to reduce the vehicle weight during the evaluation of the lower power engine. The 235 net horsepower Continental R-670, now redesignated as the W-670 for military use, was installed later to complete the suspension tests.

The combat car M1E3 was a production M1 vehicle modified at Rock Island to use the 16 inch wide Goodrich continuous rubber band track T27. Tested at Aberdeen in late 1938, the vehicle then underwent further modification. The standard rubber block track was reinstalled and it was fitted with a new power train consisting of a two speed transfer case and a three speed transmission. This arrangement lowered the drive shaft until its center line was only 6⅜ inches above the hull floor. This was to meet the Cavalry request to eliminate or reduce the height of the drive shaft tunnel under the center of the fighting compartment.

At the right is the combat car M1E3 with the Goodrich T27 rubber band track.

Above is the diesel powered combat car M2. Windshields with wipers have been mounted for use in rear areas.

Improvements such as the low height drive shaft tunnel, the trailing idler suspension, and other modifications were recommended for inclusion in the 34 combat cars scheduled for production during the fiscal year 1940. These recommendations were approved and the new vehicle was designated as the combat car M2. However, it soon became obvious that the low drive shaft modification would not be available without seriously delaying the production program. As a result, it was deleted from the requirements for the M2 and it was recommended that it be incorporated into future production vehicles as soon as possible. The M2 combat cars produced during 1940 were serial numbers 1-34.

The production of American armored vehicles now began to rapidly increase under the influence of the war in Europe. Under the Protective Mobilization Plan, the Cavalry regiments were authorized 292 of the M2 combat cars. The M2 also was to be powered by the T-1020 Guiberson diesel as that engine became available in production quantities. The Protective Mobilization Plan also recommended that approximately 88 M1 combat cars be modernized by the installation of the latest design turret and that it be fitted with protectoscopes. This was a periscope type vision device which replaced the vision slots in the earlier tanks. The modernized vehicle was to be designated as the combat car M1A2. It also was suggested at this time that the light tanks M2A1 and M2A2 be modernized, converted to combat cars, and transferred from the Infantry to the Cavalry. However this recommendation was rejected as not being economically feasible.

At the left is the combat car M2 without the windshields and with the side armor doors open.

These views show the new engine compartment design and the trailing idler suspension on the combat car M2.

Full armament has been mounted on this M2 combat car with a .50 caliber machine gun in the M15 mount and a .30 caliber machine gun in the M18 mount. The 3½ inch diameter M13 ball mount is provided for the bow gunner. The M20 antiaircraft bracket mount can be seen below with its .30 caliber machine gun.

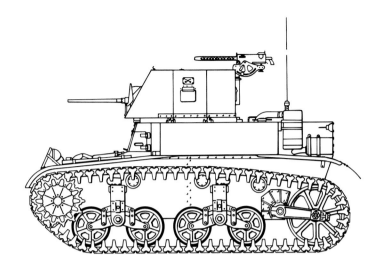

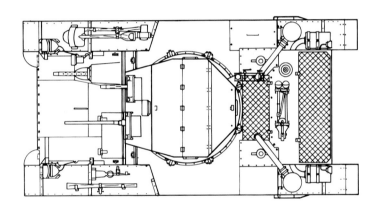

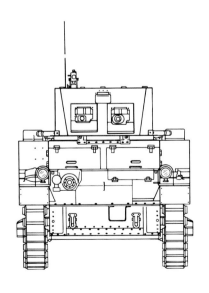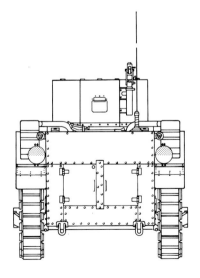

Scale 1:48

© **D.P. Dyer**

Combat Car M2

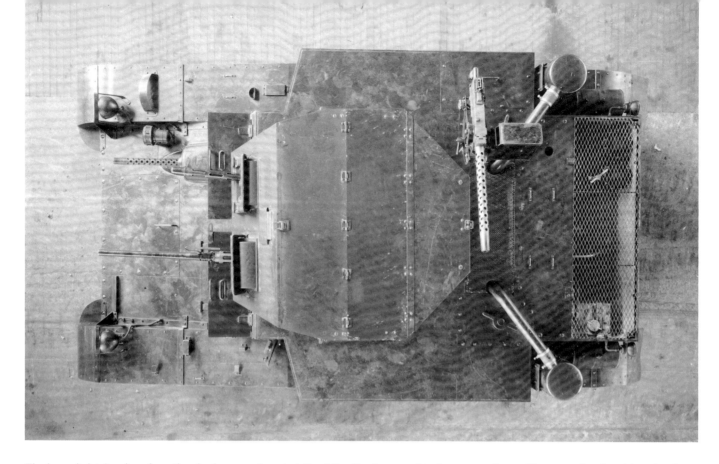

The long air intake pipes from the air cleaners, characteristic of the diesel powered tanks, appear above. Also, note that the vision slots have been omitted from the folding turret roof on the combat car M2.

With the formation of the Armored Force on 10 July 1940, the necessity for separate nomenclatures for tanks assigned to the Infantry and the Cavalry disappeared. All tanks now belonged to the Armored Force. OCM 15993, dated 22 July 1940, redesignated the combat car M2 as the light tank M1A1. The same item redesignated the modernized M1 combat car as the light tank M1A2. This action was approved on 22 August 1940 and the combat car nomenclature no longer existed. Both of the former combat cars continued to serve as training vehicles until 1942.

At the left and above are views of an experimental turret for the combat car M2. Note the vision block and the relocated M20 antiaircraft machine gun mount in the exterior photograph.

Above is an early attempt at air-ground cooperation. However, the experiments with the autogyro gave disappointing results and it was dropped from further consideration. Below, the combat cars are operating in a smoke screen during maneuvers near Plattsburg, New York in August 1939.

After completion of tests on the combat car T4, the Cavalry Board and the Ordnance Committee recommended modifications to the vehicle prior to production. The Ordnance Committee also recommended that a new convertible combat car be designed which would incorporate an engine of about 325 horsepower, improved tracks and suspension, and the maximum possible increase in fuel capacity. Although production of the T4 itself was cancelled in favor of the combat car T5, work was initiated on the design of a new convertible vehicle under the designation combat car T6. With an estimated combat weight of 24,000 pounds, the new car was to be manned by a crew of five. The proposed power plant was the Wright Whirlwind R-975 air-cooled radial engine which developed about 400 horsepower at 2400 rpm. Calculations indicated a maximum road speed of 44 miles/hour on wheels and 31.7 miles/hour on tracks. As designed, the vehicle was 204 inches long, 90 inches wide, and 102 inches high. The wheels were individually sprung by helical springs with a maximum vertical movement of 12 inches. The solid rubber tires were 28 x 7 inches and the tracks utilized an aluminum frame with steel wear inserts. The driver rode in the center front hull with a .30 caliber machine gunner on each side and slightly to the rear. Two turrets were to be installed on the center of the hull with a .50 caliber machine gun in the left and a .30 caliber machine gun in the right.

Design work on the T6 was suspended in early November 1935. The Cavalry had indicated a preference for single turret vehicles with the crew limited to four men. In view of this and the directive of the Secretary of War to limit future combat cars to a maximum weight of 7½ tons, further work on the T6 project was cancelled.

In November 1936, the Chief of Cavalry directed that development of convertible combat cars be continued and conferences concerning new designs and construction methods were held in early 1937 between Cavalry, Infantry, and Ordnance personnel. Although the Cavalry had accepted the M1 combat car, they still preferred a vehicle with smoother cross-country operation and the capability of high speed road travel on wheels. A design was proposed that was essentially a combat car M1 with a convertible suspension having the two rear wheels powered for operation without tracks. Brakes also were provided on the four rear wheels. The two front wheels were steerable when driving without tracks. Controlled differential steering was used during tracked operation. The four rear wheels were installed in two articulating bogies suspended by leaf springs. Helical springs were provided for the two independently sprung front wheels. All six wheels were fitted with 38 x 7 inch pneumatic tires with bullet resistant tubes. The level of armor protection and the armament arrangement were the same as on the combat car M1. The design was approved by the Ordnance Committee and designated as the combat car T7. The construction of one pilot was authorized for test purposes. Manufactured at Rock Island Arsenal, the T7 pilot was shipped to Aberdeen Proving Ground for tests beginning in August 1938.

Powered by the same air-cooled Continental W-670 engine as the combat car M1, the T7 had maximum road speeds of about 53 miles/hour on wheels and 35 miles/hour on tracks. The vehicle had an empty weight of 21,060 pounds. Numerous failures of wheels, wheel hubs, and suspension arms occurred during the tests requiring the redesign and strengthening of these parts. During August 1939,

Below is the convertible combat car T7 with its tracks installed at Aberdeen Proving Ground on 16 August 1938.

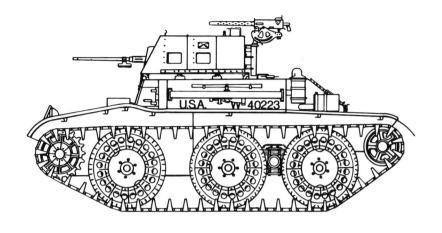

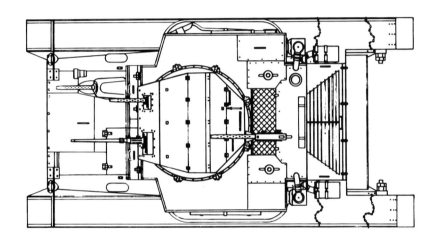

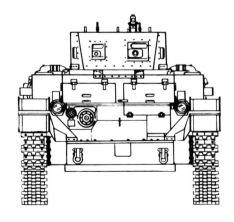
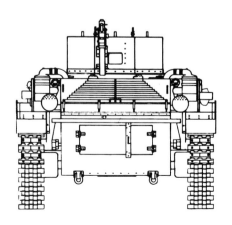

Scale 1:48

©**D.P. Dyer**

Combat Car T7

the T7 was assigned to the Mechanized Cavalry and participated in the maneuvers at Plattsburg, New York. By this time, the development of the tracked vehicle had reached the point where it could easily meet the strategic mobility requirements of the Cavalry. Thus the complexity and higher cost of the convertible vehicle could no longer be justified. On 19 October 1939, the Mechanized Cavalry Board recommended that further development and test of convertible vehicles be cancelled.

The pneumatic tires on the road wheels of the combat car T7 can be seen in these photographs. Note that the disc supports for the pneumatic tires have been removed in the bottom views. When operating on wheels, the tracks were stowed on the rear of the vehicle and suspended below the fenders.

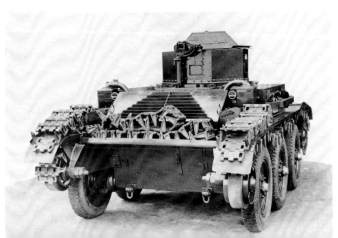

Above, the light tank T2 is at Rock Island Arsenal on 7 April 1934. Note the British Vickers type suspension installed on this pilot tank.

As mentioned previously, the light tank T2 was demonstrated along with the combat car T5 at Aberdeen Proving Ground on 23 April 1934. Like the combat car, the T2 had been manufactured at Rock Island Arsenal and utilized the same power train. It differed from the T5 by having a single turret and a suspension with a single pin track similar to that on the British Vickers six-ton tank and the light tank T1E6. This suspension consisted of two bogies per track, each with four road wheels suspended by leaf springs. Tests at Aberdeen during April and May 1934 indicated that this suspension was inferior to the volute spring suspension on the combat car T5. The ride was much rougher and it lacked durability. The T2 was returned to Rock Island for the installation of a strengthened version of the T5 type of volute spring suspension. This suspension was fitted with a new double pin, rubber block, track which provided the basic design for most of the American tank tracks used through World War II. The rubber

block was vulcanized around the steel link which contained two holes for the rubber bushed track pins. The rubber bushings were vulcanized to the track pins which were then pressed into the holes in the track block. Adjacent blocks were attached to each other by end connectors to form a continuous track. The angle between adjacent blocks of this so-called live track was half that required for the track to pass around the idler or sprocket. The additional rotation required when operating was provided by the flexure of the rubber bushings. The end connectors also served as outside guides to maintain track alignment and the lugs on their outer ends engaged and were driven by the track sprockets. These early T16 tracks underwent numerous later modifications. For example, the T16E1 was a reversible track in which the block could be reversed when worn to increase the track life. The T16E2 was not reversible, but the rubber thickness on the ground contact side was increased.

Below, the light tank T2 is at Aberdeen Proving Ground in this photograph dated 23 May 1934. No armament has been installed in the tank.

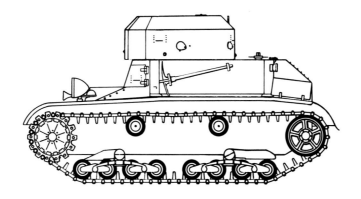

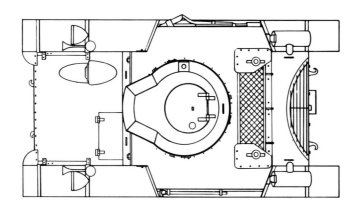

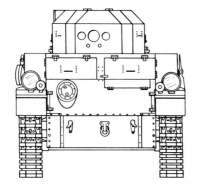 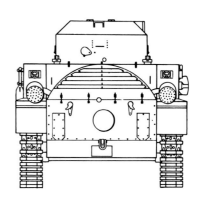

Scale 1:48

©**D.P. Dyer**

Light Tank T2

Further details of the original configuration of the light tank T2 can be seen above.

After the various modifications were complete, the vehicle was redesignated as the light tank T2E1 and returned to Aberdeen for tests which lasted from October 1934 to November 1937. From 14 January through 14 February 1935, the T2E1 was at Fort Benning, Georgia for evaluation. As a result of recommendations from the Infantry, a circular cupola was installed on top of the turret. During the test program at Aberdeen, the vehicle weight ranged from 15,000 pounds to 19,400 pounds due to the many modifications made to improve its performance. After about the first year of testing had indicated good reliability and performance, the T2E1 was standardized as the light tank

At the right and below is the light tank T2E1 during its evaluation. Note the volute spring suspension similar to that on the combat car T5.

The light tank T2E1 above retains the original turret without the cupola. No armament has been installed at this point in the test program.

M2A1. Nine of the standard tanks were manufactured at Rock Island during 1935. Including the original pilot, these vehicles were assigned serial numbers 1-10. The maximum armor thickness was $\frac{5}{8}$ inches, although the pilot T2E1 was constructed from soft steel. Fully loaded, the light tank M2A1 weighed 18,790 pounds and had a maximum road speed of 45 miles/hour. Manned by a crew of four, the armament consisted of a .50 caliber machine gun and a .30 caliber machine gun coaxially mounted in the turret, a .30 caliber machine gun in the right front hull bow mount, and a .30 caliber machine gun in an antiaircraft mount on the turret. The turret itself was cylindrical with an extension on the front for the gun mount.

The turret cupola has been added in the views above and below and the Infantry insignia is attached to the turret side wall. Note the modified stowage on the left side.

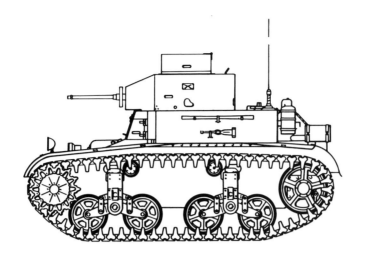

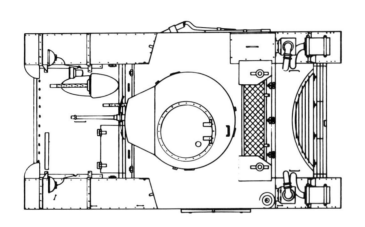

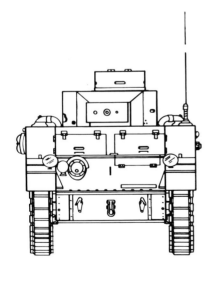

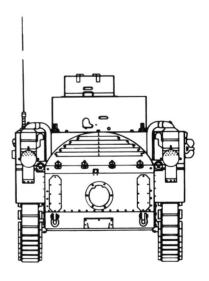

Scale 1:48

Light Tank M2A1

The full armament has been installed in light tank M2A1, serial number 7, shown in the photographs above and below. The combination gun mount T7 with the coaxial .50 caliber and .30 caliber machine guns is in the turret. The bow gunner's .30 caliber weapon is carried in the 6½ inch diameter M8 ball mount.

Details of the T7 combination gun mount can be seen at the left below. At the bottom right is a view of the bogie assembly installed on the light tank M2A1. This is a modified version of the bogie introduced on the combat car T5.

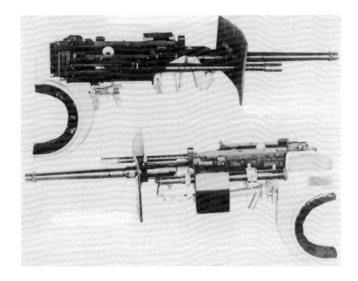

Although the armament is not carried, the M2A1 light tanks in these photographs are engaged in training exercises. The open position of the cupola cover can be seen in the view of the M2A1, serial number 10, below.

The front and side hull armor doors are shown open (above) and closed (below) in these photographs of the light tank T2E2. The full armament is clearly visible in the lower view.

Tests of the twin turret arrangement on the combat car T5 led to the selection of that configuration for the next production vehicle of the M2 series. This version was assigned the designation light tank T2E2 and then standardized at the same time as the M2A1 as the light tank M2A2. Through the fiscal year 1937, 237 of the twin turret tanks were manufactured at Rock Island Arsenal. Nine of these vehicles were referred to as the model 1935 with serial numbers 11-19. Serial numbers 20-144 were designated as the model 1936. The remaining 104 tanks were model 1937 with serial numbers 145-248. Tank number 248 was diverted from the production run for component testing.

Additional details of the light tank T2E2 can be seen below in these photographs from Rock Island Arsenal dated 16 November 1935.

98

Above, the first light tank M2A2, serial number 11, appears with the front armor doors for the driver and bow gunner open. Note that the shovel is missing from the side and its stowage bracket is damaged. To correct this problem which frequently occurred in wooded areas, a guard was installed (see bottom left).

Three of the remaining 237 production tanks were powered by the Guiberson T-1020 diesel engine and were redesignated as the light tank M2A2E1. One additional M2A2 was temporarily fitted with the Guiberson engine for evaluation at Aberdeen. After the tests were complete, it was converted back to a standard M2A2 with the Continental W-670 gasoline engine. Operations with the M2A2E1 indicated that at this stage the Guiberson diesel was unreliable and difficult to start, particularly in cold weather.

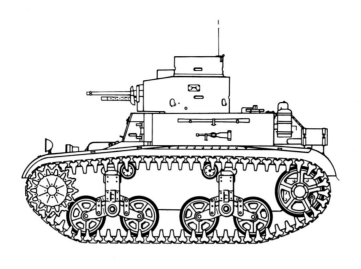

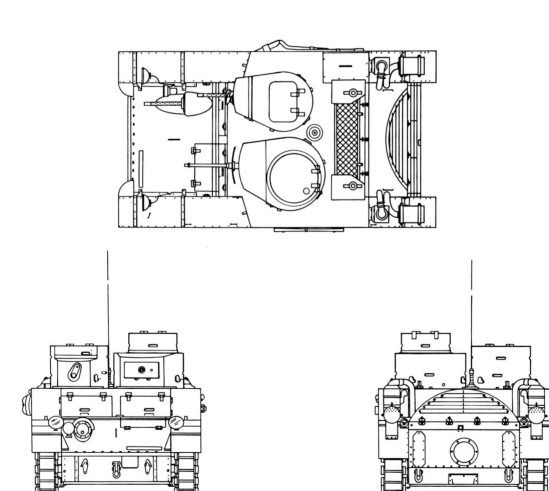

© D.P. Dyer

Light Tank M2A2

Above, the .50 caliber machine gun mount M9 (upper) and the .30 caliber machine gun mount M12E1 (lower) are at the left. The M12 mounts were installed in the right turret of M2A2 tanks 20-247 and the bow of M2A3s 249-320. At the top right, an M2A2 light tank from the 41st Tank Company is participating in the Fourth Army maneuvers during August 1940. Details of the turret cupola are visible in the view of the M2A2 below.

The twin turrets on the M2A2 were armed with a .50 caliber machine gun in the 36 inch diameter turret on the left and a .30 caliber machine gun in the 30 inch diameter turret on the right . The turrets on M2A2s with serial numbers 11 through 144 were cylindrical in shape with extensions to the front for the gun mount. On M2A2s with serial numbers 145 through 248, the turrets were assembled from flat armor plate with seven sides on the 30 inch diameter turret and eight sides on the 36 inch diameter turret. These M2A2s also were fitted with the flat faced engine compartment covers replacing the earlier round top covers. The maximum armor plate thickness on the M2A2 was still ⅝ inches. However, the two turret configuration increased the loaded weight to 19,100 pounds. The performance of the M2A2 was essentially identical to that of the M2A1 with a maximum road speed of 45 miles/hour and a cruising range of about 125 miles.

After the test of the combat car T5E1 at Fort Benning, the Infantry proposed the procurement of six light tanks with a barbette superstructure. Identical to the light tanks T2E1 and T2E2 except for the superstructure, the new vehicle was to be designated as the light tank T2E3. However, it did not enter production.

Below, light tank M2A2, serial number 20, leads a medium tank T4 and a medium tank M2 during the Third Army maneuvers at Fort Benning, Georgia in April 1940.

Above, the late model angular turret can be seen at the left on this light tank M2A2 from the 29th Tank Company of the Virginia National Guard. At the right, the M2A2 is firing its guns during training exercises. The high power to weight ratio of these light tanks is dramatically illustrated by the airborne M2A2 at the lower left.

At the right above, a late model light tank M2A2 with the angular turret is climbing onto a railway car during the 1938 Third Army maneuvers. Below is a lineup of light tanks. The .50 caliber machine gun has been dismounted from the M2A2 in front.

Above is a light tank M2A2 from the 66th Infantry (Tanks) during maneuvers at Plattsburg, New York in August 1939. Note the slack in the lower part of the track resulting from the front location of the drive sprocket. The M2A2s below are undergoing maintenance during the Carolina maneuvers on 24 October 1941.

Above are two early M2A2 light tanks with the round turrets. Note the lack of stowage guards on the hull sides. Below, M2A2s are simulating an attack on a 37mm gun manned by the Infantry.

Above are two views of the light tank M2A2E2 at Aberdeen Proving Ground on 30 July 1937. At the right is an earlier version of the same vehicle in this Rock Island Arsenal photograph dated 10 May 1937. Note the changes in the suspension system.

In July 1937, modified M2A2, serial number 248, arrived at Aberdeen Proving Ground from Rock Island. Designated as the light tank M2A2E2, it was fitted with outboard steering brakes installed with the final drive gears in special housings. The maximum armor plate thickness on this vehicle was one inch which was the major factor in the increase of the loaded weight to 21,500 pounds. Other changes included a synchromesh transmission, a modified suspension, and improved accessibility to the engine compartment. Tests of the M2A2E2 at Aberdeen continued until August 1938 to secure data for the future development of light tanks and for the medium tank T5. The tests showed that the outboard steering brakes permitted much cooler

operation of the transmission and differential, but resulted in excessive operating temperatures for the brakes and final drives.

In August 1938, the M2A2E2 was returned to Rock Island for further modification. Fitted with a General Motors liquid-cooled 6-71 diesel engine and an automatic transmission, it was now redesignated as the light tank M2A2E3. The vehicle also received a modified suspension with a trailing idler which increased the ground contact length from 94 inches to 126½ inches. Although the changes increased the weight of the vehicle by over a ton, the larger ground contact area with the trailing idler reduced the ground pressure compared to the M2A2E2.

The two photographs below, dated 6 July 1939, show the light tank M2A2E3 at Aberdeen Proving Ground. Note the modified suspension with the trailing idler. When this vehicle, serial number 248, was diverted for the experimental program, it never was fitted with the stowage guards on the hull.

Above is the light tank M2A3 at Aberdeen Proving Ground on 13 October 1938. The full armament has been installed on this tank.

As a result of the tests on the combat car M1E2, further modifications were made to the light tank scheduled for production during fiscal year 1938. The new vehicle was designated as the light tank M2A3 and it differed from the M2A2 in several respects. The suspension bogie spacing was increased changing the ground contact length from 86 to 97 inches. The angular flat sided turret design was retained, but the distance between the turret centers was increased to 38½ inches and the maximum armor plate thickness was increased from ⅝ inches to ⅞ inches. The

rear hull configuration also was modified to improve engine accessibility. With these changes, the combat weight now reached 21,000 pounds, but the larger ground contact area reduced the ground pressure compared to the M2A2. The final drive gear ratio was changed from 2:1 to 2.41:1 reducing the maximum road speed to 37.5 miles/hour. One of the M2A3s was shipped to Aberdeen in July 1938 for use in evaluating many of its new components such as battery ignition for the engine, a synchromesh transmission, and an engine governor. Seventy-three M2A3 light tanks (serial

Below, details of the turrets on the light tank M2A3 are shown in the drawings. The 30 inch diameter turret appears at the left and the 36 inch diameter turret is at the right. The increased spacing between the suspension bogies on the M2A3 is obvious in the photograph.

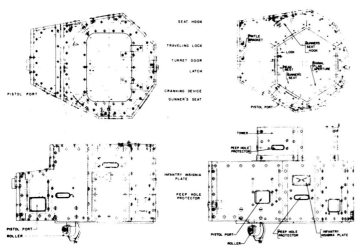

The engine compartment cover configuration can be seen in the view above of the gasoline powered light tank M2A3.

numbers 249-321) were manufactured at Rock Island Arsenal during fiscal year 1938. The M2A3 was powered by the W-670 series 9 engine. This was the latest version of the radial Continental gasoline power plant installed in the light tanks. The various designations of these engines were as follows:

The R-670 series 3C and the W-670 series 8 which developed 235 net horsepower at 2400 rpm with a compression ratio of 5.4:1.

The R-670 series 3 and 5 and the W-670 series 7, 8, 9, and 9A which developed 250 horsepower at 2400 rpm with a compression ratio of 6.1:1.

The series 9A differed from the series 9 in that the 9A was fitted with a governor. It might be noted that, according to the technical manuals, all of these light tanks were limited to a maximum speed of 30 miles/hour. Needless to say, they were capable of much greater speeds if the governors were removed as they frequently were.

Below, the gasoline powered version of the light tank M2A3 (left) can be compared with the diesel powered vehicle (right). Note the long intake pipes from the air cleaners on the latter.

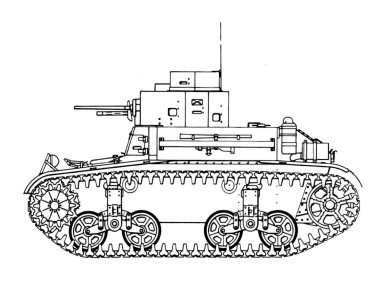

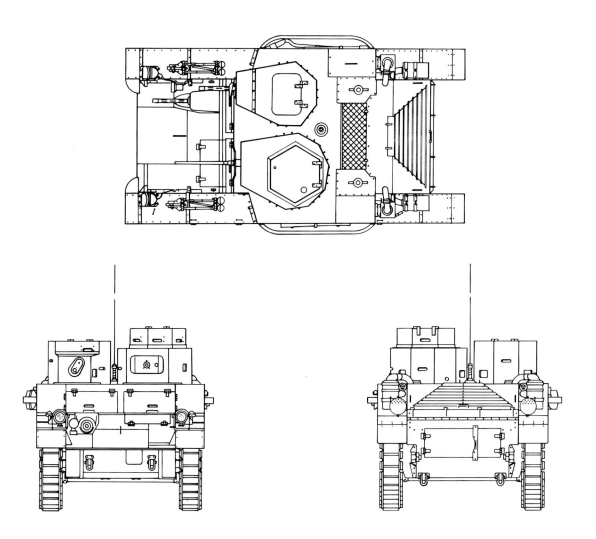

Scale 1:48

Light Tank M2A3

Above and below, further comparisons can be made between the gasoline powered light tank M2A3 (left) and the diesel powered version of the tank (right). The difference in the air intake lines is obvious in the rear views.

Below, the front armor of the light tank M2A3E2 has been removed to reveal the installation of the Timken Electrogear transmission.

Eight of the 73 production M2A3s were powered by the Guiberson nine cylinder radial diesel engine and were designated as light tanks M2A3E1. This was the Guiberson T-1020 series 3. Later vehicles were fitted with the Guiberson T-1020 series 4 which was fitted with a governor. Both engines were originally rated at 250 net horsepower at 2200 rpm. Later, this was revised to 220 horsepower at 2200 rpm. The original production M2A3s were equipped with a constant mesh sliding gear transmission. Later, these were replaced by synchromesh transmissions. Both types had five speeds forward and one reverse. The final drive gear ratio was changed form 2:1 to 2.41:1 on the M2A3 resulting in lower road speeds. One additional M2A3 was modified by the installation of the Timken Electrogear transmission and was redesignated as the light tank M2A3E2.

The general configuration of the light tank M2A3E3 is shown in these photographs. Note the trailing idler suspension required to support the heavier diesel engine.

Ordnance Committee action on 21 February 1940 approved the installation of the General Motors Corporation V-4-223 diesel engine in the M2A3. Intended for possible future use in the M2A4 light tank, OCM 15645 recommended that the engine be installed for test purposes in an M2A3 modified to the engine compartment configuration of the M2A4. The hull changes were to be made using soft steel plate. The V-4-223 was a two stroke cycle diesel engine developing 250 horsepower at 1400 rpm. The engine was to be installed with the Ordnance Department clutch, drive shaft, and synchromesh transmission. It was intended to replace the latter with a General Motors automatic transmission at a later date. To maintain the proper weight distribution with the heavier diesel engine, it was necessary to fit the tank with a trailing idler suspension. The estimated weight of the converted vehicle was 24,000 pounds. Designated as the light tank M2A3E3, it was under test at Aberdeen in January 1941.

The engine installation in the light tank M2A3E3 appears below. At the left is a view from the top. At the right, the new power plant can be seen from the rear.

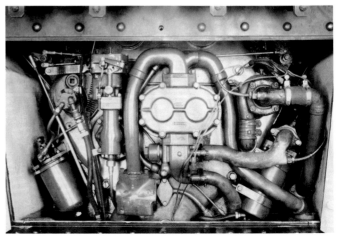

110

These photographs show the light tank T3. The view above was dated 13 March 1936. Below, the single .30 caliber machine gun has been installed.

In early 1936, Rock Island Arsenal completed a new light tank with a loaded weight less than half that of the T2 series. Designated as the light tank T3, it followed the same design concept as the World War I Ford three-ton tank. Shipped to Aberdeen in March 1936, it was under test until June 1937. Manned by a crew of two, the T3 was armed with a single .30 caliber machine gun ball mounted in the right front hull. The driver rode in the left front hull. With a maximum armor thickness of ⅜ inches, the loaded weight was only 7,080 pounds. Like its ancestor, the vehicle was driven by a standard Ford automobile engine, only now it was a V-8 developing 83 horsepower at 3800 rpm. Equipped with a four speed transmission and controlled differential steering, the T3 had a maximum road speed of 35 miles/hour. A rubber torsion type suspension was fitted during the test program, but it failed on several occasions. However, it was expected to be successful if redesigned.

At the request of the Chief of Infantry, the T3 was shipped to Fort Benning for examination. The evaluation by the Infantry showed that the vehicle was very quiet, had excellent maneuverability, and was easy to handle. However, it was considered deficient in both armament and armor protection for satisfactory use as a tank. The Infantry report pointed out that the cost of the vehicle could not be justified to carry only a single .30 caliber machine gun. They also noted that the T3 could easily be penetrated by .30 caliber ball ammunition, not to mention the effect of .30 caliber armor piercing rounds.

Despite its rejection by the user, the low cost and light weight of the T3 concept was attractive enough to have

launched projects for three modified versions before the entire program was cancelled. The first of these, designated as the light tank T3E1, was already under construction. It was powered by a Menasco air-cooled engine and fitted with a volute spring suspension. After the work on the T3 concept was stopped, the T3E1 was converted into the cross-country carrier T5. Specifications also were prepared for a light tank T3E2 with improved armor protection. This vehicle was proposed for use by the National Guard. The designation light tank T3E3 was assigned to a design study, but, like the T3E2, the vehicle was never built.

Another design study that never got beyond the drawing board was designated as the light tank T4. This vehicle was to be similar to the T3, but it was to be powered by a Guiberson five cylinder diesel engine. The designation light tank T5 was applied to another design study that was never completed.

The Marmon-Herrington light tank evaluated by the United States Marine Corps appears in these photographs. The three machine guns have not been fitted in the hull ball mounts.

The United States Marine Corps required a tank suitable for use in ship to shore operations. After early tests with the Christie amphibious vehicle, the Corps began experiments in 1935 using the Marmon-Herrington light tanks. These were light turretless vehicles with a crew of two and a loaded weight of about five tons. The Marmon-Herrington tanks were armed with one .50 caliber machine gun and two .30 caliber machine guns. All three were installed in ball mounts located in the hull front plate. The maximum armor thickness was ½ inch. A four bogie leaf spring suspension was fitted with 10½ inch wide rubber band tracks. The final version of this tank tested by the Corps was powered by an 85 horsepower Ford V-8 engine which drove the vehicle at a maximum road speed of about 30 miles/hour. Tests with this tank continued until 1939. By that time, it was obvious that the Marmon-Herrington vehicles did not meet the Marine Corps requirements and future plans were based on the use of Army light tanks.

PART II

LIGHT TANKS FOR WORLD WAR II

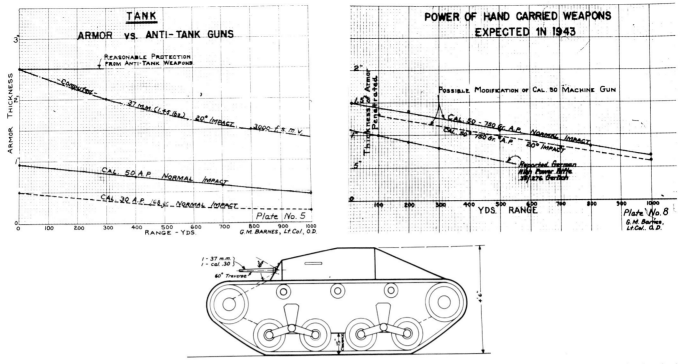

The concept proposed by Lieutenant Colonel Gladeon M. Barnes for an inexpensive, lightweight tank with relatively heavy armor is sketched above. Note the very low silhouette of this vehicle. The penetration performance of armor piercing ammunition is shown at the top left. At that time, it was not considered feasible to provide protection against the 37mm gun. Expected improvement in the performance of the .50 caliber machine gun is illustrated at the top right.

PREPARATION FOR WAR

By 1938, the development of hand carried automatic weapons had reached a stage that made thinly armored light tanks extremely vulnerable. This was emphasized by the experience in the Spanish Civil War. On 15 April 1938, Lieutenant Colonel (later Major General) Gladeon M. Barnes submitted a memorandum to the Assistant Commandant of the Army War College entitled "Tank Development Program for the U. S. Army". In his memorandum, Lieutenant Colonel Barnes reviewed the lessons of past combat experience and concluded that the light tanks then in production for the U. S. Army were inadequately armed and armored for modern warfare. He noted that both the light tank M2A2 and the combat car M1 had a maximum armor thickness of 5/8 inches. Such armor could be penetrated by the .50 caliber machine gun at ranges up to 700 yards and improvements in the near future would likely increase this range to 1000 yards. The most powerful armament on both the light tank and the combat car was the .50 caliber machine gun. A heavier weapon such as the 37mm antitank gun was required. To keep the cost low so that the vehicle could be produced in very large numbers, Lieutenant Colonel Barnes proposed the development of a two man light tank weighing about seven tons with armor 1½ inches thick. The vehicle would not have a turret and the armament would consist of a .30 caliber machine gun and a semiautomatic 37mm gun. The weapons would be installed in a combination mount in the hull front

plate permitting them to be served by one man. Such a lightweight vehicle could use many commercial automotive components resulting in an estimated production cost of $20,000 per tank. Lieutenant Colonel Barnes' proposal reflected the effect on armored vehicle design of the extremely severe budget restrictions in the period prior to World War II.

A more conventional approach to improved armor protection and more powerful armament was illustrated in two design proposal drawings submitted during July 1938 by Major (later Brigadier General) John K. Christmas. The first of these showed the chassis for a two man light tank powered by two Buick series 60 automobile engines with a combined output of about 280 horsepower. The engines drove the vehicle through two standard Buick synchromesh transmissions. The chassis was fitted with a horizontal volute spring suspension using two bogies for each track. The two front bogies on the vehicle each carried two 20 inch diameter wheels. The two rear bogies had one 20 inch wheel and one 28 inch wheel with the latter serving as a trailing idler. One inch thick armor plate was specified for all vertical surfaces on the tank. OCM 14628, dated 3 August 1938, assigned the designation light tank T6 to a similar design configuration. A single pilot T6 chassis was completed at Rock Island Arsenal in June 1939 and shipped to Aberdeen Proving Ground in July. The empty chassis weighed 19,500 pounds. Although intended for

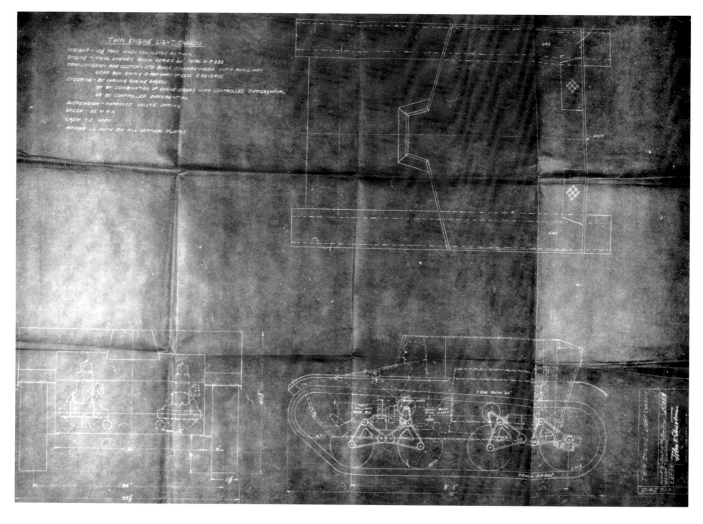

The drawing above shows the design for a twin engine light tank with a two man crew proposed by Major John K. Christmas. The drawing, dated 25 July 1938, depicts the basic chassis without the turret.

completion as a light tank with a one man turret, the turret was never installed and the vehicle was used at Aberdeen for test purposes.

The second design by Major Christmas was a three man tank armed with a 37mm antitank gun and a .30 caliber machine gun mounted coaxially in a one man turret.

A second .30 caliber machine gun was manned by a bow gunner in the right front hull. The driver was seated in the left front hull. Like the T6 design, armor plate one inch thick was specified for all vertical surfaces. This concept had an estimated weight of 10½ tons and was to be powered by the Continental W-670 radial engine with

The light tank T6 can be seen in the photographs below dated 16 June 1939. Like the design concept above, it was powered by two eight cylinder Buick automobile engines.

Above are two additional views of the light tank T6. At the right is a drawing of the horizontal volute spring suspension bogie used on the T6.

a synchromesh transmission. The vehicle was equipped with controlled differential steering and the same four bogie horizontal volute spring suspension as on the T6. With the heavier armor and armament, these concepts indicated the direction that future light tank development would take.

The concept drawing below, also submitted by Major Christmas during July 1938, shows a three man light tank with a 37mm gun as the main armament.

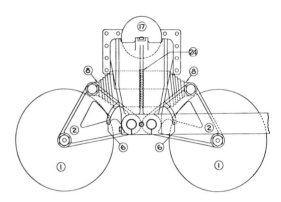

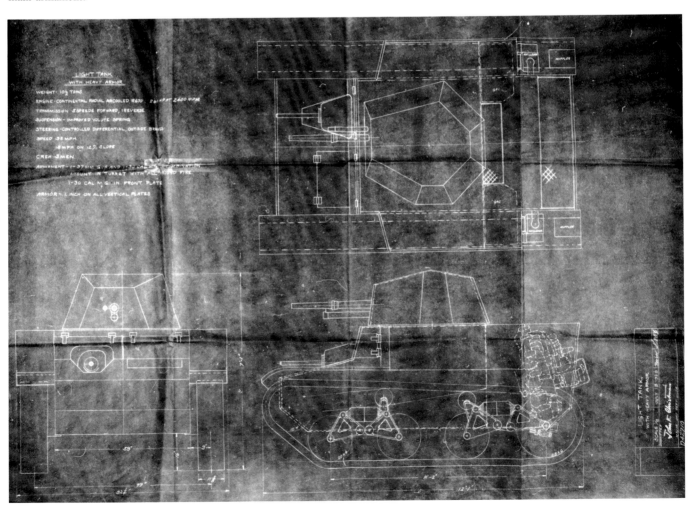

The original version of the pilot light tank M2A4 appears in these photographs dated 11 May 1939 at Aberdeen Proving Ground. Note the absence of a cupola and there is only one sponson machine gun. Also, the recoil system for the 37mm gun does not have complete armor protection.

LIGHT TANK M2A4

On 29 December 1938, OCM 14844 directed that one light tank M2A3 be taken from the production line and modified to have heavier armor and more powerful armament as requested by the Chief of Infantry. This pilot vehicle was converted from the last M2A3, serial number 321, and designated as the light tank M2A4. The necessary changes were made using soft steel plate. The major modifications included a new two man turret armed with an M3 37mm antitank gun and a .30 caliber machine gun in a coaxial mount. One inch thick armor was specified for all vertical surfaces. After the modifications were completed at Rock Island, the M2A4 pilot was shipped to Aberdeen. On 6 June 1939, a conference was held at the Proving Ground between the members of the Ordnance Automo-

tive Sub-Committee and representatives of the Infantry Board, the Chief of Infantry, the Chief of Ordnance, and the Chief Signal Officer. After examination of the pilot M2A4, the weapons were fired with the tank stationary and in motion. The Sub-Committee then convened a formal meeting and outlined the changes required before the M2A4 was placed in production. These changes included modification of the combination gun mount to increase the range of elevation and a 5.1 inch (3½ calibers) reduction in length of the 37mm gun. The latter was to prevent damage to the weapon when operating in heavily wooded areas. The original pilot had a fixed .30 caliber machine gun mounted in the left sponson for use by the driver. An additional fixed .30 caliber machine gun was specified for

These views show the pilot light tank M2A4 after its modification and return to Aberdeen. They were dated 9 October 1939. All armament is mounted except for the .30 caliber antiaircraft machine gun.

installation in the right sponson also for use by the driver. Both weapons were to be moved forward by about six inches compared to the original location. The ball mount for the bow gunner in the right front hull was retained, but it was to be modified to increase the range of elevation. A cupola with vision slots similar to that on the light tank M2A3 was to be added on the left rear of the turret roof with the hatch cover hinges on the front edge. Two pistol ports were to be added, one each in the left front and right front turret walls. All of the pistol ports were to be raised to the level of the left side pistol port in the original pilot. Armor protection was to be added for the recoil mechanism of the 37mm gun. All of the tanks were to be fitted with radio receivers and transmitters would be installed in command tanks. The pilot M2A4 was returned to Rock Island to make the requested changes and it was returned to Aberdeen in early October. By this time, steel angles also had been welded to the front armor plate to deflect bullet splash.

The first production light tank M2A4 can be seen on this page after its arrival for test at Aberdeen on 20 May 1940. The protective armor for the 37mm gun recoil system is the same as on the modified pilot tank.

Production of the light tank M2A4 began at the American Car & Foundry Company in May 1940 and continued until March 1941 with a run of 365 tanks. An additional ten M2A4s were assembled at the Baldwin Locomotive Works during April 1942 bringing the total production of the vehicle to 375. Although most of these tanks were powered by the Continental W-670 series 9A gasoline engine, some were fitted with the Guiberson T-1020 series 4 diesel. The hull and turret of the production M2A4s were assembled from rolled face-hardened steel armor plate

Light tank M2A4, serial number 382, appears in these photographs during August 1940. Note the later design protective armor for the recoil system.

Although the Armored Force had been formed a few weeks before these photographs were taken, M2A4 number 382 still retains its Infantry crossed rifles on each side of the turret.

Above are two additional views of light tank M2A4, serial number 382, taken at Aberdeen Proving Ground. The mint condition of this tank, particularly its fenders, indicate that it has not yet been subjected to much testing.

joined together by structural steel angles and nickel steel rivets. The joints between the plates were sealed with a plastic compound. The driver and bow gunner were seated in the front hull on the left and right respectively. The gunner and the tank commander rode in the turret and the tank commander also acted as loader for the 37mm gun. In the combination mount M20, a .30 caliber M1919A4 machine gun was installed on the right side of the 37mm gun and a telescopic sight was on the left. In addition to the 360 degree traverse provided by the turret rotation, the M20 mount itself could traverse 10 degrees to the left or right of center. The range of elevation was from +20 to –10 degrees.

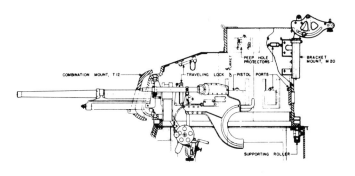

The interior arrangement of the light tank M2A4 turret can be seen in the drawing above. At the right is the combination gun mount M20. In the top view of the M2A4 below, note that the protective armor is not installed over the recoil system.

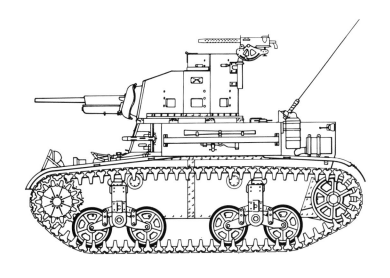

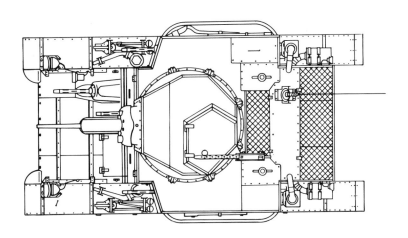

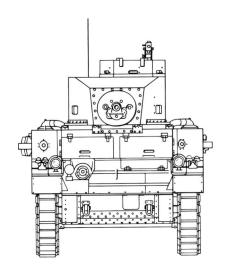

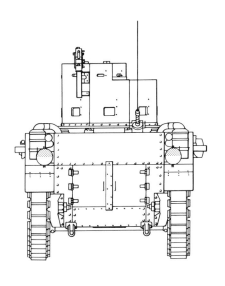

Scale 1:48

©**D.P. Dyer**

Light Tank M2A4

Above are two views of the experimental cast hull and turret assembled for possible future application to the light tank M2A4. Although the cast components followed the same general configuration as the riveted tank, many of the side surfaces were sloped for better ballistic protection.

To evaluate the problems in the possible future use of cast hulls and turrets on the M2A4, a contract was awarded to American Steel Foundries of East Chicago, Indiana. The cast sections produced under this contract were welded together by Electro-Motive Corporation in LaGrange, Illinois and then returned to Rock Island Arsenal. After some additional welding of rolled plate sections, the hull and turret were shipped to Aberdeen Proving Ground on 12 November 1940. Although the cast hull and turret were never applied to the production M2A4, the lessons learned were valuable in later development projects such as the light tank T7 program.

The two photographs at the lower left show a light tank M2A4 with the rear hull and engine compartment modified to the configuration eventually adopted for the light tank M3. At the lower right is a chart comparing the ammunition stowage in the M2A4 (dotted lines) with that in the earlier light tanks and combat cars.

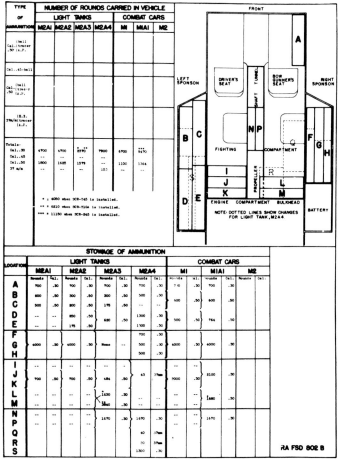

Above, Lieutenant Norris H. Perkins peers out of the driver's hatch on an M2A4 during maintenance training at Fort Knox. The views at the right show M2A4s of the 2nd Armored Division during the Tennessee maneuvers in June 1941. All of these photographs came from Dr. Norris H. Perkins.

The light tank M2A4 served with U. S. Army armored units during training and maneuvers from 1940 to 1942. When the Lend-Lease program was initiated in the Spring of 1940, 36 M2A4s were allocated to Britain, but there is no record of their being used in combat. However, some sources indicate that one or more M2A4s were transferred from the Middle East to Burma with the 7th Armoured Brigade and served with them during the retreat to India in 1942. The M2A4 also was adopted by the U.S. Marine Corps and was used in action, along with the light tank M3, during the fighting on Guadalcanal.

The 2nd Armored Division M2A4s above carry the insignia proposed for the Armored Force consisting of a blue disc on a white star with a red circle background. This was the same as the contemporary Air Corps insignia with the colors reversed. In the view just above, the tanks on the left are diesel powered and the ones on the right have gasoline engines. Below is a diesel powered M2A4. Note the long air intake pipes.

Fueling the gasoline powered M2A4 always was a hazardous process. Note the ready fire extinguisher in the photograph above from Norris Perkins. Below, an M2A4 light tank moves through Mount Carmel, Louisiana during maneuvers between the Second and Third Armies on 17 September 1941.

Above is the light tank M3 number 1. Note the large round rivet heads on the hull and turret unlike the smooth flush riveted exterior surface on the M2A4 and earlier light tanks. This photograph, taken at Aberdeen Proving Ground, was dated 14 April 1941.

LIGHT TANK M3 SERIES

Further tests and troop use of the light tank M2A4 revealed the need for numerous improvements. A trailing idler suspension was considered essential to reduce the ground pressure and to improve the weight distribution. On 3 June 1940, OCM 15864 recommended that the light tanks procured during the fiscal year 1941 have 1½ inches of frontal armor. This action was approved and OCM 15932, dated 5 July 1940, designated the improved vehicle as the light tank M3. Initially, the M3 turret was a riveted assembly of face-hardened armor plates similar to that on the M2A4. However, the pistol port design was improved and the number was reduced from seven to three. The new combination gun mount M22 replaced the M20 mount used in the M2A4. On the new mount, the recoil mechanism was redesigned and shortened so that it did not extend in front of the gun shield. Thus it did not require the long armored protector installed on the M2A4. Like the M20, the M22 mount retained the 20 degree traverse range (10 degrees left or right of center) in addition to the

360 degree traverse obtained by the turret rotation. Vision for the crew was provided by the hatches, the three pistol ports, and ten protected vision slots. Four of the latter were in the driving compartment and six in the turret cupola. A new cast steel front hull section improved the protection of the M3 in that area.

The M3, powered by the Continental W-670 gasoline engine, replaced the M2A4 on the production line at the American Car & Foundry Company starting in March 1941. Production continued without interruption until July 1942 providing 4525 tanks. A single gasoline powered M3 was delivered in October 1942 bringing the total up to 4526. In June 1941, production also began at the American Car & Foundry Company of the M3 fitted with the Guiberson T-1020 diesel engine. This run continued until August 1942 producing 1281 tanks. Four additional diesel powered M3s were completed during January 1943 increasing the total to 1285. The official designation for these vehicles was the light tank M3 (diesel).

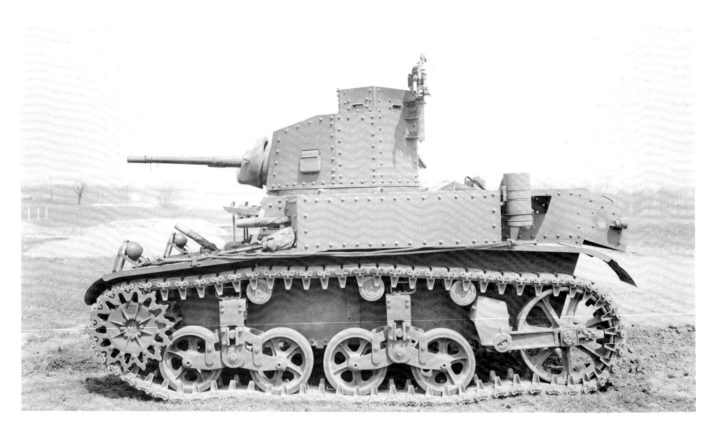

The new trailing idler suspension on light tank M3 number 1 is clearly visible in the side view above. The turret pistol ports have been fitted with hinged exterior covers replacing the internal sliding covers on the light tank M2A4.

Externally, the obvious difference between the gasoline and diesel powered tanks was the configuration of the flexible intake pipes from the air cleaners. On the gasoline driven vehicle, these pipes came out of the air cleaners and immediately curved down through the rear deck armor. On the diesel powered tanks, the intake pipes extended from the air cleaners across the deck and through the screen above the engine. This same arrangement applied to the diesel and gasoline powered versions of the M2A4 and the M3A1 as well as some of the earlier tanks.

Below, light tank M3 number 1 is fitted with windshields and wipers suitable for use in rear areas. In the rear view, note the round air cleaners which replaced the square air cleaners on the M2A4.

The photographs on this page show light tank M3, serial number 1366, at Aberdeen Proving Ground on 10 September 1941. This tank has the welded face-hardened armor turret, but it retains the bolted front plate.

Many of the production tanks were diverted to foreign aid under the Lend-Lease program. Thus 1784 gasoline driven M3s and 50 of the diesel powered version were assigned to Great Britain. In British service the tanks were named after General J. E. B. Stuart, the famous Civil War Confederate cavalry general, with the gasoline and diesel powered tanks becoming the Stuart I and the Stuart II respectively. The Soviet Union also received 1336 of the M3s with the gasoline engine.

Many changes were made during the production of the M3. Ballistic tests on the original riveted turret revealed that the 37mm M39 armor piercing projectile would penetrate at a velocity of 1842 feet/second and all hits that did not penetrate deformed and loosened the plates from the structural steel angles. Spalling of the armor also caused considerable damage inside the turret. Direct hits by .50 caliber M1 armor piercing rounds at a velocity of 2492 feet/second would drive the rivets and bolts into the turret creating a hazard for the crew. After extensive tests, the Ordnance Committee on 27 December 1940 recommended that future turrets for the light tank M3 be fabricated by welding. Tests indicated that the welded face-hardened armor retained 90 per cent of its ballistic resistance in the heat affected zone around the weld. The welded turret also eliminated the interior structural steel angles cleaning up the inside of the turret and increasing its volume. The new welded face-hardened steel turret was installed on M3 number 279 when it arrived at Aberdeen Proving Ground for acceptance tests. It was noted that the bolted turret front plate also could be welded to the remainder of the turret since its removal was not required to extract the 37mm gun. This practice also was adopted at a later date.

Other details of light tank M3 number 1366 can be seen in these views. With the armor doors closed, the vision for the driver and bow gunner is limited to the early protected vision slots. The sectional drawing at the bottom of the page shows the internal arrangement of the light tank M3.

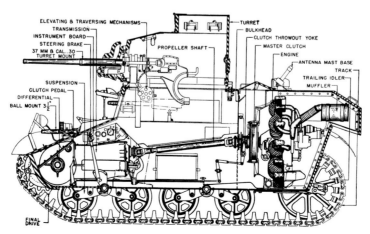

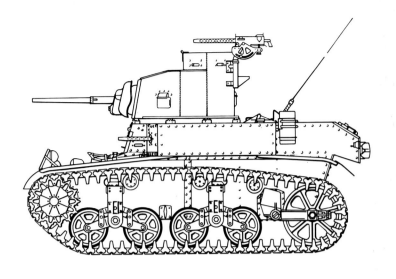

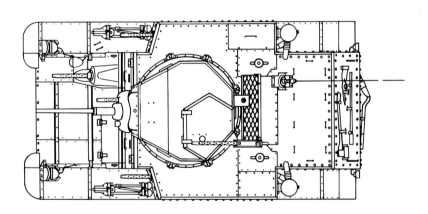

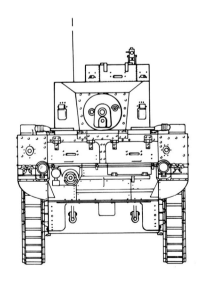

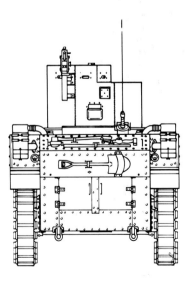

Scale 1:48

©D.P. Dyer

Light Tank M3 (early production)

Above, early production M3 light tanks are on a road near the American Car & Foundry Company plant. The lack of armament reflects the gun shortage at that time. At the left is the production line at the American Car & Foundry Company. Note the transition from riveted to welded turrets on these tanks. At the lower left are views of the driver's compartment and the top of the light tank M3. The bow gunner's station is below.

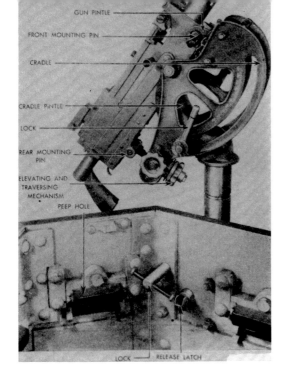

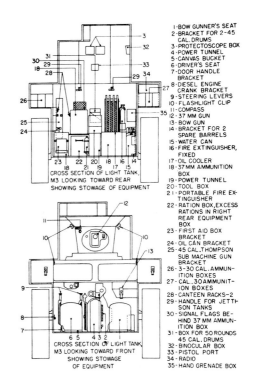

Above is the M20 antiaircraft mount and .30 caliber machine gun on the light tank M3. The stowage arrangement in the M3 is illustrated at the top right.

Interior views of the left (upper) and right (lower) sponson machine guns in the light tank M3 appear at the right.

The combination gun mount M22 armed with the 37mm gun M5 and a .30 caliber machine gun can be seen below. Later models of the light tank M3 were fitted with the M23 combination gun mount.

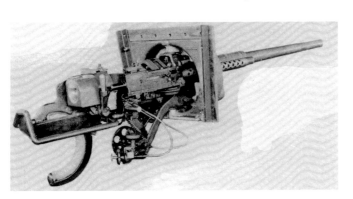

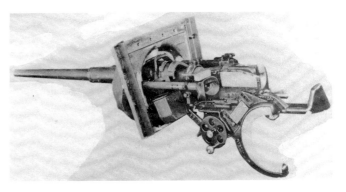

These photographs show light tank M3, serial number 1946, at Aberdeen Proving Ground on 17 November 1941. It features the new round homogeneous armor turret with a bolted front plate and protectoscopes in the pistol ports and the front hull doors.

The continuing development of armor plate resulted in further improvement. OCM 16583, dated 27 March 1941, directed that the welded face-hardened plate turret with the cast steel race ring be replaced as soon as possible. The new turret was to be formed from 1¼ inch thick rolled homogeneous steel armor and it was expected to have equal or better ballistic properties compared to the one inch thick face-hardened plate. A forged steel race ring was to be used

with the new turret. A pilot turret was fabricated by the American Car & Foundry Company and shipped to Aberdeen for evaluation. The test report indicated that the formed and welded homogeneous steel armor turret was superior to all of those previously tested. M3 number 1946 was fitted with the new turret when it arrived at Aberdeen for acceptance tests. Some additional changes also were made. The three pistol port covers were now fitted with

The driving and blackout lights are clearly visible in these additional views of light tank M3 number 1946. None of the machine guns have been installed in this tank.

protectoscopes. These periscope type viewing devices included an armor pocket to entrap a bullet or fragment penetrating the vision slot. The cupola was retained on the turret roof, but it now had a curved shape and the vision slots were eliminated. The single hatch cover on the old cupola was replaced by double hatch covers on the new model. One of these covers contained a circular opening intended for the installation of a rotating periscope. Unfor-

tunately, the location of the cupola periscope proved to be impractical for use and the opening was covered by a steel plate on the production tanks. Four protected vision slots in the curved cupola walls were introduced later in production. M3 number 1946 also was equipped with protectoscopes in the front doors for the driver and assistant driver or bow gunner. Direct vision slots with movable armor covers also were provided in the same doors.

The photograph at the left of M3 number 1946 shows the short air intake pipes of the gasoline powered tank and the new stowage boxes mounted behind the air cleaners. Above is a closeup of the new front armor doors with the protectoscopes (outboard) and the vision slots with the external moveable armor covers (inboard). The front armor doors are opened in the views below.

Below, the cupola hatch and the pistol ports on M3 number 1946 are open and closed. Note the absence of vision slots in the cupola. A plate has been installed over the circular opening in the hatch cover originally intended for a periscope. The small hole with a sliding cover was to permit the use of signal flags.

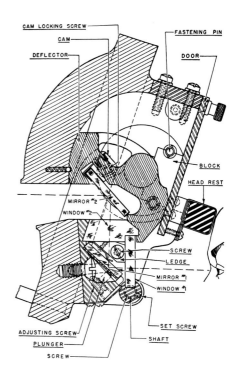

Above is an interior view of the driver's protectoscope (left) and vision slot (right) on M3 number 1946. Below, the pistol port can be seen from inside the turret. At the right are drawings of the protectoscope installed in the front armor doors (upper) and the pistol port covers (lower).

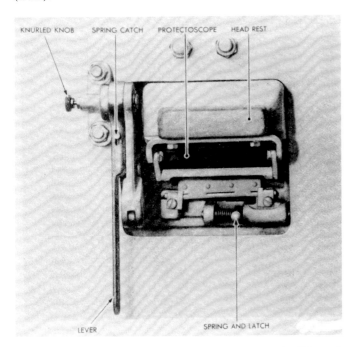

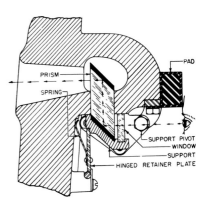

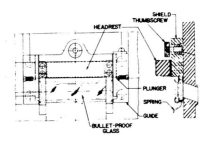

Below are two photographs of the cupola installed on the light tank M3, serial number 2188. Note the four protected vision slots in the cupola side walls. The design of these protected vision slots can be seen in the drawing at the right.

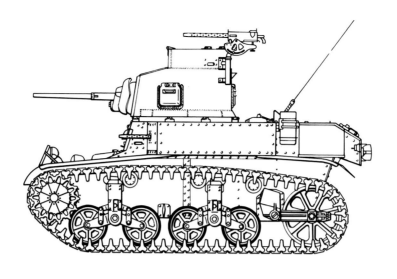

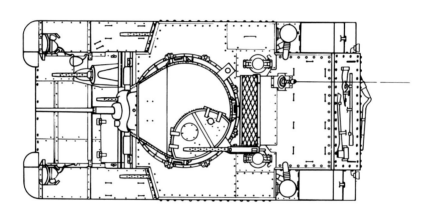

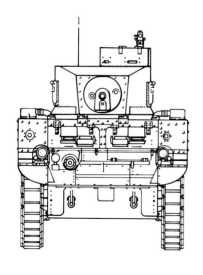

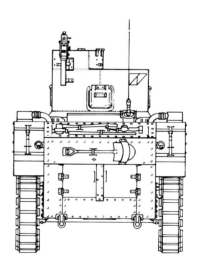

Scale 1:48

Light Tank M3 (mid production)

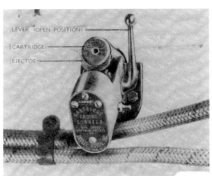

Above are front views of the Continental W-670-9 gasoline engine (left) and the Guiberson T-1020-4 diesel engine (right). The cartridge starter for the diesel engine is shown open (at left) and closed (below). At the lower left are the cartridges used with this starter.

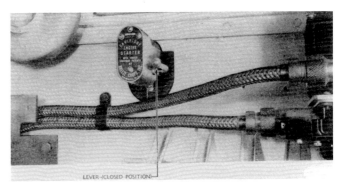

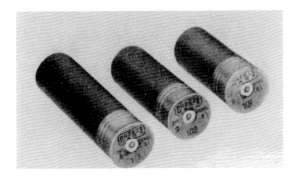

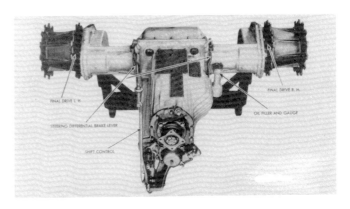

The transmission and final drives of the light tank M3 power train appear at the right. Below are details of the front bogie assembly and the trailing idler.

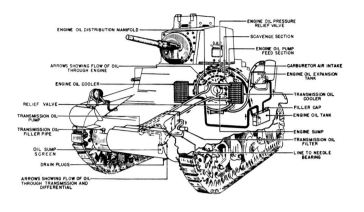

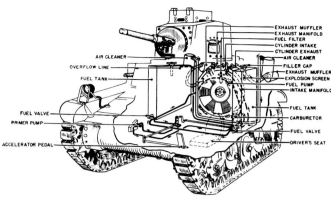

The fuel system for the light tank M3 with the Continental gasoline engine is sketched above at the right. At the top left is a drawing of the engine and transmission oil system. The oil coolers can be seen in the rear of the fighting compartment in the view at the left. Note the drive shaft tunnel dividing the fighting compartment.

The cruising range of the light tank M3 was limited to approximately 70 miles with the gasoline engine and to about 90 miles with the diesel power plant. To increase the range of operations, the Ordnance Committee in September 1941 directed that jettison fuel tanks be provided for the M3 and other vehicles at the earliest practical date. Tested at Aberdeen on M3 number 727 in November 1941, the jettison tanks consisted of two 25 gallon drums with bullet sealing covers. Mounted over the sponsons, the drums were connected to the vehicle tanks by an automatic fuel transfer coupling and a bullet sealing hose. Pulling a lanyard from within the fighting compartment detached the drums so that they rolled off the vehicle. They could be recovered later for future use. The cruising range of the M3 with the jettison fuel tanks was almost doubled.

These photographs, dated 28 November 1941, show the jettison fuel tanks installed on light tank M3, serial number 727, at Aberdeen Proving Ground. Note that the fuel tanks limited the traverse of the 37mm gun to 90 degrees left or right of center.

Above, the jettison fuel tanks are shown before (left) and immediately after (right) release. The tubes containing the release lanyards extended through the cooling air intake screen into the fighting compartment. Below, the new armor fuel cap covers can be seen on light tank M3, serial number 2346.

Ordnance Committee action in December 1941 directed that padding be installed inside the tanks to protect the crew from impacts during operations. A lifting hook also was added to each side of the hull between the front and rear bogies. Armor covers were installed to protect the fuel filler caps in December 1941 and a welded hull appeared in early 1942 on M3 number 3213. The latter was assembled by plug welding the sponson connection angles and other components to the face hardened side armor. Later, additional weld joints further simplfied the assembly.

Light tank M3, serial number 3213, with the welded face-hardened armor hull appears at the right and below. These photographs, taken at Aberdeen Proving Ground, were dated 9 January 1942. Note the lifting hook installed on the hull side wall between the bogies.

141

At the right is the stabilizer installation in the light tank M3.

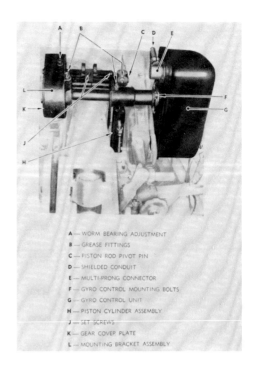

A — WORM BEARING ADJUSTMENT
B — GREASE FITTINGS
C — PISTON ROD PIVOT PIN
D — SHIELDED CONDUIT
E — MULTI-PRONG CONNECTOR
F — GYRO CONTROL MOUNTING BOLTS
G — GYRO CONTROL UNIT
H — PISTON CYLINDER ASSEMBLY
J — SET SCREWS
K — GEAR COVER PLATE
L — MOUNTING BRACKET ASSEMBLY

To improve the firing accuracy when the tank was in motion, a gyroscopic stabilizer was installed experimentally in a light tank M2A4. Tests with this vehicle indicated that greatly improved performance could be obtained with the gyrostabilizer, provided the personnel were properly trained. As a result, the stabilizer was incorporated into the production tanks starting in 1942. When properly adjusted, the gyrostabilizer maintained the manually set angle of elevation despite the movement of the tank over rough terrain. On the light tank M3, the gun was traversed manually. Successful use of the stabilizer required a high standard of training including practice with live ammunition. Unfortunately, this was not always achieved and in many cases the stabilizers were disconnected and never used.

British battle experience had indicated the desirability of an integrated fighting compartment with the tank commander and the gunner riding in a basket attached to the rotating turret. It was directed that the homogeneous steel armor turret be used to develop such an integrated fighting compartment for the light tank. The cupola was to be eliminated and replaced by a roof hatch and a periscope was to be installed for the tank commander. As described later, this turret with the 37mm gun M6 in the combination mount M23 and a power traverse system was introduced in the light tank M3A1. However, to allow the various improvements to reach the troops at the earliest possible date, the decision was made to incorporate some of the new components into the late production light tank M3. Thus the M23 mount with the 37mm gun M6 and the new turret without the cupola was introduced onto the M3 production line.

Below is the late production light tank M3, serial number 4927, without the turret cupola. However, it was not fitted with the turret basket or power traverse system. This was the tank dubbed the Stuart Hybrid in British service.

Both sides of the 37mm gun M5 can be seen at the right. Note the shoulder rest which allowed the gunner to control the free movement of the weapon.

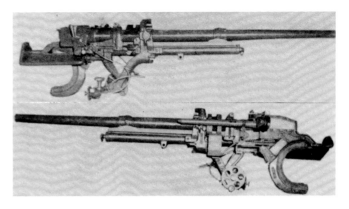

As mentioned earlier, the tube of the 37mm gun M3 was shortened by 5.1 inches (3½ calibers) when the cannon was installed in the production light tank M2A4. Originally, the modified weapon was referred to as the 37mm gun M3A1. However, Ordnance Committee action on 13 October 1939 assigned the new designation 37mm gun M5. Like the original M3 antitank gun, the M5 had a manually operated breechblock. However, development work had produced a semiautomatic breech mechanism which opened during the recoil movement ejecting the empty cartridge case. When fitted with this new breech mechanism, the weapon was redesignated as the 37mm gun M5E1. On 14 November 1940, OCM 16279 standardized the M5E1 as the 37mm gun M6 and reclassified the M5 as substitute standard. To expedite production, the full length tube was specified for the M6 making it identical to that for the 37mm antitank gun M3. Although different in length, the tubes for the M5 and M6 guns were mechanically interchangeable. However, this was prohibited since the weapon would be unbalanced and could not be used with the gyrostabilizer. The M5 gun was mounted in the light tanks M2A4 and the early M3. The M6 gun was installed in the late production M3 and subsequent vehicles of both the M3 and M5 light tank series. The M5 gun was reclassified as limited standard on 17 September 1942.

The M5 cannon on the light tanks M2A4 and early M3 were installed in the combination gun mounts M20 and M22 respectively. As mentioned previously, both types were provided with 20 degrees of traverse within the mount itself. The elevation and traverse mechanisms on these mounts could be unlocked allowing free movement of the weapon guided by the gunner's shoulder rest.

The M6 gun with its semiautomatic breech mechanism was installed in the combination gun mount M23. Like the earlier types, the M23 mount was fitted with trunnions permitting traverse about a vertical axis as well as the usual elevation and depression. When installed in a manually rotated turret, a knob actuated rack and pinion mechanism provided the 20 degrees of traverse. In a power operated turret, the rack and pinion mechanism was eliminated and the mount was locked in traverse.

The standard method of operation required two men in a manually rotated turret. The tank commander-loader would traverse the turret approximately onto the target and the gunner would use the gun mount controls to accurately aim the weapon. In a power operated turret, the gunner would lay the weapon by himself using the power traverse and the manual elevation. The shoulder rest and the free movement also were eliminated from the later mount.

M3, serial number 3722, was the first light tank to be received at Aberdeen with the new turret and gun mount, but without the basket or power traverse. Production of vehicles with this configuration was now in full swing and many were allocated to foreign aid. In Britain, they were dubbed the Stuart Hybrid. Apparently, some of these tanks were fitted with the M23 mount without the 20 degrees of internal traverse despite the fact that the turrets were manually rotated. This created an impossible situation since the manual turret traverse control was on the opposite side of the turret from the gunner. Thus the tank commander-loader had to rotate the turret on instructions from the gunner who had the only sight. Without any traverse in the mount, it was extremely difficult for the gunner to accurately lay the weapon onto the target. In any case, the British preferred one man operation by the gunner and the Stuart Hybrids were modified by relocating the manual turret control to the gunner's side of the turret. Without the turret cupola, the Stuart Hybrids were identical in external appearance to the later light tank M3A1.

Below, the 37mm gun M6 appears at the left with its recoil cylinder and breech operating mechanism. At the right, the weapon is installed in the combination gun mount M23 equipped with the stabilizer.

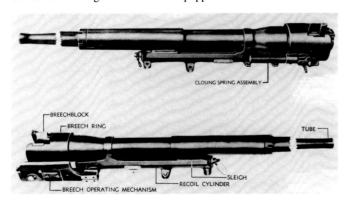

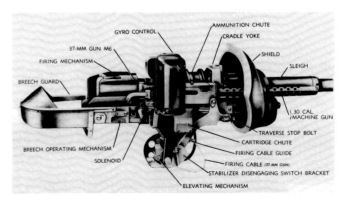

The photographs on this page show the light tank M3E1 powered by the Cummins HBS-600 diesel engine. Note the extension of the tank hull required to house the long six cylinder engine.

Possible future shortages of the radial aircraft engines resulted in a March 1941 recommendation by the Armored Force that test installations be made in light tanks using commercial in-line diesel engines. One such engine that had performance equal or superior to the standard tank power plant was the Cummins HBS-600. The Ordnance Committee recommended the test of this engine in the M3 and designated the modified vehicle as the light tank M3E1. The installation was made at the Cummins Engine Company in Columbus, Indiana and the modified tank was shipped to Aberdeen Proving Ground in November 1941. The Cummins HBS-600 was a six cylinder, four stroke cycle, diesel engine that developed 230 net horsepower at 2000 rpm. The tank was lengthened 11 inches by welding ¼ inch thick steel plate on the rear hull to enclose the cooling fan of the liquid cooled engine. The clutch and clutch housing extended 13½ inches into the fighting compartment. The drive shaft was shortened and the tunnel was lowered from 27 to 19⅞ inches. The standard transmission was retained. To increase the air flow through the two radiators, the two fuel tanks were decreased in height reducing their capacity from 28 gallons to 20 gallons each. The M3E1 was tested at Aberdeen and delivered under its own power to Fort Knox for a total driving distance of 951 miles. The test results indicated that the

Cummins engine had much higher reliability, greater operating economy, and far less maintenance requirements than the standard power plant. The major disadvantage was in its greater weight and length. The latter would have required an extensive redesign of the light tank M3. As a result, it was recommended that no further effort be made to adapt the Cummins engine to the M3, but that it be considered as a possible power plant for the light tank T7. The light tank M3E1 project was closed by Ordnance Committee action in May 1942.

In early 1941, the Ordnance Department started a program to measure and reduce the noise level of tanks. After

Further details of the light tank M3E1 are visible in the photographs at the right and below. Obviously, this test vehicle was not equipped with armament.

The installation of the Cummins diesel engine in the light tank M3E1 can be seen above. The covers, rear baffle, and air scoop have been removed. Note the two radiators mounted diagonally to the engine center line.

initial tests using two Marmon-Herrington vehicles, the Office of Scientific Research and Development awarded a contract to General Motors Corporation to evaluate various noise reduction modifications for the light tank M3. This program investigated improved mufflers and sound absorbing ducts to reduce engine noise. Rubber rings or blocks were attached to the sprockets to eliminate clatter and modified tracks were installed to reduce track rumble and hull vibration. These changes lowered the external noise to approximately one third of its original level. The internal noise in the crew compartment also was reduced by the installation of a ½ inch thick sound absorbing liner. This allowed the crew to converse without the use of the interphone. However, none of these modifications were applied to the production M3s.

The M3 continued to provide the basic vehicle for other experiments. The light tanks M3E2 and M3E3 were used to evaluate the twin Cadillac engine and Hydramatic transmission power train which appeared in the light tank M5. The light tank M3E4 tested the Straussler flotation equipment. All of these projects are discussed in later sections of this book.

Above are the rubber rings (left) and rubber blocks (right) attached to the sprocket of the light tank M3 to reduce the track clatter. Below, the exhaust duct used to reduce the engine noise appears at the left. At the right is an example of the strange combinations that frequently appeared at the Proving Ground. In this case, light tank M3, serial number 151, has been armed with the 37mm gun M5 in the M20 mount from the light tank M2A4.

Above, the 2nd Armored Division is equipped with a combination of M2A4 and M3 light tanks. Note the lack of 37mm guns in some tanks reflecting the shortage at that time. Below, a light tank M3 is upset in a ditch revealing the channel sections used to reinforce the floor of the vehicle. Both of these photographs were provided by Dr. Norris Perkins.

These views show the 1st Armored Division unloading their M3 light tanks at Rock Hill, South Carolina on 31 October 1941 during the First Army maneuvers. Once again, the shortage of 37mm guns is obvious. Note the dummy gun installed on the third tank in the upper photograph.

Above, three A20 attack planes pass over a formation of M3 light tanks. Because of the shortage, these vehicles have been designated as medium tanks for training purposes. Note the M on the turrets. Below, the crew of this M3 at Fort Benning, Georgia can be seen inside their vehicle, This photograph was dated 18 December 1941.

The round homogeneous armor turrets on the M3 light tanks above can be compared with the welded face-hardened armor turret on the M3 below. The crew of the latter vehicle is demonstrating the method of removing a wounded man from the turret.

Above, M3 light tanks of the 2nd Armored Division are engaged in training exercises at Fort Benning, Georgia during April 1942. Below, a crew peers out of their M3 and, at the right, a light tank from C Company, 70th Tank Battalion is being unloaded in Iceland in early 1942.

These photographs show the M3 light tanks of C Company, 70th Tank Battalion during operations in Iceland on 3 May 1942. All of these tanks are fitted with the round homogeneous armor turret.

The pilot model of the light tank M3A1 appears on this and the following page. These photographs from Aberdeen Proving Ground were dated 21 May 1942. Full armament has been installed in the pilot tank.

An M3 fitted with the Westinghouse gyrostabilizer and an Oilgear hydraulic traversing mechanism showed greatly improved performance during firing tests at Aberdeen. Under similar conditions, the percentage of hits from a moving tank increased from 4 to 40 per cent. However, the rapid rotation of the power operated turret created problems for the gunner and the tank commander. With the slow rotation of the manually traversed turret on the standard M3, it was easy for them to move around as the turret rotated. It was much more difficult with the rapid hydraulic power traverse. This problem was corrected by

the integrated fighting compartment which had the basket attached to the turret with a floor and seats for the gunner and the tank commander. Thus they could maintain their positions and move with the turret. This arrangement was installed along with the power traverse mechanism and the gyrostabilizer in an M3 at Aberdeen in May 1941. After successful tests by the Armored Board, the integrated fighting compartment, the power traverse mechanism, the gyrostabilizer, and other modifications were released for production and the improved tank was standardized as the light tank M3A1. It gradually replaced the M3 on the

Further details of the light tank M3A1 pilot can be seen in these views. Note that the front plate has been welded to the round homogeneous armor turret.

production line at the American Car & Foundry Company starting in May 1942. Production continued until February 1943 for a total run of 4621 M3A1 tanks. The Continental W-670 gasoline engine powered 4410 of these vehicles and the Guiberson T-1020 diesel was installed in the remaining 211. The M3 itself was reclassified as limited standard in May 1943 and declared obsolete by OCM 21015 in July of that same year. Like the M3, many of the M3A1s were destined for foreign aid. Britain received 1594 of the new tanks and 340 went to the Soviet Union. All of these

M3A1s were powered by the Continental W-670 gasoline engine. In Britain, the designations Stuart III and IV were assigned to the M3A1 and M3A1 (diesel) respectively.

The elimination of the turret cupola in the M3A1 permitted the installation of an M4 periscopic sight in the turret roof for the gunner. As mentioned earlier, the new M23 combination gun mount was locked in azimuth when used with the power turret traverse system. With this system, the turret rotation could provide the precise aiming adjustments required in azimuth. Like the M22 mount, the M23

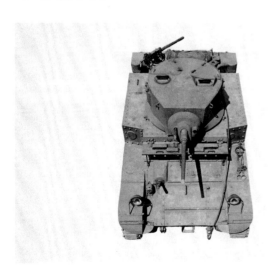 

Various components are identified and the external stowage of the light tank M3A1 is shown above and below.

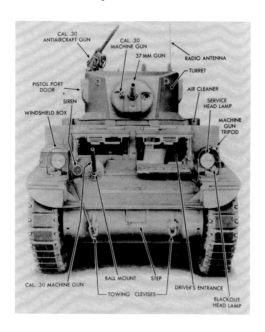

The internal arrangement of the light tank M3A1 is illustrated in the sectional drawing below.

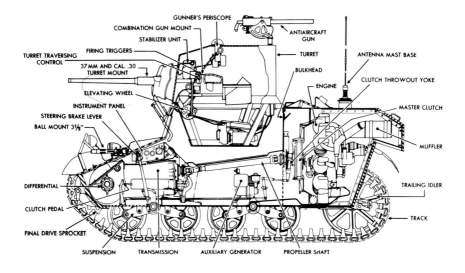

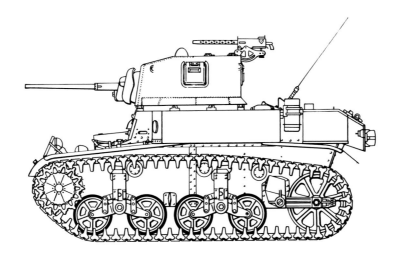

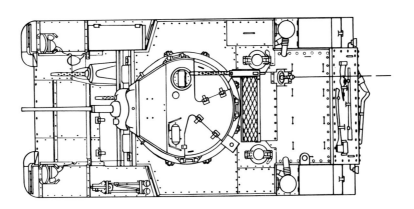

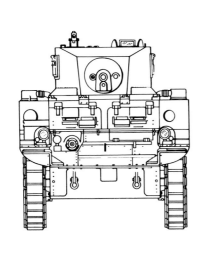

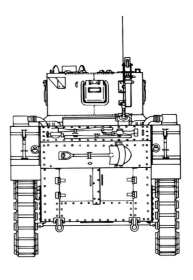

Scale 1:48

Light Tank M3A1

A — TRANSMISSION OIL PRESSURE GAGE
B — ENGINE HOUR METER
C — OIL DILUTION SWITCH
D — STARTING SWITCH
E — OIL DILUTION CHART
F — BOOSTER SWITCH
G — HAND THROTTLE
H — ENGINE OIL PRESSURE GAGE
J — COMPASS
K — BRAKE ADJUSTING APERTURE PLUG
L — TACHOMETER
M — ENGINE OIL TEMPERATURE GAGE
N — AMMETER
P — VOLTMETER
Q — SIREN BUTTON
R — CLUTCH PEDAL
S — STEERING LEVERS
T — FOOTREST
U — FOOT THROTTLE
V — LIGHT SWITCH
W — GEARSHIFT LEVER
X — HEADLIGHT DIMMER SWITCH
Y — PRIMING PUMP

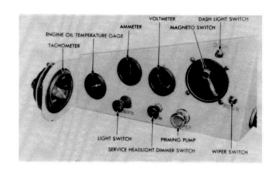

ENGINE OIL TEMPERATURE GAGE, TACHOMETER, AMMETER, VOLTMETER, MAGNETO SWITCH, DASH LIGHT SWITCH, LIGHT SWITCH, PRIMING PUMP, SERVICE HEADLIGHT DIMMER SWITCH, WIPER SWITCH

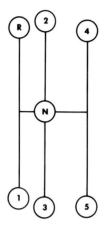

Above, the driver's station in the light tank M3A1 appears at the left and his side instrument panel is at the right with a gear shift diagram. Below, the auxiliary generator can be seen at the left.

REGULATOR ARMATURE, AMMETER, "START" BUTTON, STOP, REGULATOR FIELD, "STOP" BUTTON, EXHAUST, FUEL SHUT-OFF VALVE, OIL GAGE, OIL FILLER PIPE, BATTERY POSITIVE, BRUSH, CARBURETOR, AMMETER NEGATIVE, GENERATOR FUEL LINE, STARTER PULLEY, START (HIDDEN), AMMETER POSITIVE, TO GENERATOR REGULATOR, GROUND STRAP

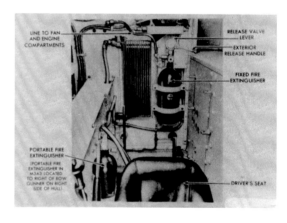

LINE TO FAN AND ENGINE COMPARTMENTS, RELEASE VALVE LEVER, EXTERIOR RELEASE HANDLE, FIXED FIRE EXTINGUISHER, PORTABLE FIRE EXTINGUISHER (PORTABLE FIRE EXTINGUISHER IN M3A3 LOCATED TO RIGHT OF BOW GUNNER ON RIGHT SIDE OF HULL), DRIVER'S SEAT

The fire extinguisher is mounted on the engine compartment bulkhead behind the driver's seat in the view above. Details of the headlight and blackout light are shown at the lower left. Below, the top front armor is being removed from the light tank M3A1.

GUARD, SERVICE HEADLAMP, BLACKOUT HEADLAMP, BRACKET, CONDUIT COUPLING, SHIELDED CONDUIT, SCREW, SCREW

LIFTING HOOK, FRONT SLOPING ARMOR, TRANSMISSION COVER PLATE, SPACER

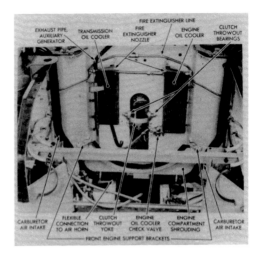

Above, removal of the top rear armor is illustrated at the left and the empty engine compartment is at the right. Below are front and rear views of the Continental W-670 gasoline engine.

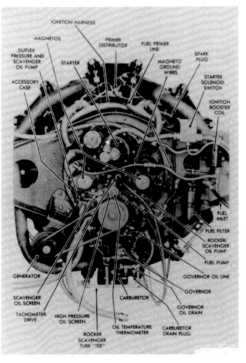

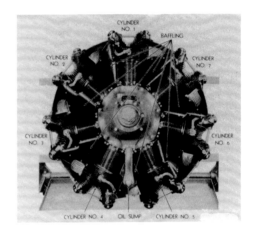

Below, the oil distribution system is at the left and the fuel system is at the center for the light tank M3A1. The internal arrangement of one vertical fuel tank can be seen in the cutaway drawing at the right.

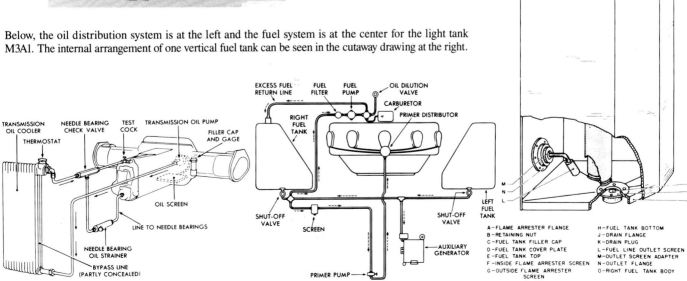

A—FLAME ARRESTER FLANGE
B—RETAINING NUT
C—FUEL TANK FILLER CAP
D—FUEL TANK COVER PLATE
E—FUEL TANK TOP
F—INSIDE FLAME ARRESTER SCREEN
G—OUTSIDE FLAME ARRESTER SCREEN

H—FUEL TANK BOTTOM
J—DRAIN FLANGE
K—DRAIN PLUG
L—FUEL LINE OUTLET SCREEN
M—OUTLET SCREEN ADAPTER
N—OUTLET FLANGE
O—RIGHT FUEL TANK BODY

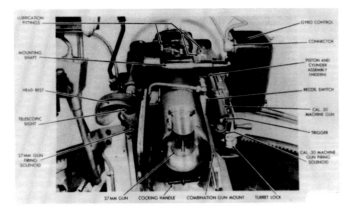

Above and below, the combination gun mount M23 is shown with the M5A1 telescope installed (left) and with it removed (right). The linkage to the gunner's M4 periscopic sight is visible in both views.

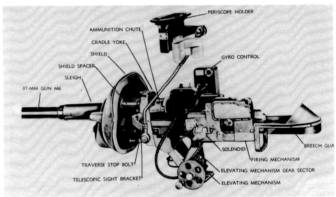

was designed to have an M5A1 telescopic sight located on the left side of the 37mm gun. However, the arrangement was such that, in practice, the gunner was unable to use the telescope at high angles of elevation. In a few cases the telescope was retained for emergency use, but in most tanks, it was removed. Thus the M4 periscopic sight coupled to the combination mount became the primary sighting device used by the gunner to aim the 37mm gun and the coaxial machine gun. A rotating M6 periscope was installed in the turret roof for the tank commander and the three pistol ports with protectoscopes were retained in the turret walls. A mount for a .30 caliber antiaircraft machine gun was located on the right rear of the turret.

Tests had shown that more hits were obtained with the driver's fixed sponson machine guns than with the flexible bow machine gun if the tank was free to maneuver and aim itself directly at the target. However, in most cases maneuverability was limited by terrain features or when the tank was restricted to roads. Under such conditions, the fixed guns were useless. As a result, they were eliminated from the M3A1 and the sponson ports were covered by steel plates. The protectoscopes and vision slots were retained in the front doors for the driver and the bow gunner. To relieve the load on the battery from the radio, gyro-stabilizer, and other components, a gasoline powered auxiliary generator was installed to supplement the engine driven generator. It was located on the hull floor behind the driver's seat.

The installation of the various stabilizer system components in the light tank M3A1 is sketched at the left.

A—TURRET COLLECTOR RING
B—DISENGAGING SWITCH
C—TRAVERSING CONTROL HANDLE
D—FLEXIBLE SHAFT
E—CONTROL BOX
F—GEAR BOX AND MOUNTING BRACKET
G—CYLINDER AND PISTON
H—GYRO CONTROL
J—RESERVOIR
K—RECOIL SWITCH
L—MASTER SWITCH
M—OIL PUMP
N—ELECTRIC MOTOR
P—TRAVERSE HYDRAULIC PUMP

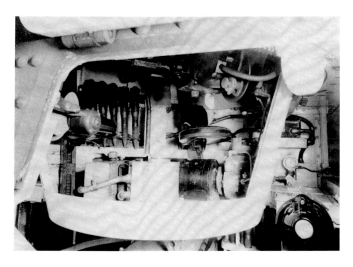

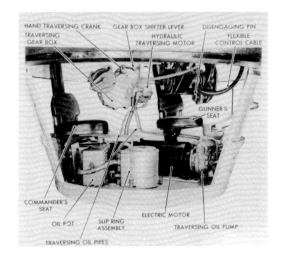

Above are two views of the turret basket in the light tank M3A1. Ammunition stowage and the internal turret arrangement are illustrated in the drawings below.

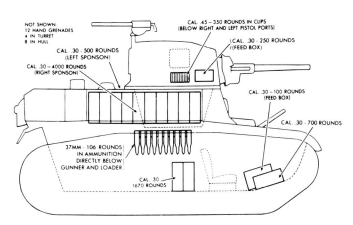

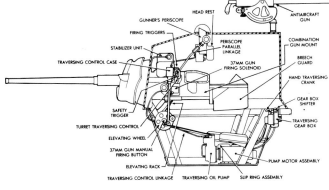

Evaluation of the light tank M3A1 at Aberdeen Proving Ground revealed that the design of the integrated fighting compartment left much to be desired and it could only be considered as a temporary solution. There was inadequate space for the crew to operate. Also, the only exit for the bow gunner was through the turret and unless the open part of the turret basket was adjacent to his position, he was trapped. Obviously, further development was required.

The various types of ammunition for the 37mm gun appear at the left. Below is the M20 bracket mount for the .30 caliber antiaircraft machine gun.

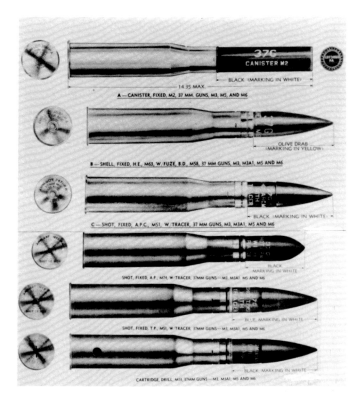

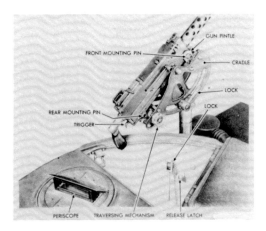

Above are views of the light tank M3A1 (diesel), serial number 5260, at Aberdeen Proving Ground for acceptance tests. These photographs were dated 28 October 1942. Note the welded hull on this tank.

In March 1942, the Adjutant General directed that, as far as practical, all diesel powered tanks be retained in the United States for training purposes. This obviously did not apply to foreign aid vehicles as many of the recipients preferred the diesel engine for their tanks. However, the U. S. Army did not want to supply two types of fuel to overseas armored units.

The light tanks M3A1 and M3A1 (diesel) were reclassified as limited standard in April 1943. As a result of the decision by the U. S. Army not to field diesel powered tanks, the M3A1 (diesel) was declared obsolete in July 1943.

OCM 17330, dated 16 October 1941, recommended that one light tank M3A1 be manufactured and tested using welded homogeneous armor with ballistic properties equal to the standard tank. This vehicle was to be designated as the light tank M3A1E1. Also, the designation light tank M3A2 was reserved by the Ordnance Committee for the production model of the welded M3A1 with the homogeneous steel armor hull. However, neither vehicle was ever built. The M3A1E1 project was combined with the program that eventually produced the light tank M5 powered by the twin Cadillac engines.

The long air intake pipes characteristic of the diesel powered tanks can be seen on M3A1 number 5260 below.

M3A1 light tanks manned by the United States Marine Corps are shown above and at the right during training for landing operations.

The Marine Corps M3A1s at the left and below are operating during maneuvers at Camp Lejeune, North Carolina in December 1942.

One of the first M3A3 light tanks (serial number 10434, registration number 3025643) appears on this page. Above, the foul weather hood has been installed for the driver. Note the early type stowage basket in the rear view below.

In April 1942, the Armored Force requested that the M3A1 be modified to have a hull similar to that developed for the light tank M5. In response to this request, a pilot tank was assembled using welded homogeneous steel armor plate following the general configuration of the M5. Equipped with the M3A1's radial gasoline engine and transmission, the new vehicle was designated as the light tank M3A3. The 1⅛ inch thick front armor was moved forward and sloped at 48 degrees from the vertical providing more space in the front hull for the driver and bow gunner. Individual hatches with rotating periscopes were installed in the hull roof above their seats. In non-combat areas, the driver and bow gunner could raise their seats and ride with their heads and shoulders exposed. Unlike the vertical sides on the M5, the 1⅛ inch thick sponson side armor on the M3A3 was sloped at 20 degrees from the vertical. The large sponsons allowed the air cleaners to be relocated under the armor and permitted the installation of two additional fuel tanks. The latter extended the cruising range of the M3A3 to about 135 miles and eliminated the need for the jettison fuel tanks.

A new turret was developed for the M3A3 with a bustle in the rear to accommodate the radio following British design practice. This cleared additional space in the left

Pistol ports were included in the original M3A3 turret design. Note that they have been welded shut on tank number 10434 above.

sponson. The turret hatches were enlarged and an additional periscope was provided for the tank commander in the right hatch cover. The radio antenna was relocated from the sponson to the rear of the turret bustle. The gun mount was redesigned with tighter tolerances to reduce dispersion. Designated as the combination gun mount M44, it included an M54 telescope on the left side of the cannon. This telescope was located in a higher position so that it could be used through the full range of elevation. A 250 round ammunition box replaced the 100 round box previously used with the .30 caliber coaxial machine gun in the M23 mount.

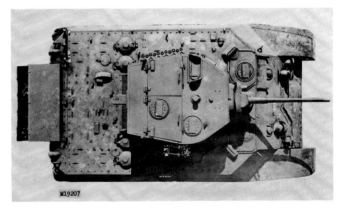

The turret pistol ports have been eliminated from light tank M3A3, serial number 10443, above. This tank, registration number 3025652, also has the later type of rear stowage basket.

The M3A3 had a combat weight of about 16 tons compared to a little over 14 tons for the M3A1. To handle the heavier weight, the final drive gear ratio was increased from 2.41:1 to 2.57:1. In line with the new policy, no M3A3 light tanks were fitted with the diesel engine. The first production M3A3 was assembled at the American Car & Foundry Company in September 1942 and a second was completed in November. Production really got underway in January 1943 and continued until September with a final total of 3427 tanks. Produced mainly for foreign aid, Britain and the French in North Africa received 2045 and 277 M3A3s respectively. Another 1000 tanks were allocated to China. In British service it was designated as the Stuart V. The M3A3 was reclassified as limited standard by OCM 20317 in April 1943.

164

A late production light tank M3A3 appears in these photographs. Note the reinforcing strip added to the rear stowage basket.

Exterior details of the light tank M3A3 can be seen in the photographs above and below.

The sectional drawing below shows the internal components of the light tank M3A3.

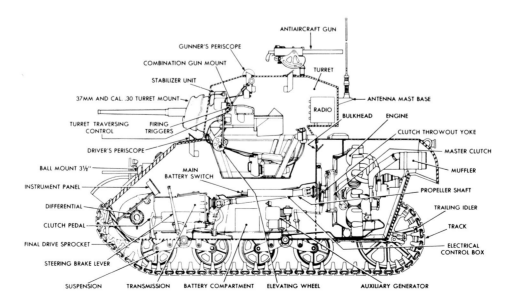

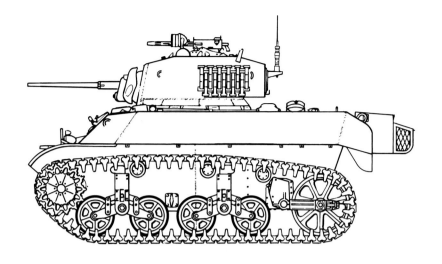

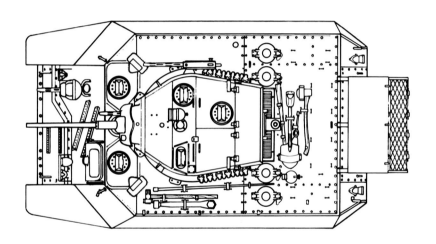

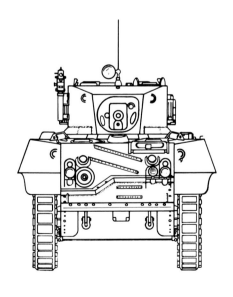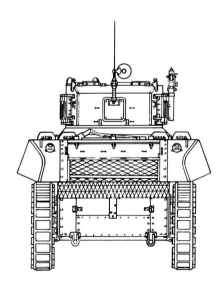

Scale 1:48

©D.P. Dyer

Light Tank M3A3

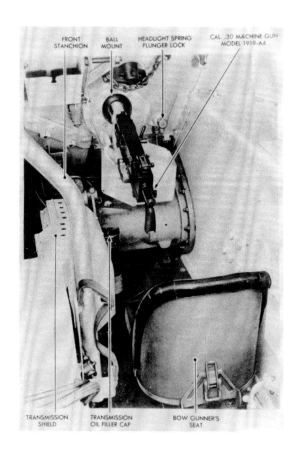

The driver's controls on the light tank M3A3 appear above at the left with a view of his instrument panel below at the left. The bow gunner's station is above at the right.

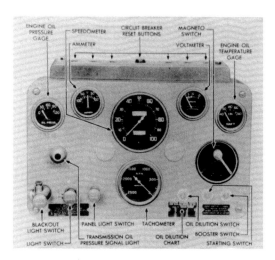

Removal of the front armor on the light tank M3A3 is shown in the views above and below. The two positions of the driver's seat can be seen at the lower left.

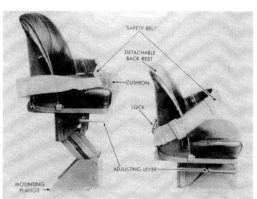

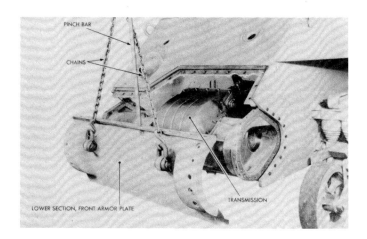

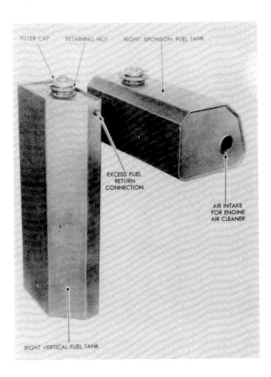

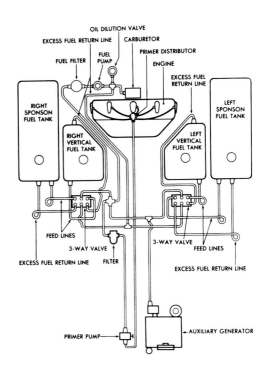

Above, the vertical and sponson fuel tanks of the light tank M3A3 appear at the left and the complete fuel system is diagrammed at the right. At the left below, the fuel tanks and air cleaners are installed in the tank hull.

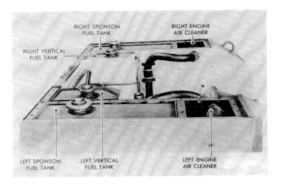

The service and blackout headlights as well as the siren on the light tank M3A3 are shown at the right. Below, the spotlight can be seen at the left and its use as a signal light is illustrated at the right.

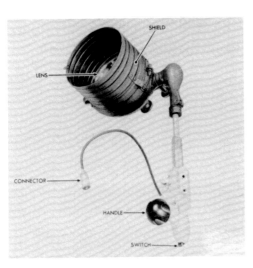

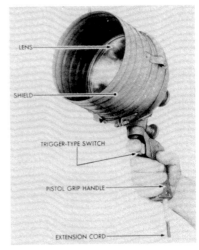

169

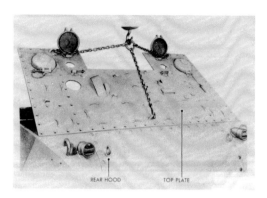

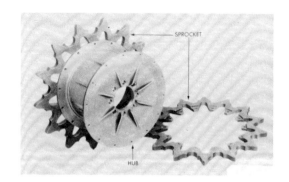

Above, the top rear armor plate is being removed at the left from the light tank M3A3 and the final drive hub with a sprocket removed appears at the right.

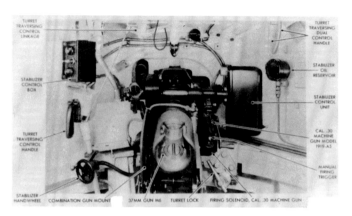

At the right is the combination gun mount M44 without the telescope in place. Note the high position of the telescope hole in the gun shield. Below is a turret seat from the light tank M3A3.

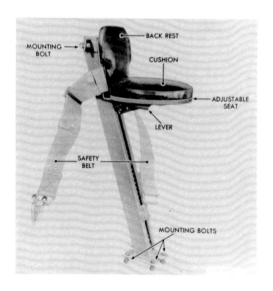

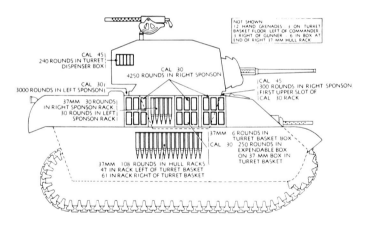

The ammunition stowage in the light tank M3A3 is sketched at the right above. Below, the turret is being removed at the left and its internal arrangement is illustrated in the sectional drawing at the right.

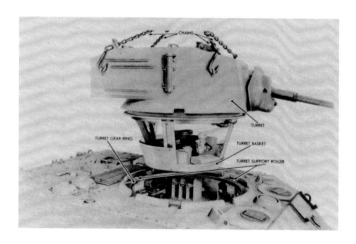

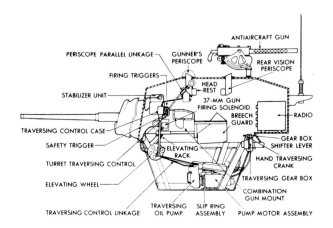

Above is light tank M3A3, registration number 3027771S, after being remanufactured and brought up to the latest production standards. Note the late type reinforcing strip on the rear hull stowage basket. The International Harvester Company remanufactured 166 M3A3 light tanks in March through May 1945.

Like its predecessors, the light tank M3A3 provided the basis for experimental test beds. In April 1943, the Ordnance Committee recommended that the Spicer automatic torque convertor transmission and gear case be installed in an M3A3. The tank retained its standard Continental W-670-9A engine and it was redesignated as the light tank M3A3E1. The Committee also recommended that a pilot installation be made with the same transmission and gear case in an M3A3 powered by the nine cylinder Continental R-950 engine. Intended to determine the effect of the latter engine's greater torque, this vehicle was designated as the light tank M3A3E2. The final drives in the M3A3E1 and the M3A3E2 were identical to those in the light tank M5A1. Also, it was proposed to install the turret from the light tank M5A1 on both tanks. This turret had the traversing equipment mounted underneath the turret basket floor unlike the M3A3 turret which located it on the basket floor. Thus more space was available inside the fighting compartment. Both the M3A3E1 and the M3A3E2 performed well during their tests at Aberdeen.

Another M3A3 was used in an effort to develop a defense against the Japanese Type 99 magnetic antitank mine. This mine had been effectively employed by Japanese antitank teams in the South Pacific and in Burma. It consisted of a circular explosive charge 4¾ inches in diameter by 1½ inches thick enclosed in a canvas cover. Four magnets were spaced equally around the edge of the charge. In use, it was tossed onto an armored vehicle where the magnets would adhere to the steel surface. The mine weighed about 2½ pounds. Tests at Aberdeen showed that the mine could blow a hole about four inches in diameter through the turret roof on the M3A3 and cause considerable damage in the surrounding area. Since the main force of the blast was perpendicular to the flat surface of the disc shaped mine, rows of steel spikes welded to a ½ inch thick mild steel plate were placed over the horizontal surfaces of the M3A3. These spikes, 6¾ inches and 5⅛ inches long, were spaced in alternate rows 4½ inches apart.

They were intended to tilt the mine at a sufficient angle to reduce the effect of the explosion. A ¼ inch thick sheet was installed around the turret to cover the engine cooling air intake. It was treated with Truscon number 260 antimagnetic coating so that any mines would slide off onto the spike covered surfaces. The tests ran from 2 September 1944 to 28 March 1945 and the report concluded that it was not possible to protect all of the horizontal surfaces on the light tank M3A3. It also noted that the weight of the protector plates was excessive and that they interfered with vision through the periscopes. The report recommended that no further work be done on this type of magnetic mine protection.

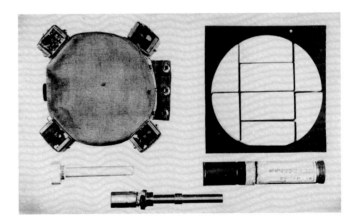

At the right is the Japanese Type 99 magnetic antitank mine (upper) and the light tank M3A3 fitted with the spike protection (lower).

171

Above is the light tank M3E2, serial number 752, fitted with the twin Cadillac engines and Hydramatic transmissions. This vehicle, registration number 303748, was photographed at Aberdeen Proving Ground on 3 November 1941.

LIGHT TANK M5 SERIES

In early 1941, the demand for air-cooled radial engines to power the rapidly increasing production of tanks and aircraft appeared likely to exceed the supply available. As a result, additional sources were sought for light tank engines with preference given to those engines already in production. On 6 June 1941, OCM 16837 authorized the installation of two Cadillac automobile engines with Hydramatic transmissions and an automatic auxiliary transmission in a light tank M3. This combination provided six speeds forward and one in reverse. The automatic auxiliary transmission also was referred to as a transfer unit or a transfer case. This same action designated the experimental vehicle as the light tank M3E2. The M3E2 was converted from M3 serial number 752 and subjected to a 2000 mile endurance test at the General Motors Proving Ground. Excellent results were obtained and the test vehicle was then transferred to Aberdeen. Although the M3E2 was

about 2500 pounds heavier than the M3A1, it had equivalent performance. In addition to the immediate availability of the standard automobile engines and transmissions, other advantages of the new power train included better low temperature starting, quieter operation, and additional space in the fighting compartment because of the lower drive shaft tunnels. The automatic transmission also reduced the driver's work load and simplified training.

The raised rear deck required to house the twin Cadillac engine installation can be seen in the view of the light tank M3E2 at the right.

Further details of the light tank M3E2 are shown in these photographs from Aberdeen Proving Ground. No armament was installed in the test vehicle. Note the weights added to the front plate to simulate a tank with a full combat load.

Above is the light tank M3E3 after its conversion from the M3E2. Note that it retains the same 303748 registration number. Below is a wooden mock-up of the new front hull on an M3A1 tank chassis. This was to be the light tank M3A1E1.

OCM 17428, dated 13 November 1941, assigned the designation light tank M4 to the new vehicle powered by the twin Cadillac engines with the Hydramatic transmissions. As mentioned earlier, the Ordnance Committee in October had authorized the construction of the light tank M3A1E1 fabricated by welding homogeneous steel armor. Since the same assembly method was planned for the light tank M4, OCM 17451 combined the projects on 21 November dropping the M3A1E1 designation. The actual course of development was that the light tank M3E2 (serial number 752) was modified by installing a redesigned homogeneous steel armor upper hull and redesignating it as the light tank M3E3. The sloped front armor on the new hull was moved forward to increase the space available for the driver and the assistant driver or bow gunner. Each of these now had a hatch over his head fitted with a rotating periscope. Direct vision for the driver and the assistant driver was

The views of the light tank M3E3 below show the raised rear deck over the engine compartment which was to be a characteristic of the light tank M5 series. All of these photographs showing the light tank M3E3 were taken at Aberdeen Proving Ground on 19 March 1942.

The full armament is mounted on the light tank M3E3 and details can be seen here of the exterior stowage. Note the fixed .30 caliber machine gun in the front hull for use by the driver.

The first production light tank M5 is shown here at the General Motors Proving Ground on 30 April 1942. Note that it retains the fixed .30 caliber machine gun for the driver.

available through a pair of two inch diameter holes in the front armor. These holes were closed by mushroom shaped steel plugs which could be pushed out from the inside. A chain attached to each plug allowed it to be pulled back to close the hole. Both men also could elevate their seats and ride with their heads exposed in the open hatches. A .30 caliber machine gun in a ball mount was provided for the bow gunner in the right front armor and a fixed .30 caliber machine gun was installed in the center of the front hull for use by the driver. Dual steering brake controls and floor mounted accelerator pedals were provided for the driver and assistant driver. The rear hull of the M3E3 was raised in order to provide clearance for the engine cooling system. The high rear and the vertical side armor on the sponsons were the major hull identification points compared to the light tank M3A3 which subsequently adopted a similar hull design.

The M3E3 was fitted with an M3A1 type turret equipped with the Westinghouse gyrostabilizer and the Oilgear power traverse system. Because of the low height of

the drive shaft tunnels, many of these components were mounted underneath the turret basket floor increasing the space available in the fighting compartment. The M23 gun mount was coupled to an M4 periscopic sight in the turret roof and a cover was installed over the port originally intended for a telescope on the left side of the cannon.

By February 1942, the new M4 medium tank was in production. To avoid confusion with the medium tank, OCM 17827 redesignated the new light vehicle as the light tank M5. Production of the M5 began in April 1942 at the Cadillac Division of General Motors Corporation in Detroit, Michigan and continued until December of the same year for a run of 1470 tanks. In August 1942, General Motors also began producing the M5 at the Southgate, California plant. This production also was terminated in December after a run of 354 tanks. The Massey Harris Company was brought into the program in July 1942. As at the other plants, M5 production ended in December after completion of 250 tanks. This brought the total light tank M5 production to 2074.

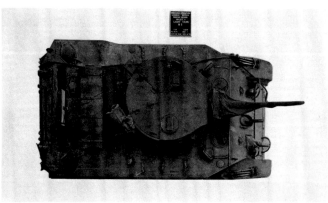

Above, an early light tank M5 is operating at the Desert Training Center, Indio, California during June 1942. Note the water can stowed on the turret. The other photographs show details of the first production M5 at the General Motors Proving Ground. At the top left is the driver's station with the steering levers pivoted at the top. The bow gunner's position is at the left and the fixed machine gun for the driver also is visible. Below, the left view shows the turret interior with the recoil guard for the 37mm gun and the loader's seat. The cooling fans and exhaust pipes for the twin Cadillac engines can be seen below looking into the rear of the engine compartment.

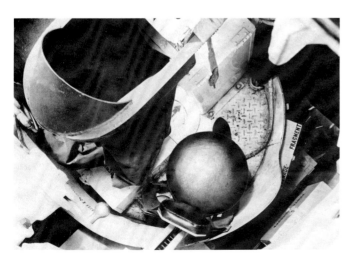

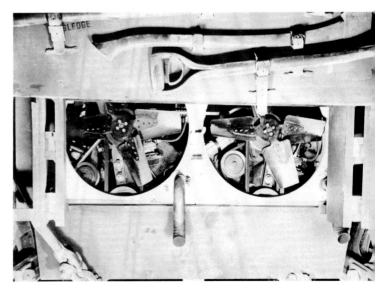

The driver's fixed machine gun has been eliminated from this early production light tank M5. However, it does not have the ventilator installed in the hull roof between the drivers' hatches.

The driver's fixed .30 caliber machine gun installed on the pilot vehicles was eliminated in accordance with the policy outlined in OCM 17906, dated 6 March 1942. This was the same directive that removed the sponson machine guns from the light tank M3A1.

At the time that the M5 was proposed for standardization, there was considerable skepticism regarding the twin engine power plant. Among these concerns was the fear that the engines and transmissions could not be properly synchronized so that the transmissions would shift together at the proper engine speed. The complexity of the Hydramatic transmissions and the transfer unit was expected to prevent field repairs and they would have to be replaced as complete units. Another objection was that the introduction of the M5 would add one more type of light tank which would require its own maintenance procedures and supply of spare parts. However, whatever problems did exist were rapidly solved and the Armored Force was enthusiastic about the new light tank. After operating a pilot M5

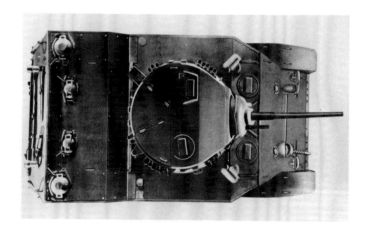

for 3370 miles in August 1942, the Armored Force Board reported that the light tank M5 was superior in performance and efficiency to any light tank previously in service.

Below, the interior arrangement of the light tank M5 can be seen in this sectional drawing.

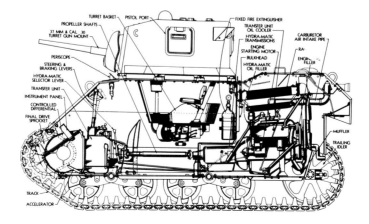

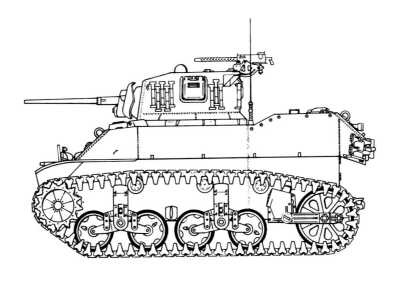

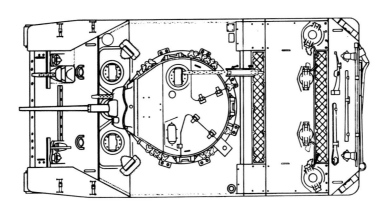

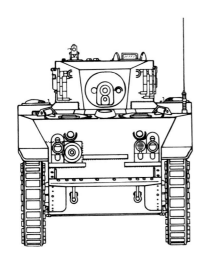

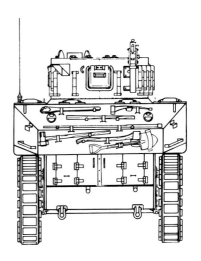

Scale 1:48

Light Tank M5

©**D.P. Dyer**

179

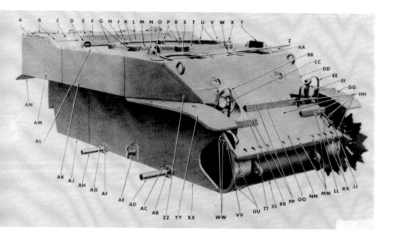

A—SCREW	S—SEAL, ASS'Y	JJ—HANDLE	YY GUARD, ASS'Y
B—SCREW	T—SEGMENT	KK—BOLT	ZZ PLATE, ASS'Y
C—PLATE, ASS'Y	U—BRACKET, ASS'Y	LL—DEFLECTOR	AB NUT / BOLT
D—BOX, ASS'Y	V—SEGMENT	MM—BOLT	AC BRACKET
E—SCREW	W—BRACKET, ASS'Y	NN—PLATE	AD AXLE, ASS'Y
F—SCREEN, ASS'Y	X—SEGMENT	OO DEFLECTOR	AE HOOK
G—BRACKET, ASS'Y	Y—HINGE, ASS'Y	PP—SCREW	AF NUT / BOLT
H—SEGMENT	Z—PLATE, ASS'Y	RR—DEFLECTOR	AG—BRACKET
J—BRACKET, ASS'Y	AA SEAL, ASS'Y	SS PLATE / SECTION, ASS'Y	AH AXLE, ASS'Y
K—SEGMENT	BB—GUARD, ASS'Y	TT—GUARD	AJ PLATE, ASS'Y
L—SEGMENT	CC—LIGHT, ASS'Y	UU—BOLT	AK—PLATE, ASS'Y
M—SEGMENT	DD—PLATE, ASS'Y	VV—EXTENSION	AL—PLATE, ASS'Y
N—HINGE, ASS'Y	EE—GUARD, ASS'Y	WW BOLT / WASHER / WASHER	AM—PLATE, ASS'Y
O—PLUG	FF—LIGHT, ASS'Y		AN GUARD
P—BRACKET, ASS'Y	GG—GUARD, ASS'Y	XX—PLATE	
R—SEGMENT	HH—PLATE, ASS'Y		

The early light tank M5 hull appears above. Note that it does not have the ventilator between the drivers' hatches. Below, one of the Cadillac engines is at the left and the Hydramatic transmission is at the right.

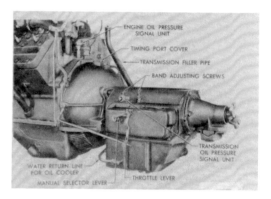

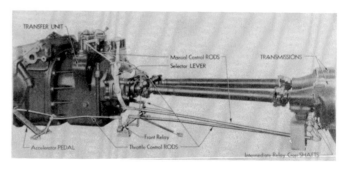

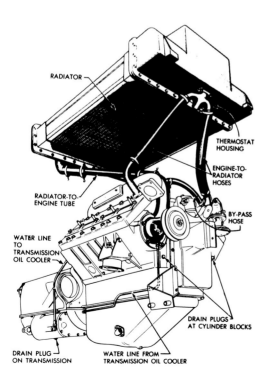

The cooling arrangement for each of the Cadillac engines is sketched at the left. Above is the automatic auxiliary transmission or transfer unit. Below, the rear top deck armor is being removed.

180

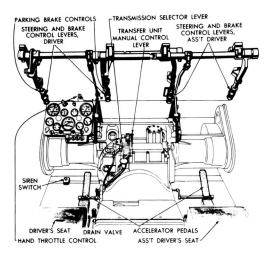

PARKING BRAKE CONTROLS — TRANSMISSION SELECTOR LEVER
STEERING AND BRAKE CONTROL LEVERS, DRIVER — TRANSFER UNIT MANUAL CONTROL LEVER — STEERING AND BRAKE CONTROL LEVERS, ASS'T DRIVER

SIREN SWITCH

DRIVER'S SEAT — DRAIN VALVE — ACCELERATOR PEDALS
HAND THROTTLE CONTROL — ASS'T DRIVER'S SEAT

STEERING LEVERS — KNOCK-OUT SIGHT PLUG

PERISCOPES

ASS'T DRIVER'S SEAT

The dual controls for the driver and the bow gunner are sketched above and the control linkage is shown below. At the right is the bow gunner's station (upper) and his hatch (lower).

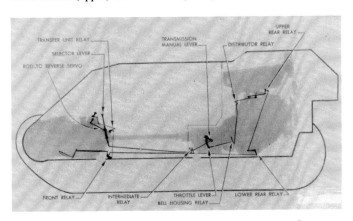

TRANSFER UNIT RELAY — TRANSMISSION MANUAL LEVER — DISTRIBUTOR RELAY — UPPER REAR RELAY
SELECTOR LEVER
ROD TO REVERSE SERVO

FRONT RELAY — INTERMEDIATE RELAY — THROTTLE LEVER — LOWER REAR RELAY
BELL HOUSING RELAY

AUX. DRIVER'S DOOR — PERISCOPE — COVER ON GUN

DOOR RELEASE LEVER — DOOR LOCKING LATCH

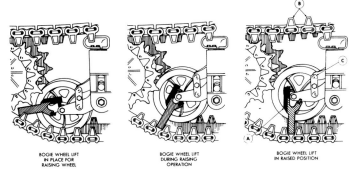

BOGIE WHEEL LIFT IN PLACE FOR RAISING WHEEL

BOGIE WHEEL LIFT DURING RAISING OPERATION

BOGIE WHEEL LIFT IN RAISED POSITION

The method for lifting a bogie wheel for replacement is sketched at the left. At the bottom left is an exploded view of the rear idler. An exploded view of the bogie assembly appears below.

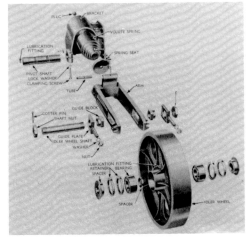

PLUG — BRACKET
VOLUTE SPRING
LUBRICATION FITTING
SPRING SEAT
PIVOT SHAFT LOCK WASHER CLAMPING SCREW
TUBE
ARM
GUIDE BLOCK
COTTER PIN — SHAFT NUT
GUIDE PLATE — IDLER WHEEL SHAFT — WASHER
NUT
LUBRICATION FITTING RETAINER — BEARING — SPACER
SPACER — IDLER WHEEL

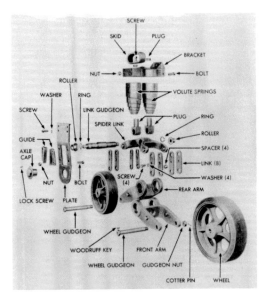

SCREW
SKID — PLUG
NUT — BRACKET — BOLT
ROLLER — VOLUTE SPRINGS
WASHER — RING — LINK GUDGEON
SCREW — SPIDER LINK — PLUG — RING
GUIDE — ROLLER
AXLE CAP — SPACER (4)
NUT — BOLT — LINK (8)
LOCK SCREW — SCREW (4) — WASHER (4)
PLATE — REAR ARM
WHEEL GUDGEON — FRONT ARM
WOODRUFF KEY — WHEEL GUDGEON — GUDGEON NUT
COTTER PIN — WHEEL

181

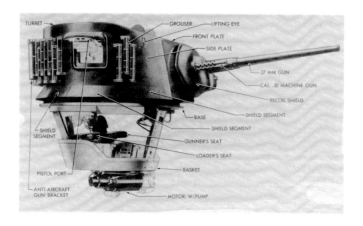

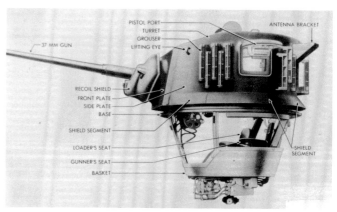

Details of the light tank M5 turret can be seen above and at the right. Note the components mounted under the turret basket floor increasing the available space for the turret crew.

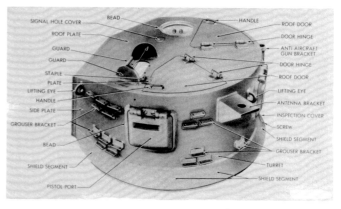

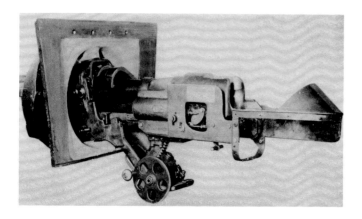

The combination gun mount M23 armed with the 37mm gun M6 is at the left and the weapon itself is below.

The seat installation in the light tank M5 turret appears below. The turret traverse mechanism is located between the two seats.

Below, this view from underneath the gun mount shows the gun controls in the M5 turret.

182

Above, a light tank M5 is crossing a ditch during training. Note that the rear bogie is completely unloaded. Below, early (left) and late (right) production M5s can be compared. Note the ventilator between the drivers' hatches on the later vehicle.

Above, two M5 light tanks are loaded on a single trailer for transportation. The high power to weight ratio of these little tanks is dramatically demonstrated at the left below. Two additional views of the M5 during training operations appear at the lower right.

A late production light tank M5 is shown above. The ventilator is visible on the front hull roof. The external stowage, including the two machine gun tripods on the front fenders, can be seen in the top view of the M5 below.

Above is a very early light tank M5A1 with pistol ports in the turret side walls.

During the development of the improved turret for the light tank M3A3, a similar design was prepared for the M5. Like the M3A3, a bustle on the new turret provided space for an SCR 508 radio and the antenna was mounted on the extreme rear. A removable plate on the rear wall of the bustle allowed the extraction of the M6 37mm gun. The .30 caliber antiaircraft machine gun mount on the M5 had been criticized as ineffective. On the new turret, the mount was improved and relocated to the right side. Later in production, a shield was installed around this mount. The two side pistol ports were redesigned at first and then eliminated completely. Some ports on early production tanks were welded shut. Another new feature was an escape hatch in the hull floor just behind the assistant driver's seat. On 24 September 1942, OCM 18295 designated the improved vehicle as the light tank M5A1 and it began to replace the

M5 on the Cadillac production line at Detroit in November. In December, production of the M5A1 started at the General Motors Southgate, California plant and at the Massey Harris Company. Production continued at Southgate until August 1943 and at Cadillac until May 1944 producing 1196 and 3530 tanks respectively. The American Car & Foundry Company was brought into the program in October 1943 manufacturing 1000 M5A1s by April 1944. The last of 1084 M5A1s built at Massey Harris was completed in June 1944 and bringing the total production of the type to 6810.

Another view of the early light tank M5A1 is at the right. Note the sandshields with the folding panels to cover the upper track run and the support rollers.

MOUNT FOR CAL. .30
ANTI-AIRCRAFT GUN

CAL. .30 MACHINE GUN

37 MM GUN

VENTILATOR COVER

ANTENNA BASE

ANTI-AIRCRAFT GUN

CAMOUFLAGE NET

PIONEER TOOLS

SAND SHIELDS

AIR DEFLECTORS

DOOR TO CARBURETOR
AIR CLEANER

SPARE TRACK BLOCKS

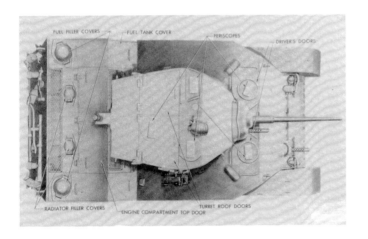

FUEL FILLER COVERS

FUEL TANK COVER

PERISCOPES

DRIVER'S DOORS

RADIATOR FILLER COVERS

ENGINE COMPARTMENT TOP DOOR

TURRET ROOF DOORS

At the top left is an early light tank M5A1 with the pistol ports welded shut. On the vehicle at the top right, the pistol ports have been eliminated. The views above and at the left show the production light tank M5A1 with the original stowage arrangement. The two photographs at the bottom show the late production M5A1 with the stowage box and basket on the rear hull and the shield around the .30 caliber antiaircraft machine gun.

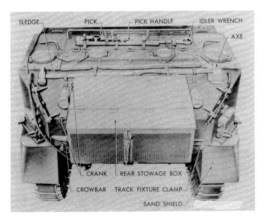

SLEDGE

PICK

PICK HANDLE

IDLER WRENCH

AXE

CRANK

REAR STOWAGE BOX

CROWBAR

TRACK FIXTURE CLAMP

SAND SHIELD

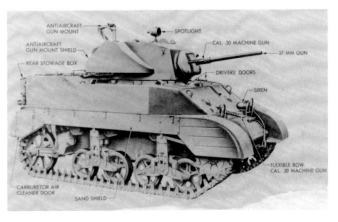

ANTIAIRCRAFT
GUN MOUNT

SPOTLIGHT

ANTIAIRCRAFT
GUN MOUNT SHIELD

CAL. .30 MACHINE GUN

REAR STOWAGE BOX

37 MM GUN

DRIVERS' DOORS

SIREN

CARBURETOR AIR
CLEANER DOOR

SAND SHIELD

FLEXIBLE BOW
CAL. .30 MACHINE GUN

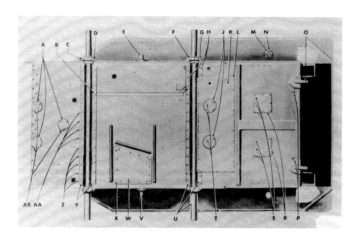

A—TRANSFER UNIT AND CONTROLLED DIFFERENTIAL DRAIN HOLE COVER

B—SCREW

C—BOGIE AXLE BRACKET CLAMPING SCREW

D—BOGIE AXLE TO HULL SIDE BRACKET

E—HOOK

F—BOGIE AXLE BRACKET CLAMPING SCREW

G—BOGIE AXLE TO HULL SIDE BRACKET

H—SCREW

J—TRANSMISSION DRAIN HOLE COVER

K—HULL REAR FLOOR COVER PLATE

L—REAR FLOOR COVER PLATE SCREW

M—FUEL TANK DRAIN HOLE COVER

N—FUEL TANK DRAIN HOLE COVER SCREW

O—TOWING BRACKET

P—ENGINE COMPARTMENT FLOOR DRAIN PLUG

R—ENGINE OIL PAN DRAIN HOLE COVER

S—ENGINE OIL PAN DRAIN HOLE COVER SCREW

T—TRANSMISSION DRAIN HOLE COVER SCREW

U—REAR BOGIE AXLE

V—HOOK

W—ESCAPE DOOR

X—ESCAPE HATCH DOOR PLATE SCREW

Y—FRONT BOGIE AXLE

Z—SCREW

AA—BOLT

AB—TRANSFER UNIT AND CONTROLLED DIFFERENTIAL DRAIN HOLE COVER STUD AND NUT

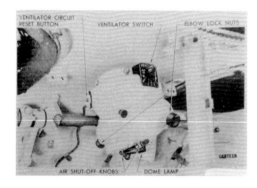

The hull bottom of the light tank M5A1 appears above.
At the left is an interior view of the floor escape hatch. Although not mentioned in the Technical Manual, this floor escape hatch also was included in the late production M5 light tanks. Below is the auxiliary generator installation on the M5A1.

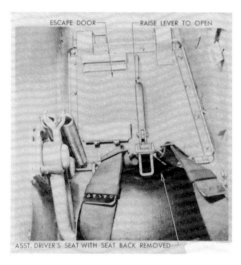

The hull ventilator on the light tank M5A1 can be seen at the left. Like the escape hatch, it also was included on the late production M5. Below, the rear of the M5A1 engine compartment is at the left and the engine compartment cover is being removed at the right.

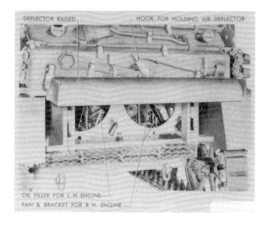

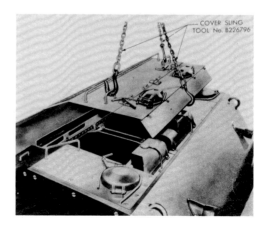

Above, the early (left) and late (right) instrument panels on the light tank M5A1 can be compared. Below, the M5A1 turret assembly is at the left and the SCR 508 radio can be seen installed in the turret at the right.

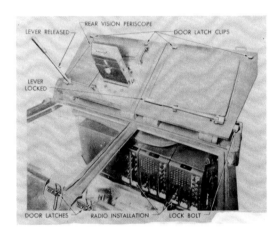

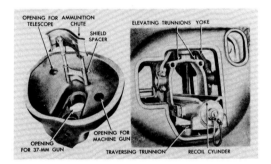

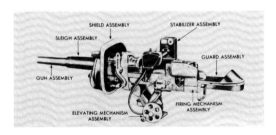

Above, the shield assembly for the combination gun mount M44 appears at the left and views of the mount itself are at the right and below. Note the higher position of the telescopic sight compared to the combination gun mount M23.

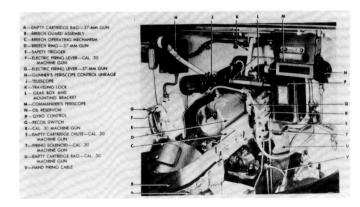

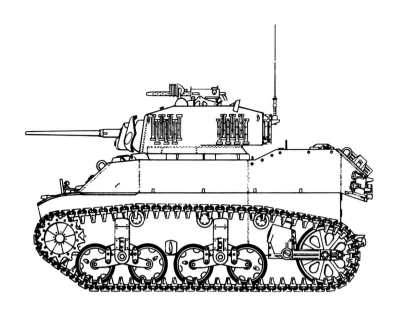

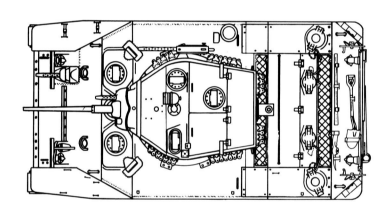

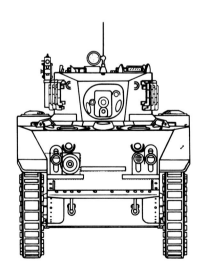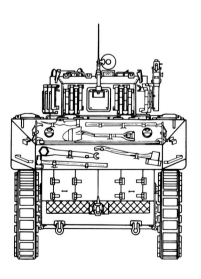

Scale 1:48

©D.P. Dyer

Light Tank M5A1 (early production)

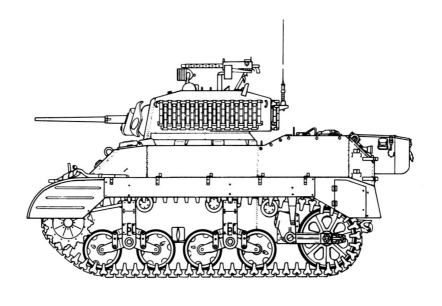

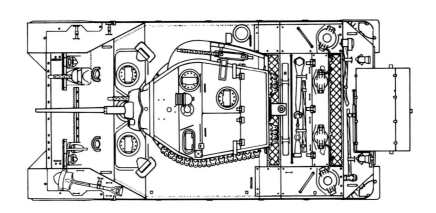

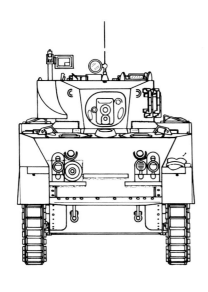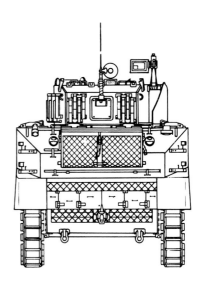

Scale 1:48

©D.P. Dyer

Light Tank M5A1 (late production)

The light tank M5A1 above is from the Demonstration Regiment at Fort Knox.

The M5s and M5A1s rapidly replaced the earlier M3 series and became the standard light tank in the U. S. Army. As the M5A1 became available, the M5 was reclassified as limited standard. Although the M5A1 was downgraded to substitute standard in June 1944 after the introduction of the light tank M24, it continued to serve as first line equipment until the end of World War II. In British service, both the M5 and M5A1 were designated as the Stuart VI, although only M5A1s were provided under the Lend-Lease program. A total of 1131 M5A1s were allocated to Britain, five to the Soviet Union, and 226 to the French in North Africa.

The light tank M5A1 below is fully stowed including the personal items belonging to the crew.

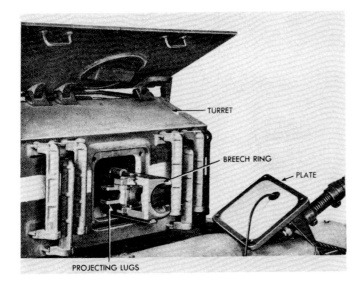

TURRET

BREECH RING

PLATE

PROJECTING LUGS

The method of removing the 37mm gun from the M5A1 light tank turret is illustrated above. Note the different stowage of track grousers on the M5A1s at the top right and the right. Details of the light tank M5A1 can be seen in the top view below from the General Motors Proving Ground.

ORDNANCE OPERATION
GENERAL MOTORS
PROVING GROUND
PROJECT 24 22
LIGHT TANK
M5A1
CADILLAC

TOP VIEW
PG 8159 ORD 2145
FEB 13 43 NEG A283

Above, the late production light tank M5A1, serial number 6261, is at the General Motors Proving Ground on 19 April 1944. Below at the left, late production M5A1, serial number 4911, displays the new rear stowage box as well as the shielded stowage for the .30 caliber antiaircraft machine gun.

Above at the right and below are views of a late production light tank M5A1 (serial number 4859, registration number 3047971) under evaluation at Fort Knox. This tank incorporated all of the improvements introduced into the final production of the M5A1.

Another late production light tank M5A1 appears above and below at the right. At the left below is an inflatable dummy intended to represent a light tank M5A1.

Below are two views of a light tank M5A1 remanufactured to incorporate late production features such as the rear hull stowage box. American Car and Foundry Company remanufactured 775 early production M5A1s in the period November 1944 through June 1945.

Above and at the right are photographs of the light tank M5A1E1 with the spaced out suspension. Here it is fitted with the standard track using extended end connectors on both sides.

The combat weight of the M5A1 was now up to about 17 tons. To reduce the ground pressure when using the standard 11⅝ inch wide tracks, a project was initiated to fit the tank with wider tracks. The Ordnance Committee in March 1943 authorized the manufacture of three tanks modified to test wider tracks and designated these vehicles as the light tank M5A1E1. Built at the Cadillac plant, the modifications consisted of 3½ inch spacers welded to each side of the hull on which the standard suspension brackets were installed. A 16½ inch wide steel, single pin, track was developed by the Burgess-Norton Manufacturing Company for evaluation on the M5A1E1. Designated as the T64 steel, rubber bushed, track, it was installed on the M5A1E1 and tested at the General Motors Proving Ground. After 785 miles of operation over the standard endurance course, nearly all of the bushing tubes had failed. Further tests were cancelled. Later, Burgess-Norton produced a 16 inch wide double pin track consisting of standard track blocks with 16 inch long pins and forged

The front view of the M5A1E1 at the right shows the increased width of the tracks with the double row of extended end connectors.

The problem of thrown tracks on the M5A1E1 with the extended end connectors is illustrated at the right. This photograph was taken during the evaluation of the vehicle at Fort Knox.

end extensions. The track life of this design using bushings similar to those in the standard production tracks was satisfactory.

A third arrangement intended to reduce the ground pressure also was tested on the M5A1E1. This consisted of installing extended end connectors on each side of the standard 11⅝ inch double pin track. This increased the total track width to 18⅜ inches. Unfortunately, this approach was unsuccessful because of excessive track throwing and cutting of the bogie tires during the tests at Fort Knox.

Another effort to lower the ground pressure involved the installation of a special 18 inch wide offset track on an M5A1, which was fitted with the standard suspension. However, tests at Aberdeen revealed that the tank was difficult to control and its speed and maneuverability were reduced. Thus the design was considered unsatisfactory and the test program was terminated.

Below is the light tank M5A1 fitted with the 18 inch wide T75 offset steel tracks. A closeup view of the track is at the right.

Above is the light tank M5A1 armed with the 37mm gun M6 in the combination gun mount T73 during its evaluation at Aberdeen Proving Ground. These photographs were dated 6 July 1944.

The Armored Board did not consider the combination gun mount M44 to be completely satisfactory. To find a better arrangement, another M5A1 was used in a program to evaluate the combination gun mount T73. Armed with the 37mm gun M6 and a coaxial machine gun, this mount was tested at Aberdeen in July 1944. However, by this time interest had shifted to heavier armament for light tanks and the project was terminated.

Below, the shape of the new shield on the T73 combination gun mount can be seen at the left. At the right is an interior view of the new mount in the M5A1 turret.

Below is the turret trainer used to prepare personnel for service in the light tank M5A1. Note the combination gun mount M44 with the telescope mounted high on the left side.

The mock-up of the proposed light tank T7 is shown above in these photographs from Rock Island Arsenal dated 20 June 1941. Note the extreme elevation range of the main armament.

LIGHT TANK T7 SERIES

Based on the service experience with the light tank M2A4, the Armored Force prepared a list of characteristics for a new light tank in January 1941. On 14 February, OCM 16582 outlined the proposed characteristics of the new vehicle and assigned the designation light tank T7. It was to weigh 14 tons or less and have a maximum armor thickness of 1½ inches. The tank was to be armed with the 37mm gun M6 and a coaxial .30 caliber machine gun in a power operated turret with a gyrostabilizer. Two fixed .30 caliber machine guns in the front hull were to be fired by the driver and another .30 caliber machine gun was mounted in the right front hull for use by the assistant driver. A .30 caliber antiaircraft machine gun was proposed for installation in the left rear of the turret roof. The specification required an engine with sufficient power to maintain a speed of 12 miles/hour on a 10 per cent grade. This engine was to be capable of starting at –40 degrees Fahrenheit and the cooling system was to permit satisfactory operation at temperatures up to 125 degrees Fahrenheit.

Construction was authorized in February 1941 for two pilot tanks. Different features were to be evaluated in these two pilots and, in May, they were redesignated as the light tanks T7 and T7E1. A wooden mock-up of the T7 was inspected by the Ordnance Subcommittee on Automotive Equipment at Rock Island Arsenal on 11 July 1941. By now, the estimated weight had increased from 14 to 16 tons and that was to be only the beginning. The low temperature

starting requirement was raised from –40 degrees to –20 degrees Fahrenheit and the engine was now also expected to provide a sustained speed of 35 miles/hour on a three per cent slope. In August, the program was expanded to include three additional pilots bringing the total to five. Some proposed features of these tanks were described as follows in the Ordnance Committee Minutes.

Light Tank T7 — Welded hull; cast turret; five speed Hydramatic transmission; individually sprung, volute spring suspension; 15⅛ inch wide rubber block track.

Light tank T7E1 — Riveted hull; formed homogeneous steel plate turret; torque convertor; horizontal volute spring suspension; 14¼ inch wide rubber block track.

Light tank T7E2 — Cast upper hull; cast turret; Warner Gear torque convertor; Wright R-975 engine.

At the right is an early concept drawing of the light tank T7 illustrating some of its new features such as the easy removal of the engine and transmission.

The method of rolling the transmission and the engine out of the tank on rails is shown above on the mock-up of the light tank T7. Below, the mock-up has been modified to include armor protected headlights.

Light tank T7E3 — Welded hull; welded turret; Detroit Gear automatic transmission; twin Hercules DRXBS diesel engines.

Light tank T7E4 — Welded hull; welded turret; twin Cadillac engines; two Hydramatic transmissions and propellor shafts and one auxiliary automatic two-speed transfer unit.

On the recommendation of the Assistant Chief of Staff, G3, the following modifications to the original characteristics were introduced. The turret side walls were to be sloped at 22½ degrees from the vertical and a bustle added at the rear to house a radio. Protective beading was to be applied around the base of the turret. Open sights were to be provided on the T7E2, T7E3, and T7E4. The +60 to –10 degrees elevation range requirement on the T7 and T7E1 was to be reduced on the T7E2, T7E3, and T7E4 to that normally used against ground targets. Also, modification of the T7E2, T7E3, and T7E4 was proposed to lower the silhouette and provide a better slope on the front armor.

The soft steel pilot of the light tank T7 was completed at Rock Island Arsenal in January 1942. This pilot was

powered by the Continental W-670 radial engine with a five speed Hydramatic transmission. The hull of the T7E1 also was assembled, but by this time, riveted structures had been shown to be inferior to cast or welded hulls and turrets and the pilot was never finished.

Below are models of the proposed light tanks T7E2 (left) and T7E4 (right). The new low silhouette design has been applied to both vehicles. Both now use cast turrets and hulls assembled by welding rolled sections and castings.

The pilot light tank T7 appears in these photographs from Rock Island Arsenal dated 16 January 1942. The machine gun armament has not been installed in the tank.

The light tank T7 pilot is compared above and below with the mock-up of the light tank T7E2. Note that the heavier 6 pounder gun is included in the T7E2 mock-up.

Armored Force representatives inspected a wooden mock-up of a low silhouette version of the new tank at Rock Island during November 1941. The hull of this new design was seven inches lower than the original version and the inside width increased from 60 to 75 inches. The Armored Force preferred this low silhouette design and directed that it be applied to the T7E2, T7E3, and T7E4. As mentioned earlier, the Armored Force recommended that the Cummins diesel engine be considered as a power plant for the light tank T7, but this was never put into effect. At one time, it was intended to install the Guiberson T-1071 diesel engine and the Livermore automatic transmission in the T7E1. However, the preference of the Armored Force for the T7E2 shifted the emphasis of the program to that vehicle

and, after the T7E1 was abandoned, it was used to supply parts for the other projects. The concentration of effort on the T7E2 also resulted in slow progress on the T7E3 and T7E4. Hercules gasoline engines were substituted for the diesels in the former and the latter was being assembled from armor plate for ballistic testing. However, both were cancelled prior to completion. One feature common to all of the T7 pilots was the design which allowed the rapid replacement of the engine and transmission. Both were mounted on rails and could be pulled out to the rear and front of the tank respectively. The objective was to permit the replacement of both components in 40 minutes. However, one practice run managed to complete the job in 20 minutes.

Below, the mock-up of the light tank T7E2 is shown alongside a medium tank M3. Note the low silhouette of the new light tank mock-up compared to the older medium tank.

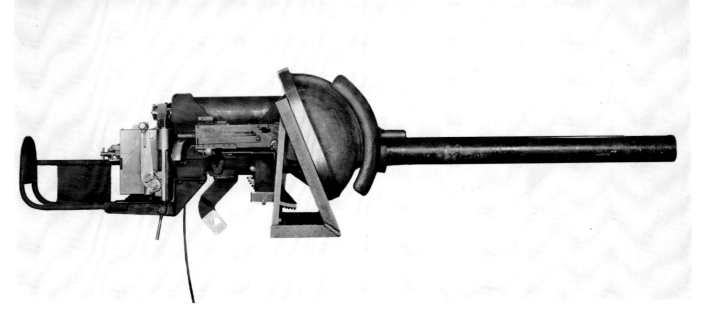

These views show the original experimental combination gun mount armed with the British 6 pounder Mark III gun and a .30 caliber machine gun. Intended for the light tank T7E2, this mount was photographed at Rock Island Arsenal on 15 May 1942.

In July 1941, General Barnes had issued instructions to develop a mount for the British 6 pounder gun which could be installed in the T7. By January 1942, the major interest was in the T7E2 and it received the 6 pounder Mark III as main armament. This 57mm gun weighed about 784 pounds and, as its name implied, fired a six pound armor piercing projectile at a muzzle velocity of over 2800 feet/second.

Below is the T63 combination gun mount which was a slightly modified version of the original mount shown above. At the right are three types of ammunition fired by the 6 pounder gun.

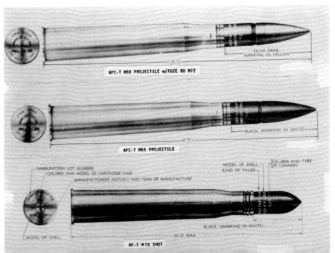

The pilot light tank T7E2 armed with the British 6 pounder Mark III gun appears in these photographs. The four volute springs in each bogie assembly are clearly visible in these views.

The low wide silhouette of the T7E2 pilot is obvious in the rear view at the left.

The T7E2 armed with the 6 pounder and powered by the Wright Whirlwind R-975-EC2 engine arrived at Aberdeen Proving Ground on 26 May 1942. This engine developed 450 gross horsepower at 2400 rpm. The Warner Gear torque converter originally intended for this vehicle proved to be unsatisfactory. It was replaced by an automatic torque converter transmission developed by the Spicer Manufacturing Company. Although the T7E2 weighed almost 26 tons, the high powered engine provided satisfactory performance and the suspension was regarded as particularly good, However, the Armored Force rejected the 6 pounder

Additional details of the light tank T7E2 pilot can be seen in the photographs on this page. The escape hatch in the left side of the hull is clearly visible above.

gun as main armament. They were enthusiastic about the tank, but insisted on the installation of the 75mm gun. By this time, Aberdeen had completed a mock-up of a suitable 75mm gun mount and it was installed in the T7E2 after the firing tests with the 6 pounder. In August, the mount with the 75mm gun was designated as the combination gun mount T64 and the tank armed with the 75mm gun became the light tank T7E5.

The pilot medium tank M7 is shown here during tests at the General Motors Proving Ground. Note that the turret pistol ports have been welded shut.

During the development program, the weight of the T7 had increased from the original specification of 14 tons to almost 27 tons. In view of this heavier weight, OCM 18582, dated 6 August 1942, standardized the light tank T7E5 as the medium tank M7. The main armament now consisted of the 75mm gun M3 with a coaxial .30 caliber machine gun on the right side in the combination gun mount M47. The turret was equipped with a power traverse mechanism and the mount was stabilized in elevation. One .30 caliber machine gun was installed in the hull bow mount and another was fitted to an antiaircraft mount on the turret. The maximum armor thickness was increased to 2½ inches and the pistol ports were eliminated from the turret. They were welded shut on the pilot tank. A new hand shift was added to the Spicer automatic transmission and the rear suspension and idler assemblies were moved forward two inches. As on the T7E2, the driver and the assistant driver were seated in the front hull with duplicate controls so that either could drive the tank. Above their heads, pivoting hatch covers each contained a rotating periscope for indirect vision and direct vision slots with armored covers were provided for both crew members in the front armor. An emergency escape door was located in the left side wall of the hull behind the driver's position. The gunner's station was on the left side of the 75mm gun in front of the tank commander. The loader was located on the right side of the cannon. The gunner was provided with a periscopic sight in the turret roof and an M5A1 telescopic sight in the left side of the M47 mount. The commander and loader each had a rotating periscope in the turret roof in front of the two double door hatches. A single nonrotating periscope was located behind the commander's hatch for viewing toward the rear. A door installed in the rear wall of the turret bustle could be opened to permit the removal of the 75mm gun. It was, of course, necessary to remove the external stowage box as well as the SCR 508 radio and other items from the inside of the turret bustle. The production tanks were powered by the Continental R-975 C1 engine since Continental Motors had taken over the production of the Wright R-975 engine for tank use.

Production facilities for the new tank were established by the International Harvester Corporation at the Quad

Cities Tank Arsenal, Bettendorf, Iowa. By 5 October 1942, International Harvester had completed three production tanks. The first was delivered to Rock Island Arsenal and the second went to Fort Knox and later to Indio, California for hot weather testing. The third tank was shipped to the General Motors Proving Ground for evaluation. The 75mm gun mounts for these three tanks were built at Rock Island. In addition, a fourth mount was shipped to Aberdeen Proving Ground to replace the 6 pounder mount on the T7E2 pilot. The fourth production M7 was winterized at Rock Island for cold weather tests in Canada. Production tanks 5, 6, 7, 9, 10, and 11 were sent to Fort Knox for evaluation by the Armored Board. The eighth production vehicle was used at Aberdeen for firing tests that could not be carried out at the General Motors Proving Ground.

Tests of the production vehicles revealed that they were much heavier than anticipated with weights of 28 to 29 tons when fully stowed. This resulted in a loss of performance and production was halted while studies were made to reduce the weight. Analysis of the problem revealed that some of the weight resulted from the use of castings that exceeded the specified thickness. Modifications were ordered for six of the production tanks to use the lightest possible castings. The power train also was revised to improve performance. In addition to torque converter modifications, the final drive gear ratio was changed from

The third production medium tank M7 appears here at the General Motors Proving Ground on 11 January 1943. The turret pistol ports have been completely eliminated on the production tank.

2.5:1 to 2.685:1 and a 13 tooth sprocket replaced the 14 tooth sprocket. The modified vehicles were referred to in some documents as the medium tank M7E2. Tests showed that the only improvement was in the lower speed range and the performance was considered inferior to the medium tank M4A3. As a result, production was cancelled after a total run of only 13 tanks. Six of these were the modified vehicles and the remaining seven were accepted as the medium tank M7. Thus the production acceptance records show a total of only seven M7 medium tanks.

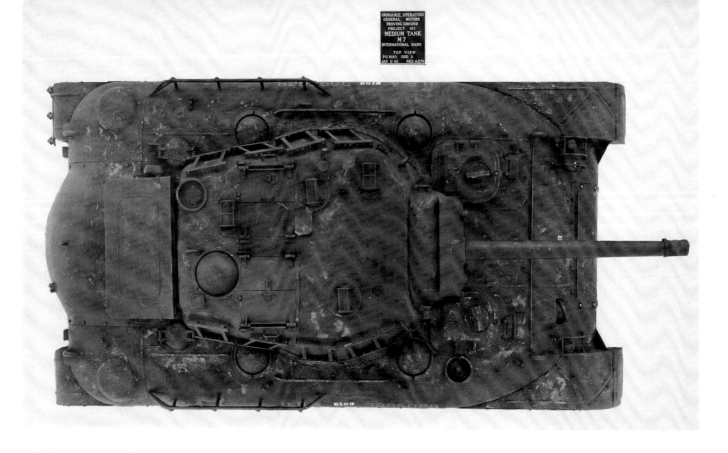

Additional details of the third production medium tank M7 can be seen in the top view above. Below are the driver's station (left) and the bow gunner's position (right). At the bottom of the page are views of the bogie assembly (left) and the engine installation (right).

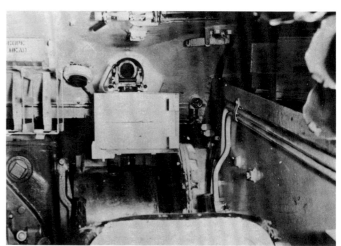

Two other production M7 medium tanks are shown in these photographs. The machine guns have been installed in the tank above. Both vehicles have some of the exterior stowage mounted on the hull and turret.

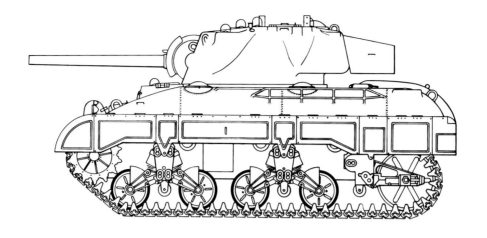

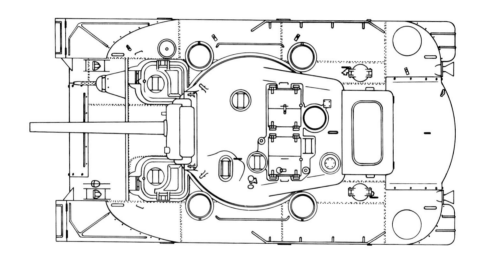

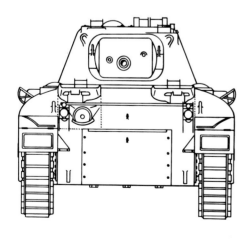
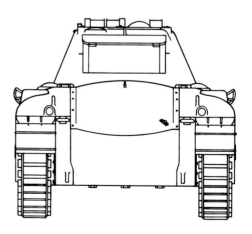

Scale 1:48

Medium Tank M7

 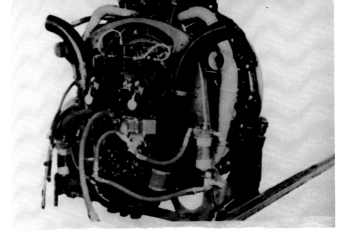

Above are front and rear views of the air-cooled radial engine in the medium tank M7. Both sides of the transmission assembly can be seen below removed from the tank.

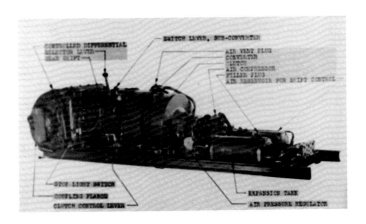 

Above are photographs of the empty engine compartment (left) and the fighting compartment (right) after the transmission has been removed. Note the seats for the driver and bow gunner on each side of the space for the transmission. Below are views of the hull interior with the turret removed looking forward (left) and toward the rear (right).

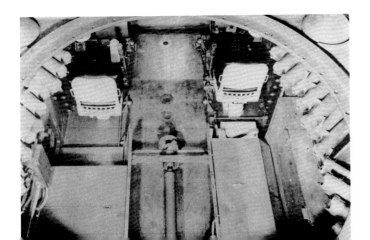 

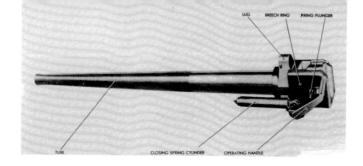
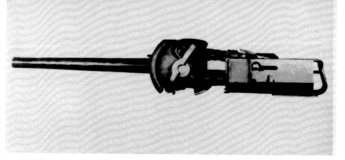

Above, the 75mm gun M3 is shown unmounted (left) and installed in the combination gun mount M47 (right). Additional views of this mount appear below.

The basket suspended from the turret of the medium tank M7 can be seen at the right. Below are various types of ammunition fired by the 75mm gun M3.

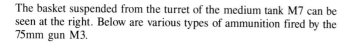
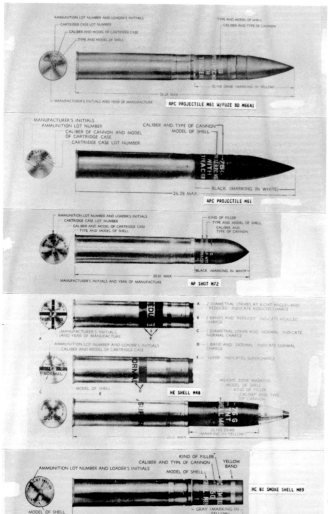

During the development program, the Ford GAN tank engine was proposed as an alternate power plant for the M7. This engine was a low silhouette version of the Ford GAA installed in the medium tank M4A3. A mock-up was prepared of the GAN installed in the M7 engine compartment and studies indicated that the low height of the new engine would permit the elimination of the bulge in the M7 upper engine compartment door. However, the weight of the vehicle would be increased by about 1500 pounds. The procurement of six tanks powered by the Ford GAN was proposed in February 1943 and the vehicle was designated as the medium tank M7E1. However, with the termination of the M7 production, the project was cancelled prior to the completion of the pilot tank. The projects for the T7E3 and T7E4 pilots also were cancelled at that time. On 20 January 1944, Ordnance Committee action reclassified the medium tank M7 as obsolete.

212

This is the Allis-Chalmers V40, also referred to as the Allis-Chalmers scout car. Note that the original V40 had seats for four including the driver.

LIGHT TANKS T13, T16, AND T21

In January 1942, the Allis-Chalmers Manufacturing Company submitted a vehicle of their own design to the Army for evaluation. Produced at no cost to the government, it was referred to as the V40 tractor or reconnaisance vehicle. With a loaded weight of 5090 pounds, the eight inch wide rubber band tracks kept the V40's ground pressure down to 5.3 psi. The 50 horsepower Allis-Chalmers gasoline engine drove the little vehicle at a maximum road speed of 40 miles/hour and it had a cruising range of about 220 miles.

After evaluation at Aberdeen Proving Ground, the Ordnance Department studied the possibility of mounting a light armored body on the V40 and arming it with the 20mm Hispano-Suiza Birkigt cannon. On 5 March 1942, OCM 17881 outlined the characteristics for such a vehicle and designated it as the light tank T13. Manned by a crew

LIGHT TANK T13

Reference Drawing E4577 26 Feb 1942

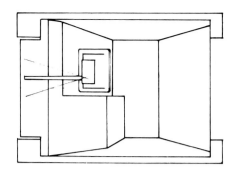

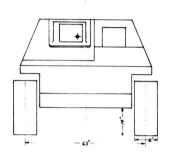

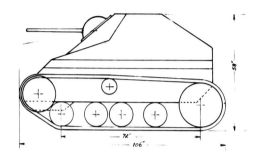

Light Tank T13 w/.50 caliber machine gun

of two, the maximum weight limit was specified as 6500 pounds. The armor was to be the maximum possible for this weight. The OCM called for maximum speeds of 35 miles/hour on level roads and 15 miles/hour on a 10 per cent grade. In addition to the 20mm Hispano-Suiza Birkigt cannon, the 20mm Oerlikon cannon and the .50 caliber machine gun were listed as alternate weapons.

After review, the Commanding General, Services of Supply, concluded that no requirement existed for such a vehicle and the project was cancelled by OCM 18148 on 30 April 1942.

Two concept studies for the light tank T13 are shown here. They were redrawn by Phil Dyer from very poor originals located in the files of the United States Army Tank Automotive Command.

Light Tank T13 w/20mm gun

20mm HISPANO SUIZA BIRGIKT GUN MOUNTED IN SPECIAL ALLIS CHALMERS TANK

Reference Drawing E4575 31 Jan 1942

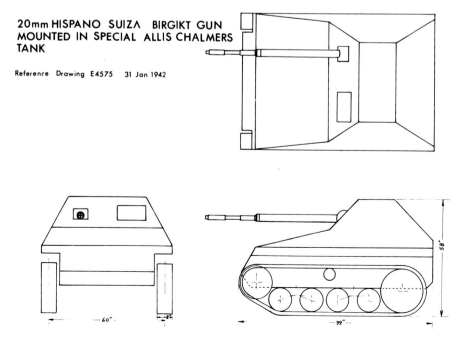

214

These photographs show details of the light tank T16 accepted for service on an emergency basis by the United States Army. Note the early type vision slots. Below is a lineup of T16s at the Marmon-Herrington plant.

After the attack on Pearl Harbor and the entry of the United States into World War II, the government took over numerous contracts for war materiel being produced for allied nations under the Lend-Lease program. Among these was a contract with the Marmon-Herrington Company to construct 240 light tanks for China. These were small two man vehicles weighing about eight tons. The armor was ½ inch thick except on the front where the plates were doubled to give a total thickness of one inch. The tanks were armed with three .30 caliber machine guns. One of these was located in a small turret with a manual traverse of 240 degrees. The other two were installed in the front hull plate with one fixed and the other in a flexible ball mount. Direct vision slots were provided in the hull and turret. Powered by a Hercules WXLC-3 gasoline engine, the maximum road speed was about 30 miles/hour. On 23 July 1942, OCM 18526 designated these Marmon-Herrington model CTLS-4TAC tanks as the light tank T16. They were distributed to the troops on an emergency basis with some ending up in Alaska.

This light tank T16 was assigned to the Provisional Tank Company at Fort Glenn, Umnak Island, Alaska in 1942. The slotted vision port covers can be seen rotated to the open position. None of the T16s were equipped with periscopes.

The Marmon-Herrington CTMS-1TB1 produced for the Netherlands Purchasing Commission is shown on this page. The machine guns have not been installed on this vehicle.

The contracts for two other tank models produced by Marmon-Herrrington for the Netherlands Purchasing Commission also were taken over by the Services of Supply. The first of these was for three man tanks, Marmon-Herrington model CTMS-1TB1. The armament on this vehicle consisted of a 37mm 44 caliber automatic cannon manufactured by the American Armament Corporation and a coaxial .30 caliber Colt machine gun. Both were in a manually rotated turret with 360 degree traverse. Three additional .30 caliber Colt machine guns were installed in the hull front plate with two of them fixed for use by the driver. The third was in a flexible ball mount. The armor plate was ½ inch thick on the front, sides, and rear. A telescope was provided for aiming the cannon and the coaxial machine gun. Direct vision slots with protective glass blocks were located in the hull and turret. With a loaded weight of about 13 tons, the tank was fitted with a vertical volute spring suspension and 15 inch wide steel tracks. This resulted in a ground pressure of slightly less than 9 psi. The six cylinder Hercules RXLD gasoline engine was rated at 174 horsepower at 2600 rpm. It drove the tank through a manually operated sliding gear transmission with five speeds forward and one reverse. The vehicle had a maximum road speed of 25 miles/hour and it could climb a 50 per cent slope.

The tank was driven 454 miles during tests at Aberdeen from 25 February 1943 to 3 May of the same year. By this time, far superior light tanks were in full production and there was no need for stopgap vehicles. Thus the CTMS-1TB1 was considered unsatisfactory and rejected for use by the United States.

This is the Marmon-Herrington MTLS-1G14 light tank manufactured for the Netherlands. A top view drawing of the twin 37mm gun mount is at the bottom of the page.

The second vehicle contract taken over from the Netherlands Purchasing Commission was for a four man tank also manufactured by Marmon-Herrington. Designated as the MTLS-1G14, it was similar in many respects to the three man vehicle. However, the armament now consisted of the American Armament Corporation dual 37mm 44 caliber automatic cannon in the turret. A .30 caliber Colt machine gun was ball mounted in the front side wall to the right of the twin 37mm guns. Another .30 caliber Colt machine gun was installed on an external antiaircraft mount at the rear of the turret. The turret had a 360 degree manual traverse. Three additional .30 caliber Colt machine guns were located in the hull front plate. Two of these were fixed and the third was in a flexible ball mount. Like the

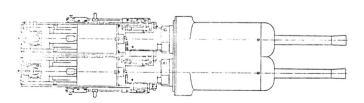

three man tank, the armor consisted of bolted plates, but the thickness ranged from 1½ inches on the front to ½ inch on the top. The MTLS-1G14 weighed about 21 tons and the vertical volute spring suspension was fitted with 18 inch wide steel tracks. Driven by a 240 horsepower Hercules gasoline engine, it had a maximum road speed of about 25 miles/hour. Tested at Aberdeen starting in April 1943, the MTLS-1G14 also was considered unsatisfactory and rejected for use by the United States.

Representatives of the Ordnance Department and the Armored Force held a conference at Fort Knox on 18 August 1942 to discuss the characteristics of an ideal light tank. Ordnance agreed to prepare design studies which would reflect those characteristics most desired by the Armored Force. The general design was to be based on the new medium tank T20. A mock-up of the latter had been completed in May at the Fisher Body Division of General Motors Corporation. Originally, it was intended to arm the new light tank with the 75mm gun M3, but an even more powerful weapon was desired if possible within a weight limit of 20 tons. The armor was to provide protection against .50 caliber machine gun fire. The original concept proposed the use of the suspension from the medium tank M7.

After initial studies, OCM 19655, dated 4 February 1943, listed the general characteristics of the new vehicle and assigned the designation light tank T21. It was now a five man vehicle with a loaded weight of 47,000 pounds. Armament was specified as the 76mm gun with a coaxial .30 caliber machine gun in a power operated turret with the gun mount stabilized in elevation. Another .30 caliber machine gun was located in the front hull ball mount and a .30 caliber antiaircraft machine gun was installed on the turret. The armor plate ranged in thickness from 1⅛ inches on the front to ½ inch on top. A maximum sustained road speed of 35 miles/hour was specified with a cruising range of 150 miles at 25 miles/hour.

Final layout drawings of the T21 were completed at the Fisher Body Division during March 1943 and submitted to Fort Knox. By this time, the estimated weight had increased to 51,000 pounds. Based on past experience, Fort Knox concluded that additional weight increases would occur during development and the end result would be an inadequately armored medium tank. As a result, the Armored Force recommended that the T21 project be terminated without the construction of any pilot tanks. Ordnance Committee action cancelled the program in July 1943.

Below is the mock-up of the medium tank T20 which provided the basis for the design of the light tank T21. The T21 had the same configuration with lighter armor.

LIGHT TANKS T24, M24, AND T24E1

Combat experience in North Africa had indicated the need for more powerful armament in the light tanks. The effect of this experience has been noted earlier in the T7 program and the T21 design study. In late 1942, a project was approved to mount the 75mm gun M3 in the open top turret of the 75mm howitzer motor carriage M8. This vehicle had the same chassis as the M5 light tank and the purpose of this project was to determine the effect of firing the more powerful M3 gun on the M5 chassis. The tests at Aberdeen were successful with the light tank chassis providing a stable firing platform for the M3 cannon. However, the limited space in the M5A1 tank turret did not permit the installation of the larger weapon.

In March 1943, the Ordnance Committee listed the characteristics of a new light tank based on the power train of the M5A1 and designated the new vehicle as the light tank T24. The proposed characteristics called for the 75mm gun M3 to be installed in the turret using the T19 concentric recoil mechanism developed during the T7 program. Such a mechanism reduced the space requirements by eliminating the separate recoil cylinders and using a hollow recoil cylinder around the gun tube itself. The T19 recoil mechanism with the M3 gun had been fired in the light

Above is the early wooden mock-up of the light tank T24. Details of the turret and armament had not been fully determined at that time.

tank T7E2 at Aberdeen, but it was not adopted for the medium tank M7 because of the limited amount of testing that had been completed at that time. However, as noted during the earlier studies, the use of the 75mm gun M3 with an appropriate mount made it extremely difficult to design a tank with a combat weight of 20 tons or less. A

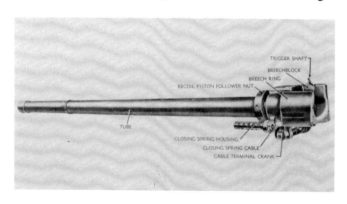

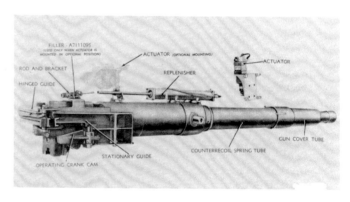

Above, the 75mm gun M5 (T13E1) appears at the left and, at the right, it is installed in the long recoil AN-M9 aircraft mount. Below at the left, the lightweight 75mm gun is in the short recoil M64 (T90) mount developed for use in the light tank T24 turret. At the bottom right is a cross section drawing of the T33 concentric recoil mechanism used in this mount.

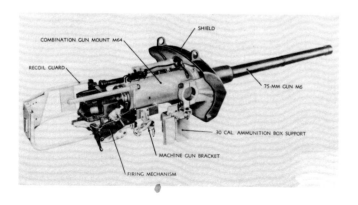

solution to this problem that now appeared was the use of the lightweight 75mm gun T13E1 which had been developed for aircraft use. Ballistically identical to the M3 gun, the thin wall tube heated up more rapidly during firing and

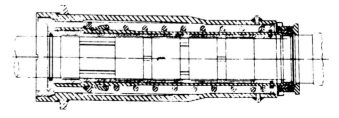

220

The first pilot light tank T24 is shown above and below on 21 October 1943 after it arrived at Aberdeen Proving Ground. Note the lack of a cupola for the tank commander and there is no pistol port in the turret right side wall. The tank is fully armed with all of its machine guns.

had a shorter life. However, the T13E1 weighed slightly over 400 pounds compared to 893 pounds for the M3. Eventually standardized as the 75mm gun M5, the T13E1 was fitted with a long recoil mechanism and installed in the B25H bomber. A new concentric short recoil mechanism, designated as the T33, was developed that limited the recoil distance to a maximum of 12 inches which could be tolerated inside a tank turret. Using the T33 recoil mechanism, the T90 combination gun mount was designed for the lightweight cannon and a coaxial .30 caliber machine gun. A T92 telescopic sight was installed on the left side of the mount. A new turret with a 60 inch inside diameter ring was designed for use with the T90 combination gun mount. In this turret, the gunner and the tank commander were located on the left side of the cannon with the loader on the right.

On 2 September 1943, OCM 21446 classified the T24 as a limited procurement type and the Services of Supply directed that 1000 light tanks T24 be built in lieu of 1000 light tanks M5A1. Thus no expansion of manufacturing facilities was required. The first pilot T24 was delivered on 15 October 1943 and shipped to Aberdeen Proving Ground. The second T24 pilot arrived at Aberdeen in December. Firing tests revealed problems with the concentric recoil mechanisms on both tanks and they were returned to Rock Island for modification. Other failures during the test program involved the road wheels, cooling fan drive shafts, shock absorbers, and the transfer unit. These components were modified before production began.

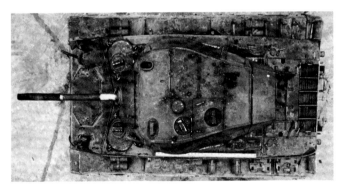

Below, the first pilot light tank T24 appears on 7 February 1944 after 2821 miles of operation during tests at Aberdeen Proving Ground. Note that the gun mount has been removed for modification during the automotive evaluation.

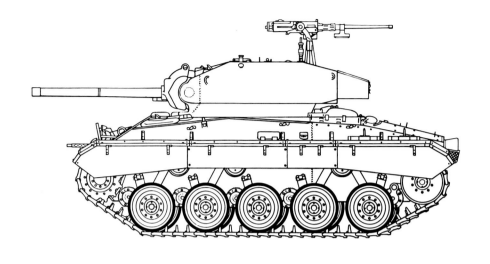

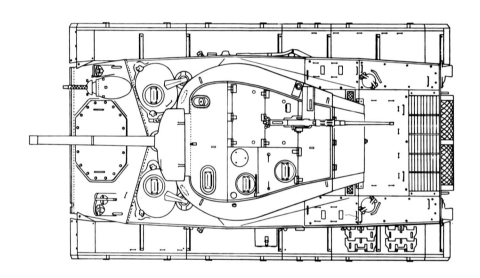

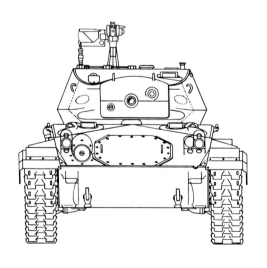

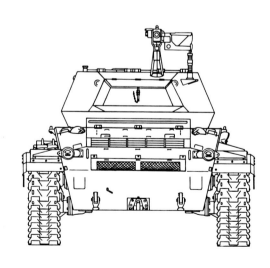

Scale 1:48

Light Tank T24, 1st Pilot

©D.P. Dyer

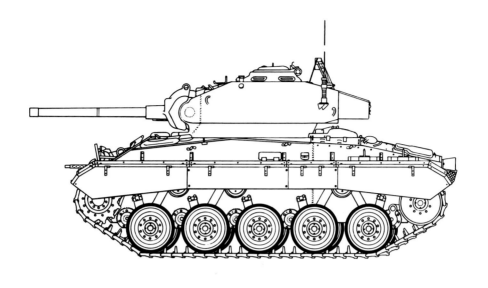

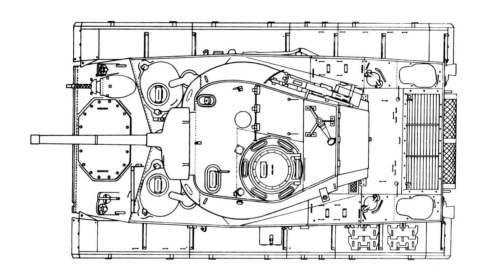

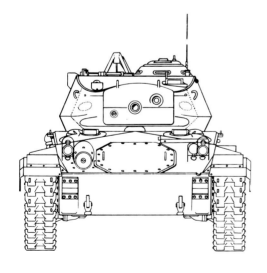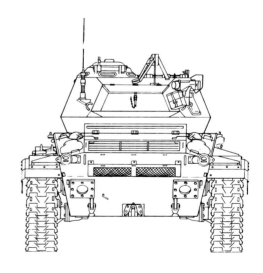

Scale 1:48

Light Tank M24

223

The configuration standardized as the light tank M24 can be seen here on the second production vehicle at Aberdeen on 23 June 1944. A vision cupola has been provided for the tank commander and a pistol port is installed in the turret right side wall.

Various components and items of external stowage on the light tank M24 are identified above and at the right. Note the port for the smoke mortar in the right front of the turret roof.

A new chassis was developed based on the M5A1 power train with the twin Cadillac engines and Hydramatic transmissions. Problems in the field with the automatic transfer unit in the M5 and M5A1 resulted in its replacement by a manual transfer unit with two speeds forward and one reverse. The new transfer unit and reverse gear were included in the gear train that coupled the two power plants together. The new design resulted in a 22 per cent increase in the overall low gear ratio providing improved gradeablilty despite the tank's weight increase compared to the M5A1. The combination of the new transfer unit and the Hydramatic transmissions provided a total of eight speeds forward and four in reverse. The latter permitted a maximum speed of 18 miles/hour in the reverse direction, a handy feature for a rapid withdrawal.

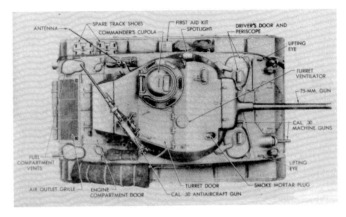

At the right is the empty hull and suspension system of the light tank M24 without the tracks. The internal components of the complete tank are visible in the sectional drawing below.

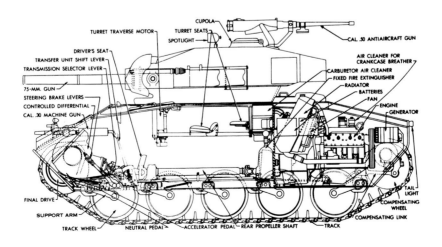

225

Above, one of the two Cadillac engines with its Hydramatic transmission is shown at the left and it is assembled with its cooling system at the right. Below, the twin engines are installed in the hull at the left and the rear deck is in place at the right.

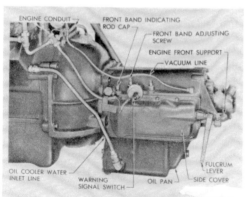

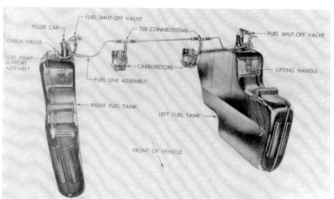

One of the Hydramatic transmissions appears above at the left and the fuel system of the light tank M24 is directly above. The bottom of the tank hull can be seen at the left. Note the square opening for the floor escape hatch.

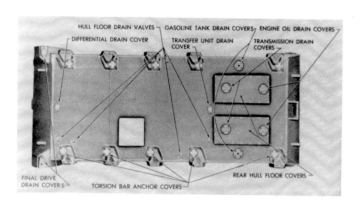

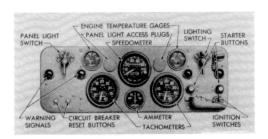

The driver's station in the light tank M24 is at the left and his instrument panel is above. The exterior of the driver's hatch appears below at the left and an inside view is directly below.

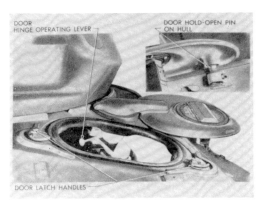

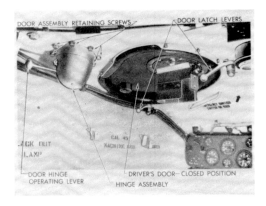

At the right, the floor escape hatch can be seen inside the tank just behind the assistant driver's seat.

Dual controls were provided for the driver and the assistant driver, but the steering brake levers were pivoted at the bottom, unlike the top pivoted levers on the M5 and M5A1. The drivers' hatches were enlarged over those on the earlier light tanks and they were designed to open regardless of the turret position. Each of these hatches was fitted with a rotating periscope. An emergency escape hatch was located in the hull floor behind the assistant driver's seat. A .30 caliber machine gun in a ball mount was installed in the right front armor for use by the assistant driver.

An interior view of the ventilator mounted in the hull roof between the driver and assistant driver is at the left. Below, the pioneer tool stowage can be seen on the outside of the tank.

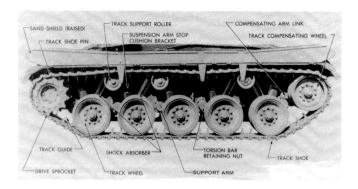

Above, the suspension and tracks on the light tank M24 are exposed at the left with the sandshield raised. At the right are two shoes for the T72 single pin track.

The tests on the M5A1 by the Armored Board and at Aberdeen had shown the necessity for an improved suspension with wider tracks. To meet this requirement, a new torsion bar suspension was designed with individually sprung dual road wheels. This suspension was fitted with T72 cast steel tracks. These were 16 inch wide, single pin, center guide tracks with a pitch of 5½ inches. Tests indicated that the new suspension improved the ride, provided a more stable gun platform, and increased the cross-country mobility. The armor plate on the T24 was highly sloped with a maximum thickness of one inch except for the gun shield. The latter was a casting 1½ inches thick. The loaded weight of the new tank was approximately 20 tons and the twin Cadillac engines drove it at a maximum road speed of about 35 miles/hour.

Production of the light tank T24 began in April 1944 at the Cadillac Division of General Motors Corporation and in July 1944 at the Massey Harris Company. It continued at both plants until the end of World War II for a total of 4731 tanks. OCM 24175, dated 22 June 1944, recommended the standardization of the T24 as the light tank M24 and the reclassification of the M5A1 as substitute standard. This action was approved in July. The M24 was furnished to allied nations under the Lend-Lease program with 289 tanks being allocated to Great Britain and two to the Soviet Union. Following the precedent established by the Stuart, the M24 also was named after a famous cavalryman. This time it was Major General Adna R. Chaffee, the first commander of the Armored Force.

Below, the propeller shaft can be seen between the ammunition stowage spaces in this view with the floor plates removed. At the right are the bulkhead doors at the rear of the fighting compartment (upper) and a view of the compartment with the turret removed (lower).

228

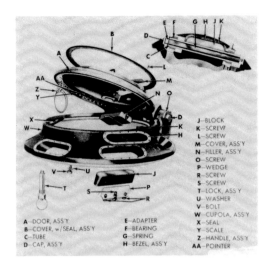

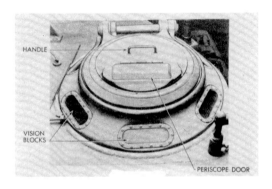

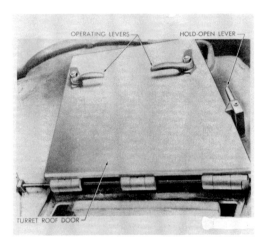

J—BLOCK
K—SCREW
L—SCREW
M—COVER, ASS'Y
N—FILLER, ASS'Y
O—SCREW
P—WEDGE
R—SCREW
S—SCREW
T—LOCK, ASS'Y
U—WASHER
V—BOLT
W—CUPOLA, ASS'Y
X—SEAL
Y—SCALE
Z—HANDLE, ASS'Y
AA—POINTER

A—DOOR, ASS'Y
B—COVER, w/SEAL, ASS'Y
C—TUBE
D—CAP, ASS'Y

E—ADAPTER
F—BEARING
G—SPRING
H—BEZEL, ASS'Y

The commander's cupola on the light tank M24 is shown here with the hatch open (above) and closed (below). An exploded view of this cupola appears at the upper right. At the lower right is the flat turret hatch over the loader's position.

The production tanks differed from the first pilot in several features. A new vision cupola replaced the flat commander's hatch on the left side of the turret roof. This cupola with six vision blocks and a periscope in the hatch cover replaced the commander's two rotating periscopes in the pilot. A pistol port was installed in the right side of the turret for the loader and wet stowage was provided for the 75mm ammunition. The latter consisted of water filled containers surrounding the 75mm ammunition racks. The T90 gun mount was standardized as the combination gun mount M64. The lightweight tank mounted cannon became the 75mm gun M6. This included the T13E1 and M5 aircraft guns which, when installed in the tank, were redesignated as the M6. The former aircraft weapons could easily be identified by the grooved collar near the front end of the tube. This collar was used to attach the concentric long recoil mechanism of the AN-M9 gun mount used in the aircraft installation. On later production M6 guns, the collar was omitted.

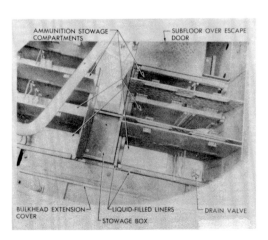

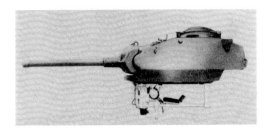

The wet stowage arrangement in the floor ammunition spaces can be seen at the left. Below, the turret is removed from the M24. Although the seats for the tank commander, gunner, and loader are attached to the turret, it does not have a basket.

The armament is installed in the light tank M24 turret above with a closeup view of the smoke mortar at the upper right. At the lower right is the .50 caliber antiaircraft machine gun. Below, the SCR 508 radio is in the turret bustle.

In addition to the .30 caliber coaxial and bow machine guns, the M24 was armed with a .50 caliber antiaircraft machine gun on the turret roof. A 2 inch M3 smoke mortar was installed in the right front of the turret roof, however, it was eliminated after World War II. The Chaffee was manned by a crew of four or five. With a four man crew, the assistant driver also acted as loader for the 75mm gun.

In early 1945, the 75mm gun T21 was installed in a light tank M24 for evaluation at Fort Knox. The T21 was an improved version of the M6 cannon with a stronger and heavier breech assembly. It also had an improved firing mechanism, a fixed breech operating handle, and a hand cocking lever accessible to the gunner, loader, or the tank commander. The new gun also was fitted with the T13 single baffle muzzle brake. After minor modifications, the improved cannon eventually was standardized as the 75mm gun M17 with the muzzle brake M5. By this time, the war was over and production of the light tank M24 had ended.

Below, the gun mount is being installed in the light tank M24 turret at the left and an interior view of the bow machine gun mount is at the right.

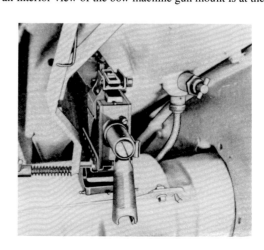

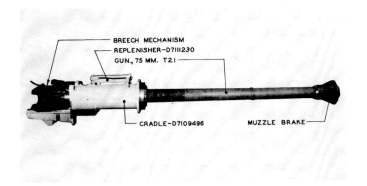

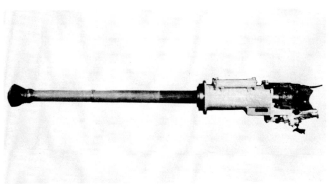

BREECH MECHANISM
REPLENISHER-D7III230
GUN, 75 MM. T21
CRADLE-D7I09496
MUZZLE BRAKE

The 75mm gun T21 appears above in the T33E3 recoil mechanism. At the right and below are views of the T21 gun breech. The recoil guard installed on the mount in the light tank M24 turret can be seen below.

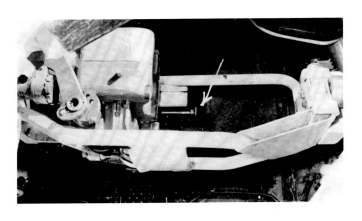

In an effort to provide greater machine gun firepower for the medium tanks, a new commander's cupola was developed based upon a gun turret installed on bomber aircraft. Designated as the twin machine gun mount T121, it was installed on the medium tanks M4A3 and M26. In July 1947, a lighter weight version was completed for use on the M24 and designated as the twin machine gun mount T122. It was armed with two .50 caliber M2 HB machine guns, although two .30 caliber machine guns could be installed as alternate armament. Protected by ½ inch thick steel armor, the new mount required an adapter ring when it replaced the commander's cupola on the M24. It had

The light tank M24 below is fitted with the twin machine gun mount T122 replacing the commander's cupola. Weights have been added to the tank hull to simulate a full combat load.

The installation of the two .50 caliber machine guns on the T122 mount is clearly visible in the top view at the left. Below, the silhouette of the tank with the T122 mount is compared with that of a standard light tank M24.

retained the same diameter as the heavier T121 which was designed to fit the 31.5 inch diameter cupola bolt circle on the medium tanks. The bolt circle on the M24 commander's cupola was only 30.5 inches in diameter. The overhang of the new mount interfered with the loader's hatch cover on the M24 and a redesign would have been required. The test program continued until June 1948, but the T122 was never standardized. However, the test report recommended the development of an improved mount to provide 360 degree machine gun fire independent of the turret position.

The late production tanks were fitted with mounting pads for flotation gear on the hull which replaced the front steps on each side. In May 1945, tests were run at the Tank Arsenal Proving Ground on an M24 equipped with long steel grousers to lower the ground pressure. These grousers were 28⅜ inches long and they were attached to the T72E1 tracks. These tracks differed from the original T72 tracks by the addition of three holes for the attachment of the grousers. Tests showed that the grousers had a life in excess of 1000 miles and that they were very effective in improving the tank's mobility over soft ground. Later, a new 14

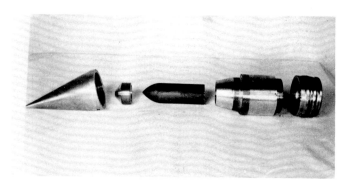

In an effort to improve the armor penetration performance of the 75mm gun, some new types of ammunition were developed. At the left is a disassembled view of the 75mm HVAP-T shot T45. With a muzzle velocity of 2850 feet per second, it penetrated six inches of homogeneous armor at low angles of obliquity and a range of 500 yards during tests at Fort Knox. At the lower left is the 75mm AP-T shot M338A1. It had a muzzle velocity of 2340 feet per second and provided penetration performance superior to the AP-T M79 and APC-T M61 rounds, particularly at high angles of obliquity.

Below are the track shoes for the T85E1 double pin track.

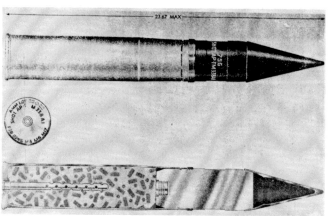

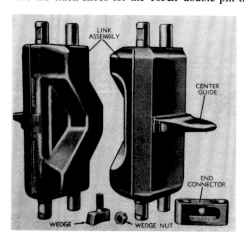

Light tank M24, registration number 30112598, is shown here at the Tank Arsenal Proving Ground on 11 May 1945. It has been fitted with the 28 inch rolled section grousers. A closeup view of the grouser attached to the T72E1 track shoe is at the bottom right.

inch wide, double pin, rubber chevron track was developed for the M24. Designated as the T85E1, it had the same 5½ inch pitch as the earlier T72 and T72E1 tracks and it could be installed with extended end connectors to give a track width of 16½ inches. A new 13 tooth sprocket was required for use with the T85E1 track.

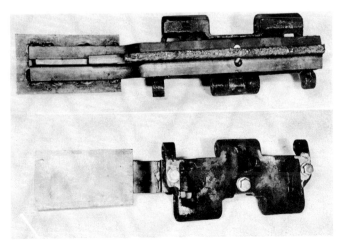

The light tank M24 appears here during its evaluation at Fort Knox.

Above is light tank M24, serial number 108, at the General Motors Proving Ground on 2 August 1944. None of the machine guns have been mounted on this vehicle.

At the right and below are two additional views of the light tank M24. The tank below is on the firing range.

This light tank M24 was one of those supplied to Britain under the Lend-Lease program.

Above is the light tank T24E1 pilot at Aberdeen Proving Ground on 31 January 1945. Note the threaded gun muzzle where the muzzle brake has been removed. Since the T24E1 was converted from the first pilot T24, it lacked a cupola for the tank commander.

When the light tank T24 was classified as a limited procurement type in September 1943, the same Ordnance Committee action authorized the construction of a pilot tank powered by the Continental R-975 engine with a Spicer automatic torque converter transmission. This version was designated as the light tank T24E1. This vehicle was expected to weigh approximately the same as the T24, but the power to weight ratio would be raised to about 20 horsepower/ton. After completion of the tests at Aberdeen and Fort Knox, the original T24 pilot was shipped on 15 March 1944 to the American Car & Foundry Company in Berwick, Pennsylvania for conversion to the T24E1. After the work was complete, it was transferred to Aberdeen Proving Ground for tests beginning on 10 October 1944. During the original evaluation of the T24 pilot, a double baffle muzzle brake was installed on the 75mm gun T13E1. This muzzle brake was still in place when the tank was converted to the T24E1. It was removed later during the tests at Aberdeen.

The top of the engine compartment on the T24E1 was raised and it was extended to the rear to accommodate the large Continental R-975-C4 engine. Two fuel tanks for 80 octane gasoline were installed in the engine compartment. A 65 gallon tank on the right side and a 75 gallon tank on the left brought the total capacity to 140 gallons compared to 115 gallons in the M24. The engine compartment in the T24E1 was designed so that the R-975-C4 power plant could be pulled out to the rear on rails. These rails were installed on the floor of the engine compartment and on

At the right are additional views of the light tank T24E1 pilot. The large bulged engine compartment required to house the R-975-C4 radial engine is particularly obvious.

the rear door. When this door was lowered to the horizontal position, the rails on the inside surface aligned with those on the engine compartment floor forming a track on which the engine could be moved.

The Spicer automatic torque converter transmission was controlled by a shift lever with five positions. These were normal, high, low, reverse, and neutral. The latter was used when starting the engine. In the normal range, power was transmitted through the torque converter until

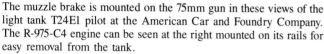

The muzzle brake is mounted on the 75mm gun in these views of the light tank T24E1 pilot at the American Car and Foundry Company. The R-975-C4 engine can be seen at the right mounted on its rails for easy removal from the tank.

a speed of about 18 miles/hour was reached. At that point, it automatically shifted to direct drive. The maximum speed obtainable in the normal range was about 34 miles/hour. For faster speeds, the transmission was shifted to the high range which engaged an overdrive gear behind the torque converter. If the tank was started in the high range, the shift from the torque converter to direct drive occurred at approximately 23 miles/hour. The maximum speed in the high range was about 45 miles/hour. For operation in rough terrain, the low range introduced a further gear reduction behind the torque converter. With the higher power available in the T24E1, the final drive gear ratio was 1.37:1 compared to 1.57:1 in the T24.

The tests at Aberdeen confirmed the superior performance of the T24E1 compared to the M24. However, the reliability of the Spicer transmission was considered to be unsatisfactory. One particular problem was with torsional vibration in the transmission direct drive shaft. The test program at Aberdeen continued until November 1945. By that time, World War II had ended and no further consideration was given to the production of a light tank based on the T24E1.

Another experimental project installed the tracks and suspension from the 12-ton German half-track vehicle (Sonder Kraftfahrzeuge 8) on the chassis of the M24. This suspension from the Diamler Benz "DB 10" featured overlapping road wheels and padded, lubricated, tracks. The turret was not installed on the M24 during these tests. Since the new suspension did not show a significant improvement in performance, further work was cancelled.

The modified chassis of the M24 provided the basis for a combat team of vehicles. These included the 40mm gun motor carriage M19 and the 155mm howitzer motor

carriage M41 as well as their respective companion vehicles, the cargo carriers T23E1 and T22E1. All of these had the engine shifted forward to just behind the driving compartment. The 105mm howitzer motor carriage M37 also utilized the modified M24 chassis, but the engine was in the rear.

The end of the line for the light tank T24E1 is at the right. Here it is in the storage area at Aberdeen Proving Ground in December 1946. Once again, it is fitted with the muzzle brake.

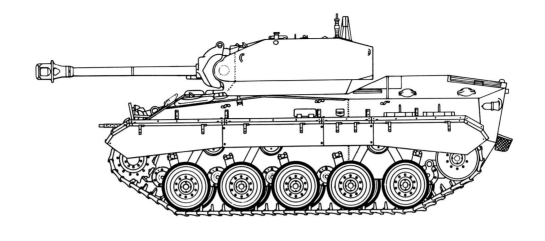

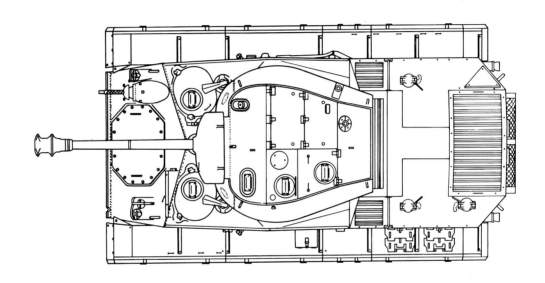

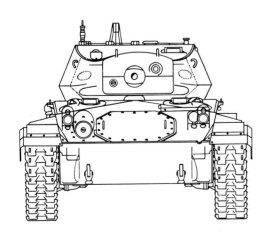

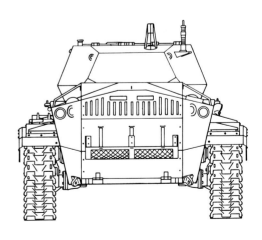

Scale 1:48

©D.P. Dyer

Light Tank T24E1

The Chaffee continued to serve long into the postwar period. Between 1946 and 1950, 1600 of the M24s were rebuilt and brought up to the latest standards. In early 1947, the Cadillac Division of General Motors installed 21 inch wide tracks on a modified M24. To permit this installation, the standard suspension components were spaced out 2½ inches from the hull by welded extensions. Two types of tracks were installed. The first was the single pin T86, rubber bushed, forged steel design with an octagonal pin. The second was the T87 double pin track. The shoes of the latter were molded rubber blocks with steel grousers. Long steel track grousers and special ice grousers were provided for use with the T86 single pin track.

The Chaffee was widely distributed to foreign countries after World War II. In this service it was frequently modified and modernized by the installation of new power trains and more powerful armament.

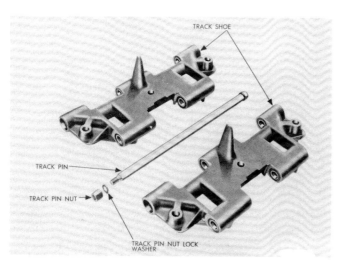

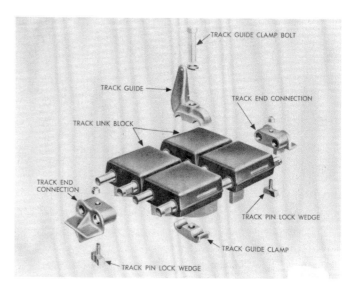

Above, the 21 inch wide track shoes T86 and T87 appear at the left and right respectively. Below, these tracks are shown installed on the spaced out suspension of the light tank M24.

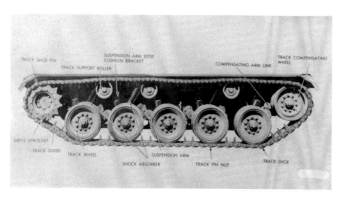

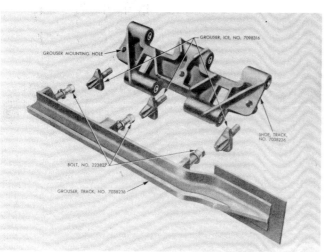

At the left is a view of the track and ice grousers provided for use with the single pin T86 track.

240

The early light tank T9 mock-up appears above with the vertical volute spring suspension and a trailing idler. A T16 rubber block track is installed on the left side. The bogies are mounted on the right side, but the trailing idler, sprocket, and track have not been fitted.

AIRBORNE TANKS

Representatives of the Armored Force, the Air Corps, and the Ordnance Department met on 27 February 1941 to consider the required characteristics of an airborne light tank and a suitable aircraft to carry it. A letter from Major General D. H. Pratt of the British Purchasing Commission indicated their strong interest in such a tank. OCM 16747, dated 22 May 1941, outlined the characteristics of the proposed vehicle and designated it as the light tank T9. Most of these characteristics were approximate since the details of the proposed carrier aircraft were not yet available. It was estimated that the vehicle would have a maximum weight of 7½ tons without crew or stowage and stripped of all readily removable equipment. The approximate dimensions were 138 inches in length, 84 inches in width, and a maximum height of 66 inches. Armament was to be either a 37mm gun or a 57mm gun in a combination mount with a .30 caliber machine gun. These weapons were to be installed in a power operated turret with a 360 degrees traverse and fitted with an elevation gyrostabilizer. The tank also was to be armed with as many

additional machine guns as practical. A crew of two or preferably three was specified.

In July 1941, Mr. J. Walter Christie was invited to present a proposal for the design and manufacture of a pilot airborne tank which would meet the required characteristics previously described. For a price of $126,000, Mr. Christie agreed to design and build such a pilot tank. Unfortunately, his preliminary design did not meet the dimensional requirements. A second Christie design in November 1941 also did not meet the specifications previously outlined and it would have required the construction of a special aircraft for transportation. After this, no further consideration was given to the Christie designs.

In August 1941, a preliminary wooden model of the T9 was inspected by representatives of the Air Corps, the Ordnance Department, and the Douglas Aircraft Company. The new C54 transport designed by the latter was being considered as the aircraft to carry the new tank. The Marmon-Herrington Company proposed to build a pilot tank of the new design powered by a Lycoming aircraft

Below, the light tank T9 mock-up has the short pitch Marmon-Herrington track installed on the right side with an appropriate sprocket. It retains the T16 rubber block track on the left side. The machine gun armament was included on the mock-up at this stage.

Light Tank T9, Pontiac concept

Scale 1:48

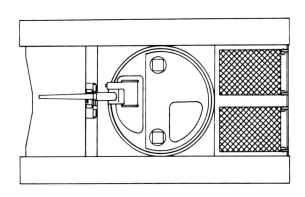

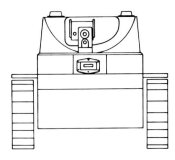 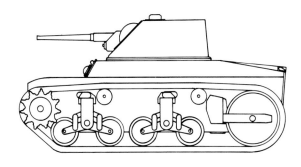 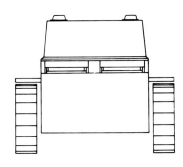

The drawing above depicts the Pontiac proposal for the light tank T9. Below is the mock-up for this vehicle without the turret.

engine and using the Marmon-Herrington suspension with steel tracks. In September, a proposal also was received from the Pontiac Division of General Motors Corporation for the construction of a T9 pilot powered by two Pontiac six cylinder engines. However, the estimated costs of this design were higher and the development contract was awarded to Marmon-Herrington.

A partial wooden mock-up of the Marmon-Herrington tank's upper hull structure was completed in November 1941. It was shipped to the Douglas Aircraft Company to check the carrier installation on the C54. Apparently, some minor modifications were required, but there were no serious problems with this arrangement which suspended the tank without the turret underneath the C54 fuselage. The turret was designed to be easily removable so that it could be carried with the crew inside the aircraft.

The light tank T9 pilot was completed at Marmon-Herrington in April 1942 and shipped to Fort Benning,

Georgia to further check the carrier arrangement on a mock-up of the C54. Tests indicated that the suspension lugs on the tank should be strengthened and some redesign was required for the aircraft hydraulic hoisting mechanism.

Below is the light tank T9 pilot after completion at Marmon-Herrington. Note that the single pin Marmon-Herrington tracks with a 3 inch pitch have been installed on the vehicle.

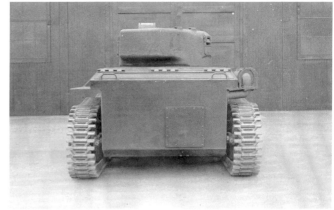

The two photographs above and the three below show the light tank T9 pilot as originally completed at Marmon-Herrington. Note the two fixed .30 caliber bow machine guns for use by the driver in addition to the .30 caliber machine gun coaxial with the 37mm gun in the turret.

Constructed of soft steel plate and manned by a crew of three, the T9 pilot was armed with the 37mm gun M6 and a coaxial .30 caliber machine gun in the turret combination mount. As specified, the turret was power operated in traverse and the mount was stabilized in elevation. The gunner and the tank commander-loader were located on the left and right sides of the gun mount respectively. The driver was seated in the left front hull. Two fixed .30 caliber machine guns were installed in the right front hull for use by the driver.

By May 1942, the carrier installation on the C54 was satisfactorily completed and additional tests of the tank were underway at Fort Bragg, North Carolina and at the General Motors Proving Ground. As often happened during a

Below and at the right is the light tank T9 pilot after modification. Bogie braces have been added to the suspension and carrying brackets are installed on each side to suspend the hull under the C54 aircraft.

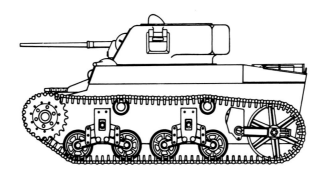

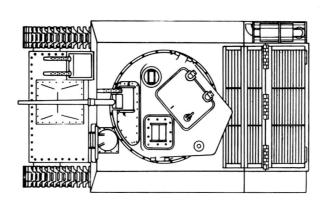

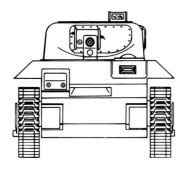

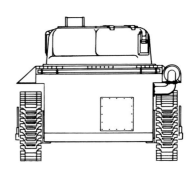

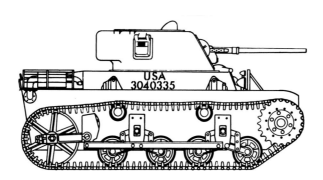

AFTER MODIFICATION

Scale 1:48

©D.P. Dyer

Light Tank T9, Marmon-Herrington

244

The bogie braces added to the light tank T9 can be seen in the closeup view of the modified suspension at the left above. At the top right, the hull of the light tank T9 pilot is suspended underneath the C54 aircraft.

development program, the weight of the tank had increased and now exceeded the original specification. As a result, its performance was reported as somewhat sluggish. Representatives of the Armored Force and the Ordnance Department met at Marmon-Herrington 31 May 1942 to consider the weight problem. Information from the Army Air Force and the British indicated that the maximum empty weight would have to be limited to 15,800 pounds. To meet this requirement, it was agreed to eliminate the gyrostabilizer, the power traverse mechanism, and the two fixed bow machine guns. The differential gears were changed to provide a lower steering ratio and the tank was

subjected to further tests at Marmon-Herrington and at the General Motors Proving Ground. In November 1942, the T9 was shipped to California for actual flight tests and in January 1943 it was returned to Marmon-Herrington. Some minor modifications were required resulting from the test program. The T9 pilot was then used as a test vehicle to support the development of the improved airborne tank intended for production.

Rapid progress had been made in tank components as well as overall design since the selection of the original configuration for the T9. To incorporate these latest features, design studies for an improved airborne tank began

Below is the mock-up of the light tank T9E1. Note that the fixed .30 caliber machine guns in the bow have been eliminated and the front hull has been redesigned.

These photographs show the first pilot light tank T9E1 at Aberdeen Proving Ground on 5 December 1942. The tank is equipped with full armament and the external stowage is installed. Note the pistol port on each side of the turret. Dimensions of the pilot taken at the Proving Ground have been added to the side view.

in February 1942. Designated as the light tank T9E1, the front hull was redesigned to improve the ballistic protection and to provide better vision for the driver. On the new turret, separate hatches for the gunner and the tank commander replaced the single hatch on the T9 and two M6 periscopes were provided for the tank commander compared to one on the earlier vehicle. A wooden mock-up of the T9E1 was shipped to Fort Benning in April 1942 to check its installation on the mock-up of the C54 aircraft.

Two T9E1 pilot tanks were authorized for construction and the first was completed in November 1942 and shipped to Aberdeen Proving Ground for initial tests. In February 1943, it was transferred to the Armored Force

Board for evaluation. The second T9E1 pilot was shipped directly to Britain accompanied by an ordnance officer familiar with the development program.

Procurement of the T9E1 was authorized prior to standardization and production began at Marmon-Herrington in April 1943. It continued through February 1944 for a total run of 830 tanks. In September 1944, the vehicle was classified as limited standard and designated as the light tank M22. Although it was never used in combat by American troops, it did see action with the British during the airborne crossing of the Rhine river. Named the Locust, 260 of the little airborne tanks were allocated to the British under the Lend-Lease program.

Additional details of the first pilot light tank T9E1 can be seen here. Note the changes in the turret hatch arrangement compared to the light tank T9. Below at the left is a closeup view of the suspension during the automotive tests.

Below is the first pilot T9E1 fitted with a Goodyear rubber band track on the left side of the vehicle. At the lower right is an experimental Food Machinery Corporation track which also was evaluated on the T9E1. Neither track was adopted for production.

The early production version of the light tank M22 (T9E1) is shown in the photograph above at Aberdeen Proving Ground dated 5 May 1943. Note the original driver's head cover and vision slot.

The production M22 (T9E1) had a fully loaded weight of about 16,400 pounds and the 162 net horsepower Lycoming O-435T air-cooled gasoline engine gave it a maximum road speed of about 35 miles/hour. The front armor on the vehicle was equivalent to one inch of vertical rolled homogeneous steel, although the actual thickness was only ½ inch on the highly sloped upper front hull. A 57 gallon fuel capacity provided a cruising range of about 110 miles. An escape hatch was located in the hull floor to the right front of the turret basket. A vision slot with an armored cover was provided for the driver in addition to his periscope on the first 27 production tanks. On later vehicles, this slot was replaced by a vision port closed by a steel plug.

The early type of sandshields can be seen in these views of the production tank. The pioneer tools and other external stowage have not been installed. Also, note that the turret pistol ports have been eliminated on the production vehicle.

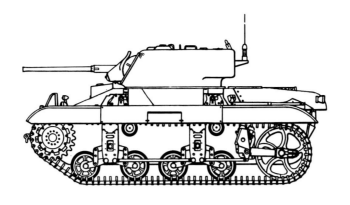

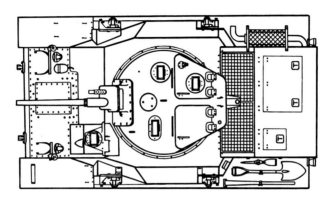

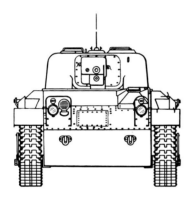

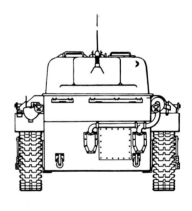

Scale 1:48

©D.P. Dyer

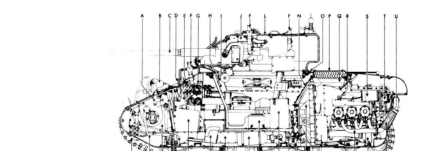

A. HEAD LIGHT SOCKET AND RELEASE·
B. SIREN
C. 37 MM. GUN
D. LOOKOUT HOLE PLUG
E. DRIVER'S HEAD COVER MECHANISM
F. PERISCOPE

G. INSTRUMENT PANEL
H. TURRET BASKET PHONE BOX
I. GUN ELEVATING MECHANISM
J. VENTILATING FAN
L. TURRET HATCH DOOR
N. BULKHEAD

O. TURRET RACE
P. AIR INLET SCREEN AND LOUVERS
Q. DIFFERENTIAL OIL COOLER
R. ENGINE OIL LEVEL GAUGE
S. GENERATOR
T. DIFFERENTIAL OIL PUMP

U. STARTER
V. EXHAUST PIPE
W. TRAILING IDLER WHEEL
X. ENGINE OIL COOLER
Y. EXHAUST MANIFOLD
Z. CLUTCH HOUSING

AA THROTTLE SLAVE CYLINDER
AB TRANSFER CASE
AC 37 MM. AMMUNITION BOX
AD SLIP RING
AE FIRE EXTINGUISHER CYLINDER
AF HEATER AIR DUCT

AG DRIVER'S SEAT
AH TRANSMISSION
AI STEERING BRAKE LEVER
AJ CONTROLLED DIFFERENTIAL
AK CLUTCH PEDAL
AL DRIVING SPROCKET

Light Tank M22 (T9E1)

249

The late production light tank M22 appears here with full armament and stowage installed. Note the later type of sandshields.

The new design driver's head cover with the vision slot replaced by the view port and plug can be seen in these photographs of the late production light tank M22.

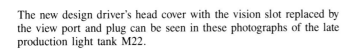

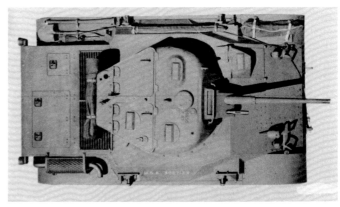

HEAD LIGHT RELEASE
BRAKE LOCKING HANDLES
COMPASS
HYDRAULIC FLUID SUPPLY TANK
STEERING LEVERS
HEAD COVER OPERATING MECHANISM
CONTROLLED DIFFERENTIAL

FINAL DRIVE CASE ASS'Y
UNIVERSAL JOINT COVER
SHIFTING LEVER
SHIFTING DIAGRAM PLATE
CLUTCH PEDAL
ACCELERATOR PEDAL
TRANSMISSION

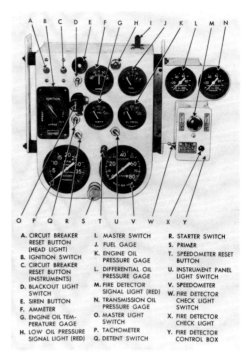

A. CIRCUIT BREAKER RESET BUTTON (HEAD LIGHT)
B. IGNITION SWITCH
C. CIRCUIT BREAKER RESET BUTTON (INSTRUMENTS)
D. BLACKOUT LIGHT SWITCH
E. SIREN BUTTON
F. AMMETER
G. ENGINE OIL TEMPERATURE GAGE
H. LOW OIL PRESSURE SIGNAL LIGHT (RED)

I. MASTER SWITCH
J. FUEL GAGE
K. ENGINE OIL PRESSURE GAGE
L. DIFFERENTIAL OIL PRESSURE GAGE
M. FIRE DETECTOR SIGNAL LIGHT (RED)
N. TRANSMISSION OIL PRESSURE GAGE
O. MASTER LIGHT SWITCH
P. TACHOMETER
Q. DETENT SWITCH

R. STARTER SWITCH
S. PRIMER
T. SPEEDOMETER RESET BUTTON
U. INSTRUMENT PANEL LIGHT SWITCH
V. SPEEDOMETER
W. FIRE DETECTOR CHECK LIGHT SWITCH
X. FIRE DETECTOR CHECK LIGHT
Y. FIRE DETECTOR CONTROL BOX

Above, the driver's station in the light tank M22 with the early type head cover appears at the left and his instrument panel is at the right. Below, the early driver's head cover (left) is compared with the later design (right).

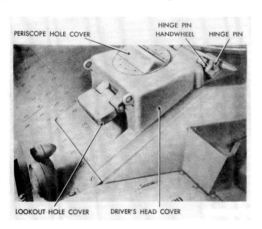

PERISCOPE HOLE COVER
HINGE PIN HANDWHEEL
HINGE PIN
LOOKOUT HOLE COVER
DRIVER'S HEAD COVER

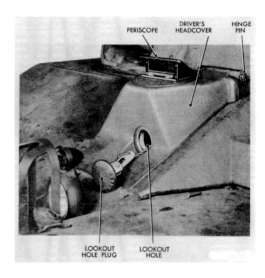

PERISCOPE
DRIVER'S HEADCOVER
HINGE PIN
LOOKOUT HOLE PLUG
LOOKOUT HOLE

An interior view of the later type driver's head cover is at the bottom right. Below is the escape hatch in the right front of the hull floor in the light tank M22.

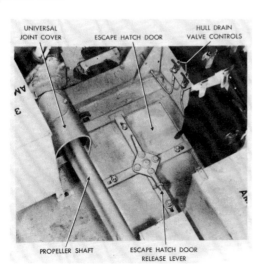

UNIVERSAL JOINT COVER
ESCAPE HATCH DOOR
HULL DRAIN VALVE CONTROLS
PROPELLER SHAFT
ESCAPE HATCH DOOR RELEASE LEVER

PERISCOPE HOLDER
CHAIN
LEVER
LOOKOUT HOLE PLUG

251

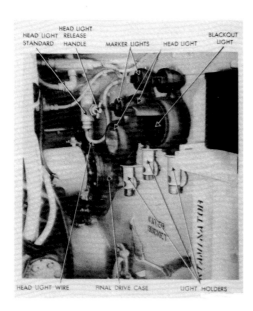

HEAD LIGHT
HEAD LIGHT RELEASE
STANDARD HANDLE MARKER LIGHTS HEAD LIGHT
BLACKOUT LIGHT

HEAD LIGHT WIRE FINAL DRIVE CASE LIGHT HOLDERS

BATTERY CABLE TANK HEATER BATTERIES BATTERY STRAP

HEATER DUCT CO₂ FIRE EXTINGUISHER CYLINDER

Above, the various lights are stowed in the right front hull. At the top right, the batteries and the tank heater can be seen in the left rear hull. Below is the Lycoming O-435T air-cooled engine that powered the light tank M22. This power plant is being removed from the tank engine compartment at the lower right.

Below, details of the carrying brackets used to suspend the light tank M22 hull under the C54 aircraft are shown at the left and the pioneer tools stowed on the left rear fender are at the right.

MUFFLER GUARD AIR INLET SCREEN LIFT BRACKET

MUFFLER TRACK INSPECTION DOOR CARRYING BOLT

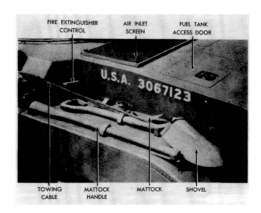

FIRE EXTINGUISHER CONTROL AIR INLET SCREEN FUEL TANK ACCESS DOOR

U.S.A. 3067123

TOWING CABLE MATTOCK HANDLE MATTOCK SHOVEL

252

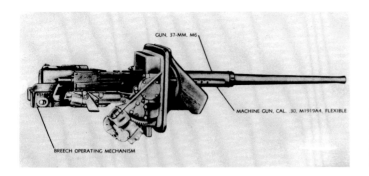

GUN, 37-MM, M6

MACHINE GUN, CAL. .30, M1919A4, FLEXIBLE

BREECH OPERATING MECHANISM

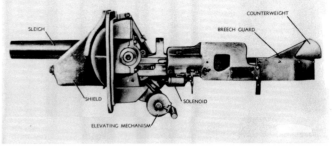

SLEIGH

SHIELD

ELEVATING MECHANISM

SOLENOID

COUNTERWEIGHT

BREECH GUARD

The combination gun mount M53 (T55) appears above armed with the 37mm gun M6 and a .30 caliber coaxial machine gun. An exploded view of the mount is at the right. The weapons are installed in the light tank M22 turret below.

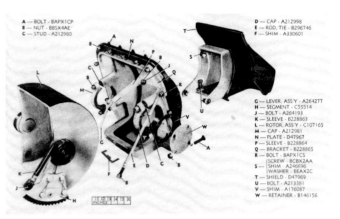

A — BOLT - BAPX1CP
B — NUT - BBSX4AE
C — STUD - A212980

D — CAP - A212998
E — ROD, TIE - B296746
F — SHIM - A330601

G — LEVER, ASS'Y - A264277
H — SEGMENT - C55514
J — BOLT - A264193
K — SLEEVE - B228863
L — ROTOR, ASS'Y - C107165
M — CAP - A212981
N — PLATE - D47967
P — SLEEVE - B228864
Q — BRACKET - B228865
R — BOLT - BAPX1CS
    (SCREW - BCBX2AA
S — {SHIM - A246696
    (WASHER - BEAX2C
T — SHIELD - D47969
U — BOLT - A213381
V — SHIM - A176087
W — RETAINER - B146156

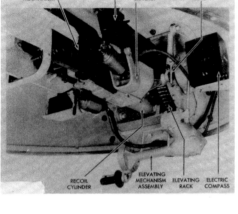

BREECH OPERATING MECHANISM

CAL. 30 MACHINE GUN

SOLENOID AND GUN MOUNT BRACKET

ELEVATING GEAR LOCKING LEVER

RECOIL CYLINDER

ELEVATING MECHANISM ASSEMBLY

ELEVATING RACK

ELECTRIC COMPASS

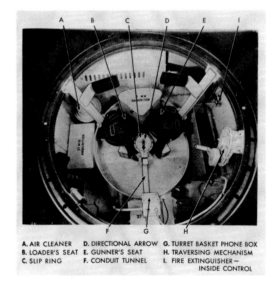

A. AIR CLEANER
B. LOADER'S SEAT
C. SLIP RING
D. DIRECTIONAL ARROW
E. GUNNER'S SEAT
F. CONDUIT TUNNEL
G. TURRET BASKET PHONE BOX
H. TRAVERSING MECHANISM
I. FIRE EXTINGUISHER — INSIDE CONTROL

Above, the turret is being removed from the light tank M22 at the left and the crew seats can be seen in the turret basket at the right. The ammunition stowage is visible in the views below.

TRAVERSING GEAR LOCK

TURRET TO RING GEAR DOWEL PIN

HAND GRENADE STOWAGE BOXES

COMMANDER'S TELESCOPE HEAD STOWAGE BOXES

BRACKETS FOR THOMPSON SUBMACHINE GUN

CAL. .45 AMMUNITION STOWAGE BOXES

TURRET TO RING GEAR DOWEL PIN

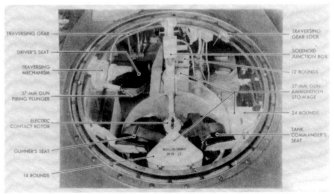

TRAVERSING GEAR

DRIVER'S SEAT

TRAVERSING MECHANISM

37-MM GUN FIRING PLUNGER

ELECTRIC CONTACT ROTOR

GUNNER'S SEAT

14 ROUNDS

TRAVERSING GEAR LOCK

SOLENOID JUNCTION BOX

12 ROUNDS

37-MM GUN AMMUNITION STOWAGE

24 ROUNDS

TANK COMMANDER'S SEAT

Above, the early production light tank M22 (left) can be compared with the late production tank (right) during training exercises. At the right and below are additional views of the late production vehicle during tests and training operations.

At the left below, the light tank M22 is shown with the C82 aircraft in which it could be carried in battle ready condition. The light tank M24 also could be transported by the C82, but it required two aircraft. One of these, as shown at the right below, carried the stripped hull which weighed about nine tons. The turret and remaining parts required a second C82.

Above, the British Locust is armed with the standard 37mm gun M6 at the left. The gun on the tank at the right has been fitted with the Littlejohn device. Both tanks are early production models. A sketch of the Littlejohn device intended for the British 2 pounder gun is shown below. The version attached to the 37mm gun was similar, but lighter in construction.

Although originally designed to be suspended without its turret under a C54 transport, later aircraft such as the C82 could carry the M22 fully assembled. In British service, the Locust was carried ready for battle in the Hamilcar glider. Modifications to the British tanks included smoke grenade launchers and, in some cases, the installation of the Littlejohn device on the 37mm gun. The latter was a muzzle attachment with a smooth tapered bore which squeezed a special armor piercing projectile down to a diameter of 1.195 inches from its original diameter of 1.46 inches (37mm). This projectile had a tungsten carbide core and achieved a muzzle velocity of about 4000 feet/second when it passed through the Littlejohn device. Originally developed for the British 2 pounder (1.575 inch bore), the device was adapted for use with the 37mm gun. The tube of the M6 37mm gun was shortened for this installation.

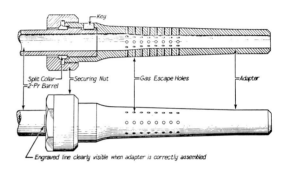

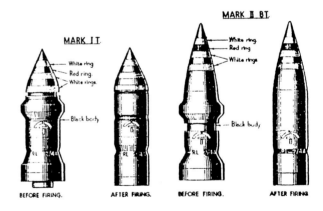

Two types of ammunition for the British 2 pounder equipped with the Littlejohn device appear at the right showing the configuration before and after firing. Below are rear views of the tanks at the top of the page. Note the different rear sandshield section on the tank at the left.

Above, the light tank M22 with the standard 37mm gun M6 (left) can be compared with one armed with the shortened gun (right) for use with the Littlejohn device.

In November 1943, a project was initiated to determine the feasibility of mounting an 81mm mortar in the turret of the light tank T9E1. Preliminary studies indicated that such an installation was practical and in August 1944, Ordnance Committee action recommended the development of the 81mm breech loading mortar T24E1. This mortar was to be installed in the light tank turret using the T51 concentric recoil mechanism. With this new armament, the vehicle was redesignated as the light tank T9E2. The smooth bore T24E1 mortar was fitted with an interrupted screw type breech. Once leveled, a cant mechanism in the mortar mount maintained the weapon in a level position during turret rotation, even if the tank was on a slope. An 81mm shaped charge round was under development for use against armored targets.

Because of a relatively low priority, work progressed at a slow pace and was still incomplete at the end of World War II. Along with many other experimental projects, the program for the T9E2 was then cancelled.

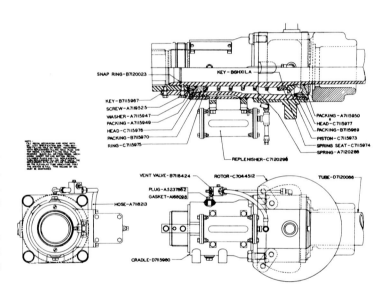

Below are two views of the breech loading mortar T24E1 with the concentric recoil mechanism T51. Above at the right, is a drawing of the T51 recoil mechanism.

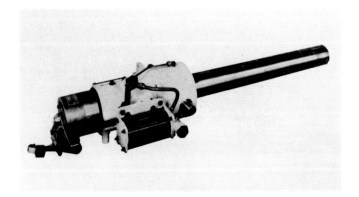

256

PART III

SPECIALIZED LIGHT ARMORED VEHICLES

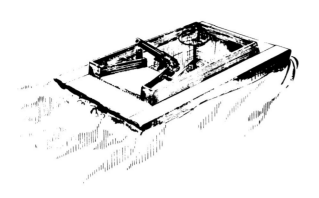

Above, the first version of the Christie amphibian is shown in the photograph at the right and afloat in the sketch at the left.

AMPHIBIAN TANKS AND TRACTORS

Britain experimented with amphibious modifications of the Medium D tank at the end of World War I. However, the first American amphibian armored vehicle was completed by J. Walter Christie in June 1921. Although referred to as an amphibian tank, it actually was an open top self-propelled 75mm gun. This was a convertible wheel or track vehicle driven in the water by twin propellors. The running gear consisted of six dual road wheels, three per side, with coil springs only on the front pair. When running without tracks, the rear and center wheels were connected by roller chains on the hub sprockets. For cross-country operation, the vehicle was fitted with tracks consisting of flat steel links 10 inches wide with a pitch of 10 inches. The maximum speeds were 30 miles/hour on wheels, 18½ miles/hour on tracks, or 7½ miles/hour in water. The vehicle was powered by a Christie six cylinder 90 horsepower engine. Alternate armament was a 37mm

gun or a machine gun. The armor was ¼ inch thick resulting in a vehicle weight of about 6½ tons. Later modifications raised the rear wheels slightly when running without tracks.

In 1923, the vehicle was rebuilt with an additional pair of dual road wheels. Coil springs were now provided on all but the rear set of wheels. Additional modifications were completed in November 1923 which raised the sides of the vehicle to make it more seaworthy. In demonstrations, it successfully crossed the Potomac and the Hudson rivers. During winter maneuvers in 1924, the latest version was tested by the United States Marine Corps during a ship to shore movement off Culebra, Puerto Rico. In this operation, it swam from the battleship Wyoming to the beach. However, the vehicle was rejected for service use as it was still considered to be unseaworthy and the armor protection was inadequate.

Below, the Christie amphibian has been modified to the second version at the left and rebuilt as the third type at the right. Note that the armament could be varied.

The final version of the Christie amphibian is shown in these four photographs. Although the sides were raised and the top partially enclosed, it was still considered to be unseaworthy. At the left below, the amphibian is on the deck of a submarine during its evaluation by the Marine Corps.

With the approach of World War II, interest was revived in amphibian tanks. On 4 December 1941, OCM 17494 recommended the construction of pilot vehicles and assigned the designation light tank T10 (amphibian). The proposed characteristics described a four man tank weighing about 12½ tons. The approximate dimensions were 192 inches in length, 102 inches in width, and 96 inches in height with armor protection ranging from ¾ inches on the turret front to ⅜ inches on the top and rear. The power operated turret was to be armed with a 37mm gun M6 and a coaxial .30 caliber machine gun in the combination mount M24. The mount was to be stabilized in elevation. The specified maximum speeds were 30 miles/hour on roads and 5 miles/hour in water.

A contract was awarded to the Food Machinery Corporation for engineering studies to determine the optimum hull shape and the best method of propulsion. The contract also provided for the construction of a pilot tank after completion of the preliminary studies. Experiments at Food Machinery and the University of California indicated that a shrouded grouser type of track propulsion would result in the most efficient use of the power available. A wooden model of a proposed grouser was shipped to Aberdeen

Proving Ground in March 1942 to determine if it could be applied to the T36E1 track. The report from Aberdeen was favorable and Food Machinery started the manufacture of a full set of grousers to be tested on the light tank M3.

However, by this time, the work to develop an amphibian tank based upon the Navy landing vehicle, tracked (LVT) had been successful and there was no further interest in the light tank T10. In April 1942, it was directed that the program be cancelled upon completion of the design studies without the construction of a pilot tank. Ordnance Committee action in May 1942 formally closed the project.

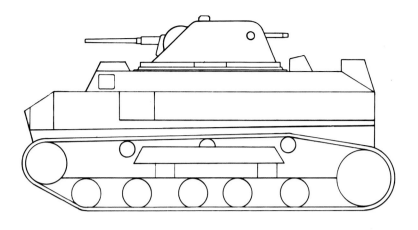

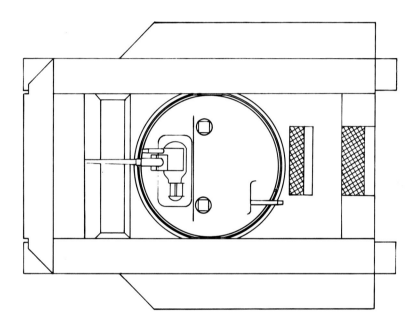

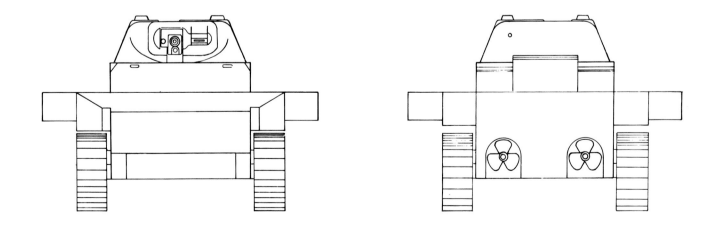

Scale 1:48

©D.P. Dyer

Light Tank T10 (Amphibian)

261

Two views of the early Alligator are above showing the vehicle development in 1935 (left) and 1937 (right). Below is the production line for the early LVT(1) at the Food Machinery Corporation in Dunedin, Florida. Note the wide spacing of the front windows on the early LVT(1).

The LVT resulted from the early experiments of Donald Roebling to develop a vehicle that could operate in water, in swamps, or on land. The damage resulting from a severe hurricane in the Okeechobee area of Florida during 1932 indicated the value of such a vehicle. Conceived as a rescue vehicle for use in the Florida Everglades or in hurricane devastated areas, it was a tracked amphibian propelled in the water by the cleats or grousers on its tracks. Dubbed the Alligator, by 1938 this vehicle had evolved to the point that it was capable of 25 miles/hour on land and 8.6 miles/hour in water. In May 1940, a new model, named the Crocodile, incorporated improvements resulting from the tests of the earlier vehicles. Its ground clearance also was increased to 19 inches to aid in negotiating obstacles such as stumps or logs. The United States Navy purchased a Crocodile for use as a rescue vehicle for airmen forced down in the Everglades.

Following the outbreak of World War II, the Navy awarded a contract to Roebling to build 200 vehicles based upon the Alligator, but constructed of steel in place of aluminum. Designated as the landing vehicle, tracked mark I, LVT(1), production was continued into 1943 with a total run of 1225 vehicles. An improved version, the landing vehicle, tracked mark II, LVT(2) was larger with a cargo

The later version of the LVT(1) appears below. Note the closer spacing of the front windows.

The unarmored LVT(2) is shown on this page in photographs from Aberdeen Proving Ground. They were dated 10 September 1943.

capacity of 5940 pounds or 24 fully armed men. Like the LVT(1), the LVT(2) was unarmored. The six cylinder Hercules engine and the Spicer transmission in the LVT(1) were replaced in the LVT(2) by the power train from the light tank M3. Despite its larger size and heavier weight, the more powerful Continental W-670-9A engine increased the maximum speed of the LVT(2) to 20 miles/hour on land and to 7.5 miles/hour in water. This compared to 18 miles/hour and 7 miles/hour respectively for the LVT(1). The cruising range for the LVT(2) was about 150 miles on land and 50 miles in water.

The LVT(2) was fitted with the new torsilastic suspension which utilized rubber springs to support the vehicle. The rubber was bonded between an outer sleeve attached to the suspension wheel arm and a hollow inner shaft mounted on the pontoon. When the wheel moved up or down, the torsional force was transmitted through the rubber spring. One advantage of the rubber springs was that they were not subject to corrosion in sea water. Another improvement introduced on the LVT(2) was the use of a rear idler sprocket and bracket to adjust the track tension. This design replaced the hydraulic jack on the LVT(1). The tracks themselves were assembled from a double steel chain of inner and outer links each with a pitch of four inches. The inner links were connected by steel cross plates and the grousers with their support plates served the same purpose for the outer links. The overall width of the assembled track was 14¼ inches.

The LVT(2) had a length of 313 inches, a width of 128 inches, and a height of 98 inches. Its weight was 24,400 pounds empty and 30,900 pounds loaded. Like all of the LVTs, the hull of the LVT(2) was rectangular in plan form with the interior divided into the cab in front, the cargo compartment in the center, and the engine room in the rear. A floor in the cargo compartment was mounted on supports providing a bilge space in the bottom of the hull. The cargo compartment was divided in the center by a control tunnel containing the engine drive shaft which extended from the engine room to the transmission in the cab. Two large windows in the cab front provided forward vision for the crew. Pontoons fabricated from 12 gauge sheet steel were welded to each side of the hull inside the tracks to increase the buoyancy. Later documents refer to these as pontons. Armament was specified as one .50 caliber M2 HB machine gun and three .30 caliber M1919A4 machine guns. All were mounted on M35 skate mounts attached to two gun tracks. The .50 caliber weapon usually was fitted on the gun track attached to the rear of the cab. The .30 caliber guns normally were divided between the front gun track and the track that extended across the rear and up the sides of the cargo compartment. However, this arrangement was sometimes modified in the field. The rear gun track on the later version of the LVT(2) extended farther to the front along the sides of the cargo compartment than that on the earlier vehicles. The gun mounts were frequently modified by the addition of shields to protect the gunner. Like

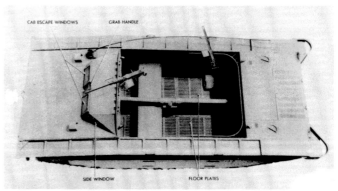

Various components of the unarmored LVT(2) are indicated above. The power transmission tunnel dividing the cargo compartment can be seen in the top view. Only one .30 caliber machine gun is shown, but as many as three were frequently installed on the M35 skate mounts.

the LVT(1), the LVT(2) was mass produced by Food Machinery Corporation, Borg-Warner Corporation, Graham-Paige, and the St. Louis Car Company. A total of 2963 LVT(2)s were manufactured between 1942 and 1945. Originally, the Army planned to designate the LVT(1) and LVT(2) as the T33 and T34 amphibian tractors respectively. However, since the production of these vehicles remained a Navy reponsibility, the Navy nomenclature was retained.

Developed in 1941, the landing vehicle, tracked (armored) mark II, LVT(A)(2), was manufactured to Ordnance Department specifications which replaced the 10 to 14 gauge sheet steel of the LVT(2) with ½ inch thick armor plate on the most vulnerable parts and with ¼ inch thick armor on the less vulnerable areas. Actually, the ½ inch thick armor was limited to the cab front and the ¼ inch plate was located on the hull front, sides, and rear and the sides of the cab. The armored cab was fitted with two roof hatches and a front panel that could be opened to provide

direct forward vision for the driver. Indirect vision for the driver and the assistant driver or radio operator was through two rotating periscopes in the roof hatches.

The power train and general configuration of the LVT(A)(2) were identical to those of the LVT(2). The armor increased the weight of the LVT(A)(2) to 27,600 pounds empty and 32,800 pounds loaded. The armament was the same as on the LVT(2). The cargo capacity was reduced to 4950 pounds on the LVT(A)(2) compared to 5940 pounds on the unarmored vehicle. The Army originally designated the armored vehicle as the amphibian tractor T35, but, as with the earlier types, this was dropped in favor of the Navy nomenclature. Total production of the LVT(A)(2) reached 450 vehicles.

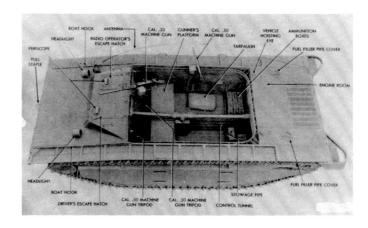

Details of the armored LVT(A)(2) are visible at the right and below. Again, only one .30 caliber machine gun is installed on the M35 skate mount. Note the difference in the armored cab compared to that on the unarmored LVT(2) at the top of the page.

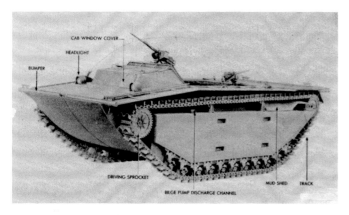

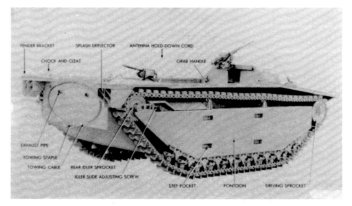

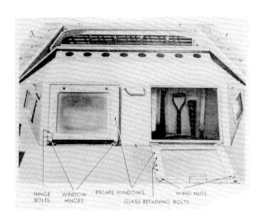

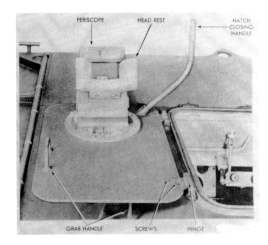

Above, the cab escape windows on the LVT(2) (left) are compared with the cab roof escape hatch on the LVT(A)(2) (right). The cab interior can be seen below at the left with the cover removed. The driver's controls are below at the right.

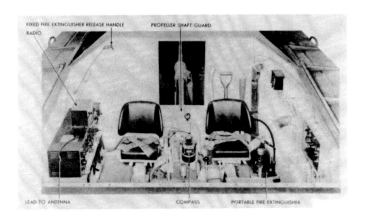

Above, the driver's instrument panel appears at the left and the radio installation is at the right. Below, the bulkhead at the rear of the cargo compartment is at the left. The louvers covering the engine cooling air intakes have been removed. At the bottom right is the rear deck showing the hinged cover with the engine cooling air exhaust grill.

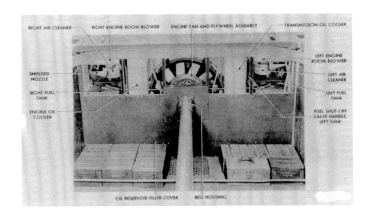

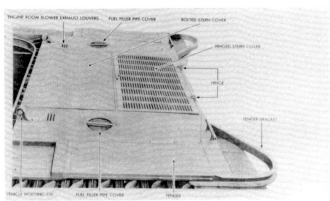

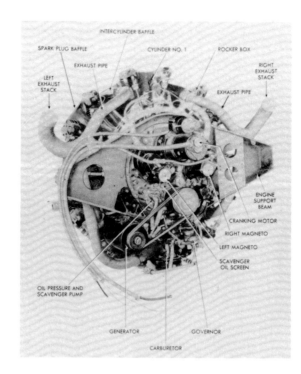

The air-cooled Continental W-670-9A engine is above and at the upper right. The power plant is installed in the engine compartment at the lower right. The hull structure is illustrated in the drawing below.

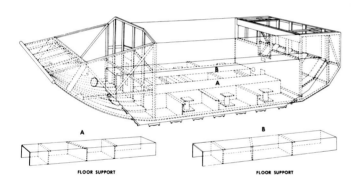

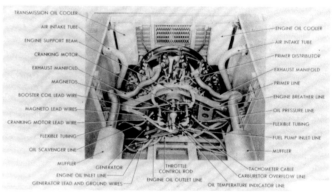

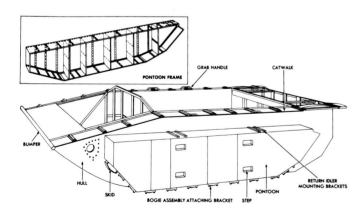

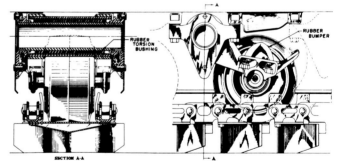

The drawing above shows the pontoons attached to the hull. The rubber torsion suspension system can be seen in the drawing at the upper right and the track assembly appears at the lower right.

The variation in the armament for the LVT(A)(2) is obvious in these photographs. The vehicle in the water above is armed with two .30 caliber machine guns. Below, the LVT(A)(2) at the left carries one .50 caliber machine gun and two .30 caliber weapons. At the right, two .50 caliber and at least one .30 caliber machine guns have been installed.

No armament is fitted on the LVT(A)(2) below at Aberdeen Proving Ground on 29 April 1944. The towing eyes welded to the front and rear of the hull near the bottom were not standard features.

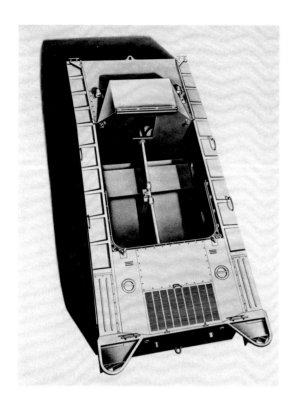

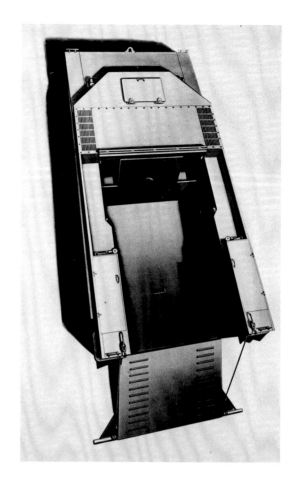

The configuration of the original LVT(2) above can be compared with that of the proposed CT-3 design at the right. Note the greater space in the cargo compartment with the stern ramp arrangement.

The center cargo compartment and the high sides of the early LVTs made it difficult to load or unload cargo. Various types of hoisting equipment, ramps, and troughs were improvised for use in the field. Also, troops were exposed to enemy fire while climbing over the sides of the vehicles. Work at Food Machinery and Borg-Warner sought to correct this problem by designing a vehicle with a rear loading ramp. The project at the latter eventually resulted in the LVT(3) which will be discussed later. At Food Machinery Corporation, a design study dated 10 July 1943 rearranged the components of the LVT(2). The Continental engine was moved forward to just behind the cab

eliminating the tunnel dividing the cargo compartment. A ramp was installed at the rear of the hull, pivoted at the bottom, and operated by a hand winch. Torsilastic springs reduced the effort at the winch crank handle to 15 pounds or less. Designated as the CT-3, the new design increased the cargo compartment volume from 364 cubic feet in the LVT(2) to 541.3 cubic feet and the stern ramp provided easy loading or unloading. The overall dimensions of the vehicle remained essentially the same. The improved vehicle entered production as the landing vehicle, tracked (unarmored) mark IV, LVT(4), and a total of 8348 were manufactured before the end of World War II.

Below, the static trim of the new CT-3 design (left) is compared with the standard LVT(2) (right). As indicated, both were carrying a 7500 pound cargo.

CT3   LVT (2)

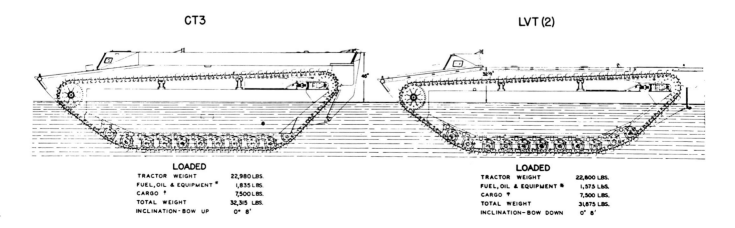

LOADED			LOADED	
TRACTOR WEIGHT	22,980 LBS.		TRACTOR WEIGHT	22,800 LBS.
FUEL, OIL & EQUIPMENT *	1,835 LBS.		FUEL, OIL & EQUIPMENT *	1,575 LBS.
CARGO †	7,500 LBS.		CARGO †	7,500 LBS.
TOTAL WEIGHT	32,315 LBS.		TOTAL WEIGHT	31,875 LBS.
INCLINATION - BOW UP	0° 8'		INCLINATION - BOW DOWN	0° 8'

The unarmored LVT(4) appears in the photographs above and below at Aberdeen Proving Ground on 11 March 1944. No armament has been installed at this time. Details of the grouser type track used to propel the LVTs in the water are clearly visible in the view above.

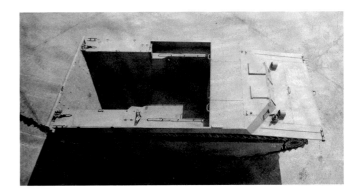

As constructed, the hull of the LVT(4) was unarmored. However, approximately 3000 pounds of steel applique armor could be added to the sides and front when required. This armor was ½ inch thick on the front and ¼ inch thick on the sides. This reduced the payload of the vehicle by an equal amount. The unarmored cab was fitted with two large front glass windows and two roof hatches. This cab was interchangeable with three versions of an armored cab. All three of the latter were protected by ½ inch thick armor on the front and ¼ inch thick armor on the top and sides. The early model armored cab featured a solid front panel which could be opened to provide direct vision for the driver. Rotating periscopes were installed in the two roof hatches for use by the driver and the assistant driver or radio operator. Initially, these periscopes were protected by hemispherical transparent plastic covers, but they were eliminated on the later vehicles. Later versions of the cab had a .30 caliber machine gun in a ball mount for use by the assistant driver. The final production model of the armored cab also was armed with a .30 caliber machine gun in a ball mount. However, in this version, the driver's

front vision panel was eliminated and vision blocks were installed in the front and sides of the cab. The periscope also was eliminated from the driver's roof hatch. The LVT(4) was armed with two .50 caliber machine guns in pivot mounts on the engine compartment bulkhead at the front of the cargo compartment. Two .30 caliber machine guns were installed, one at each side of the cargo compartment, on the front of the rear sponsons boxes. As mentioned before, the late model cabs had an additional .30

Below, the LVT(4) with the early armored cab (left) is compared with one having the late armored cab (right). Note the applique armor on the front hull of both vehicles and the plastic periscope covers on the early LVT(4).

269

Above, the unarmored LVT(4) (left) is compared with one featuring the very early armored cab without a bow machine gun (right). The unarmored vehicle is fitted with four .30 caliber machine guns and the armored LVT(4) carries two .50 caliber and two .30 caliber weapons. Below, various components of the LVT(4) are illustrated at the left and the hull escape hatch is at the right.

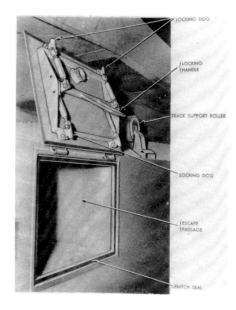

caliber machine gun in the right front ball mount. Some late production LVT(4)s were fitted with an escape hatch in the hull side wall through the pontoon. Although it was not the first LVT designed with a rear ramp, the LVT(4) was the first to see action in the Pacific war.

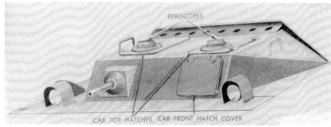

The early armored cab with the bow machine gun above can be compared with the late armored cab below. The LVT(4) at the left features the early armored cab without the bow machine gun.

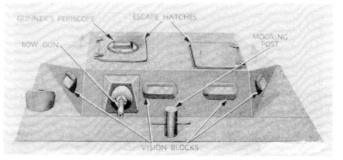

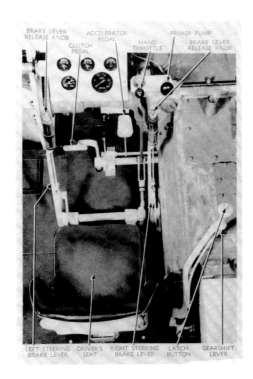

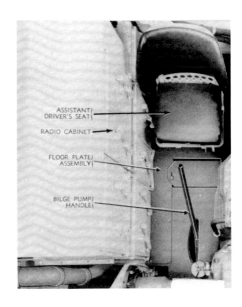

The stations for the driver and assistant driver in the LVT(4) appear at the upper left and above respectively. At the lower left, the LVT(4) is carrying a 105mm howitzer. The ballast and bilge pump system in the late LVT(4) is illustrated below.

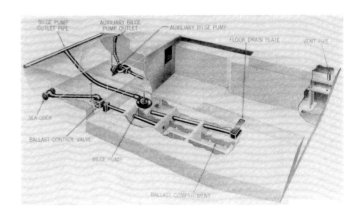

In early 1945, the T54 launcher for the 7.2 inch T37 demolition rocket was installed in an LVT(4). This 20 rail launcher was a slightly modified version of the standard M17 launcher. It was fixed in traverse and had an elevation range of +45 to –5 degrees. The 20 rockets could be launched as single rounds or by ripple fire at intervals of 0.3 to 2 seconds. The front, sides, and bottom of the launcher were protected by ¼ inch thick steel armor. A rack for 40 additional rockets was installed in the LVT(4). The launcher with its armor protection and ammunition supply increased the weight of the LVT(4) by about 6000 pounds.

At the bottom left, the T54 rocket launcher is installed in the LVT(4). Below, a 7.2 inch T37 rocket is being fired from the launcher.

Above at the left is the Borg-Warner Model A amphibian. Although rejected for production, this was the first American amphibian tank in World War II. Note the two bow machine guns. At the right above is the Borg-Warner Model B which provided the basis for the successful LVT(3).

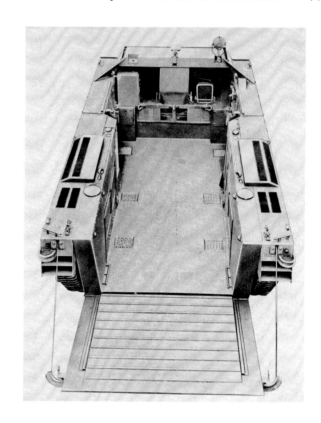

The landing vehicle, tracked mark III, LVT(3), resulted from development work at the Borg-Warner Corporation. In 1941, a prototype amphibian tank was submitted to the Navy Bureau of Ships for evaluation. Designated by Borg-Warner as the Model A, it was armed with a turret mounted 37mm gun and several machine guns. However, the Model A was considered to be unsatisfactory and was rejected for production. In 1943, Borg-Warner produced a second prototype designated as the Model B. This was the first LVT designed with a rear ramp. However, it also was considered to be unsatisfactory, but it provided useful data for the third design which was accepted for production as the LVT(3). Production started in 1944 and 2962 LVT(3)s were completed before the end of the war.

Although somewhat similar in appearance to the LVT(4), the cab on the LVT(3) was located farther forward and it was fitted with double pin tracks 12 inches wide with a pitch of 5½ inches. They carried grousers similar to those on the other LVTs. The LVT(3) also had a new power train consisting of two 110 horsepower V-8 Cadillac engines, one in each sponson, driving the vehicle through two Hydramatic transmissions and a single steering unit. Like the other LVTs, the LVT(3) had a torsilastic suspension. Although the LVT(3) was unarmored as constructed,

The interior of the LVT(3) can be seen in the rear view above with the stern ramp in the lowered position. Below, the LVT(3) is shown with the applique armor installed (left) and without armor (right).

 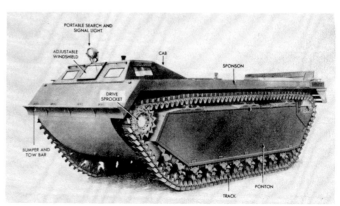

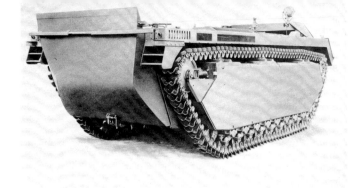
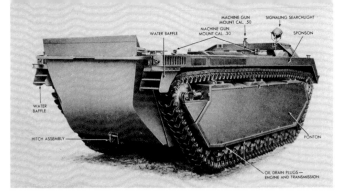

Above, the LVT(3) is fitted with the applique armor on the left and is without armor on the right. Below is a view of the driving compartment in the LVT(3).

applique armor could be added to the front and sides of the vehicle when required. A mount was provided for a a single .50 caliber machine gun at the front of the cargo compartment, although twin .50 caliber guns were installed experimentally. Mounts for two .30 caliber machine guns were located one on each side of the cargo compartment.

Without applique armor, the LVT(3) weighed 29,600 pounds with fuel, equipment, and a three man crew. This weight increased to 38,600 pounds with a full cargo load. With the applique armor added, the weight with fuel, equipment, and crew increased to 32,500 pounds. Since the maximum weight was held at 38,600 pounds, the cargo load was reduced. Maximum speeds were about 17 miles/hour on land and six miles/hour in water.

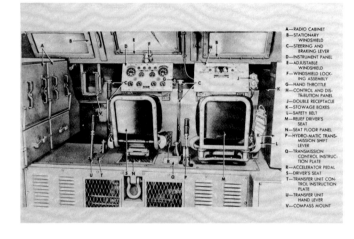

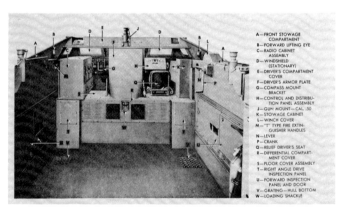

Above, the interior of the LVT(3) can be seen looking forward (left) and looking aft (right). The LVT(3) below was photographed at Aberdeen Proving Ground on 24 March 1945. Note the twin .50 caliber machine gun mount. The front applique armor is visible on the floor of the cargo compartment in the top view at the right.

Above, LVT(3), number 302, was photographed at Aberdeen Proving Ground on 17 March 1945. It is obvious that the jeep could be driven into the cargo compartment with space to spare. No armament is installed on the three mounts.

In 1945, the Bureau of Ships approved a project to develop lightweight versions of the LVT(3) and LVT(4). Since they were intended for cargo purposes only, the weight reduction was achieved by reducing the sheet metal thickness, substituting aluminum for steel in some parts, and eliminating the armament. This increased the cargo capacity by about two tons. With the end of the war, the lightweight vehicles did not enter production.

Early in the postwar period, the Marine Corps selected the LVT(3) for modification to improve its efficiency. An easily opened aluminum cover was installed over the cargo compartment and a small turret was added with a .30 caliber machine gun. Another .30 caliber machine gun was carried in the bow mount. This new design kept the crew and cargo dry and provided some protection against artillery air bursts. The modified vehicle was designated as the LVT(3)(C). It could be fitted with removable armor and was manned by a crew of three. It retained the standard LVT(3) power train, suspension, and tracks, but the weight increased by about three tons. A total of 1200 LVT(3)s were converted to the LVT(3)(C) configuration by the Long Beach Naval Shipyard. The LVT(3)(C) was successfully employed during the Korean War along with the original LVT(3).

At the left are views of the lightweight LVT(3) (upper) and LVT(4) (lower). Below is the LVT(3)C with the cover for the cargo compartment.

The first successful American amphibian tank, the LVT(A)(1), appears in the photographs on this page. Later production models were provided with a bow machine gun as illustrated for the LVT(4) on page 270.

The first successful amphibian tank was developed during 1942. Designated as the landing vehicle, tracked (armored) mark I, LVT(A)(1), it utilized the same chassis as the LVT(A)(2). A superstructure was fitted over the cargo compartment extending back from the cab. This provided the base for the installation of a lightly armored turret armed with an M6 37mm gun and a coaxial .30 caliber machine gun in the combination gun mount M44. This

turret was ½ inch thick on the sides and ¼ inch thick on the top. Behind the turret were two mark 21 mounts for .30 caliber machine guns, one on each side of the hull roof.

With its crew of six, the LVT(A)(1) weighed 32,800 pounds. During its production run, a total of 509 LVT(A)(1)s were completed. The Army assigned these vehicles to amphibian tank battalions. These battalions were organized with four amphibian tank companies consisting

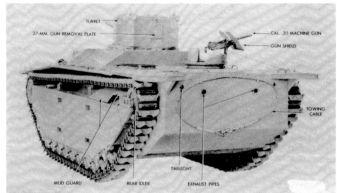

Various components of the early production LVT(A)(1) are indicated in the views above and below. Only one of the two mark 21 machine gun mounts has been installed on this vehicle. The lightweight turret is at the right below.

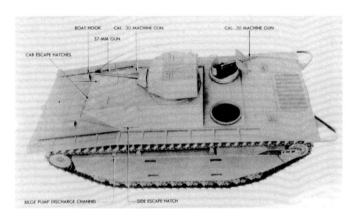

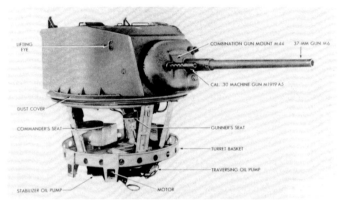

Below are details of the turret hatches and viewing devices. A cutaway view of the lightweight turret is at the right.

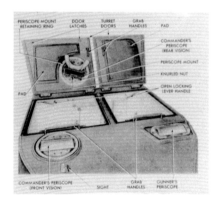

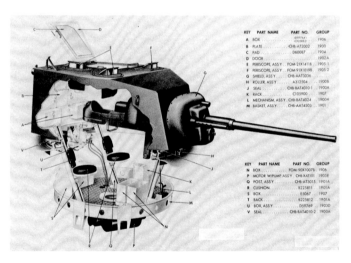

KEY	PART NAME	PART NO.	GROUP
A	BOX	D59761-(D50982)	1906
B	PLATE	CHB-AT2002	1900
C	PAD	D60087	1904
D	DOOR		1902A
E	PERISCOPE, ASS'Y	FOM-21X14118	1905-1
F	PERISCOPE, ASS'Y	FOM-91X10198	1905-2
G	SHIELD, ASS'Y	CHB-AAT3036	1900
H	ROLLER, ASS'Y	A312504	1900B
J	SEAL	CHB-BAT4010-1	1900A
K	RACK	C105900	1907
L	MECHANISM, ASS'Y	CHB-BAT4024	1900H
M	BASKET, ASS'Y	CHB-AAT4503	1901

KEY	PART NAME	PART NO.	GROUP
N	BOX	FOM-90X10075	1906
P	MOTOR W/PUMP ASS'Y	CHB-XAT301	1903E
Q	POST, ASS'Y	CHB-AT3015	1901A
R	CUSHION	8225811	1901A
S	BOX	E5067	1907
T	BACK	8225812	1901A
U	BOX ASS'Y	D59769	1903D
V	SEAL	CHB-BAT4010-2	1900A

Below, the early production LVT(A)(1) is underway in calm water. The hatches and vision ports are closed and the periscopes are being used to guide the vehicle.

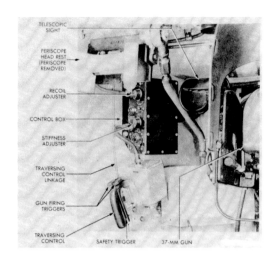

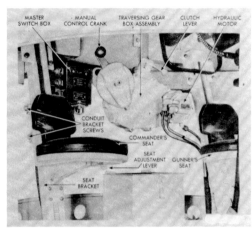

At the left are left front (upper) and rear (lower) views of the turret interior. The right front appears above and the equipment mounted on the bottom of the turret basket can be seen below.

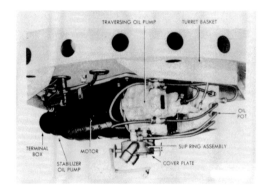

The interior arrangement of the LVT(A)(1) is visible in the sectional drawing below.

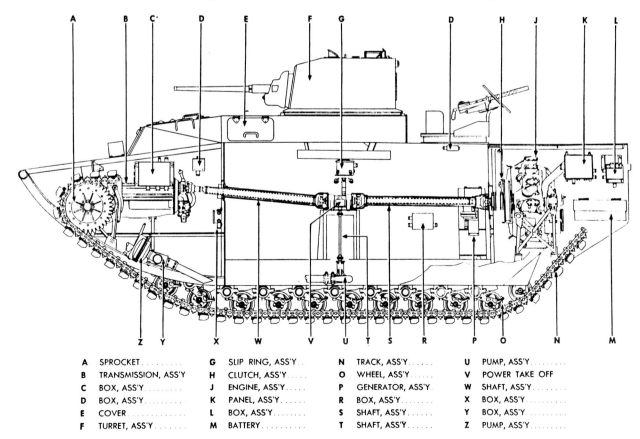

A	SPROCKET	**G**	SLIP RING, ASS'Y	**N**	TRACK, ASS'Y	**U**	PUMP, ASS'Y
B	TRANSMISSION, ASS'Y	**H**	CLUTCH, ASS'Y	**O**	WHEEL, ASS'Y	**V**	POWER TAKE OFF
C	BOX, ASS'Y	**J**	ENGINE, ASS'Y	**P**	GENERATOR, ASS'Y	**W**	SHAFT, ASS'Y
D	BOX, ASS'Y	**K**	PANEL, ASS'Y	**R**	BOX, ASS'Y	**X**	BOX, ASS'Y
E	COVER	**L**	BOX, ASS'Y	**S**	SHAFT, ASS'Y	**Y**	BOX, ASS'Y
F	TURRET, ASS'Y	**M**	BATTERY	**T**	SHAFT, ASS'Y	**Z**	PUMP, ASS'Y

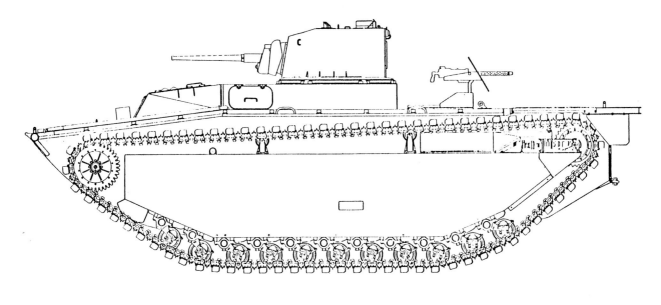

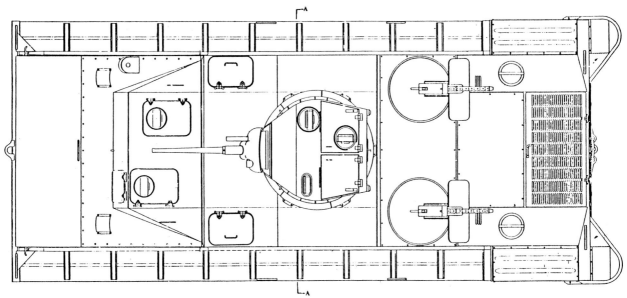

These are original drawings of the early production LVT(A)(l).

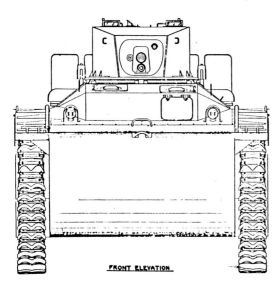

FRONT ELEVATION

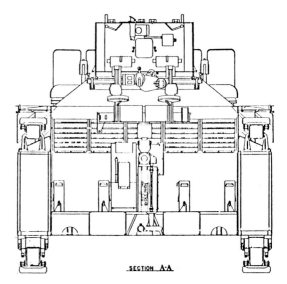

SECTION A-A

Scale 1:48

LVT(A)(1)

Above and at the right are additional views of the early production LVT(A)(1). Both mark 21 machine gun mounts have been installed on the vehicle at the right. On later production vehicles, the engine cooling air exhaust grill on the rear deck was replaced by armored louvers.

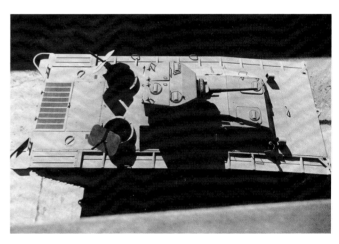

Below, the crew members are manning the two mark 21 .30 caliber machine gun mounts.

Above, the LVT(A)(l) is underway. Note that the engine cooling air exhaust is lifting the canvas cover on the rear deck. Below, the LVT(A)(l) makes an impressive sight firing tracer ammunition at night.

of a company headquarters and three platoons. Each platoon was equipped with five amphibian tanks. The vehicles were employed as tanks during the early stages of an amphibious landing until standard tanks could be brought ashore. However, their success was limited because of their light armor and firepower. To improve the firepower situation, the landing vehicle, tracked (armored) mark IV, LVT(A)(4), was introduced in March 1944. It retained the chassis of the LVT(A)(1), but it was fitted with a new turret armed with the 75mm howitzer M3. In addition to the howitzer, the early LVT(A)(4) turrets carried an M2 HB .50 caliber machine gun on a ring mount. Later, the turret was redesigned and the ring mount was replaced by two separate mounts for .30 caliber machine guns, one on each side at the rear of the turret. A .30 caliber machine gun in a ball mount was located in the right front of the armored cab. Both the early and late versions of the armored cab were fitted to the LVT(A)(4). Vision blocks were installed in the rear and each side wall of the late model turrets.

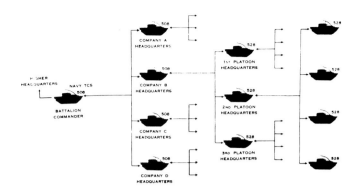

The organization of the Amphibian Tank Battalion is illustrated by the radio net above. Below is an LVT(A)(4) with the early armored cab fitted with a bow machine gun. At the bottom of the page, an early LVT(A)(4) comes ashore. Note the lack of a bow machine gun.

The early production LVT(A)(4) in these photographs is armed with a .30 caliber bow machine gun and a .50 caliber machine gun on the turret ring mount. It also is fitted with armored louvers over the engine cooling air exhaust ports.

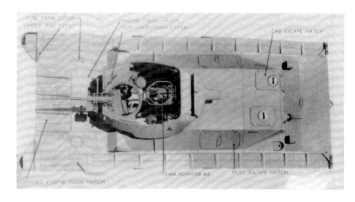

The early LVT(A)(4) below does not have the bow machine gun, but it is provided with the armored louvers over the engine cooling air exhaust ports.

Above are front and rear views of the early LVT(A)(4) afloat. Below, the early LVT(A)(4) is engaged in training exercises.

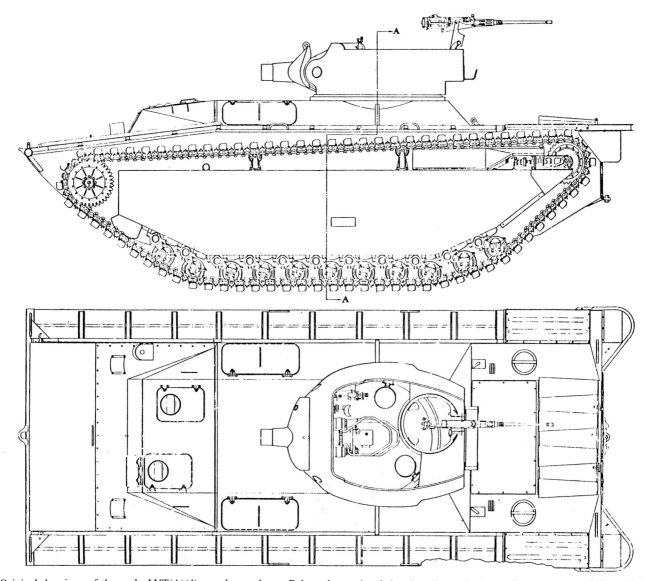

Original drawings of the early LVT(A)(4) are shown above. Below, the sectional drawing shows the internal arrangement of the vehicle.

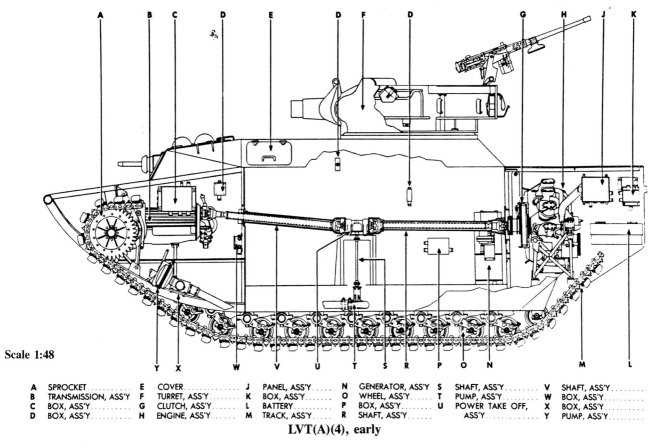

Scale 1:48

A SPROCKET	**E** COVER	**J** PANEL, ASS'Y	**N** GENERATOR, ASS'Y	**S** SHAFT, ASS'Y	**V** SHAFT, ASS'Y
B TRANSMISSION, ASS'Y	**F** TURRET, ASS'Y	**K** BOX, ASS'Y	**O** WHEEL, ASS'Y	**T** PUMP, ASS'Y	**W** BOX, ASS'Y
C BOX, ASS'Y	**G** CLUTCH, ASS'Y	**L** BATTERY	**P** BOX, ASS'Y	**U** POWER TAKE OFF,	**X** BOX, ASS'Y
D BOX, ASS'Y	**H** ENGINE, ASS'Y	**M** TRACK, ASS'Y	**R** SHAFT, ASS'Y	ASS'Y	**Y** PUMP, ASS'Y

LVT(A)(4), early

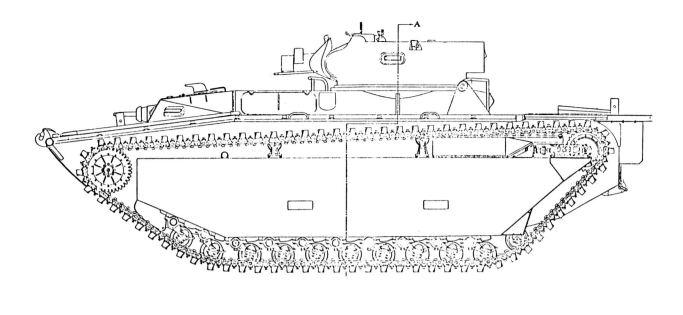

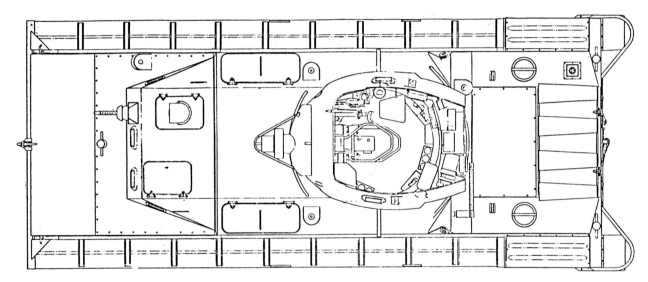

These original drawings depict the late production LVT(A)(4). Note that the ring mount for the .50 caliber machine gun has been eliminated and vision blocks have been installed in the cab and turret.

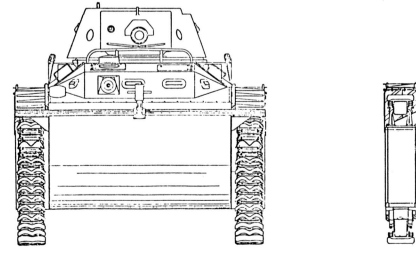

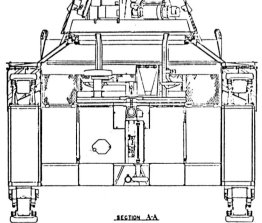

SECTION A-A

Scale 1:48

LVT(A)(4), late

These photographs of the LVT(A)(4) were dated 18 October 1944. The ring mount for the .50 caliber machine gun has been eliminated, but the vision blocks have not been installed. A counterweight is mounted to balance the 75mm howitzer, but it was not required without the stabilizer.

CAL. .30 MACHINE GUN M1919A4
75-MM HOWITZER M3
PERISCOPE M12
CAL. .30 MACHINE GUN M1919A4
HULL ESCAPE HATCH
FINAL DRIVE SPROCKET
BILGE PUMP DISCHARGE CHANNEL
PONTON
STEP POCKET

These photographs, dated 19 June 1945, show the LVT(A)(5) with the two turret mounted .30 caliber machine guns and the vision blocks in the cab and turret. The counterweight is installed to balance the 75mm howitzer for use with the stabilizer.

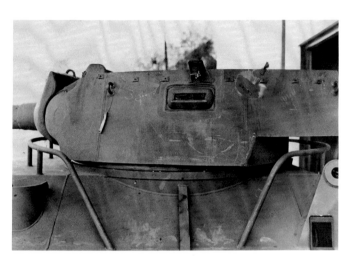

In April 1945, the LVT(A)(4) was equipped with a power traverse mechanism for the turret and an elevation stabilizer for the 75mm howitzer. With these changes, the vehicle was redesignated as the landing vehicle, tracked (armored) mark V, LVT(A)(5). Two auxiliary generators replaced the single auxiliary generator in the original LVT(A)(4) to handle the increased load.

The turret mounted .30 caliber machine guns can be seen in the photographs of the LVT(A)(5) above. Below, the driver's station appears at the left and the assistant driver's station is at the right. The .30 caliber bow machine gun is visible in the latter view.

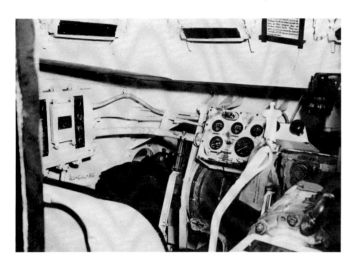

At the right are the two auxiliary generators in the LVT(A)(5). On the LVT(A)(4), the single auxiliary generator was mounted on the right side of the vehicle.

The rear (left) and front (right) of the LVT(A)(5) turret interior can be seen below.

Above, an LVT(A)(5) enters the water during a public demonstration.

In another effort to improve the firepower of the amphibian tank, the Army on 8 June 1944 requested the experimental installation of the turret from the light tank M24 on the LVT(A)(1). This required some modification to fit this turret with its 60 inch diameter ring to the LVT(A)(1) chassis. The transmission and final drives were modified to handle the increased weight and the stowage was rearranged to carry 100 rounds of ammunition for the M6 75mm gun. Tests by the Bureau of Ships indicated that the 75mm gun could be safely fired when afloat, but that the vehicle was unstable during water maneuvers. It was recommended that the hull be reduced in height by nine inches and the turret moved forward by two inches to improve stability. It also was recommended that the turret be modified to reduce its weight. These changes had not been carried out when the war ended and the project was cancelled.

As mentioned previously, the use of the LVTs as tanks was not very successful and they were usually employed as self-propelled artillery. As a result, late in the war, the amphibian tank battalions were reorganized to reflect this role. The new battalion consisted of 48 LVT(A)s organized like batteries in 12 platoons of four vehicles each. Fire control centers were established in the four company headquarters, each of which controlled three platoons. Field Artillery personnel performed observation and liaison duties.

Although they were officially designated as landing vehicles, tracked, amphibian tanks or tractors, the LVTs also received the name Water Buffalo. Among the troops they were called amtracks, amptracks, alligators, or just LVTs.

The LVT(A)(1) appears in these two photographs fitted with the turret from the light tank M24.

Above is the amphibian 76mm gun motor carriage T86. The stack for the engine cooling air and exhaust gases is in the folded position.

In late 1943, the National Defense Research Committee was requested by the Ordnance Department to investigate the possibility of converting the 76mm gun motor carriage T70 (M18) into an amphibian vehicle. The preliminary study, conducted under contract by Sparkman & Stephens, Inc. of New York City, indicated that such a conversion was practical. Based on these conclusions, the Ordnance Department initiated a design program in February 1944 and in September, construction was authorized for two pilot vehicles. Designated as the 76mm gun amphibian motor carriages T86 and T86E1, they differed mainly in the method of propulsion. The T86 was propelled in the water by its tracks and the T86E1 was fitted with propellors. The two were to be built concurrently in order to determine the most efficient means of propulsion for future production vehicles. However, because of delays in obtaining the propellor drive gears, the T86 was completed first on 16 June 1944.

The T86 utilized the M18 chassis with the hull removed above the sponson level. It was replaced by a larger light-weight hull designed to provide the necessary buoyancy for the vehicle. The original M18 turret was retained, but it was mounted 30 inches higher on the new hull and the gun mount was equipped with an elevation stabilizer. The stowage of 76mm ammunition remained at 45 rounds. The weight of the loaded T86 with crew was approximately 45,000 pounds. To reduce the ground pressure, a new 21 inch wide track was installed. This track was developed from the 16 inch wide single pin track used on the light tank M24. The tracks were shrouded by hinged skirts to assist propulsion and to reduce the drag in the water. A surf plate and deflectors on the turret were provided to assist in shedding water. The surf plate folded back to a stowed position to permit better visibility for the driver during land operations. New hoods were fitted for the driver and assistant driver and each man had an additional periscope in

Below, the hoods are installed for the driver and assistant driver in the T86. The exhaust stack is erected and is shown with (right) and without (left) the hood attached.

Above, the surf plate (A) can be seen stowed (left) and in the operating position (right). Note the details of the drivers' hatches with and without the hoods. Below, the rudders are retracted (left) and in the operating position (right). The (A) indicates the stack and its operating lever and the (B) identifies the fuel filler caps.

the hull roof forward of their hatches. Steering in the water was by means of two rudders mounted at the stern which folded up for operations on land. The rudders were actuated by a crank located in the top front of the driving compartment. A folding stack that could be fitted with a hood was installed for the exhaust gases and engine cooling air. The air intake was through a grill under the turret bustle or through the turret when in the water.

The amphibian hull resulted in a large vehicle with an overall length of 367 inches, a width of 122 inches, and a height to the turret top of 115 inches. The side armor below the sponson was the same ½ inch as on the M18. However, above the sponson on the sides, as well as the front and hull bottom, it was only ¼ inch. The top and rear were ⅛ inch thick.

The performance of the T86 on land was comparable to that of the M18 with a maximum road speed of about 45 miles/hour. In water, the maximum speed was 5.2 miles/hour. The cruising range was approximately 150 miles on land and 40 miles in water.

The T86E1 was completed in November 1944. The original version was driven by two 26 inch diameter propellors. However, its performance was disappointing with only a slight water speed increase over the T86. Its weight also had increased to about 46,000 pounds with the new propul-

At the right are two views of the propellor driven 76mm gun motor carriage T86E1. Obviously, this is the original version with the twin propellors.

sion system. Modifications were made replacing the twin screws with a single 32 inch diameter propellor. However, the maximum water speed was still only 6.2 miles/hour, well below the design objective of 7.5 miles/hour. The cruising range was estimated as 150 to 175 miles on land and 60 to 85 miles in water.

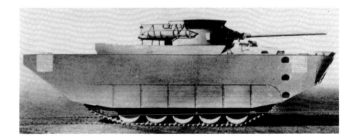

Above, the amphibian 105mm howitzer motor carriage T87 appears as originally delivered. The .50 caliber machine gun has not been mounted.

A third pilot had been authorized, but its development was held up until November 1944 when the results of the earlier tests were available. The track propulsion system was then adopted. As the designation, 105mm howitzer amphibian motor carriage T87, indicated, the new vehicle was armed with the 105mm howitzer M4. The turret was similar to that manufactured for the 105mm howitzer motor carriage T88. This, in turn, was a modified version of the turret for the 76mm gun motor carriage M18. The ring mount for the .50 caliber machine gun on the earlier vehicle was replaced by a pedestal mount at the front of the turret and a sheet metal cover was added to protect the crew when operating in water. The gunner was shifted to the right side of the turret with the loader on the left. The commander was located at the right rear and was provided with an M12 panoramic sight. The gunner had an M10 periscopic sight replacing the M4A1 in the M18. The direct sight telescope was eliminated and replaced by an emergency peep sight.

The hull of the T87 was considerably shorter than that on the T86 with a length of about 325 inches when the rudders were retracted. The width remained at 122 inches with a height of 125 inches. The armor thicknesses were the same as on the earlier pilots. The driver remained in the left front hull, but was now seated under a vision cupola. The assistant driver was on the right, but was moved to the rear, just in front of the turret. He was slightly higher in the superstructure and also had a vision cupola. Dual controls permitted either driver to operate the vehicle on land, but only the assistant driver had rudder controls for water operation.

The water speed of the T87 was estimated as 5.4 miles/hour. However, tests at Aberdeen Proving Ground reached only 4.4 miles/hour. Tests with canvas grousers attached to the tracks increased the speed by about .25 miles/hour. However, 42 of the 78 canvas grousers were torn off during the test and further experiments with them were cancelled. It was recommended that future vehicles have LVT type grousers welded to the tracks. With the end of World War II, further development of the T86, T86E1, and T87 was cancelled.

Below, the T87 appears after modification with the protective cover added to the turret. The .50 caliber machine gun has been installed on the pedestal mount at the front of the turret. The rudders are shown in the retracted and operating positions.

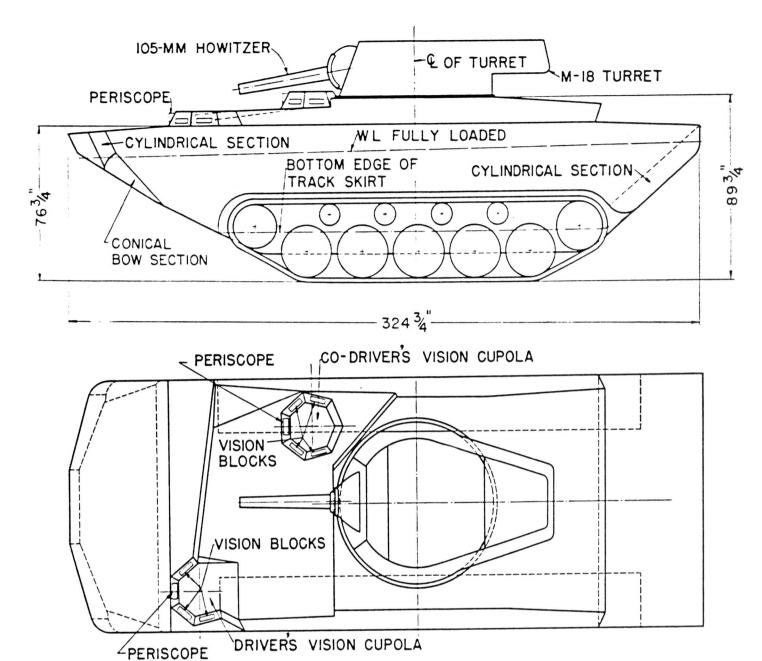

105-MM HOWITZER

CL OF TURRET

M-18 TURRET

PERISCOPE

CYLINDRICAL SECTION

WL FULLY LOADED

BOTTOM EDGE OF
TRACK SKIRT

CYLINDRICAL SECTION

76¾"

89¾"

CONICAL
BOW SECTION

324¾"

PERISCOPE

CO-DRIVER'S VISION CUPOLA

VISION
BLOCKS

VISION BLOCKS

PERISCOPE

DRIVER'S VISION CUPOLA

This sketch shows the dimensions and original layout of the 105mm howitzer motor carriage T87.

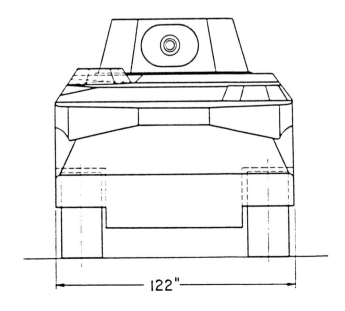

122"

105mm Howitzer Motor Carriage T87

The 1.85 inch tank support gun in its turret mount on the light tank M2A1 chassis can be seen above. The gun is at maximum elevation.

TANK DESTROYERS

Although tank destroyers as a separate organization in the United States Army did not appear until World War II, the employment of self-propelled guns in this role had been proposed much earlier. After World War I, some of the new self-propelled artillery was considered for this mission, but little progress was made during the postwar years. On 9 October 1936, the Infantry Board outlined the characteristics for a tank support gun and carrier. Procurement was then authorized for one soft steel turret armed with a 1.85 inch (47mm) gun for installation on the hull of an M2A1 light tank. The weapon was based on the Browning 37mm M1 automatic antiaircraft gun with a larger diameter bore and the mechanism modified for semiautomatic fire. The ammunition was loaded in five round clips and the projectile muzzle velocity was 1500 feet per second.

The soft steel turret with the 1.85 inch gun was fitted to the hull of a light tank M2A1 in July 1937 at Fort Benning. Although the main justification for the tank support gun was to destroy enemy antitank guns which would be difficult targets for the tanks with their limited vision, the new self-propelled weapon also was tested against moving targets to determine its effectiveness in the antitank role. Unfortunately, the improvised 1.85 inch gun jammed frequently and the test results were considered unsatisfactory. The gun also did not meet the specified penetration requirements. These were 1¼ inches of armor plate at 20 degrees obliquity at a range of 800 yards. After these tests, further work on the project was cancelled.

At the right is the gunner's position on the left side of the 1.85 inch gun in its turret mount. The ammunition feed rack for the semiautomatic weapon is just above the telescopic sight.

294

The views on this page show the 3 inch gun motor carriage T1 in the original configuration that was standardized as the 3 inch gun motor carriage M5. These photographs from Aberdeen Proving Ground were dated 13 January 1942.

After the start of World War II in Europe, there was renewed interest in self-propelled antitank weapons. Many of these were improvised by mounting antitank guns on various wheeled chassis. One such experiment installed an M3 37mm antitank gun on the Dodge ¾ ton truck. This vehicle was standardized as the 37mm gun motor carriage M6 and it served as an interim antitank weapon in North Africa. The halftrack chassis also provided the basis for an interim tank destroyer as the 75mm gun motor carriage M3. Other experiments mounted antitank guns on the chassis of the medium tank. One of these was standardized as the 3 inch gun motor carriage M10 which served successfully throughout the war and was later upgraded to the 90mm gun motor carriage M36.

Efforts to produce a lightweight, heavily armed tank destroyer had begun as early as December 1940 when the Ordnance Committee authorized the development of the 3 inch gun motor carriage T1. Based on the seven-ton high

speed tractor produced by the Cleveland Tractor Company (Cletrac), the T1 was armed with a modified version of the 3 inch antiaircraft gun T9. The ballistic performance

Above are two additional views of the 3 inch gun motor carriage M5 on 13 January 1942. At the right, the gun is at the maximum depression. Below, in these two photographs dated 18 April 1942, the M5 has been modified adding the spades at the rear and rearranging the crew positions and the stowage. The shield has been removed during the modification at the right.

of this weapon, which was standardized as the 3 inch gun M6, was identical to that of the 3 inch gun M7 that appeared later. The maximum weight for the new gun motor carriage was originally estimated as eight to nine tons. However, during the development program this grew to about 12 tons. The only armor protection was the gun shield and the armor installed at the stations for the driver and the assistant driver. This all consisted of ½ inch thick homogeneous steel plate. The T1 was powered by a 160 horsepower supercharged Hercules diesel which drove it at a maximum speed of about 38 miles/hour.

In January 1942, the T1 was standardized as the 3 inch gun motor carriage M5 with the 3 inch gun M6 and production was authorized for 1580 vehicles. However, development problems delayed production with numerous modifications to the general arrangement of the vehicle. The 3 inch ammunition stowage was increased from 24 to 33 rounds, but this was still short of the 42 rounds specified in the military characteristics. By this time, rapid progress had been made in the development of the 3 inch gun motor carriage M10 based upon the medium tank. As a result, production of the M5 was cancelled in August 1942.

The final version of the 3 inch gun motor carriage M5 appears in these photographs from Aberdeen dated 4 August 1942. Note the muzzle brake on the gun and the new arrangement of the crew and stowage.

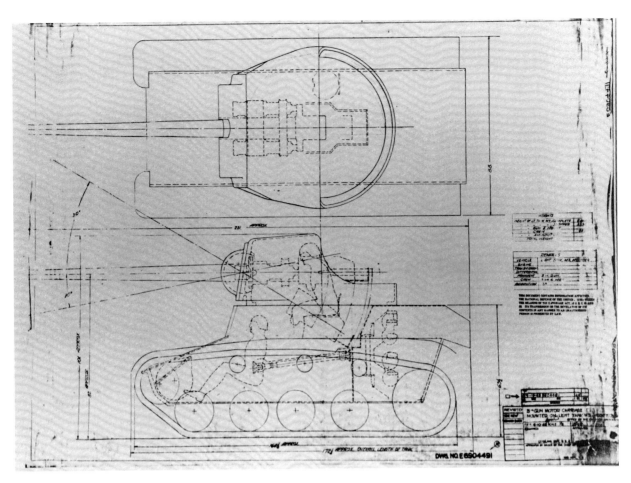

The proposal drawings above and below for the 3 inch gun motor carriage T50 were dated 10 June 1942 and 24 June 1942 respectively. The concept of the ideal tank destroyer was rapidly changing during this period.

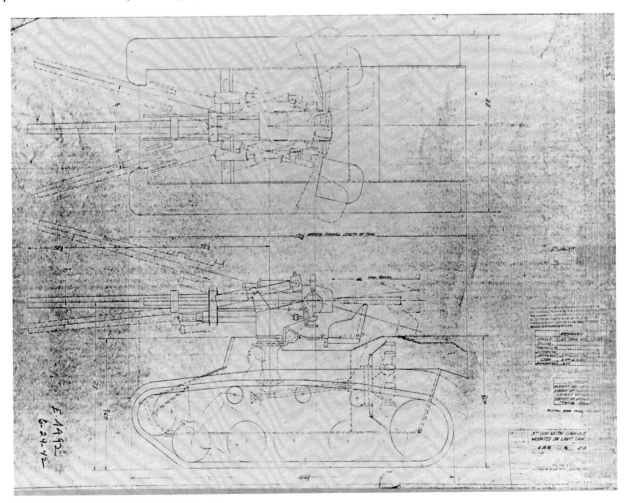

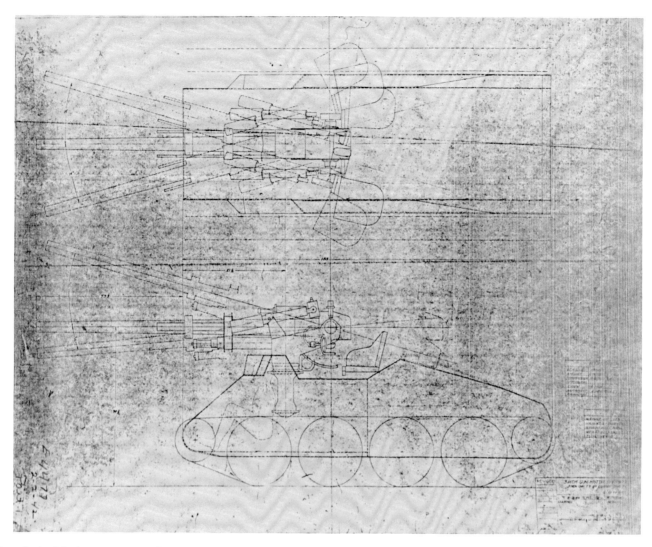

Above is the 3 inch gun motor carriage T50 concept based upon the chassis proposed for the 37mm gun motor carriage T42. This chassis was subsequently enlarged with an additional road wheel for the 57mm gun motor carriage T49.

A design was proposed in September 1941 for mounting the 3 inch gun T9 on the chassis of the light tank M3. Designated as the 3 inch gun motor carriage T20, the original intention was to lower the vehicle silhouette by replacing the M3's radial engine with a twin engine power plant similar to that which appeared later in the light tank M5. In October 1941, it was concluded that the 3 inch gun was too powerful a weapon for installation on the light tank chassis and the T20 project was cancelled.

After the unfavorable conclusion of the project for the 3 inch gun motor carriage T20, another program was proposed in May 1942. Designated as the 3 inch gun motor carriage T50, it was to be a five man vehicle carrying the 3 inch antitank gun either in an open top turret or on a pedestal mount. The front, sides, and rear were to be armored for protection against .50 caliber machine gun fire. In July, the use of a chassis similar to that being developed for the 57mm gun motor carriage T49 was recommended. However, the T49 evolved into the 75mm gun motor carriage T67 and later became the 76mm gun motor carriage T70. The latter was standardized as the 76mm gun motor carriage M18. As a result, the T50 project was cancelled in March 1944.

Despite the earlier failure, another effort to develop a 3 inch gun motor carriage on a light tank chassis was started in September 1942. After the appearance of the light tank M3A3 with its sloped front armor, the Ordnance Committee proposed that this vehicle be used as the basis for two new 3 inch gun motor carriages. Designated as the T56 and T57, they differed mainly in the power plant. The T56 was driven by the Continental W-670 series 12 engine which was a higher horsepower version of the W-670-9A in the M3A3 light tank. The series 12 engine developed 288 gross horsepower at 2600 rpm. The T57 was powered by the Continental R-975-C1 engine which produced 400 gross horsepower at 2400 rpm. The front and side armor of the M3A3 hull was retained on both vehicles, but the engine was relocated forward to just behind the drivers' compartment. This left the rear of the chassis free for the pedestal mounted 3 inch gun M7. A rear plate of ½ inch thick armor was hinged so that it could be lowered for use as a loading platform.

Although the T57 with its more powerful engine was considered to be the best design, the T56 could be completed at an earlier date. Thus it was delivered to Aberdeen in November 1942 to permit early evaluation of the

298

These photographs, dated 17 November 1942, show the 3 inch gun motor carriage T56 at Aberdeen Proving Ground.

These additional views also show the 3 inch gun motor carriage T56 at Aberdeen for evaluation. The engine can be seen through the open compartment doors above. Below, the gun is at maximum elevation.

The 3 inch gun motor carriage T57 appears here at Aberdeen Proving Ground on 13 January 1943. Below, the gun is at maximum elevation.

gun mount. In this installation, the 3 inch gun M7 had an elevation range of +25 to –5 degrees and it could be traversed 15 degrees to the left or right of center. The gun shield armor on the T56 was 1½ inches thick on the front and sides and had a ½ inch thick top. Stowage was provided for 40 rounds of 3 inch ammunition. A .30 caliber machine gun was specified for antiaircraft and ground fire, but it was not installed on the T56 or T57 pilots.

Both the Special Armored Vehicle Board and Aberdeen Proving Ground concluded once again that the 3 inch gun was too heavy a weapon for installation on the light tank chassis. The T57 pilot arrived at Aberdeen in December 1942 shortly after the unfavorable report of the Special Armored Vehicle Board had been submitted. In addition to its more powerful engine, it differed from the T56 in not being fitted with a gun shield. However, it was subject to the same criticism as the T56 and the Ordnance Committee cancelled the program for both vehicles in February 1943 without any tests of the T57.

Details of the 3 inch gun M6 can be seen in the view of the 3 inch gun motor carriage T57 at the right.

301

Above, the M8 motor carriage armed with the 75mm gun M3 is at Aberdeen Proving Ground on 13 January 1943. The M8A1 was not an official designation. Below, the vehicle was under evaluation by the Tank Destroyer Command and, at the bottom of the page, it was being tested at Fort Knox.

In late December 1941, the Ordnance Committee proposed the installation of a modified version of the turret from the medium tank M4 on the hull of the light tank M3. The layout drawings indicated that the armor would be thinned down and the rear section removed. This proposed vehicle was designated as the 75mm gun motor carriage T29. The using arms showed no interest in this project and it was cancelled by OCM 18126 on 20 April 1942.

As mentioned earlier, the 75mm gun M3 was installed in the turret of the 75mm howitzer motor carriage M8 to determine the feasibility of mounting this weapon on the light tank chassis. On 30 January 1943, the new self-propelled weapon was demonstrated at Aberdeen Proving

Ground. Impressed by its performance, a representative of the Tank Destroyer Command requested that it be shipped to Camp Hood, Texas for evaluation as a tank destroyer.

In order to mount the M3 gun in the M8 turret, the front opening was enlarged. The roof at the rear of the turret and the .50 caliber machine gun ring mount were removed. This resulted in a completely open top turret. The new gun motor carriage performed well during the tests at Camp Hood and it was considered suitable as an interim tank destroyer until the new 76mm gun motor carriage T70 became available. Subsequently, it was determined that production quantities of the modified M8 could not be available prior to the appearance of the T70 and the program was cancelled.

None of these projects satisfied the original requirement for a lightweight, highly mobile tank destroyer. In late 1941, a development program had been initiated that was to finally produce the required tank destroyer.

Initially, the new project called for the installation of the 37mm gun in a turret on the chassis of the airborne light tank T9. Designated as the 37mm gun motor carriage T42, the concept went through several changes. Drawings dated 27 October 1941 show the 37mm gun with a coaxial .30 caliber machine gun in an open top turret on the T9 chassis. The weapons were installed in the combination gun mount M22. A later drawing, dated 11 December 1941, shows the hull lengthened and indicated that the road wheels were independently sprung. The final version in a drawing dated 5 January 1942 was lengthened even more and was equipped with a Christie type coil spring suspension having four large road wheels on each side of the vehicle. Manned by a crew of four, all three versions were fitted with a .30 caliber machine gun in the right front hull in addition to the turret armament. The turret armor was $\frac{7}{8}$ inches thick. On the hull, the armor varied from a maximum of $\frac{7}{8}$ inches on the front to $\frac{3}{8}$ inches on the sides and top.

At the right is the concept study drawing of the 37mm gun motor carriage T42 dated 11 December 1941. Below, the final version of this vehicle has been redrawn by D.P. Dyer from the original Ordnance Department drawings indicated. Note the Christie type independent coil spring suspension on this vehicle.

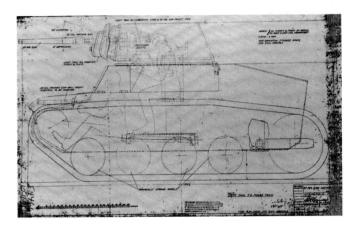

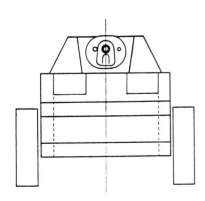

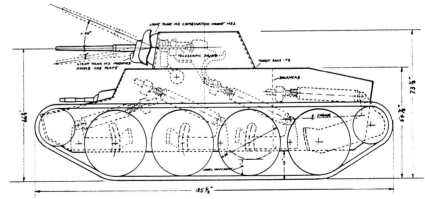

Elevation reference Drawing E4470 5 Jan 1942

37mm Gun Motor Carriage T42, late concept

LIGHT TANK T9 POWER TRAIN

ARMOR 7/8" ON TURRET, 7/8" & 5/8" ON FRONT OF VEHICLE,

3/8" ON SIDES & OVER ENGINE COMPARTMENT

CREW 4 MEN

Plan reference Drawing E4470A 29 Dec 1941

The pilot 57mm gun motor carriage T49 appears in these photographs, some of which were dated 30 July 1942. The coil spring suspension is visible in the side view above.

On 3 April 1942, the Ordnance Committee recommended that the 37mm gun in the T42 be replaced by the more powerful 57mm gun M1. This recommendation was approved by OCM 18119 and the modified vehicle was designated as the 57mm gun motor carriage T49. Two pilot vehicles were authorized for construction at the Buick Motor Car Division of General Motors Corporation. The gun mount produced by Rock Island Arsenal was fitted with the 57mm gun M1 and a coaxial .30 caliber machine gun. This combination gun mount was installed in a power operated turret of welded construction. An additional .30 caliber machine gun in a ball mount was located in the right front of the hull. As on the T42, the maximum armor thickness was ⅞ inches. The T49 was manned by a crew of five and powered by two 165 horsepower Buick series 60 engines. They drove the vehicle through a Twin Disc torque convertor and a three speed, manually controlled, transmission. The final drives and sprockets were mounted at the rear of the vehicle. Five large road wheels on each side were independently sprung by vertically mounted coil springs. The new single pin, rubber bushed, steel tracks with center guides were 12 inches wide.

The first pilot T49 was completed at Buick during July 1942 and shipped to the General Motors Proving Ground for tests. These tests revealed excessive power losses in the torque convertor which reduced the estimated maximum speed of 55 miles/hour to only 38 miles/hour. However, the new suspension gave the vehicle excellent ride characteristics and the lightweight center guide tracks reduced track throwing tendencies permitting fast operation over rough terrain.

304

The photographs on this page show the T67 gun motor carriage after the 75mm gun M3 was replaced by the 76mm gun M1. Again, the independent coil spring suspension is clearly visible.

In the meantime, the Tank Destroyer Command had concluded that the 75mm gun M3 was superior to the 57mm gun M1 for tank destroyer operations. In response to this conclusion, the Ordnance Committee on 10 October 1942 recommended that the second pilot be armed with the 75mm gun M3 in an open top turret. This action was approved in December and the modified vehicle was designated as the 75mm gun motor carriage T67. The first pilot also was returned from the General Motors Proving Ground so that the 75mm gun could be installed.

The second pilot T67 was completed at Buick and delivered to Aberdeen Proving Ground in November 1942. Like the first pilot, it was powered by two Buick series 60 engines. A new open top turret was installed with the 75mm gun M3 in a modified M34 mount. Although the port remained in the gun shield, the coaxial machine gun was not installed. The hull also was redesigned eliminating the .30 caliber bow machine gun. Tests at Aberdeen showed that the power plant still was inadequate and it was recommended that a standard, higher horsepower, engine be installed. Although the results of the firing tests with the 75mm gun were satisfactory, this weapon was replaced in late November 1942 by the new 76mm gun M1. The Tank

Destroyer Command had indicated a preference for the more powerful weapon. Tests with the 76mm gun had shown its superior armor piercing performance and it was specified by the Tank Destroyer Command for installation in the new vehicle. The project for the 75mm gun motor carriage T67 was closed by Ordnance Committee action in January 1943 and OCM 19438, dated 7 January 1943, recommended the development and manufacture of six pilots of the 76mm gun motor carriage T70.

305

These are additional views of the T67 gun motor carriage armed with the 76mm gun M1. Note the overhang of the long cannon barrel.

Below, the driver's compartment in the T67 gun motor carriage is at the left and the two Buick engines can be seen installed in the engine compartment at the right.

This is the 76mm gun motor carriage T70, pilot number 3, at Aberdeen Proving Ground on 11 June 1943. The USA registration number visible in the original photograph was 40128386. Note the bulge in the left front turret wall and that a stowage box is welded only to the right side of the turret.

The first pilot was completed in early April 1943. By July, all six pilots were delivered for testing at the General Motors Proving Ground, Camp Hood, and Aberdeen Proving Ground. To improve its performance over the T67, the T70 was powered by the Continental R-975-C1 radial engine which delivered 400 gross horsepower at 2400 rpm. The 900T Torqmatic transmission with multiple disc clutches for the first and reverse gears replaced the 3700 Torqmatic transmission with band clutches used in the T67. The heavier gun installation required that the weight be redistributed in the T70. Thus the transmission and final drives were shifted to the front of the vehicle. The engine as well as the transmission and final drive assembly were mounted on rails to permit them to be moved out for servicing. The same type of independently sprung dual road wheels were used as on the T67. However, the coil springs on the latter were replaced by torsion bars on the T70.

The test program on the pilots revealed a number of deficiencies. These included the automotive type starter and weak shock absorbers. The latter were the largest commercially available, but they still were inadequate for a vehicle whose weight had now increased to almost 20 tons. By mounting two shock absorbers on the front road wheel arms, the life was increased to an acceptable level. Later, a shock absorber was designed specifically for the T70. Short track life also was a problem and considerable effort was directed toward a track improvement program. The performance of the 76mm gun in the T1 mount was satisfactory, but the mount was extremely difficult to remove and replace in the turret. The gun was shifted two inches to the right of the turret center line to provide more room for the gunner. As a result, firing the high velocity gun in the lightweight turret applied a moment which caused a jerk in the manual traversing mechanism. However, this was not a problem when the power traversing mechanism was used.

Production was underway in June 1943 with the first T70s being accepted in July. This was the beginning of a

The 76mm gun motor carriage T70, serial number 7, appears above and below at the General Motors Proving Ground on 9 August 1943. Note that the track pins extend out on each side of the shoe increasing the overall track width. Stowage boxes are now welded to both sides of the turret.

run which reached 2507 vehicles by the time production ended in October 1944. Standardization of the T70 as the 76mm gun motor carriage M18 was approved in March 1944. This same action directed that vehicles with serial numbers 685 through 1096 be modified to incorporate a new gear ratio before overseas shipment. All vehicles below serial number 685 were to be returned to the factory for modification. Eventually, 640 of these were converted into M39 armored utility vehicles. The M18, sometimes referred to as the Hell Cat, was first committed to battle in Italy during the Spring of 1944.

Above and at the left below are additional views of the 76mm gun motor carriage T70, serial number 7. The USA registration number was 40108110. At the bottom right is the 76mm gun motor carriage T70, serial number 35. Note that the bulge under the left front turret stowage box has been eliminated.

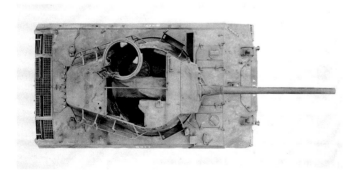

308

Above, M18 76mm gun motor carriages are coming off the production line at the Buick Motor Car Division of General Motors Corporation. The muzzle of the 76mm gun in the late model M18 at the right is threaded for the use of a muzzle brake and a thread protector is installed. Below, M18 serial number 726 is armed with the 76mm gun M1A1 which could not be fitted with a muzzle brake. This photograph was dated 28 April 1944.

These photographs show the 76mm gun motor carriage M18, serial number 1709, at Aberdeen Proving Ground on 16 June 1944. The USA registration number for this vehicle was 40145585. All of the external stowage has been installed.

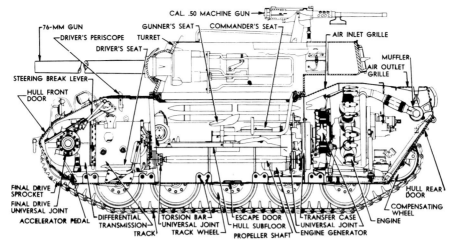

The internal arrangement of the 76mm gun motor carriage M18 can be seen above. Below, these two late model M18s are armed with 76mm guns fitted with muzzle brakes. The bottom photograph shows M18 serial number 2508 at the General Motors Proving Ground on 7 November 1944.

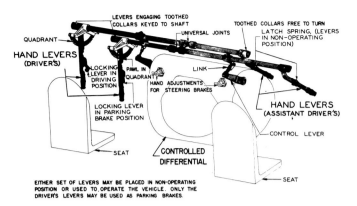

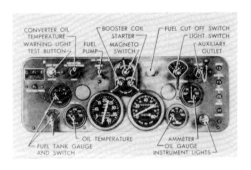

The steering and brake controls in the 76mm gun motor carriage M18 are sketched at the left. The driver's instrument panel is above.

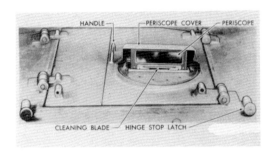

Above, the driver's hatch in the M18 is shown open (left) and closed (right). Below, the driver's seat is at the left and the hull of the vehicle is at the right.

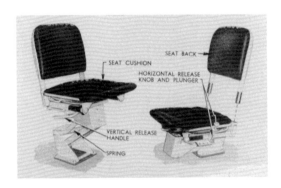

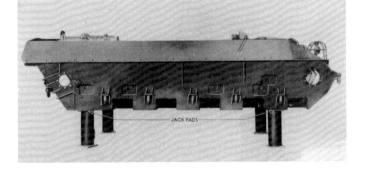

The driver and assistant driver rode in the left and right front of the M18 hull respectively. They were provided with dual controls so that either one could drive the vehicle. Two double section doors were installed in the hull roof for the driver and the assistant driver. A periscope was mounted in the outer section of each door. A floor escape hatch was located in the right front of the hull. The hull itself was assembled by welding rolled homogeneous steel armor plate ½ inch thick on the front, sides, and rear. A 77½ inch diameter opening in the hull roof center plate provided space for mounting the turret which rotated on a 69 inch inside diameter bearing race ring.

At the left is the driver's hood and the floor escape hatch in the M18 is below.

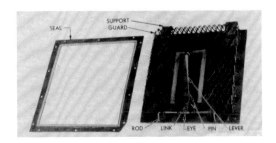

312

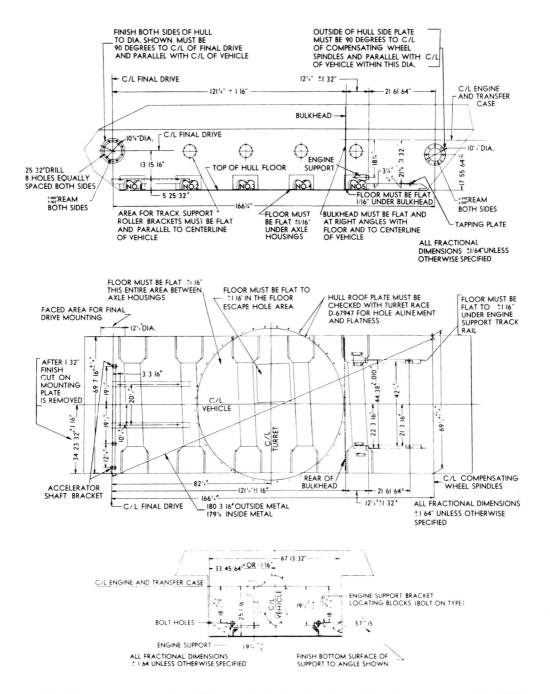

The hull dimensions of the 76mm gun motor carriage M18 appear in the drawings above. Below, the components of the M18 suspension system are illustrated at the right and the subfloor doors and plates can be seen at the left. Access to the floor escape hatch was through the right front subfloor door.

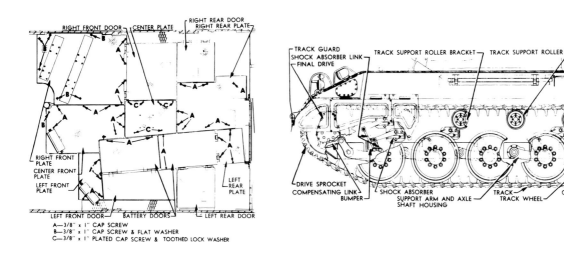

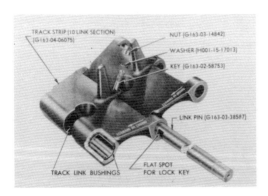

Links of the single pin track used on the 76mm gun motor carriage M18 are above. At the right, the Continental R-975-C1 engine is installed in the vehicle. The exhaust manifold and mufflers are visible in the latter view.

The transmission was located in the front hull between the driver and assistant driver, but the engine was installed in the rear of the vehicle behind the fighting compartment. M18s with serial numbers 1 through 1350 were powered by the Continental R-975-C1 radial engine. Vehicles with higher serial numbers were equipped with the improved R-975-C4 which developed 460 gross horsepower at 2400 rpm. Transfer cases at the transmission and at the engine lowered the drive shaft which passed underneath the turret thus reducing the height of the vehicle. The final drives at the front drove the single pin steel tracks through two 37 tooth sprockets. The width of the track links was 12 inches, but the track pins were 14⅜ inches long extending out on each side of the links. In addition to the double shock absorbers on the front road wheel arms, single shock absorbers were installed at the second, fourth, and fifth road wheel stations.

The turret was a welded assembly of rolled homogeneous steel armor plate ½ inch thick on the sides and rear.

A cast armor plate was welded across the turret front to support the M1 gun mount. The thickness in front varied from ¾ to 1 inch with the gun shield. In the M1 mount, the 76mm gun was tilted to the right at an angle of 45 degrees. Three versions of the 76mm gun were installed in the production M18s. These were the 76mm guns M1A1, M1A1C, and M1A2. The M1A1 and M1A1C were identical except that the muzzle of the latter was threaded for the installation of a muzzle brake. When the brake was not installed it was replaced by a thread protector. The uniform right-hand twist rifling in the M1A2 had one turn in 32 calibers compared to one turn in 40 calibers for the M1A1 and M1A1C. The slightly tighter twist of the rifling in the M1A2 gun improved the projectile stability at the longer ranges. The muzzle of the M1A2 also was threaded for a muzzle brake. The 76mm gun fired the armor piercing projectile APC-T M62 at a muzzle velocity of 2600 feet per second. The HVAP-T M93 shot had a muzzle velocity of 3400 feet per second.

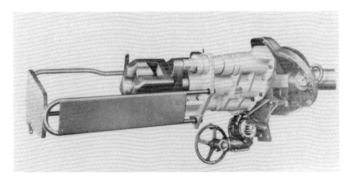

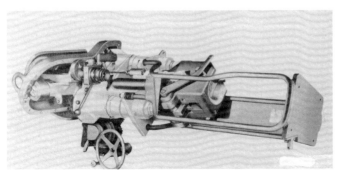

The 76mm gun in the M1 mount appears in the photographs at the left. The gun mount and its controls are sketched below. Note that the weapon is installed at an angle of 45 degrees in the mount. The numbers in the sketch indicate lubrication points on the gun and mount.

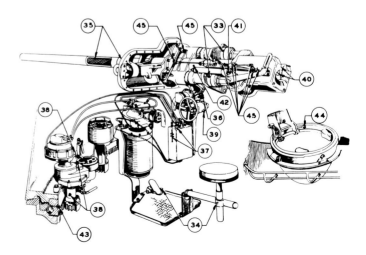

314

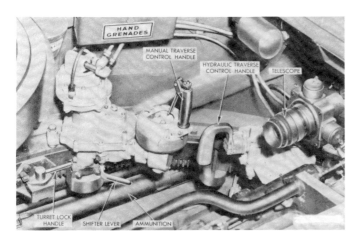

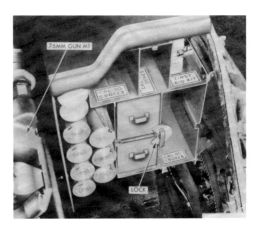

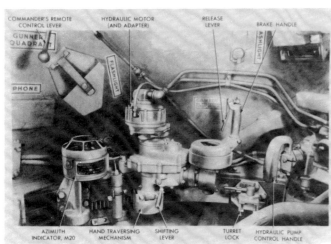

At the left are views of the early (upper) and late (lower) gunner's controls on the M18. The ammunition ready rack in the right front of the turret is above. The .50 caliber machine gun on its ring mount is below.

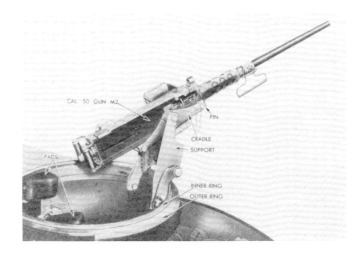

The gunner was seated in the turret on the left side of the cannon and was provided with an M72C or an M76 direct sight telescope in addition to the M4A1 periscopic sight in the top front of the turret. The commander was located to the rear of the gunner under the ring mount for the .50 caliber antiaircraft machine gun. The latter was the only secondary armament on the M18. The loader's station was on the right side of the cannon. The turret had an open top except for the small partial roof at the front and a roof plate welded into the right front corner which supported a ready rack for nine 76mm rounds as well as ammunition for the .50 caliber machine gun. Eighteen rounds in each hull sponson brought the total 76mm ammunition stowage to 45. An SCR 610 radio was installed in the turret bustle. Stowage racks for tarpaulins and blanket rolls were welded to the turret sides and two boxes were welded to the front turret corners to stow the drivers' hoods.

In late July 1943, the Army Ground Forces directed the Armored Board to consider the 76mm gun motor carriage T70 for possible use as a light tank. A test program was initiated at Fort Knox and the T70's automotive performance, armor protection, and armament were evaluated and compared to the requirements for a light tank.

At the right, the M18 turret has been damaged by .30 caliber AP rounds at a range of 75 yards. Nine out of 30 hits penetrated the turret.

The report completed in January 1944 rejected the T70 as a possible light tank. The major objections were the light armor which could be penetrated by .30 caliber armor piercing ammunition at ranges up to 75 yards and insufficient secondary armament which consisted of only the .50 caliber machine gun. The antiaircraft mount of the latter required the gunner to expose himself above the open top turret. Also, the open top turret exposed the crew to artillery air bursts. As a result, the report concluded that the T70 was unsuitable for tactical employment as a light tank.

The photographs on this page show the turret from 90mm gun motor carriage M36 installed on the hull of the 76mm gun motor carriage M18. Note the overhang of the long 90mm cannon.

As previously mentioned, the Ordnance Committee in September 1944 approved the construction of two pilot amphibian vehicles based on the M18. Designated as the 76mm gun motor carriages T86 and T86E1, they differed mainly in the method of propulsion in the water. The T86 was propelled by its tracks and the T86E1 utilized a propellor. Both are described in greater detail in the section on amphibian vehicles.

By the end of World War II in Europe, both tanks and tank destroyers were being armed with the 90mm gun M3. It also was expected that this more powerful weapon would be required for use against the Japanese. It would have been particularly effective in reducing bunkers and other fortifications. In this regard, it was desirable to mount the M3 on a highly mobile, lightweight chassis. In June 1945, the turret from the 90mm gun motor carriage M36 was installed on the M18 chassis at Aberdeen Proving Ground. Only minor modifications were required such as raising the half floor of the turret and the slip rings by two inches. It was concluded that the modification could be made in the field. Test firing with and without the muzzle brake indicated that it was a definite requirement. Without the muzzle brake installed, the vehicle rolled back 22 inches

when the gun was fired in the forward direction and it rocked violently when firing to the side. With the muzzle brake, only slight movement was noted. Installation of the M36 turret increased the empty vehicle weight to 43,075 pounds. Later in the program, the 21 inch wide T82 tracks were installed to reduce the ground pressure and a gun travel lock from an M26 tank was mounted on the rear of the hull. With the stowage rearranged to accommodate 90mm ammunition, the M18 chassis and the M36 turret were a successful combination. However, the end of the war in the Pacific cancelled further development.

An earlier attempt had been made to provide a lightweight 90mm gun tank destroyer. In July 1943, a new tank destroyer was proposed based on the chassis of the light tank T24 fitted with the gun mount from the 90mm gun motor carriage T71 (M36). The proposed vehicle was designated as the 90mm gun motor carriage T78. However, the Army Ground Forces believed that the T24 light tank should be adequately tested and proved to be satisfactory before it was modified as a gun motor carriage. As a result, the program was cancelled in August 1943 and it was never revived after the successful development of the T24.

The large bustle in the M36 turret required to balance the 90mm gun is obvious in the views below.

Above, the Christie (left) and the Holt (right) self-propelled mounts for the 75mm gun M1920 or the 105mm howitzer M1920 are compared. The Christie vehicle is shown with its tracks installed.

SELF-PROPELLED ARTILLERY

The development of self-propelled artillery in the United States Army began during World War I. Some projects that were initiated during that war extended for several years afterward. These ranged from light to heavy self-propelled guns and howitzers. The heavy weapons included the 8 inch howitzer motor carriage built by J. Walter Christie and the 155mm gun motor carriage mark II. Among the lightweight designs, the 75mm gun M1916 was installed on the small Holt tractor providing a self-propelled weapon weighing about 10,600 pounds. A later design mounted the 75mm gun M1920 or the 105mm howitzer M1920 on the Holt tractor. This combination weighed 13,200 pounds. Christie also produced a chassis for these two weapons which weighed about 16,000 pounds. Another Christie design provided a chassis for the 155mm gun which only weighed 39,800 pounds. Development work on this

motor carriage continued through 1924. Both of the Christie vehicles featured the combination wheel or track design.

Additional views of the Christie (left) and Holt (right) self-propelled mounts appear below. At the right is the Holt vehicle with armor protection installed.

Above is the Christie self-propelled mount for the 155mm gun. This wheel or track vehicle is shown with the tracks installed.

As mentioned in an earlier section, the chassis of the light tank T1E1 was used in 1928 as the basis for the 4.2 inch mortar motor carriage T1. After the new 75mm pack howitzer M1 was standardized in 1927, it was mounted experimentally on the Holt light tractor. In 1930, James Cunningham, Son and Company produced the 75mm howitzer motor carriage T1 armed with the same weapon. Based on the track development chassis T2, it utilized the components of the light tank and had an unloaded weight of 11,300 pounds. An 89 horsepower LaSalle V-8 engine drove the vehicle at a maximum road speed of 21 miles/hour. The crew of four was protected by armor which ranged in thickness from ¼ to ⅜ inches. The suspension consisted of two bogies on each side of the vehicle with leaf springs. The steel tracks had integral grousers and were 10½ inches wide with a pitch of five inches.

Below, the howitzer in the 75mm howitzer motor carriage T1 is at maximum elevation.

Above, the 75mm howitzer motor carriage T1 (left) is compared with the new 75mm howitzer motor carriage T3 (right). The howitzer on the T3 is in the travel position in this photograph from Aberdeen Proving Ground dated 26 January 1940.

Produced during the depths of the depression, procurement of the T1 was limited to the single pilot vehicle. However, its evaluation provided valuable data on the employment of self-propelled artillery in support of mechanized units.

During 1938, a board of officers reviewed the use of mechanized artillery and submitted recommendations for the further development of such equipment. On 9 March 1939, OCM 14931 approved the construction of a pilot 75mm howitzer motor carriage T3 based on the chassis of the combat car M1. The vehicle was armed with the 75mm pack howitzer M1A1 mounted in the right front of a superstructure installed on the combat car chassis. The driver remained in his usual position in the left front of the hull. A 30 inch diameter turret was located on the left side of the superstructure roof. As originally constructed, this turret was fitted with a one meter base range finder in addition to a .30 caliber machine gun. However, it proved to be extremely difficult to maintain the proper adjustment of the range finder and a second turret was built omitting this feature. It was replaced by a portable one meter base range finder and an M1917 panoramic sight. The turret armor was ⅝ inches thick except for the ¼ inch thick top. The hull was ⅝ inches thick in front, ½ inch thick on the

sides, and ¼ inch thick on the rear. A pair of doors in the front closed around the howitzer barrel. When closed they still permitted the full elevation range of the howitzer from +20 to –10 degrees, but no traverse. With the doors open, the weapon could be traversed from 10 degrees left to 15 degrees right of center.

The T3 was manned by a crew of three consisting of a driver, a gunner, and a loader. The gunner fired the .30 caliber machine gun as well as the howitzer. Space was provided for 60 rounds of 75mm ammunition in the sponsons and below the howitzer mount. The loaded weight of the T3 was about 20,000 pounds and it had a maximum road speed of 45 miles/hour.

The Field Artillery Board considered the T3 unsuitable for Field Artillery use mainly because of insufficient crew space. As would be shown later, a single loader was inadequate for rapid time fire or when it was necessary to adjust the propellant charge. However, Aberdeen Proving Ground concluded that the T3 would be suitable for use as an assault gun by Armored Force units. It was recommended that a battalion be equipped for evaluation. However, no additional T3s were built, but the data obtained from the pilot were applied to the development of later howitzer motor carriages.

Below, the interior of the T3 is at the left and, at the right, the howitzer is in firing position at 20 degrees elevation and 15 degrees right traverse.

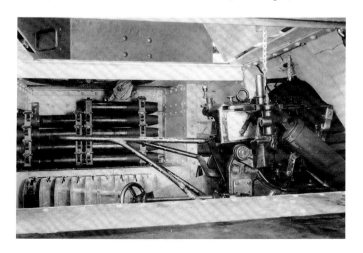

Above is the Firestone mock-up of the 75mm howitzer motor carriage T18 on 26 December 1941. Below, the T18 pilot is at Aberdeen Proving Ground on 5 June 1942. Note the change in the superstructure.

In June 1941, the Adjutant General directed that studies be made to determine the feasibility of mounting either the 75mm howitzer or the 105mm howitzer on the chassis of the light tank M3. The restricted space in the light tank and the unbalance created by the heavy howitzer made the installation of the 105mm weapon impractical. However, two design layouts for mounting the 75mm howitzer appeared promising. The first of these was designated as the 75mm howitzer motor carriage T17 and it utilized the chassis of the experimental combat car M1E3. As mentioned previously, this vehicle had a low power tunnel which provided more space in the fighting compartment. However, this design was dropped at the drawing board stage since the Adjutant General required the use of the standard light tank M3.

The second concept was based on the light tank M3 and was designated as the 75mm howitzer motor carriage T18. In October 1941, the Ordnance Committee approved the construction of two soft steel pilot vehicles and the Firestone Tire and Rubber Company built a wooden mock-up on the chassis and lower hull of a light tank M3. The upper hull and turret were replaced by a large superstructure with vertical sides. The 75mm howitzer M1A1 was installed in the right front using a modified version of the M1 mount for the 75mm gun in the medium tank M3. This mount permitted the howitzer to traverse 15 degrees to the left or right of center. The elevation range was from +20 to −5 degrees. Provision was made for the installation of two fixed .30 caliber machine guns, one in each sponson. Forty-

Additional views of the 75mm howitzer motor carriage T18 appear here. The vehicle is fitted with a protectoscope in the front door and two roof hatches compared to the vision slot and single roof hatch on the mock-up.

two rounds of 75mm ammunition and 4900 .30 caliber rounds were stowed in the vehicle. After inspection of the mock-up, Firestone was authorized to proceed with the construction of the two pilot vehicles. Based on the recommendations of Aberdeen Proving Ground, several changes were incorporated. Two hatches were provided in the superstructure roof compared to one in the mock-up. The battery box on the right side was moved to the rear permitting

the steel superstructure casting to be the same on both sides. This superstructure casting was 2 inches thick in front, 1¼ inches thick on the top and sides, and 1 inch thick in the rear. An M1 periscopic sight was installed in the roof for the gunner. The vision slot in the driver's front door on the mock-up was replaced on the pilots by a protectoscope.

The first pilot T18 was received from Firestone in May 1942. By that time, superior 75mm howitzer motor carriages had appeared. The best of these was the T47 which was standardized as the 75mm howitzer motor carriage M8. In fact, before the pilot T18 was received, the Ordnance Committee had recommended in April 1942 that the T18 program be cancelled.

To meet the immediate requirements of the new armored divisions for a 75mm howitzer motor carriage, the Ordnance Department in December 1941 ordered the manufacture of 312 75mm howitzer motor carriages T30. Produced as an expedient vehicle, the T30 mounted the 75mm pack howitzer M1A1 on the half-track personnel carrier M3. Later, the production of the T30 was increased to a total of 500 vehicles and they served in Africa, Italy, and the Pacific until they no longer could be repaired.

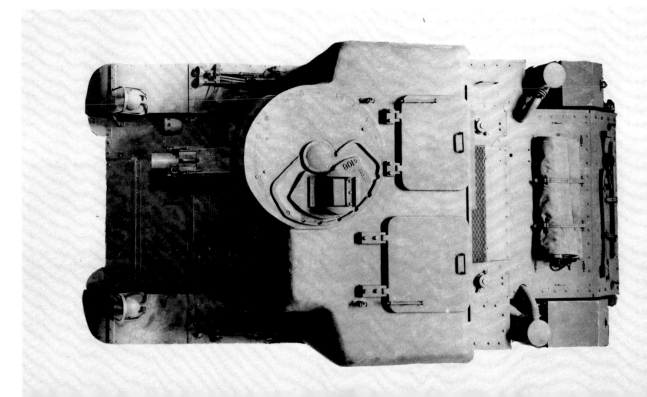

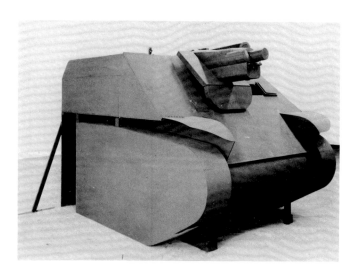

The first mock-up of the 75mm howitzer motor carriage T41 is shown above. The howitzer is mounted on the vehicle center line.

The requirements of the Armored Force were changing and the development of a new 75mm howitzer motor carriage had been initiated by the Ordnance Department in December 1941. The new design studies were based on the chassis of the light tank M5. The T18 had been criticized for the poor ballistic protection provided by its vertical armor. On the new vehicle, the sides were sloped at 30 degrees from the vertical resulting in a width 12 inches greater than the light tank M5. The 75mm howitzer was located on the vehicle center line with a traverse of 15 degrees to each side and an elevation range of +20 to –10 degrees. A shield attached to the howitzer itself improved the protection from bullet splash. A mock-up was constructed and, in April 1942, the vehicle was designated as the 75mm howitzer motor carriage T41. The procurement of a pilot was authorized.

The T41 mock-up was modified by relocating the howitzer to the right of the vehicle center line. The external shield was eliminated and additional armor was fitted inside the vehicle, but the design of the pack howitzer prevented complete shielding of the weapon in a vehicle mount. On 1 April 1942, the Chief of Ordnance directed that the design be modified to use the chassis of the light tank M3. Apparently, it was expected that the availability of the latter chassis would be greater than that of the newer M5. However, before a pilot could be completed, the mock-up of the new 75mm howitzer motor carriage T47 was available for review. It was considered to be far superior to any design presented up to that time. As a result, the T41 was not considered even as an interim vehicle. When the T47 was standardized as the M8, further development of the T41 was cancelled.

The modified mock-up of the T41 is below. Note that the howitzer has been shifted to the right of the vehicle center line.

The mock-up of the 75mm howitzer motor carriage T47 with the original turret design can be seen above at Aberdeen Proving Ground on 15 April 1942. Below, the mock-up is fitted with a modified turret.

The original mock-up of the T47 was based on the chassis of the light tank M3 in view of its expected greater availability. However, this was soon changed to the light tank M5 chassis. Several versions of a fully rotating turret were considered, all of which were armed with a modified version of the 75mm howitzer. A major difficulty on the earlier designs had been to find a way to provide proper shielding around the pack howitzer M1A1. On the T47, this problem was solved by modifying the howitzer. Only the tube and breech assembly were retained from the pack howitzer and they were adapted for installation in a new mount which utilized components from the M34 mount of the Sherman tank. The new design provided full shielding over an elevation range of +40 to –20 degrees in a

A later turret design is shown on the T47 mock-up in these photographs taken at Cadillac on 15 May 1942.

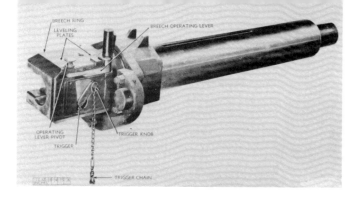

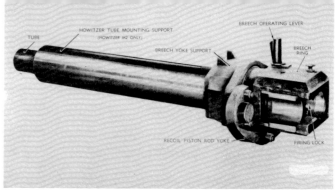

Above is the 75mm howitzer M3. The 75mm howitzer M2 was identical except that the howitzer tube mounting support was a separate part. Below and at the right are views of the howitzer in the M7 mount.

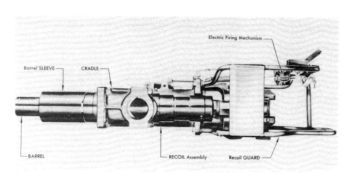

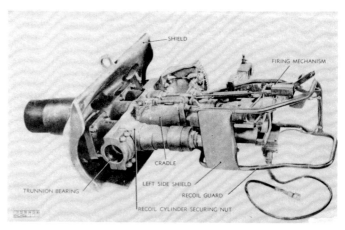

manually rotated turret with 360 degree traverse. This design was standardized as the 75mm howitzer mount M7. The modified weapon was designated as the 75mm howitzer M2 and it consisted of the breech assembly and tube from the M1A1 with a barrel support sleeve added to provide a cylindrical recoil surface 6.5 inches in diameter and 34 inches in length with a keyway to prevent rotation. The

M2 howitzer was classified as limited standard and only 197 were produced. Later vehicles were armed with the 75mm howitzer M3. This new production weapon used the same breech assembly as the M2, but the recoil surface and keyway were machined directly on the tube and it did not require a separate barrel support sleeve. The M2 and M3 howitzers were interchangable in the M7 mount.

Below, the pilot 75mm howitzer motor carriage M8 is at Aberdeen Proving Ground on 22 September 1942. Note the long flash deflector on the 75mm howitzer.

These photographs show the external stowage on the pilot 75mm howitzer motor carriage M8. The long flash deflector is particularly obvious in the side view.

The T47 had been standardized in May 1942 as the 75mm howitzer motor carriage M8 and in September, the first pilot vehicle arrived at Aberdeen Proving Ground. Tests at Aberdeen, Fort Knox, and by the Desert Warfare Board produced satisfactory results with recommendations for only a few minor modifications. Production began at the Cadillac Motor Car Division of General Motors Corporation in September 1942 and continued through January 1944 for a total of 1778 vehicles. None of the M8s were allocated to Britain, the Soviet Union, or China under the Lend-Lease program.

The 75mm howitzer muzzle is visible in the front view below despite the long flash deflector. The vehicle is fitted with steel tracks. The direct sight telescope can be seen on the right side of the howitzer in the top view.

The 75mm howitzer motor carriage M8, serial number 5, is shown here at Aberdeen Proving Ground on 7 January 1943. With the shorter flash deflector, the muzzle of the howitzer is easily seen in the view at the top left. The front vision doors have been lashed open and windshields installed for the test program. The seats for the driver and assistant driver in the front hull can be seen below at the right.

In appearance, the hull of the M8 was similar to that of th light tank M5. However, with the open top turret for access, the hatches in the M5 hull roof for the driver and the assistant driver were eliminated. Two large vision doors in the hull front plate provided each with a direct view forward. Each driver had two M9 periscopes in the hull roof. As on the M5, dual controls enabled either man to drive the vehicle.

Below are front (right) and rear (left) views of the turret interior. The howitzer controls and sighting equipment are visible in the right photograph and some of the 75mm ammunition stowage appears at the left.

Above, the 75mm howitzer motor carriage M8 is firing on the range. Below, this late production M8 is fitted with sandshields and track grousers are stowed on the turret. Late production vehicles also were provided with rear hull stowage boxes as on the late light tank M5A1. The internal arrangement of the M8 can be seen in the sectional drawing at the bottom of the page.

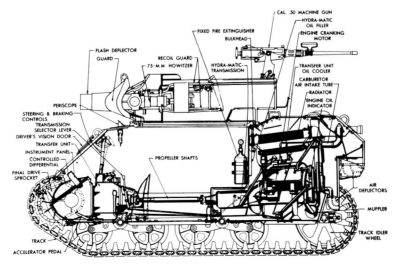

327

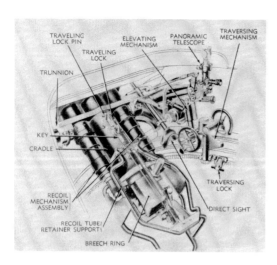

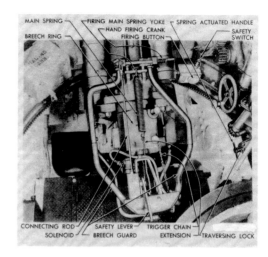

The turret and howitzer controls as well as the fire control equipment in the M8 turret are sketched above. The photographs at the right show further details of the howitzer controls (upper) and the turret controls (lower).

The M8 turret was installed on a 54½ inch inside diameter ring compared to the 46¾ inch diameter ring on the light tanks. The two man turret crew rode with the gunner on the left and the loader on the right. In addition to an M12A5 panoramic telescope, the gunner was provided with the M56 direct sight telescope. The latter was replaced later by the M70C direct sight telescope. Secondary armament on the M8 consisted of a .50 caliber M2 HB machine gun on a ring mount at the right rear of the turret. Forty-six rounds of 75mm ammunition and 400 .50 caliber rounds were stowed in the vehicle. Late production M8s were fitted with sand shields and track grousers were carried on the turret. By the end of the war in September 1945, 862 M8s were overseas with the U. S. Army.

The driver's vision door in the 75mm howitzer motor carriage M8 appears at the upper right in the open and closed positions. The ammunition stowage in the M8 is below. At the lower right are three types of 75mm ammunition fired by the howitzer.

The photographs on this page show the pilot 105mm howitzer motor carriage T76 at Aberdeen Proving Ground on 17 July 1944. The external stowage has been installed and the open top vehicle is fitted with canvas covers.

As mentioned earlier, there were several unsuccessful attempts to install the 105mm howitzer M2A1 on a light tank chassis. At one point, a modified Cletrac MG-2 tractor was considered as a possible mount. When fitted with the 105mm howitzer, this vehicle, manufactured by the Cleveland Tractor Company, was to be designated as the 105mm howitzer motor carriage T9. However, the project was dropped without the completion of a pilot vehicle.

The urgent need for a 105mm howitzer motor carriage to equip the armored divisions resulted in the production of an expedient vehicle designated as the 105mm howitzer motor carriage T19. Consisting of the 105mm M2A1 howitzer mounted on the M3 half-track personnel carrier, it was rushed into production in January 1942 and 324 vehicles were completed by the end of March. These vehicles served in North Africa until they could be replaced by the 105mm howitzer motor carriage M7 based on the medium tank. The latter became the standard weapon for the armored field artillery battalions during the remainder of the war.

Although the M7 was highly successful, a lighter weight vehicle was expected to be even more useful. Reports from the field also indicated the desirability of a direct sight telescope and improved armor protection for the crew. Consideration was given to installing the howitzer on the chassis of the 4.5 inch gun motor carriage T16. However, this chassis required that the howitzer be mounted at the rear and such a location would have required an excessively high mount in order to obtain a depression of 10 degrees over the front.

The chassis of the light tank T24 also was considered as a possible howitzer motor carriage. If the turret and top deck plates were removed, the 105mm howitzer M4 could be pedestal mounted between and just behind the driver and the assistant driver. The M4 howitzer had been developed for installation in the turret of the medium tank M4. It was ballistically identical to the M2A1, but it had been redesigned for use inside the tank turret.

On 10 June 1943, OCM 20679 recommended the development and procurement of pilot vehicles and assigned the designation 105mm howitzer motor carriage T76. This action was approved on 8 July. A wooden mock-up was constructed and it was reviewed in August by artillery officers from the Armored Board. They recommended that the crew be increased from six to seven men to permit rapid fire in support of tank operations. The mock-up was modified and the chassis lengthened to increase the size of the fighting compartment. Since the assistant driver was not required, the howitzer was shifted to the right of the vehicle center line and moved forward. A .50 caliber machine gun on a ring mount was then located in the right front hull. The revised mock-up was inspected in September 1943 by representatives of the Army Ground Forces, the Armored Board, and the Tank-Automotive Center. In December, the Army Service Forces approved the revised military characteristics of the T76. To expedite the manufacture of pilot vehicles, the Tank-Automotive Center procured the new T14 howitzer mounts and the first was proof fired on 17 March 1944. Some modifications were required and, after they were completed, the mount was successfully proof fired in early June at Rock Island Arsenal. The first T76 pilot vehicle was shipped to Aberdeen Proving Ground arriving in early July. After extended firing tests, pilot number 1 was transferred to the Armored Board at Fort Knox.

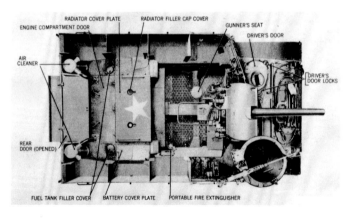

The canvas covers have been removed from the 105mm howitzer motor carriage T76 in these photographs. Note the large M49C ring mount for the .50 caliber machine gun. The vertical stowage of the 105mm ammunition is visible in the top view.

The tests at Aberdeen and Fort Knox resulted in several modifications. The 42 inch diameter M49C ring mount for the .50 caliber machine gun was replaced by the 36 inch diameter T107 mount. The SCR 510 radio was eliminated to provide space for additional 105mm ammunition. The 105mm rounds were rearranged and the vertical stowage was replaced by separate bins with the ammunition loaded horizontally. The total number of 105mm rounds was increased from 68 to 126. The rear door on the hull was redesigned to permit its use as a loading platform when open. With these changes, standardization of the T76 as the 105mm howitzer motor carriage M37 was approved in January 1945. However, the end of the war limited the total production to 150 vehicles and none were shipped overseas. The M37 served in the postwar period and saw action during the Korean War.

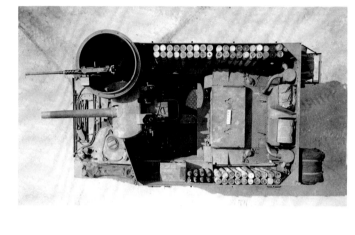

The standardized 105mm howitzer motor carriage M37 at the right and below can be compared with the T76 prototype at the top of the page. The smaller T107 ring mount for the .50 caliber machine gun is particularly obvious as well as the changes in ammunition stowage and rear hull configuration.

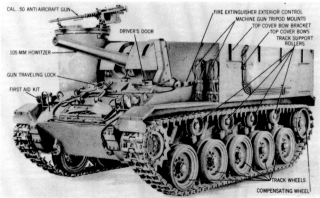

Components of the suspension system on the 105mm howitzer motor carriage M37 are indicated in the view at the top right. Below, the rear door and engine compartment cover can be seen at the left and the vehicle is fitted with canvas covers at the right.

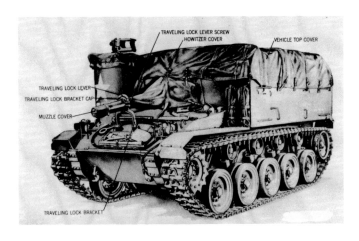

Details of the engine compartment bulkhead appear at the left and the howitzer and fire control equipment are at the lower left. The controls for the howitzer and mount are below.

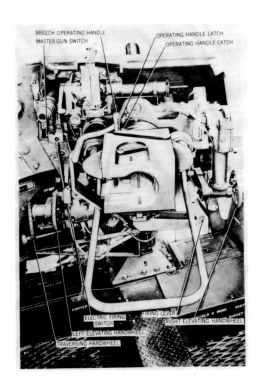

Above is the original pilot of the 105mm howitzer motor carriage T82 as converted from a light tank M5A1 at Aberdeen Proving Ground.

In November 1943, Major General Barnes directed Aberdeen Proving Ground to install a 105mm howitzer M3A1 on a light tank M5A1 after removing the turret and the upper hull armor. The M3A1 was a lightweight weapon intended for use by airborne troops, but it fired the same projectiles as the 105mm howitzer M2A1 at a slightly lower velocity. It was expected that such a lightweight howitzer motor carriage would be useful in jungle terrain that might be impassable for heavier vehicles.

The howitzer was mounted in the right front of the M5A1 hull alongside the driver. Steel plate ½ inch thick was added for a front shield and ¼ inch thick plate covered the sponson sides, top, and rear. The vehicle carried 23 rounds of 105mm ammunition. With full fuel tanks and fitted with 14 inch wide T55E2 tracks, the little vehicle weighed 25,400 pounds.

On 30 December 1943, OCM 22522 approved the development of the vehicle now designated as the 105mm howitzer motor carriage T82. Two pilots were authorized and a contract was awarded to the Heil Company of Milwaukee, Wisconsin for their construction. Both pilot

The pilot 105mm howitzer motor carriage T82 as converted by the Heil Company is shown in these three photographs. Compare this vehicle with the original Aberdeen conversion above.

vehicles were completed and shipped to Aberdeen on 15 August 1944. The first T82 was the original Aberdeen pilot after rework.

The T82 pilots differed in several ways from the original vehicle improvised at Aberdeen. Two pedestal mounts were installed for a .50 caliber antiaircraft machine gun. The howitzer mount was relocated three inches forward and an SCR 510 radio was installed in the left sponson. The 105mm ammunition stowage was increased to a total of 58 rounds with 34 inside the fighting compartment and 24 over the engine compartment. Manned by a crew of four, the T82 had a combat weight of 32,000 pounds and a maximum road speed of 36 miles/hour. New 16 inch wide tracks were installed to reduce the ground pressure.

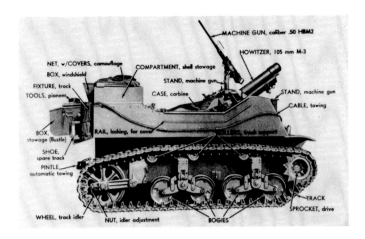

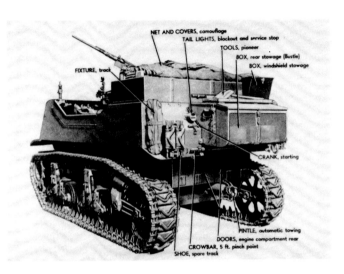

The various components of the 105mm howitzer motor carriage T82 are designated in these views. Note the extended end connectors which increased the track width to 16 inches. The suspension components were spaced out from the hull to provide clearance.

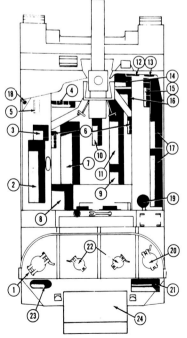

Originally, it had been intended to ship the second pilot to Fort Knox, but the Armored Board had no interest in the project. Because of the priority of other work at Aberdeen, firing and performance tests were delayed until January 1945. In February, the second pilot was proof fired and shipped to Fort Benning, Georgia for evaluation by the Infantry Board. Although the T82 passed all of its tests successfully, no military requirement was established for the vehicle and the project was terminated on 21 June 1945.

The driver's station in the T82 can be seen below at the left. At the right is a stowage diagram for the vehicle.

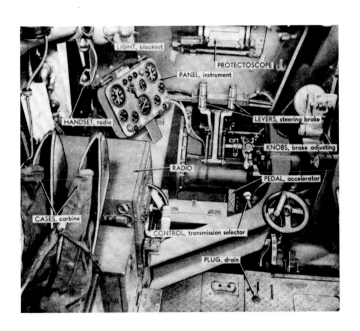

1. COVER, filler, left gasoline.
2. BOX, battery.
3. BOX, panoramic sight.
4. BOX, grenade.
5. BRACKET, first aid kit.
6. BOX, grenade.
7. BOX, ammunition, left floor stowage.
8. COMPARTMENT, tool.
9. COMPARTMENT, miscellaneous stowage.
10. COMPARTMENT, ration stowage.
11. BOX, right floor ammunition stowage.
12. BRACKET, gunners quadrant.
13. BRACKET, range drum.
14. COVER, 105 MM ammunition.
15. BOX, flare.
16. BOX, gun spare parts.
17. BOX, 105 MM SPONSON stowage.
18. SOCKET, cover bow.
19. BRACKET, fire extinguisher.
20. COVER, filler, right gasoline.
21. BOX, windshield stowage.
22. COVERS, radiator filler.
23. BOX, first aid.
24. BOX, rear stowage.

The pilot 105mm howitzer motor carriage T88 is shown here at Aberdeen Proving Ground on 5 December 1944. The 105mm howitzer M4 was fitted with a counterweight on the muzzle to balance the weapon for use with the stabilizer.

On 31 August 1944, OCM 24943 recommended the development of a 105mm howitzer motor carriage based on the 76mm gun motor carriage M18. This action was approved on 14 September. The vehicles were to be armed with two types of 105mm howitzers. The first was the 105mm howitzer M4 developed for use in the medium tank. The vehicle armed with this cannon in the mount T20 was designated as the 105mm howitzer motor carriage T88. The second weapon was a modified version of the lightweight 105mm howitzer T12 originally developed for aircraft use. As modified for installation in the motor carriage, it was redesignated as the 105mm howitzer T51. The T12 and T51 differed only in external contour. The vehicle using the T51 howitzer with the T55 concentric recoil mechanism in the T21 mount was designated as the 105mm howitzer motor carriage T88E1.

After a preliminary study to determine the feasibility of the project, a contract was awarded to the Buick Motor Car Division of General Motors Corporation to build the pilot vehicles. Two M18 turrets were modified to the T88 configuration armed with the M4 howitzer in the T20 mount. One of these was installed on a modified M18 chassis and the other was shipped to the Marmon-Herrington Company for water proofing and further modification. It then was installed on the amphibious 105mm howitzer motor carriage T87.

On the T88, the M18's ring mount for the .50 caliber machine gun was replaced by a pedestal mount at the top

front of the turret. Another change to the M18 turret on the T88 was the relocation of the gunner's station from the left to the right side of the cannon. The direct sight telescope was eliminated and replaced by an emergency peep sight. An M10 periscopic sight replaced the M4A1 and a panoramic telescope was located on the right rear turret wall for the vehicle commander. The howitzer mount was fitted with an elevation gyrostabilizer. Sixteen 105mm ready rounds were located on the left turret wall near the loader. Twentyfour rounds in the hull brought the total 105mm ammunition stowage to 40.

In addition to the ammunition stowage modifications, the T88 conversion of the M18 hull was provided with a bilge pump and connectors for use with the T7 flotation device. When the conversion was complete, the T88 was shipped to Aberdeen Proving Ground for tests. After the correction of minor problems with the recoil cylinders, the T88 was transferred to Camp Hood for evaluation by the Tank Destroyer Board.

Buick also modified an M18 turret for the T88E1. The T55 concentric recoil mechanism was developed at Rock Island Arsenal where it was proof fired with the lightweight 105mm howitzer T51. The combination of the concentric recoil mechanism and the lightweight cannon was expected to provide more room in the turret and reduce the weight of the vehicle. The T88E1 was complete except for the installation of the howitzer and mount when both the T88 and T88E1 projects were cancelled at the end of the war.

Details of the shield on the T20 howitzer mount can be seen in the front view of the T88 pilot above. The rear view shows the track shoes attached to the turret bustle.

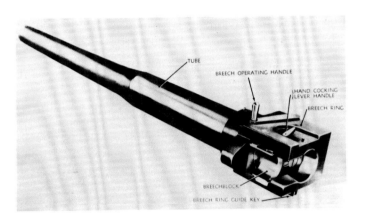

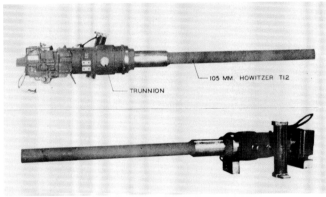

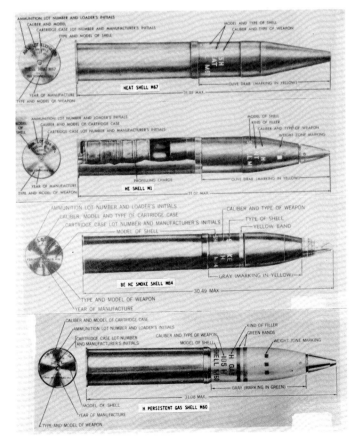

Above at the left is the 105mm howitzer M4. Two views of the lightweight 105mm howitzer T12 are above. Three types of standard 105mm howitzer ammunition are illustrated at the left and below is the limited procurement armor piercing round APHE T24E2. This 28.1 pound projectile had a muzzle velocity of 1925 feet per second in the M4 howitzer.

Above is the 4.5 inch gun motor carriage T16 at Aberdeen Proving Ground on 2 June 1944. The vehicle is fitted with steel T36E6 tracks. The motor carriage is in travel order with the cannon in the travel lock and the spade elevated.

Ordnance Committee action in August 1941 approved the development of a lightweight self-propelled gun based on the chassis of the light tank M3 or T7. After further study, the light tank M5 chassis was selected as the basic vehicle. In September 1942, a contract was awarded to the Cadillac Motor Car Division of General Motors Corporation to design and manufacture two pilot vehicles now designated as the 4.5 inch gun motor carriage T16. As its designation indicated, the main armament of the new self-propelled weapon was the 4.5 inch gun M1. The M5 light tank chassis was lengthened by 12 inches and the twin

engine power plant was relocated to the middle of the vehicle just behind the drivers' compartment. The overall width was increased to 109 inches. An additional set of bogie wheels was installed on each side and a conventional rear idler replaced the trailing idler on the M5 suspension. The Burgess-Norton T36E6 steel tracks were 11⅝ inches wide with a pitch of 5½ inches. The 4.5 inch gun mounted at the rear of the chassis was aimed forward and could be traversed 17 degrees to the left and 20 degrees to the right of the vehicle center line. The elevation range was +40 to 0 degrees.

Above and at the right below, the 4.5 inch gun motor carriage T16 is in the firing position with the spade lowered. The ammunition stowage racks can be seen in the rear view. At the lower left is the 4.5 inch gun M1.

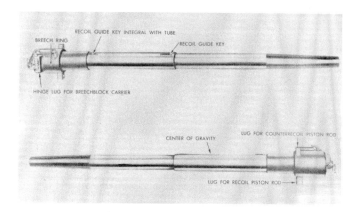 

336

Above, the 155mm howitzer motor carriage T64 is in travel order at Aberdeen on 1 February 1943. Like the T16, it is fitted with steel tracks.

In December 1942, the contract with Cadillac was amended to provide only one 4.5 inch gun motor carriage T16. The second pilot was to be armed with the 155mm howitzer M1 and it was assigned the designation 155mm howitzer motor carriage T64. The basic chassis of the T64 was identical to that of the T16. On the T64, 18 rounds of 155mm ammunition replaced the 26 4.5 inch rounds on the T16.

The T16 was shipped to Aberdeen for preliminary tests on 11 January 1943 followed by the T64 later that same month. In February, both vehicles were driven to Fort Bragg, North Carolina for evaluation by the Field Artillery Board. In general, the two motor carriages performed satisfactorily during their tests, but there were a few problems. The inability to depress the main weapon below the horizontal was a disadvantage and the spade at the rear of the vehicle required strengthening. There was insufficient ventilation in the drivers' compartment and the muzzle blast from the short barreled 155mm howitzer damaged the stowage on the front of the T64.

The spade on the T64 can be seen in the raised and lowered positions in the photographs above and at the upper left. Below and at the lower left, the T64 is under test by the Armored Force Board at Fort Knox.

Above, the 155mm howitzer motor carriage T64E1, pilot number 1, is in travel order. Below, the howitzer has been raised to its maximum elevation.

The Field Artillery Board noted some of the same problems revealed at Aberdeen and also recommended the use of an improved suspension and some stowage modifications. On 29 June 1943, the two vehicles were shipped to Fort Knox for examination by the Armored Board. At this time, a redesign of the howitzer motor carriage was in progress using the chassis of the light tank T24. The Armored Board recommended that this design, designated as the 155mm howitzer motor carriage T64E1, be completed and put into production as soon as possible. A similar version of the T16 based on the light tank T24 was designated as the 4.5 inch gun motor carriage T16E1. However, the Armored Board rejected the 4.5 inch gun pointing out that its explosive charge was less than that of the 105mm howitzer round. They also noted that the 105mm howitzer, the 155mm howitzer, and the 155mm gun provided complete range coverage and that there was no need for the 4.5 inch gun. As a result, a pilot of the T16E1 was not authorized.

On 20 January 1944, OCM 22683 approved the manufacture of a pilot T64E1 and a contract was issued to Cadillac in May. The T64E1 was completed in December and shipped to Aberdeen. The tests revealed that the front stowage and fenders were still damaged by the muzzle blast. In January 1945, the pilot vehicle was shipped to the Field Artillery Board at Fort Bragg. After some changes to the stowage and the relocation of the radio antenna from the gun shield to the top of the hull over the engine compartment, the Field Artillery Board recommended that the vehicle be standardized. On 28 June 1945, OCM 28165 reclassified the vehicle as the 155mm howitzer motor carriage M41.

The rear of the pilot T64E1 in travel order can be seen at the left in this photograph at Detroit Arsenal on 5 January 1945.

The standard 155mm howitzer motor carriage M41 appears in these photographs. Note the guard installed over the drivers' periscopes to protect them from the muzzle blast of the howitzer.

 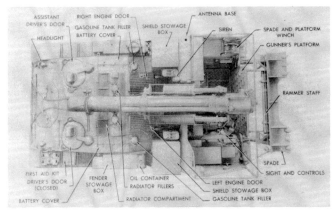

The howitzer mount on the M41 was improved providing an elevation range of +45 to –5 degrees compared to the +40 to 0 degrees on the T64. The 155mm ammunition stowage also was increased from 18 to 22 rounds. The new torsion bar suspension with the 16 inch wide center guide tracks reduced the ground pressure and improved the ride. Like other members of the combat team based on the light tank M24, the chassis was lengthened increasing the ground contact length to 124 inches.

During the development of the 4.5 inch gun motor carriage T16 and the 155mm howitzer motor carriage T64, it was noted that neither vehicle had the required space for ammunition or crew to properly serve the weapon. It was recommended that a companion vehicle based upon the same chassis be produced to carry the extra crew members as well as a supply of ammunition. Designated as the cargo carrier T22, this vehicle utilized the same chassis as the T16 and T64. When the T64 was converted to the light tank T24 chassis, a similar change was made for the companion vehicle now designated as the cargo carrier T22E1.

Production of the M41 began at the Massey Harris Company, but it was limited by the end of the war to 85 vehicles. One M41 was shipped to Britain for evaluation, but none reached the Army in the field. The M41 was used during the postwar period and saw active service in the Korean War.

Above, the 155mm howitzer motor carriage M41 is in firing position. Note the ammunition racks below the howitzer mount.

Above at the left, 155mm howitzer motor carriage M41, registration number 40192778, is at Aberdeen Proving Ground on 11 August 1945. At the top right, the M41 is in firing position. Below, details of the M41's suspension and tracks can be seen at the left and the hull and suspension appear at the right.

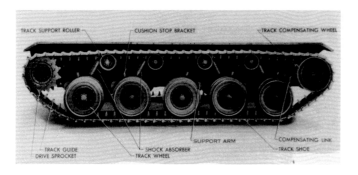

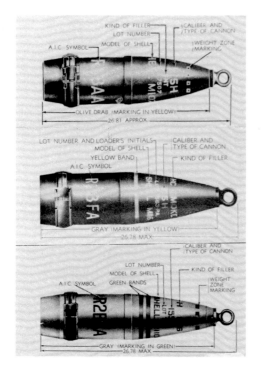

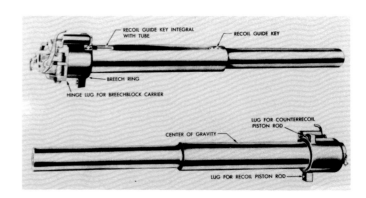

Above is the 155mm howitzer M1. At the left and below are examples of the projectiles and propelling charge used by this weapon. The shells from top to bottom are HE M107, BE HC M116 smoke, and H M110 gas.

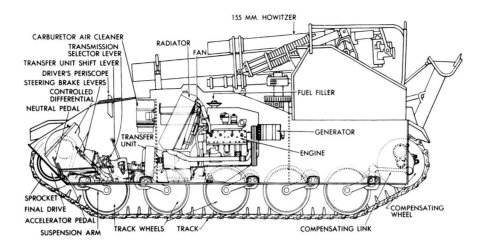

The internal arrangement of the 155mm howitzer motor carriage M41 appears in the sectional drawing above. The dimensions of the M41 hull are shown on the drawings below.

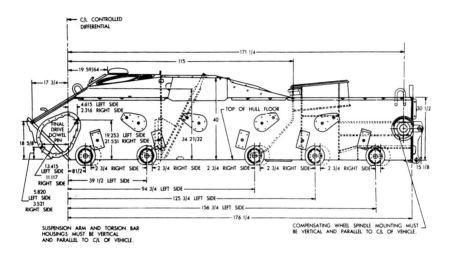

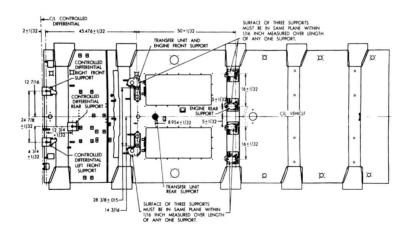

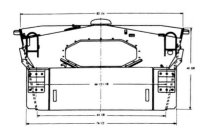

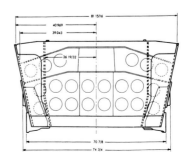

341

Above, the early 4.2 inch mortar motor carriage T1 converted from the cargo carrier T1E1 is at the left. At the top right is the 4.2 inch mortar motor carriage T2 constructed by James Cunningham, Son & Company.

As mentioned earlier, the cargo carrier T1E1 was converted into the 4.2 inch mortar motor carriage T1 in the late 1920s. In early 1935, another 4.2 inch chemical mortar was installed experimentally by James Cunningham, Son & Company on a light full track chassis. This vehicle was designated as the 4.2 inch mortar motor carriage T2.

In November 1943, the Army Ground Forces requested the construction of two 81mm mortar carriers based on the light tank M5A1. The turret and top hull armor were to be removed and extra vertical side armor added for the protection of the mortar crew. The two vehicle designs differed in the height of the mortar mount and, as a result, in the height of the protective side armor. The 81mm mortar M1 was to be mounted with approximately 35 degrees of traverse in addition to that available in the mortar mount itself. Ordnance Committee action designated the two vehicles as the 81mm mortar carriers T27 and T27E1.

None of the experimental mortar motor carriages were produced in quantity and during World War II, the 81mm mortars in the armored units were mounted in half-track vehicles. The 81mm mortar carriers M4, M4A1, and M21 served successfully until the end of the war. The space inside these vehicles provided ample room for the mortar crew and ammunition. The 4.2 inch mortar was installed in the half-track mortar carrier T21, but it never reached production. Although the half-track mortar carriers provided satisfactory service, it was desirable to have a vehicle with mobility equal to the tank so that it could accompany the armored units on all types of terrain.

After further study, the program was revised to produce a lower silhouette vehicle, but it retained the designation 81mm mortar carrier T27. The T27E1 pilot was cancelled and replaced by a vehicle similar to the new version of the T27, but mounting the 4.2 inch chemical mortar. The latter vehicle was designated as the 4.2 inch mortar carrier T29. The new T27 and T29 were fitted with one inch thick armor extensions above the front and sides of the M5A1 hull to protect the mortar crew. On both vehicles, the driver and the assistant driver rode in their usual positions and the latter manned the .30 caliber bow machine gun. The other two crew members were located alongside the mortar. A .50 caliber antiaircraft machine gun was mounted on a pedestal at the rear of the mortar compartment and an alternate socket mount was provided at the

Below, the 81mm mortar carrier T27 appears at the left and the 4.2 inch mortar carrier T29 is at the right. Note the base plate stowed on the front hull so that the mortar could be removed from the vehicle and fired from the ground.

As indicated by their markings, the 81mm mortar carrier T27 is at the top left and the 4.2 inch mortar carrier T29 is at the top right. The T27 at the left is under test by the Armored Force Board at Fort Knox. Both vehicles have stowage boxes on the rear hull similar to those on the late production light tank M5A1.

front. Ninetyfour 81mm rounds or 55 4.2 inch rounds were stowed in the vehicle. A mortar base plate was carried on both the T27 and the T29 so that, if necessary, the weapon could be set up and fired from the ground.

The T27 was completed by the Chevrolet Division of General Motors Corporation in early March 1944 and shipped to Aberdeen Proving Ground. The tests at Aberdeen produced satisfactory results indicating that the T27 was a stable mount for the 81mm mortar. In April, it was shipped to Fort Knox for tests by the Armored Board. Here it was rejected primarily on the grounds that the four man crew was inadequate to properly serve the weapon. Apparently, a companion vehicle was not considered. The T29, which also was completed in March 1944, met a similar fate and OCM 26143 terminated both projects on 21 December 1944.

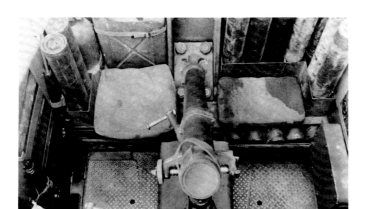

The photograph at the left shows the 81mm mortar installed in the T27. In the top views below, the 81mm mortar can be seen in the T27 (left) and the 4.2 inch mortar is visible in the T29 (right). Both vehicles retained the .30 caliber bow machine gun in addition to the pedestal mounted .50 caliber weapon.

Above, the 4.2 inch mortar carrier T38 is at Aberdeen Proving Ground on 8 March 1949. Note that the base plate provided for ground firing is stowed to cover the gap in the front armor resulting from the removal of the 105mm howitzer.

After it became known that the T29 was being rejected, the Chief of the Chemical Warfare Service requested the development of a new 4.2 inch mortar carrier. Ordnance Committee action in May 1945 officially initiated the project and designated the proposed vehicle as the 4.2 inch mortar carrier T35. At first, it was intended to use the armored utility vehicle T13 as the basis for the new mortar carrier. However, changes in the T13's characteristics shifted the project to the armored utility vehicle T16. Unfortunately, the development of the T16 was delayed and the production date was indefinite. As a result, the program now turned to the 105mm howitzer motor carriage M37 and OCM 29029 recommended the use of this chassis on 13 September 1945 and designated the new vehicle as the 4.2 inch mortar carrier T38. This was approved on 4 October and the same action cancelled the T35 project. By this time, World War II had ended and development proceeded at a slower pace. Two pilot vehicles had been authorized and a requirement was included for installing the 75mm recoilless rifle or the 4.2 inch recoilless mortar in place of the .50 caliber machine gun on the ring mount. Tests with these

weapons on the M37 indicated that such an arrangement was impractical. The field of fire would have to be so restricted to prevent injury to the crew or damage to the vehicle from the back blast that the weapons would be relatively ineffective. OCM 31747, dated 2 October 1947, eliminated the requirement for the recoilless weapons on the machine gun mount and reduced the number of pilot vehicles to one.

The T38 was designed at the York Safe and Lock Company of York, Pennsylvania. It was intended to be a kit which could be used in the field to convert the 105mm howitzer motor carriage M37 to the mortar carrier. The drawings were transferred to Detroit Arsenal where an M37 was converted and shipped to Aberdeen Proving Ground in December 1948.

The T38 was converted from the M37 by removing the 105mm howitzer and mount and installing a ½ inch thick armor shield across the opening in the front hull. A beam was fitted across the bottom of the hull at the rear of the fighting compartment to support the mount for the 4.2 inch mortar M2. The mount itself could be rotated and locked in several fixed positions. This, combined with the

Below, the 75mm recoilless rifle T21 (left) and the 4.2 inch recoilless mortar (right) are installed for test purposes on the 105mm howitzer motor carriage M37. The danger from the back blast of both weapons is obvious.

 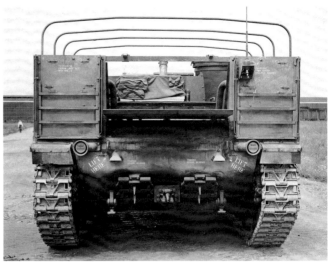

The front and rear views of the 4.2 inch mortar carrier T38 above show the great similarity of the converted vehicle to the original M37. Except for the mortar base plate replacing the howitzer, the appearance is essentially the same.

screw traverse mechanism on the mortar, resulted in a total traverse range of 180 degrees, or 90 degrees to the left or right of the vehicle center line. The mortar, which was aimed forward, had an elevation range of +60 to +45 degrees. Manned by a crew of six, the T38 had a combat weight of 38,500 pounds. The M37 stowage was rearranged to provide space for 140 rounds of 4.2 inch ammunition. The regular base plate and standard for the 4.2 inch mortar were stowed on the vehicle so that the mortar could be removed and fired from the ground.

In April 1949, the T38 was transferred to Fort Benning for tests by the Army Field Forces Board Number 3. These tests were to determine the tactical utility of such a self-propelled mortar and no further conversions were planned.

The 4.2 inch mortar M2 and its mount can be seen in the interior view of the T38 at the right. This mortar mount and the internal stowage also are visible in the top view at the bottom right. A side view of the T38 is below.

Above, four 75mm T21 recoilless rifles are mounted on the chassis of the twin 40mm gun motor carriage M19. Note the open rear of the turret installation to provide a clear space for the back blast of the recoilless weapons.

Although the installation of the recoilless rifle and mortar on the M37's machine gun mount was impractical, it was desirable to provide a suitable motor carriage for recoilless weapons. In June 1945, the Director of the Ordnance Research and Development Center at Aberdeen Proving Ground proposed the installation of a full battery of four 105mm recoilless rifles on a suitable vehicle. Since there were no 105mm recoilless rifles immediately available, four T21 75mm recoilless rifles were selected and installed on a modified twin 40mm gun motor carriage M19. The 40mm guns were removed and replaced by the recoilless weapons on the modified M12 mount. The test firing at Aberdeen proved to be successful and it was recommended that the development program continue using the T19 105mm recoilless rifles when they became available. The 105mm installation was completed in April 1946 and evaluated at Aberdeen. However, now that the war was over, no additional M19s were converted.

In these photographs, the 75mm weapons have been replaced by four 105mm recoilless rifles T19. The turret design has been improved to provide some protection for the bulky ammunition stowed on each side.

346

Above is the original concept study (left) and the pilot installation (right) of the quadruple .50 caliber machine gun mount on the M3 light tank chassis. Additional views of the pilot vehicle are below.

ANTIAIRCRAFT VEHICLES

Prior to World War II, multiple .50 caliber machine gun mounts had been installed experimentally on trucks for the protection of mechanized columns. The experience in Europe in 1939 and 1940 indicated that such antiaircraft protection was essential in modern warfare. The Ordnance Committee in October 1940 recommended the further development of multiple gun motor carriages. This action eventually resulted in the standardization of several such weapons based on the half-track chassis. The multiple gun motor carriages M13 and M14 were armed with two .50 caliber machine guns in a power operated turret and were based on the M3 and M5 half-track personnel carriers respectively. Later the M13 and M14 were succeeded by the M16 and M17 each of which was armed with four .50 caliber machine guns in the power operated M45 mount. They also were based on the M3 and M5 half-track personnel carriers respectively. The M15 and M15A1 multiple gun motor carriages combined a 37mm automatic gun and two .50 caliber machine guns in a single power operated turret on the chassis of the half-track personnel carrier M3. All of these weapons based on the half-track chassis served effectively during World War II and the M15A1 and the M16 remained in active service during the Korean War.

Although the multiple gun motor carriages based on the half-track vehicle were very effective, it was desirable to have such weapons mounted on a full-track chassis so that their mobility would equal that of the tanks and other full-track vehicles in the armored units. A quadruple .50 caliber mount was installed experimentally on the M3 light tank chassis, but it was not produced.

At the right, an armor shield has been added to the quadruple .50 caliber machine gun mount on the M3 light tank chassis.

347

Above is an experimental installation of two .50 caliber aircraft machine guns using a Navy Mark 17 mount on the chassis of the light tank M5A1.

On 22 July 1943, OCM 21109 recommended the development of a multiple gun motor carriage based on the chassis of the light tank T24. The vehicle was designated as the multiple caliber .50 gun motor carriage T77 and it was to be armed with a quadruple .50 caliber machine gun mount developed by the United Shoe Machinery Corporation and the United States Army Air Forces. This mount, designated as the T89, was extremely compact and utilized a remote control system that allowed the gunner to be positioned at some distance from the guns. This arrangement permitted better observation unobscured by smoke or flash. The Ordnance Committee recommendations were approved in October and a mock-up was assembled by December for inspection by the Antiaircraft Command and the Ordnance Department. After the inspection, the military characteristics were revised to increase the number of .50 caliber machine guns in the T89 mount from four to six and in April 1944 the procurement of two pilot vehicles was approved. A mock-up of the revised configuration was completed in June and, after review, some minor changes were made to facilitate production. In October, firing tests were performed on the first .50 caliber gun rotor and the construction of the first pilot vehicle began in November. The first T77 pilot was completed in July 1945 and it was shipped to Aberdeen Proving Ground where tests began on both the vehicle and the gun mount.

Below, the multiple .50 caliber gun motor carriage T77 is at Aberdeen Proving Ground on 23 July 1945. The .30 caliber bow machine gun has not been installed in its mount.

Details of the T77 with its six .50 caliber machine guns can be seen in these additional views of the vehicle during its evaluation at Aberdeen.

The T77 was manned by a crew of four with the two man gun crew in the turret and the driver and assistant driver in the front hull. The .30 caliber bow machine gun was retained on the pilot vehicles. In the six gun power operated turret, 1100 rounds of .50 caliber ammunition were provided for each of the two outboard guns and the four remaining guns had 900 rounds each. An additional 1200 .50 caliber rounds were stowed in the hull. The turret was ½ inch thick on the front, sides, rear, and top and it was mounted on the 60 inch diameter turret ring of the light tank M24 with full 360 degree traverse. Fire control equipment consisted of two mark IX or two T5E1 computing sights. An SCR 528 radio was installed in the turret bustle. The six .50 caliber machine guns had an elevation range

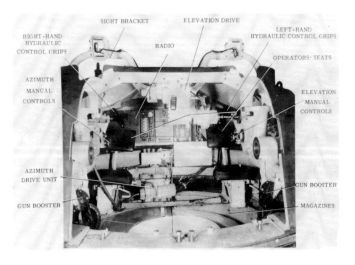

Above, the interior of the T77 turret appears at the left with the multiple machine gun rotor removed. At the right is a rear view of the rotor with the six .50 caliber machine guns mounted.

of +85 to –10 degrees in the T89 mount. The specifications called for a maximum power elevation or traverse rate of at least 65 degrees per second.

The second pilot T77 was equipped with a more sophisticated fire control system including a target selector and a vector type computing sight. With these changes,

the second pilot was redesignated as the multiple caliber .50 gun motor carriage T77E1 and the redesigned gun mount became the T89E1. With the end of the war, the T77 and the T77E1 were never released for production and they served as test vehicles to develop new weapons during the postwar period.

The multiple .50 caliber gun motor carriage T77E1 is shown here. In the photographs above, the domes over the gunners' seats are in the open and closed positions. Below, the left gunner's controls can be seen at the left and, at the right, is a top view with the gunners' domes closed. Note that the .30 caliber bow machine gun has been installed.

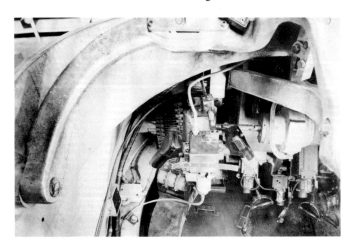

Above is the multiple 20mm gun motor carriage T85 utilizing the chassis of the twin 40mm gun motor carriage T65. The four 20mm Oerlikon guns are in the T18 mount.

In May 1943, the Ordnance Committee recommended the development of a quadruple 20mm gun mount to be installed on a highly mobile chassis for antiaircraft use. This action was approved in June and a program was outlined to study four different designs. The first two were based on the .50 caliber M45 Maxson mount. One of these was armed with four Oerlikon mark IV 20mm antiaircraft guns and it was designated as the multiple 20mm gun mount T18. The same mount armed with four Hispano-Suiza 20mm automatic guns AN-M2 was designated as the T18E1. The remaining two designs were based on the twin 20mm gun mount T4 equipped with an hydraulic drive and a Sperry type K sight. The designations multiple 20mm gun mounts T19 and T19E1 were assigned to these mounts when armed with four Oerlikon or Hispano-Suiza guns respectively. In October 1943, the projects for the T18E1 and T19E1 using the Hispano-Suiza guns were cancelled.

In June 1944, the Ordnance Committee recommended that the T18 and T19 mounts be installed on the chassis of the twin 40mm gun motor carriage T65 based on the light tank M5. Two of these were available since interest

had shifted to the twin 40mm gun motor carriage T65E1 based on the light tank M24. It was noted that if these installations were successful, the gun mounts could easily be transferred to the modified M24 chassis for production.

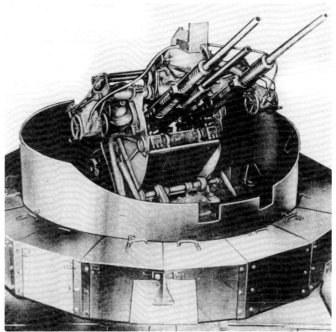

At the right is the quadruple 20mm gun mount T18. Below are two additional views of the mount installed in the T85 gun motor carriage.

The sketch at the right shows the dimensions and general configuration of the multiple 20mm gun motor carriage T85.

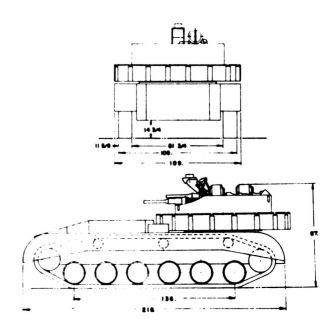

The vehicle with the T18 mount was designated as the multiple 20mm gun motor carriage T85 and the one with the T19 mount became the multiple 20mm gun motor carriage T85E1.

The T85 arrived at Aberdeen for tests during March 1945. These tests were still in progress when the end of the war closed out the program. Later, the T85E1 was fitted with the multiple 20mm gun mount T19E2 armed with the new 20mm gun M3. This weapon was a lightweight version of the 20mm gun AN-M2 with the barrel shortened by 15 inches. The T85E1 with the T19E2 mount was completed in September 1945 and in November it was received at Aberdeen Proving Ground. Its tests provided useful information for the further development of light self-propelled antiaircraft guns.

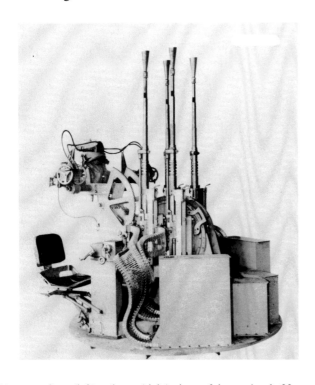

Above are front (left) and rear (right) views of the quadruple 20mm gun mount T19E2 with the guns at maximum elevation. Below, the multiple 20mm gun motor carriage T85E1 is fitted with the T19E2 mount.

Above, the first pilot twin 40mm gun motor carriage T65 is at Aberdeen Proving Ground prior to its evaluation by the Antiaircraft Artillery Board.

Combat experience with the multiple gun motor carriages M15 and M15A1 based on the half-track chassis was very favorable. As a result, the Ordnance Committee in November 1943 recommended that a project be initiated to develop a multiple gun mount consisting of a 40mm automatic gun and two .50 caliber machine guns. It also recommended that this mount be installed on the chassis of the twin 40mm gun motor carriage T65E1. This action was approved in December and the new mount and vehicle were assigned the designations combination gun mount T98 and the combination gun motor carriage T81 respectively. The mount was to be equipped with the computing sight T63 which was a modified version of the computing sight T41. The final version of the mount was power operated in azimuth and elevation and was controlled by the T14 drive controller.

The 40mm gun M1 and the two .50 caliber machine guns were mounted in an open top turret with an armor shield on the tipping parts. The mount had an elevation range of +90 to –5 degrees and a 360 degree traverse. While the development program was in progress, the twin 40mm gun motor carriage M19 was standardized. Since this vehicle filled the requirement for which the T81 was intended, the project was terminated on 30 November 1944.

In May 1942, the Army Ground Forces approved the requirement of the Antiaircraft Artillery Board for a new twin 40mm gun motor carriage. Initially, the chassis of the 3 inch gun motor carriage M5 was considered for the new self-propelled mount. However, this vehicle was not readily available and interest shifted to the chassis being developed for the 4.5 inch gun motor carriage T16 and the 155mm howitzer motor carriage T64. As mentioned previously, this design was based on the light tank M5 with the twin engine power plant relocated to just behind the drivers' compartment. The suspension of the lengthened chassis had three bogies per side and the rear provided a platform for the gun mount. Designated as the twin 40mm gun motor carriage T65, two pilots were approved for construction. The first T65 pilot was completed at the Cadillac Motor Car Division of General Motors Corporation in early 1943. It was shipped first to Aberdeen Proving Ground for a short test and then to the Antiaircraft Artillery Board at Camp Davis, North Carolina. Several changes were recommended as a result of the test program including the use of an M7 computing sight in a new pilot.

At the right, the twin 40mm guns on the T65 are at maximum elevation.

The T65 was manned by a crew of six and had a combat weight of about 38,000 pounds. The two M1 40mm guns were installed in the T12 mount with a full 360 degree traverse and an elevation range of +90 to –5 degrees. The mount was power operated in both traverse and elevation. The four man gun crew, consisting of two gunners and two loaders, rode on the mount and the driver and assistant driver occupied their usual positions in the front hull. The sloped front hull armor was $\frac{5}{8}$ inches thick. The hull sides and rear were $\frac{1}{2}$ and $\frac{3}{8}$ inches thick respectively. The gun mount shields were were $\frac{1}{2}$ inch thick in front and $\frac{1}{4}$ inch thick on the sides and rear. A total of 336 rounds were carried for the 40mm guns. There was no secondary armament on the T65 except for the personal weapons of the crew.

A pilot companion vehicle was completed at the same time as the first T65. Designated as the cargo carrier T23, it was intended to carry an additional supply of ammunition. The T23 utilized the same chassis as the T65 and was similar to the cargo carrier T22 used with the 4.5 inch gun motor carriage T16 and the 155mm howitzer motor carriage T64.

On 25 May 1943, OCM 20583 approved the procurement of a pilot based on the lengthened chassis of the light tank T24. Designated as the twin 40mm gun motor carriage T65E1, the new pilot was completed at Cadillac in early 1944 and shipped to the Antiaircraft Artillery Board after preliminary tests at Aberdeen Proving Ground. The companion vehicle also was redesigned to use the lengthened T24 chassis and was redesignated as the cargo carrier T23E1.

After evaluation by the Antiaircraft Artillery Board, the Army Ground Forces approved the recommendation that the T65E1 be standardized after minor modifications. On 14 June 1944, OCM 24133 approved the standardization of the new vehicle now designated as the twin 40mm gun motor carriage M19.

The twin 40mm gun motor carriage M19 appears below and at the right as originally standardized. Unlike the T65E1 pilot vehicle, the radio antenna has been shifted from the fixed mount on the differential cover plate to a flexible mount on the upper hull front.

The tests by the Antiaircraft Artillery Board resulted in the recommendation that the requirement for the cargo carrier T23E1 be cancelled and that it be replaced by an ammunition trailer towed by the gun motor carriage. As a result, the project for the T23E1 was terminated and the one-ton cargo trailer was modified to carry 320 rounds of 40mm ammunition. Standardized as the ammuntion trailer M28, it was to be issued on the basis of one trailer for each M19 gun motor carriage.

As standardized, the M19 had a combat weight of about 39,000 pounds. With the power plant located just behind the drivers' compartment, the rear of the chassis was free for the installation of the twin 40mm automatic gun mount M4 just above a stowage compartment. The diameter of the gun mount was 85 inches. The two 40mm guns were now designated as the 40mm dual automatic gun M2. The 40mm rounds were inserted into the automatic loader of each gun using four round clips. Each automatic loader had a seven round capacity. The dual gun had a maximum firing rate of 240 rounds per minute (120 rounds per tube) in short bursts. The empty cartridge cases were discharged to the ground through the shell chute located at the front of the gun mount. A total of 352 40mm rounds were stowed on the gun motor carriage. With the 320 rounds in the M28 trailer, 672 40mm rounds were available.

As on the M24 tank, duplicate controls were provided for the driver and assistant driver. An SCR 510 or an AN/VRC-5 radio was shock mounted in the front hull for use by the assistant driver. Interphone stations were

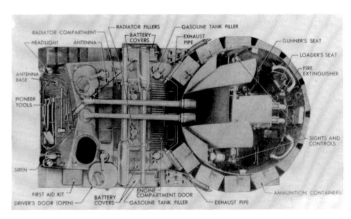

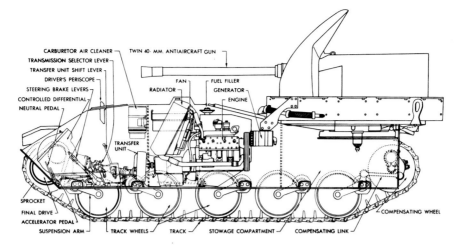

The internal components of the twin 40mm gun motor carriage M19 are visible in the sectional drawing above.

provided for each crew member. On the T65E1, the radio antenna was mounted on the left front hull roof. To eliminate interference with the traversing gun tubes, it was shifted to the cover plate for the controlled differential on the hull front. On the production vehicles, the antenna was relocated to just above the controlled differential cover plate. Here it was provided with a new mount so that it could be raised or lowered by using a crank in the drivers' compartment.

Production of the M19 began at Cadillac during April 1945, but with the end of the war, it was terminated in August after a run of 300 vehicles. All but one of these were delivered without turrets and were completed later after some changes. The cylindrical turret now featured two bulges, one on each side. The smaller bulge was on the left side and the larger on the right. The latter was used to house a second radio set with the antenna mounted on the forward wall of the bulge.

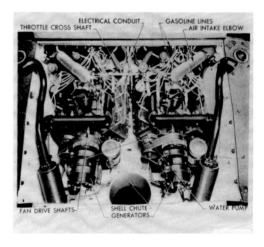

Above at the left, the engine compartment covers can be seen looking aft and, at the right, the covers are removed looking toward the front of the vehicle. Below, the external part of the exhaust system is at the left and the track and suspension system is at the right.

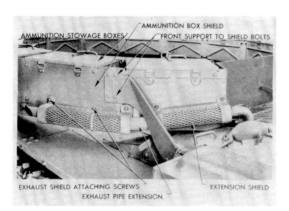

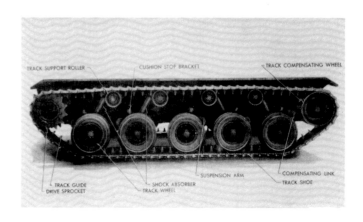

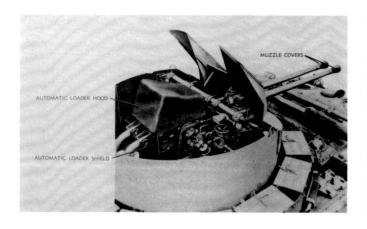

Above are two views of the twin 40mm gun mount M4 on the M19. Components of the M13 computing sight are shown below at the right and the hull bottom of the M19 is at the left. Note the opening for the shell chute.

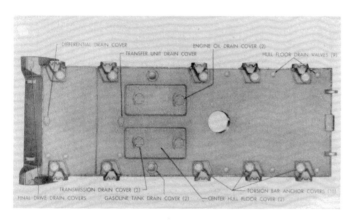

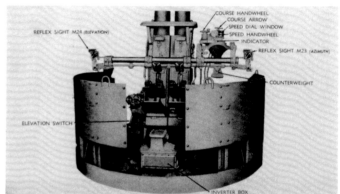

Further modification of the M19 resulted in the vehicle being redesignated as the twin 40mm gun motor carriage M19A1. The modified vehicle was equipped with a 200 ampere, 24 volt auxiliary generator driven by a two cylinder gasoline engine. This unit was installed on the right fender behind the battery box. The location of the auxiliary generator on the right fender required a redesign of the exhaust pipes. On the original M19, an exhaust pipe extended out to each side of the vehicle. The auxiliary generator prevented this so the two pipes were joined and extended out to the left side with a guard installed to prevent personnel from contacting the hot surfaces. The radio equipment on the M19A1 consisted of the AN/VRC-5 in the driving compartment and either the SCR 593 or the AN/GRR-5 in the right turret bulge. Combat loaded, the M19A1 weighed about 41,000 pounds. It continued to serve in the United States Army until after the Korean War.

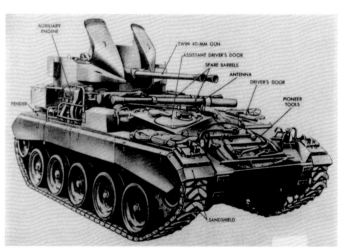

At the right are two views of the twin 40mm gun motor carriage M19A1. Note the auxiliary generator on the left fender.

356

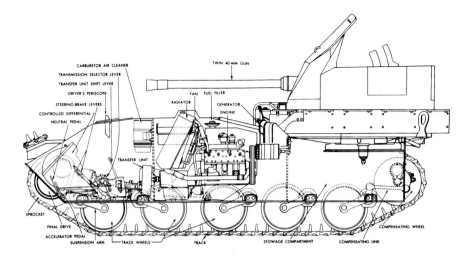

The arrangement of components in the twin 40mm gun motor carriage M19A1 can be seen above and side views of the vehicle are below.

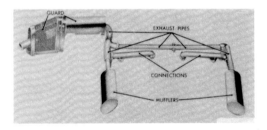

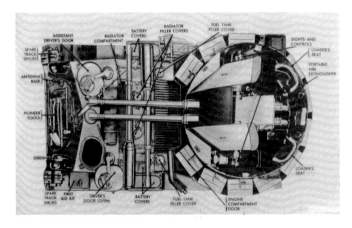

The exhaust system of the M19A1 appears above and a top view of the vehicle is at the upper right. The auxiliary generator installation is below and the AN/VRC-5 radio is at the lower right at the assistant driver's station.

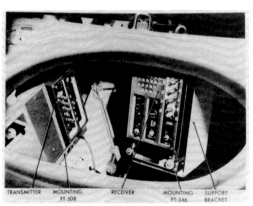

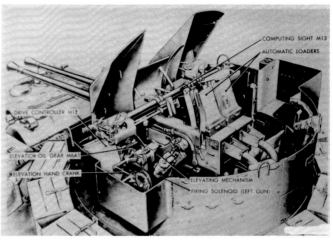

Above is the twin 40mm gun mount M4 as installed on the M19A1. Note the bulges in each side of the turret compared to the original M19. At the lower left, the SCR 593 radio is mounted in the right turret bulge. The direct fire sights and their packing case can be seen at the lower right.

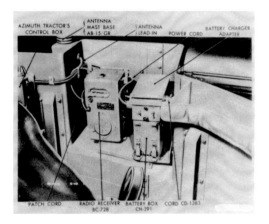

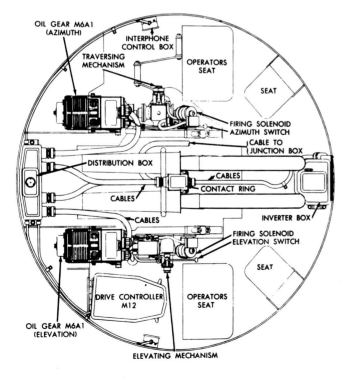

The drawing at the left shows the M16A1 local control system used to power the dual 40mm gun in azimuth and elevation. Below are two types of ammunition fired by the 40mm gun. From top to bottom they are the armor piercing AP-T M81A1 and the high explosive HE-T Mk II.

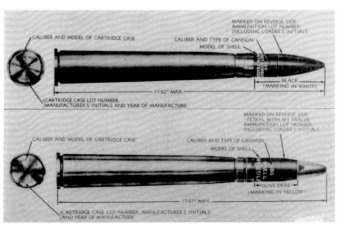

358

The motor carriage for the 75mm gun T22 appears on this page. The 75mm gun in the T18 mount replaced the M4 twin 40mm mount on the M19 chassis.

On 1 February 1945, OCM 26544 recommended the development of a self-propelled mount for the 75mm gun T22. This weapon was intended for use as an antiaircraft gun at short to medium ranges using the new radio proximity fuze. At that time, the 75mm projectile was the smallest that could be fitted with such a fuze. The 75mm gun T22 was installed on the mount T18 with a recoil operated loader-rammer. Using this arrangement, the gun was designed to fire automatically at a rate of 40 to 45 rounds per minute.

The chassis of the twin 40mm gun motor carriage M19 was selected for the installation of the T22 gun and the T18 mount. The mount for the dual 40mm gun was removed and an adapter ring was used to install the T18 mount.

Tests at Aberdeen Proving Ground ran from February 1946 to June 1948. Problems with the loader-rammer made

it extremely difficult to obtain automatic fire and then only when the gun was in a horizontal position. This may have been fortunate since it was determined that the natural frequency of the vehicle suspension was approximately the same as the firing rate of the automatic cannon. Needless to say, this would have resulted in destructive vibration during automatic fire. Further tests with the M19 chassis were discontinued, but the experience was useful during the development of the postwar Skysweeper antiaircraft gun.

The general arrangement of the T18 gun mount installation can be seen in the top view at the right.

Above, the collapsible canvas hull on the light tank M3E4 is fully erected. In the right view, the canvas cover has been removed revealing the tubular support columns and the horizontal metal frames.

FLOTATION AND DEEP WATER FORDING EQUIPMENT

In April 1941, the Office of Scientific Research and Development initiated a study of methods which could be used to land tanks under conditions where it was not possible to use landing craft. This study was carried out under contract by Sparkman & Stephens, Inc. of New York City. An exchange of information with Great Britain led to the development of equipment similar to the Straussler apparatus for application to the light tank M3. OCM 18373, dated 11 June 1942, initiated the project and designated the vehicle under development as the light tank M3E4. The tank hull was waterproofed and the original fenders were replaced by a watertight base which supported a collapsible canvas hull. Stiffened by horizontal metal frames, the canvas hull could be raised to its full height by compressed air in the vertical tubular support columns made of fabric covered fire hose. The canvas hull then formed a boat-like structure around the tank with sufficient displacement for it to float. Propulsion and steering in the water were provided by two 9.7 horsepower fully reversible outboard motors, one of which was mounted on each side at the rear of the vehicle. The M3E4 modification was completed in September 1942 by the Studebaker Corporation. After preliminary tests in Lake Michigan, it was shipped to Fort Knox. The Armored Board did not believe that the flotation device was practical in its present form and the project was cancelled in November 1942.

Below, the light tank M3E4 is afloat at the left and coming ashore at the right. Note the outboard motors used for propulsion and steering.

360

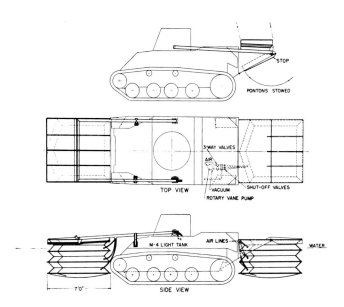

The flotation system using the collapsible fabric pontons proposed for the light tank M5 is sketched at the right. At that time, the tank still carried the M4 designation.

The major requirement was to provide flotation and deep water fording apparatus for the medium tanks, however, development also continued in the application of such equipment to the light vehicles. After the rejection of the M3E4, collapsible fabric pontons were considered for application to the light tank M4, later redesignated as the light tank M5. These pontons were inflatable rubberized fabric bags which were stowed in a metal container at the rear of the tank when not in use. One ponton was intended to support each end of the tank. Before inflation, the forward ponton was swung into position from the rear stowage container. Each ponton consisted of three bag sections to minimize damage from enemy fire.

A later flotation device, consisting of rigid fore and aft pontons, was developed for use with the 76mm gun motor carriage M18. Referred to as the Berg or Ritchie device, it was officially designated as the swimming device T7. For security reasons, this was later abbreviated to just the device T7. On 29 November 1943, the Buick Motor Car Division of General Motors Corporation was requested to construct a set of pontons for installation on the M18, then still designated as the 76mm gun motor carriage T70. The flotation device was tested on 29 December in the boat slip at the River Rouge Plant of the Ford Motor Company. Driven by the action of its tracks in the water, the swimming vehicle reached a speed of 4.24 miles/hour and had a turning radius of 74 feet. Four additional sets of flotation equipment for pilot vehicles were authorized on 1 January 1944 and the first, incorporating a mechanical float

release, was demonstrated on 15 February. Other new features such as improved rudders, running lights, fording stacks, splash shields, and muzzle blast reinforcements were evaluated on pilots 2, 3, and 4. The latter two also were fitted with elevation gyrostabilizers for the 76mm gun. On 16 March 1944, OCM 23206 authorized the procurement of 250 T7 conversion kits.

The combat weight of the M18 with the T7 device was 47,700 pounds. With the gyrostabilizer, the gun could be effectively fired while afloat, but the traverse was limited to 305 degrees by the fording stacks. During operations, the driver and the assistant driver were provided with underwater breathing equipment for emergency use.

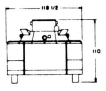

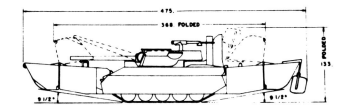

The dimensions of the 76mm gun motor carriage M18 fitted with the T7 device appear in the drawing at the right. Below is a model of the M18 with the proposed flotation device during the design study. The M18 with the T7 device installed is at the lower right.

361

Above, the 76mm gun motor carriage M18 with the T7 device is shown during the test program. Below, details can be seen of the front (left) and rear (right) pontons. The rudders are raised to prevent damage during launching.

Below, the M18 fitted with the T7 device is afloat. In the right view, the gun is firing.

The T7 device also was installed on the 105mm howitzer motor carriage T88 as shown in these photographs from Aberdeen dated 4 May 1945. In the views below, the rudders are lowered in the operating position and raised to prevent damage when on land.

The light tank M5A1 above has been fitted with deep water fording equipment and modified for the installation of a swimming device. Note the LVT type grousers attached to the tracks for propulsion in the water.

On 8 March 1944, the Cadillac Motor Car Division was requested to design swimming apparatus for the light tanks M5A1 and M24. The major effort was devoted to the M24 with design work beginning in July. The first pilot flotation apparatus for the M24 was ready for test on 30 October. The new design was evaluated at Aberdeen and Fort Pierce, Florida. Some problems were noted in the steering mechanism and in the float release system. The equipment was returned to Cadillac for modifications which were completed on 14 February 1945. The construction of a second pilot set of flotation gear for the M24 was started in December 1944 and was completed during the Spring of 1945. To facilitate the assembly of the flotation equipment on the M24, float adapters were incorporated into the production tanks. The rear adapters were introduced at Cadillac on M24 serial number 713. The front adapters were included at serial number 1101. At Massey Harris, both adapters were installed starting with tank number 250.

With the flotation equipment added, the combat weight of the light tank M24 reached 54,500 pounds. The swimming device alone weighed about 14,000 pounds. The track propulsion gave a maximum speed of 5.2 miles/hour in still water with a minimum turning radius of about 60 feet. Special 28½ inch long grousers could be attached to the T72E1 tracks to reduce the ground pressure and improve the performance in the water. These grousers provided a track similar to that on the LVTs. The fording stacks on the rear deck of the tank limited the turret traverse to 310 degrees.

The light tank M24 with the swimming device installed appears in these photographs from Aberdeen Proving Ground on 28 November 1944. Note the jettison fuel tanks added to increase the cruising range.

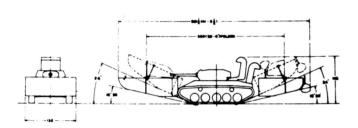

Above, the swimming device on the light tank M24 can be seen with the rudders in the folded position. They are extended for water operation at the top right. At the right is a view of the 24 inch LVT type grousers attached to the tracks for water propulsion. The dimensions of the light tank M24 with the swimming device are shown in the drawing below.

When the landing craft could bring the vehicles close to the beach, swimming ability was not required. Under these conditions, the vehicles were waterproofed and equipped for deep water fording. Fording kits were developed for all of the vehicles that might be expected to participate in amphibious landings. Among the light vehicles, such kits were available for the light tanks M3A1, M3A3, M5, M5A1, and M24 as well as the 76mm gun motor carriage M18, the 105mm howitzer motor carriage M37, and the 155mm howitzer motor carriage M41. Openings in the vehicles were closed with special fittings and sealed using waterproofing compounds. Stacks were installed for the engine air intake and exhaust. Many of the standard deep water fording modifications also were applied to the vehicles fitted with the swimming devices.

At the right are two photographs of the deep water fording gear pilot for the light tank M3. This particular vehicle is a strange combination. Note the turret from the light tank M2A4 fitted with the M23 combination gun mount.

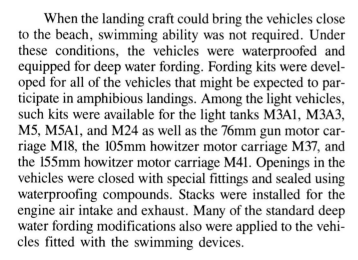

Above and at the left are views of a British light tank M3A1 equipped with deep water fording gear. Stacks are fitted for both the engine cooling air intake and the exhaust. All openings below the turret top have been sealed.

REAR EXHAUST STACK (S)
UPPER ATTACHING STRAP (K)
SASH CORDS
STOWAGE BOX FOLDED FORWARD
LATCHES
REAR EXHAUST ADAPTER (M)
EXHAUST ADAPTER PAN (P)
TOP ATTACHING PLATE (J)

At the right, the light tank M3A3 is prepared for deep water fording according to U.S. specifications. Note that the engine cooling air intake is sealed. This limited the operating time to about 15 minutes and the cover had to be removed immediately after landing. Below, the British M3A3s have a separate stack for the engine cooling air intake and were not subject to the same limitation.

Above, the light tank M5 has the U.S. deep water fording kit installed. Note the single exhaust stack and the engine cooling air intake is sealed limiting its time of operation.

The light tanks M5A1 above and at the right are prepared for deep water fording using the U.S. kit. Note the sealed engine cooling air intake. Lines connected to the sealed cover and the exhaust stack allowed them to be jettisoned immediately after landing.

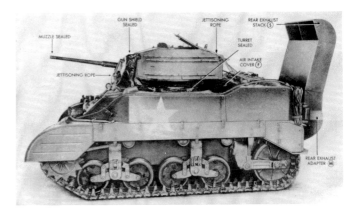

The two views below show the light tank M24 with the deep water fording kit installed. This kit featured separate stacks for the engine cooling air and the exhaust.

Above, the pilot recovery vehicle T6E1 appears as originally completed with the .30 caliber bow machine gun and the 81mm mortar. The boom and anchor spades are in the travel position.

RECOVERY AND ENGINEER VEHICLES

Most of the tank recovery vehicles employed by the United States Army during World War II were based on the medium tank. However, in early 1943, a project was initiated to produce a recovery vehicle using the chassis of the light tank. Designated as the tank recovery vehicle T6, it was based on the light tank M5A1. On 11 August 1943, a project was started to use the light tank T24 as the basis for the new light recovery vehicle. OCM 21824, dated 14 October 1943, approved this development and it was designated as the tank recovery vehicle T6E1. Subsequently, the project for the T6 based on the light tank M5A1 was terminated.

The T6E1 used the standard T24 (later M24) light tank chassis modified for use as a recovery vehicle. The turret and ammunition racks were removed and replaced by an irregular hexagonal fixed turret with a ring mount on top for a .50 caliber machine gun. As originally designed, an 81mm mortar was installed on the front hull to provide smoke screens and the .30 caliber bow machine gun was retained for use by the assistant driver. An A frame boom

Additional details of the pilot recovery vehicle T6E1 can be seen in the views below and at the right.

of fabricated steel construction was attached to the front hull. It was folded to the rear for travel and raised over the front of the vehicle for operations. A 60,000 pound winch was installed on the hull floor forward of the turret center. The T6E1 had a combat weight of about 41,000 pounds and it was manned by a crew of four.

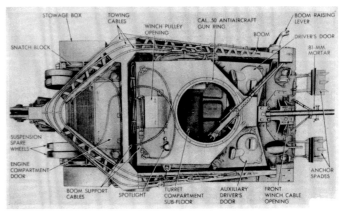

Above, the turret compartment of the recovery vehicle T6E1 is shown looking forward (left) and to the rear (right). After the 81mm mortar was eliminated, the removal of the ammunition provided additional space in the turret. Below, the T6E1 is lifting the turret off of a light tank M24 during its evaluation at Fort Knox.

The first pilot T6E1 was completed by the Cadillac Motor Car Division on 5 September 1944 and shipped to the Armored Board for tests which were concluded on 30 November. As a result of these tests, the final drive gear reduction was increased from 2.57:1 to 2.94:1, the winch spades and tow bar arrangement were modified, and the 81mm smoke mortar and bow machine gun were eliminated. The T6E1 pilot was shipped to the American Car & Foundry Company on 2 December 1944 for these modifications. However, with the end of the war in August 1945, the T6E1 did not enter production. Other vehicles were modified in the field for use in the recovery role. For example, the LVT(2) was fitted with a winch and a hoist for such operations in the Pacific during 1942.

The T6E1 at the left is towing a light tank M24. The dimensions of the T6E1 are in the sketch below and, at the lower left, the drawing shows a recovery vehicle improvised from an LVT(A)(2).

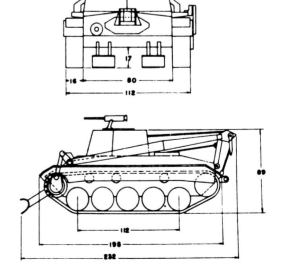

369

Although poor in quality, the view at the top left shows the LVT(A)(1) equipped with a dozer blade. This installation reduced the water speed of the vehicle by only ½ knot. At the top right is the light tank M24 fitted with two T95 rocket launchers using the Navy 4.5 inch barrage rocket.

The LVT(A)(1) was equipped with a dozer blade for engineer operations and, as described earlier, the 7.2 inch rocket launcher T54 was installed in the LVT(4). The M24 light tank also was equipped with two T95 4.5 inch rocket launchers. To provide earth moving capability, a bulldozer was installed on the M24. Designated as the T4, it was a modified version of the M1 bulldozer developed for the Sherman. Later, an improved design was developed and standardized as the M4 bulldozer. Unlike the T4, it did not require attachment to the tank's suspension system.

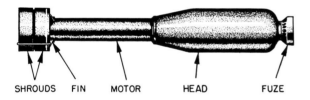

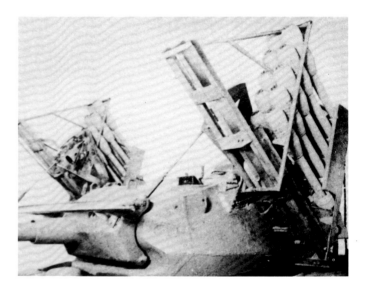

Above is a sketch of the Navy 4.5 inch barrage rocket and the installation of the T95 launcher for this rocket on the light tank M24 can be seen at the right. Below are two views of the T4 dozer mounted on the light tank M24.

Additional views of the T4 dozer installation on the light tank M24 are above. At the right is the later M4 dozer mounted on the M24. Note the lack of any connection to the suspension system.

Although later mine clearance equipment was adapted to the medium tank, the early mine exploder T2 was tested using the light tank M3. The T2 was a drag weight type exploder suspended from a boom structure on the front of the tank. The six drag weights totaled 4410 pounds. Tests at Aberdeen Proving Ground during the Summer of 1942 showed that the T2 was relatively ineffective and it was dropped in favor of improved designs used with the medium tank. Some components of the early roller type mine exploders were tested using the light tank.

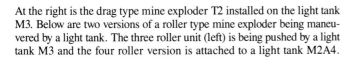

At the right is the drag type mine exploder T2 installed on the light tank M3. Below are two versions of a roller type mine exploder being maneuvered by a light tank. The three roller unit (left) is being pushed by a light tank M3 and the four roller version is attached to a light tank M2A4.

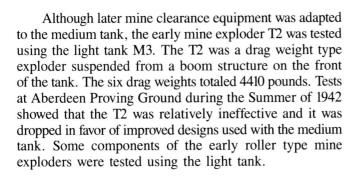

371

Above, a light tank M3A1 is firing a flame thrower installed in the bow machine gun mount. This photograph was taken on New Caledonia and dated 10 October 1943. The flame gun is obviously using unthickened fuel.

FLAME THROWER VEHICLES

The fighting on Guadalcanal in late 1942 and early 1943 emphasized the need for a mechanized flame thrower protected by armor. Such a vehicle would allow the flame thrower to be brought within effective range of the heavily fortified enemy bunkers. After the battle was over, there was considerable experimentation among the troops to adapt the portable M1A1 flame thrower to a tank mount. Several efforts were made to modify the flame gun so that it could replace the .30 caliber machine gun in the bow mount of the light tank. The 3rd Marine Division cut 13½ inches off of the machine gun barrel so that it could be easily withdrawn and replaced by the modified flame gun. A rack was fitted inside the tank for either the flame gun or the machine gun when not in use. Two containers for flame gun fuel were installed and plans were made to provide two flame thrower tanks in each light tank platoon. The Army also experimented with replacing the bow machine gun with the portable flame thrower. During October 1943, such an installation was demonstrated on New Caledonia using a light tank M3A1.

Either a flame gun or a .30 caliber machine gun could be fired from the bow mount of this light tank M3A1. The bow gunner is removing the machine gun in the right view. The flame gun is installed in the left photograph.

Above, the light tank M3A1 is firing unthickened fuel from its bow mount flame gun. Note the pierced plank landing mat sections added to the front hull. This was intended to prevent the Japanese magnetic mines from sticking to the armor. A closeup view of the flame gun installation appears at the right. Both photographs from New Caledonia were dated 10 October 1943.

Despite the efforts of the troops to modify it for use in a vehicle mount, the portable M1A1 flame thrower was not suitable for such an application. Frequently, the fuel failed to ignite and the vibration of the tank damaged the flame gun components. However, these improvised flame thrower installations remained in use until something better could be provided.

Below, another improvised installation attached the flame gun to the .30 caliber bow machine gun so that either weapon could be used without the delay required for a change. These photographs were taken on New Caledonia on 15 March 1944.

Above is the Satan flame thrower tank with the British Ronson flame thrower installed in the light tank M3A1 turret. The right photograph shows the turret at its maximum right traverse.

On 3 February 1944, the British Ronson flame thrower was introduced to the United States Army in Hawaii. Designed for vehicle installation, it was mounted in an LVT for the demonstration. After a conference on 4 February, the 43rd Chemical Laboratory Company was assigned the task of mounting the Ronson in a medium tank. Unfortunately, no suitable medium tanks were available at that time. However, the M3 series light tanks were then being replaced by the newer M5 and thus they were readily available for conversion. The project was then changed to use the light tank by replacing the 37mm gun in the turret with the flame gun. The .30 caliber coaxial machine gun was retained. The crew was reduced to two consisting of the driver and the gunner who also was the tank commander. Four tanks of flame gun fuel were installed in the hull and the cylinder of carbon dioxide used to pressurize the system was fitted into the right sponson. Since there was no assistant driver, the .30 caliber bow machine gun was eliminated. The flame gun was installed in the turret and fitted with a shroud which resembled the 75mm howitzer. Dubbed the Satan, the new main armament flame thrower tank was demonstrated on 15 April 1944. The Marine Corps was particularly interested and requested that 24 M3A1 light tanks be converted to flame tanks in time for the invasion of the Marianas. This request was approved and by 17 May,

the 24 tanks had been rearmed with the flame thrower, test fired, waterproofed, and loaded aboard the ships bound for the Marianas. It would have been preferable to have medium tanks, but, as noted before, none were available for conversion in time to meet the invasion schedule.

The Satan flame thrower tanks had a capacity of 170 gallons of fuel for the flame gun which provided a two minute duration of fire. The operating pressure was 180 to 250 psi and the effective range with napalm thickened fuel was 60 to 80 yards. The turret basket and power traverse system were removed. The only manual turret traverse mechanism available limited the traverse range to about 90 degrees, 10 degrees left and 80 degrees right of center, and there was no time for a redesign. The elevation range of the flame gun was +18 to –15 degrees. The gun mount was modified to permit some free traverse and elevation. It was not possible to obtain armor for the flame gun shrouds so steel pipe was used with an outside diameter of 6⅝ inches and a ½ inch thick wall. The periscope assembly was shifted from the left side of the turret roof to the center line of the flame gun. The seat for the gunner was adapted from an original turret seat and located between the upper two flame fuel tanks directly behind the flame gun and periscope. A piece of one inch thick armor was bolted over the port for the bow machine gun.

Below are exterior and interior views of the flame thrower installation in the Satan turret. Note the steel pipe used to provide a shroud for the flame gun.

The Satan flame thrower tank is in action above on Saipan during July 1944. Below, another Satan is firing during tests of the new flame thrower tank.

The 24 Satan flame thrower tanks were issued, 12 to the 2nd Marine Division and 12 to the 4th Marine Division. On 17 June 1944 (D+2), they were landed on Saipan and were employed continuously until 13 July. On 24 July, they took part in the assault on Tinian.

Below are two additional views of the Satan in action on Saipan during July 1944.

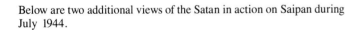

At the right is the Navy mark I flame thrower. The large size of this unit is obvious.

As a result of the lessons learned at Tarawa, The Navy Bureau of Ordnance developed a heavy duty flame thrower with a range of over 100 yards. Originally, it was intended to mount these flame throwers in landing craft so that they could sweep and neutralize a beach to a depth of 100 yards. However, because of their weight of over three tons, they were considered too heavy for amphibious operations. Designated as the Navy mark I flame thrower, five of the units were shipped to the 43rd Chemical Laboratory Company in Hawaii. After examination, it was obvious that they could not be installed in a tank. On 3 June 1944, three of the mark I flame throwers were assigned to the 1st Marine Division on Guadalcanal. Here, despite their weight, they were mounted in LVTs for use during the invasion of Peleliu. The mark I had a fuel capacity of 200 gallons and a firing duration of 74 seconds.

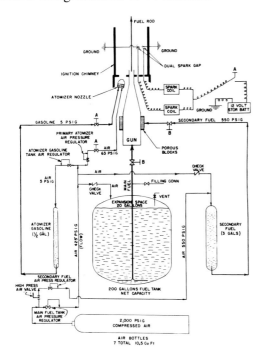

Before sailing for Peleliu, three additional mark I flame throwers were received and taken aboard the transports. After the initial landing, they were installed in LVT(4)s and served with the first three units throughout the battle. However, because of the thin armor and open tops on the LVTs, they were vulnerable to enemy fire.

In preparation for the invasion of Yap, the XXIV Corps requested the installation of the Ronson flame thrower in the turret of the LVT(A)(1) amphibian tank. It replaced the 37mm gun in the turret similar to the Satan arrangement. The new amphibian flame tank was completed in Hawaii on 5 August 1944. Subsequently, the Army installed nine more Ronson flame throwers in the turrets of M3A1 light tanks. After the Yap invasion was cancelled, these tanks, as well as the single LVT(A)(1) armed with the Ronson flame thrower, were used during the invasion of Leyte in October 1944.

Above is the schematic diagram of the Navy mark I flame thrower. Below, the mark I is installed in an LVT(4) for operation on Peleliu.

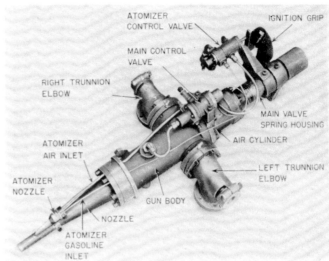

Above, the E7-7 flame thrower turret developed for installation on the light tank M5A1 appears at the left and at the right is the E7 flame gun intended for use in this turret.

The large number of improvised flame throwers was a result of the slow start in developing this equipment in the United States. In 1942, the Ad Hoc Reviewing Committee concluded that there was a definite requirement for portable flame throwers, but that the need for mechanized flame throwers was much less certain. Also, the Armored Force, concerned with the long range tank battles in the Western Desert, showed little interest in the short range mechanized flame thrower which was basically an infantry support weapon. Despite this attitude on the part of the future user, some progress was made. The National Defense Research Committee (NDRC) held a meeting at the Massachusetts Institute of Technology on 3 March 1942. This resulted in several design studies and the construction of three experimental flame throwers. None of these entered production, but they contributed information used in the development of the model "Q" flame thrower produced by the Standard Oil Development Company. The model "Q" was successfully demonstrated in January 1943 as part of a trailer mounted pilot system. After testing and

modification, the improved model "Q" was officially designated as the flame gun E7 and it was adopted as part of the Navy mark I flame thrower. Also in January 1943, the Standard Oil Development Company received a contract to install the E7 flame gun in an M5A1 light tank for service tests. The combination of the fuel system E7 in this installation and the flame gun E7 was designated as the E7-7. The conical M5A1 turret basket was replaced by one with a cylindrical shape to provide additional space for flame fuel tanks and compressed gas cylinders. The hull stowage was modified to allow clearance for the wider base of the new basket.

The three man crew in the E7-7 consisted of the driver and the assistant driver in the front hull and the gunner in the turret. The flame gun replaced the 37mm cannon and the turret periscopes were relocated to accommodate the gunner. The coaxial .30 caliber machine gun was retained on the right side of the flame gun. The hydraulic power traverse equipment was shifted to the turret bustle replacing the radio which was moved to the right sponson

Below are two views of the E7-7 mechanized flame thrower based on the light tank M5A1. Note that the tank retains both its coaxial and bow machine guns.

377

Above, the E7-7 can be seen firing unthickened fuel (left) and fuel thickened with napalm (right). Note the increased range in the latter photograph.

for use by the assistant driver. The .30 caliber bow machine gun was retained also for use by the assistant driver. The power operated turret had a 360 degree traverse and the elevation range of the flame gun was from +30 to –10 degrees. The shroud installed around the flame gun had approximately the same silhouette as the 75mm howitzer.

The compressed gas propellant for the primary flame gun fuel could be air, nitrogen, or inert gas and it was stored in 21 interconnected cylinders at a pressure of 2000 psi. Two interconnected gas cylinders were provided for the expulsion of the secondary fuel. The primary flame gun fuel was a seven per cent napalm-gasoline gel and it was carried in five drums connected in series. The total net capacity of 107 gallons provided a 45 second duration of fire. The three gallon secondary fuel supply was unthickened gasoline used to enhance ignition. The effective range of the E7-7 was sightly over 100 yards.

The prototype E7-7 was tested in November 1943 and three additional pilots were converted. After further tests and some modifications, the four pilots were shipped to the Pacific. By this time, interest in main armament flame throwers had shifted to the use of the medium tank and

no further units were assembled on the light tank chassis. The four E7-7s were assigned to the 13th Armored Group and used in action with the 25th Infantry Division on Luzon during April 1945.

In January 1944, the Chemical Warfare Service requested that a main armament flame thrower be installed in an LVT(A)(1) amphibian tank. The work was carried out by the Lima Locomotive Works with the Standard Oil Development Company acting as engineering consultants. The flame gun was a slightly modified version of the E7 designated as the E7R2. During the test of the prototype, the flame thrower was referred to as the E7-LVT-A1. Later, the fuel system was designated as the E14 and the complete mechanized flame thrower became the E14-7R2.

To arm the LVT(A)(1) with a flame thrower, the 37mm cannon was removed and replaced by the E7R2 flame gun and, as on the E7-7, the flame gun was installed inside a shroud resembling a 75mm howitzer tube. The turret front was widened to permit retention of the .30 caliber coaxial machine gun, but the direct sight telescope was eliminated. The stabilizer and elevation controls were removed and hand grips were attached to the flame gun allowing free

The schematic diagram at the left shows the flow plan of the E7-7 flame thrower. Below, the E7-7 flame thrower tanks of the 13th Armored Group are on Luzon in the Philippine Islands on 3 August 1945.

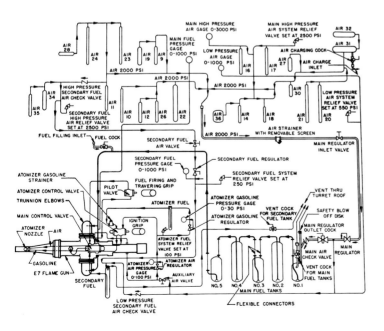

378

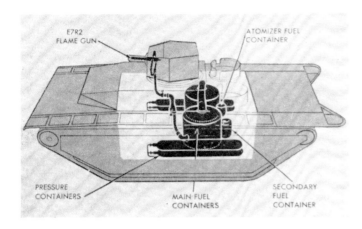

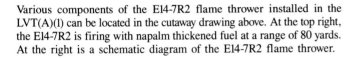

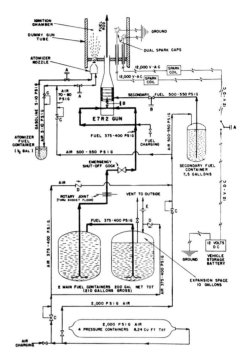

Various components of the E14-7R2 flame thrower installed in the LVT(A)(1) can be located in the cutaway drawing above. At the top right, the E14-7R2 is firing with napalm thickened fuel at a range of 80 yards. At the right is a schematic diagram of the E14-7R2 flame thrower.

movement in elevation from +30 to –10 degrees. The power operated turret was controlled by a foot pedal, but mechanical stops were installed limiting the traverse to 240 degrees. This was to prevent the flame gun from firing over the heads of the gunners in the two machine gun mounts behind the turret.

The E14 fuel and pressure system was installed in the hull. It consisted of four interconnected gas propellant bottles at a pressure of 2000 psi and two main fuel containers with a total net capacity of 200 gallons. The main flame gun fuel was gasoline thickened by 6 to 8 per cent napalm. A 7.5 gallon tank of gasoline was provided as secondary fuel to enhance ignition. With no wind and 20 degrees elevation, the maximum range was 105 yards using a ½ inch diameter nozzle. With a ¾ inch diameter nozzle, the maximum range under these conditions increased to 125 yards.

As originally assembled with full combat stowage, the E14-7R2 was somewhat overweight and bow-heavy when in the water. However, this problem was corrected by reducing the weight of the flame thrower and shifting the location of the pressure vessels down and to the rear. The full six man crew was carried with two men in the turret and four in the hull.

Ten of the E14-7R2s were completed, but World War II ended before they could be used in combat.

Another experimental project was initiated in January 1943 under contract with C. F. Braun & Company. The objective of this program was to develop a large fuel capacity flame thrower with a range of about 200 yards that could be easily installed as a self-contained unit. Designated as the E8 flame thrower, it was designed to fit in a modified M5A1 light tank. The tank was modified by

removing the turret and fitting a fireproof bulkhead just behind the drivers' seats. The engine compartment bulkhead was retained and the hull roof was removed between the two bulkheads leaving an open top compartment in the middle of the vehicle. Around this compartment a superstructure was installed that was wider and almost as high as the original turret. The components of the new flame thrower were attached to a roof installed on the superstructure, so that the complete assembly could be removed or replaced as a unit. The flame gun was mounted in a small turret at the front of the superstructure with the traverse limited to 180 degrees (90 degrees to the left or right of front center). The elevation range was from +25 to –7 degrees. The flame gun was controlled by a single vertical lever which moved it in traverse when pushed to the side. The elevation was controlled by pushing the lever forward or backward. Two bottles for the flame gun fuel were connected in series and mounted vertically in the front of the flame thrower compartment. They had a total fuel capacity of 240 gallons. A prototype of the E8 flame thrower was constructed and demonstrated at Edgewood Arsenal during the Summer of 1944. Although it operated satisfactorily, the M5A1 carrier vehicle was obsolescent and further development work was terminated.

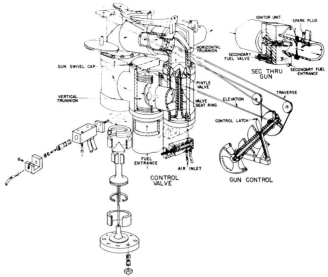

Above is the E9 flame thrower with its large fuel trailer attached to a light tank M5A1. The system of pulleys and cables used to aim the flame gun can be seen in the diagram at the right.

In April 1943, Standard Oil Company of Indiana received a contract to develop a new flame thrower, also for use with the light tank M5A1. The objective of the program was to produce a unit which would have a large fuel capacity, a maximum range of about 200 yards, and would not reduce the standard firepower of the M5A1 tank.

To achieve these objectives, the E9 flame thrower was designed to locate all components except for the flame gun in a two wheel trailer approximately the same height and width as the M5A1 light tank. About 800 gallons of fuel for the flame gun were carried in a 1200 gallon armor steel bottle in the trailer. The additional space in the bottle served as an air cushion. Two air compressors supplied 800 psi air which was stored in the bottle above the fuel. Fully loaded, the trailer weighed about 12 tons. It was attached to the tank through a ten inch diameter ball and socket joint which allowed the trailer to turn through an angle of 105 degrees each way from the center line. The fuel passed through the ball and socket joint and the trailer could be jettisoned in an emergency. Special valves prevented loss of fuel when the trailer was disconnected.

The flame gun was mounted on the front of the tank hull and could be traversed 60 degrees to the left or right of center. The elevation range was from +30 to –15 degrees and all movement in both elevation and traverse was controlled by a system of pulleys and cables. The duplex flame gun consisted of two separate systems with two different nozzles sizes mounted in parallel. One had a ¾ inch diameter nozzle and the other was ¼ inch in diameter. They could not be fired at the same time.

Tests on the E9 were never completed. For the actual firing trials, a batch of napalm thickened gasoline was prepared in the fuel bottle and pressurized to 500 psi. A compressor failure occurred and shortly thereafter the fuel bottle exploded destroying the trailer and causing fatal injuries to the personnel. The project was terminated shortly thereafter.

Efforts to develop a mechanized flame thrower on the chassis of a light armored vehicle continued after World War II. Two pilot vehicles were converted from M39 armored utility vehicles at Detroit Arsenal and shipped to Aberdeen Proving Ground for evaluation. Designated as the self-propelled flame thrower T65, they were armed with the Canadian Iroquois flame thrower in the front hull. The flame gun could be turned 30 degrees to the right or left of center and elevated from +25 to –15 degrees. A .50 caliber machine gun was installed on the vision cupola mount on top of the vehicle. The T65 was tested at Aberdeen from 17 September to 27 October 1952 and then transferred to Fort Knox. The ½ inch thick armor of the T65 would have made it extremely vulnerable to enemy fire and no further vehicles were converted.

Below, the view at the left shows the self-propelled flame thrower T65 based on the armored utility vehicle M39. The dimensions of this vehicle are indicated on the drawing at the right.

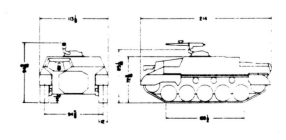

Above, the cargo carrier T1 appears at the left and the cargo carrier T1E1 is at the right. The T1E1 is being used as a camera vehicle during a test program.

TRACKED CARRIERS, PRIME MOVERS, COMMAND AND RECONNAISSANCE VEHICLES

The first examples of the American light tank chassis being used as cargo carriers were the T1 and T1E1 converted from the light tanks T1 and T1E1 respectively. Later, the cargo carriers T2 and T5 also were based upon light tank components. This practice continued during World War II with the development of both light and medium cargo carriers as companion vehicles for self-propelled artillery. Among the light vehicles, the cargo carriers T22 and T23 used the same chassis as their artillery motor carriages, both of which were based upon the light tank M5.

The cargo carriers T22 and T23 had a combat weight of about 38,500 pounds. As mentioned in a previous section, the T22 was intended to be the companion vehicle for the 4.5 inch gun motor carriage T16 or the 155mm howitzer motor carriage T64. The T23 was to accompany the twin 40mm gun motor carriage T65. The cargo carriers utilized the same arrangement as the motor carriages with the twin Cadillac engines installed just behind the drivers' compartment. They also used the modified light tank suspension with three bogies per side. A ring mount for a .50 caliber machine gun was installed above the assistant driver's hatch. This was the only armament on the vehicle except for the individual weapons of the five man crew. The armor protection was $\frac{5}{8}$ inches thick in front, $\frac{1}{2}$ inch thick on the sides, and $\frac{1}{4}$ inch thick on the rear. The ammunition stowage racks in the T22 were interchangeable allowing it to carry either 112 4.5 inch rounds or 75 155mm rounds depending upon which motor carriage was being serviced. The cargo carrier T23 had stowage space for 960 rounds of 40mm ammunition.

Below, the pilot cargo carrier T22 is under test by the Armored Force at Fort Knox. The cargo carrier T23 was similar, but it provided stowage for 40mm ammunition.

The rear of the cargo carrier T22 is shown above with the rear doors open and closed. Below at the right is a dimensional sketch of the T22.

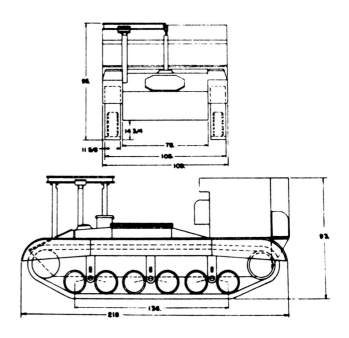

After the redesign of the motor carriages to use the newer chassis based upon the light tank T24, a similar change was made for the cargo carriers. They now became the cargo carriers T22E1 and T23E1. The T22E1 was to be used with the 155mm howitzer motor carriage T64E1 which was standardized later as the M41. The 4.5 inch gun had been rejected by the user and the T16E1 project was terminated. The cargo carrier T23E1 was to be used with the twin 40mm gun motor carriage T65E1, later standardized as the M19. However, the user replaced the companion vehicle with an ammunition trailer towed by the motor carriage itself and the project for the T23E1 cargo carrier was terminated.

With the switch to the chassis based upon the light tank T24, the combat weight of the cargo carriers T22E1 and T23E1 increased to about 40,500 pounds. The armor was ½ inch thick on the front and sides and ¼ inch thick on the rear. The .50 caliber machine gun was retained as the sole armament on the ring mount above the assistant driver's hatch. With the end of the war, the T22E1 was not put into production.

Below is the cargo carrier T22E1 and its dimensions are indicated on the sketch at the right. Compare the latter with the dimensions of the cargo carrier T22 above.

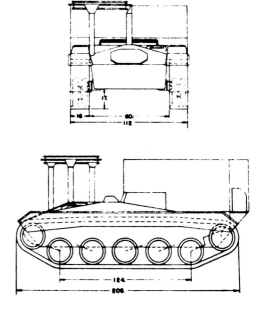

The light tractor T18 appears in these photographs at Aberdeen Proving Ground on 26 March 1943. Note the close resemblance to the light tank M22 (T9E1).

The T9 light airborne tank also was modified for use as a light armored prime mover. Designated as the light tractor T18, it had a loaded weight of 15,500 pounds. The armor varied from a maximum of ½ inch thick on the front and sides to ⅜ inches thick on the rear. The open top vehicle was 167½ inches long, 88½ inches wide, 56 inches high and carried five men including the driver. It had stowage space for 25 rounds of 105mm ammunition when used as a prime mover for the howitzer. Using the same power train as the T9 light tank, the T18 had a maximum road speed of 40 miles/hour and a cruising range of about 200 miles. Converted by Marmon-Herrington, the T18 arrived at Aberdeen Proving Ground during March 1943. However no additional vehicles were produced.

During World War II, light tanks were frequently modified in the field for use as command or reconnaissance vehicles. To evaluate such use, the Army Ground Forces directed in January 1944 that two light tanks M5A1 be converted into reconnaissance vehicles. This conversion consisted of removing the turret, modifying the stowage, and adding a ring mount for a .50 caliber machine gun. Designated as the full-track reconnaissance vehicles

T8 and T8E1, they differed only in the location of the M49C ring mount for the .50 caliber machine gun and the tracks installed. On the T8, the ring mount was located over the right rear of the opening in the hull roof and the vehicle was fitted with the standard 11⅝ inch wide rubber tracks. On the T8E1, the M49C mount was lowered and it was

Below, the T8 and T8E1 reconnaisance vehicles are at the left and right respectively. Note the 16 inch wide Burgess-Norton steel tracks on the T8E1.

The difference in the location of the .50 caliber machine gun mount can be clearly seen above on the T8 (left) and the T8E1 (right). The smoke mortar replaced the ventilator on the light tank between the driver and assistent driver. An additional view of the stowage arrangement on the T8E1 is below at the right.

concentric with the opening in the hull roof. The T8E1 also was fitted with Burgess-Norton 16 inch wide steel tracks. Both the T8 and the T8E1 were equipped with SCR 506 and SCR 528 radios in the left and right sponsons respectively. The combat weights with a crew of six were 28,200 pounds for the T8 and 30,900 pounds for the T8E1. A two inch smoke mortar was installed in the hull roof between the driver and the assistant driver and a rack for ten land mines was attached to the outside of the right sponson.

The T8 and T8E1 were evaluated by the Armored Board and compared to the armored cars M8 and M20 as well as the light tank M5A1. As was expected, the tracked vehicles had superior cross-country performance, but the armored cars were much quieter. None of the vehicles were considered to have sufficient armament. The Armored Board recommended the use of the light tank M24 with its 75mm gun as a reconnaissance vehicle.

At the right is a dimensional sketch of the T8E1 reconnaisance vehicle. Below, the lower silhouette of the T8E1 (right) compared to the T8 (left) is obvious.

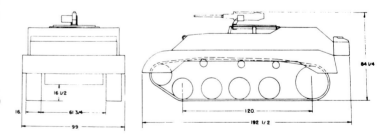

The photographs on this page show the armored utility vehicle T41, serial number 4, at Detroit on 15 November 1944. The vehicle is fully stowed and its sole armament of one .50 caliber machine gun is mounted.

Operations with the 76mm gun motor carriage M18 revealed that its tactical employment was frequently restricted by the limited speed and mobility of the other vehicles in the tank destroyer units. To correct this problem, the Tank Destroyer Board modified an M18 by removing the turret and relocating some components to permit its use as a reconnaissance vehicle or a prime mover for towed antitank guns. Preliminary tests were highly successful and on 7 March 1944, the Army Service Forces authorized the conversion of two M18s for use as prime movers for the 3 inch gun carriage M6. The first of these pilots was completed and shipped to the Tank Destroyer Board for evaluation. However, the second pilot was redesigned to permit easy conversion from a full-track prime mover to a command and reconnaissance vehicle. The first and second

pilots were tentatively designated as the armored utility tractors T41 and T41E1 respectively. Tests showed that the design of the second pilot was far superior and no further consideration was given to the first pilot. The nomenclature was now revised dropping the tractor designation. The second pilot became the armored utility vehicle T41 when fitted with the stowage and necessary equipment for use as a prime mover. When equipped as a command and reconnaissance vehicle, the designation was the armored utility vehicle T41E1.

With the same armor protection as the 76mm gun motor carriage M18, the combat loaded T41 and T41E1 weighed about 36,000 pounds. Both were armed with a .50 caliber machine gun on a ring mount at the front center of the open top crew compartment. The driver and the

The general arrangement of the armored utility vehicle T41 can be seen in the top view of T41, serial number 4, above.

assistant driver rode in their usual positions in the front hull. A low open top superstructure was installed on the center hull behind the driving compartment. The T41 was manned by a crew of ten including the driver and assistant driver. The eight men in the open top compartment rode on two lateral bench type seats. An SCR 610 radio was installed in the right sponson for use by a man facing toward the rear on the forward seat. Stowage space was available for 42 rounds of 3 inch ammunition in the T41.

For its role as a command and reconnaissance vehicle, the T41E1 was provided with an SCR 506 or SCR 608 radio in addition to the SCR 610. An auxiliary generator also was installed to handle the increased electrical load. The crew was reduced to nine men and a 2.36 inch rocket

Above, armored utility vehicle M39, serial number 19, is towing the 3 inch gun carriage M6. Below, an M39 has the 90mm gun T15 on the T14 carriage. Note the misaligned muzzle brake on the long 90mm tube. In this position, it would kick up a lot of dust if fired.

Above, the SCR 506 and SCR 508 radios are in the left and right sponsons respectively of the armored utility vehicle T41E1. In external appearance, the T41E1 was identical to the M39 except for the additional radio antenna.

launcher as well as three antitank mines were carried. Both the T41 and the T41E1 were capable of level road speeds up to 50 miles/hour with a cruising range of 150 miles.

On 26 June 1944, OCM 24262 approved limited procurement of the T41. Approximately 650 vehicles were to be converted from the early production M18 gun motor carriages which had been returned to Buick. Originally, it had been intended to upgrade these vehicles as gun motor carriages by incorporating the latest production features. Subsequently, the number of T41s converted was reduced to 640 and in November 1944, they were standardized as the armored utility vehicle M39. At the request of the European Theater of Operations, ten additional vehicles were converted to the T41E1 configuration for evaluation in the field, but they were never standardized.

The crowded seating arrangement in the armored utility vehicle M39 is obvious in the top view above. An additional photograph of the M39 is below.

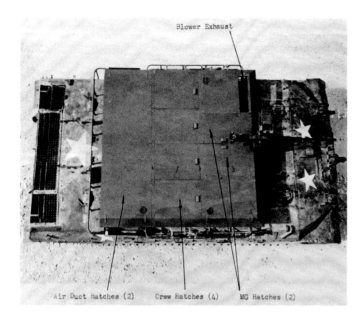

The armored cover on the armored utility vehicle M39 appears above closed (left) and open (right). The many hatchs permitted access to various components and allowed the crew to man the .50 caliber machine gun.

March 1945, reports from Europe indicated a need for the installation of armored covers on the open top vehicles such as the M39 and the T41E1. The Tank Destroyer Board designed such a cover and constructed a mock-up. It was intended to use ⅜ inches thick armor plate mounted eight inches above the open crew compartment. Eight hatches in this cover permitted access to the engine compartment air ducts, the crew compartment, and the .50 caliber machine gun mount. The latter was extended eight inches

to provide clearance above the armor cover. With the end of the war, there was no production of the armor covers for the M39 and the T41E1.

By the end of World War II, the 3 inch and 90mm towed antitank guns were no longer in use. The M39s were then converted for use as personnel carriers or command and reconnaissance vehicles. They served through the Korean War and were declared obsolete by OTCM 36468 on 14 February 1957.

The gunner's position in the M39 with the cover open can be seen below at the left. The drawing at the right shows the configuration of the armored cover.

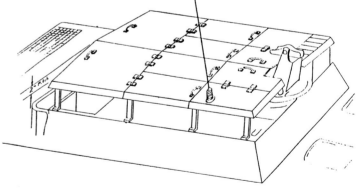

PART IV

LIGHT TANKS IN ACTION

Above at the left, a light tank M3, Stuart I, is being unloaded in the Middle East. This vehicle has the turret with the welded face-hardened armor. At the top right, a British crew looks over a newly arrived Stuart with the riveted turret.

DESERT BATTLES

The first American built light tanks to see action in World War II were manned by British crews in the Western Desert. After the fighting in Greece and Crete during the Spring of 1941, the strength of the British armored force in the Middle East was greatly reduced. Since the number of vehicles available from Britain was strictly limited, it was necessary to locate another source for replacements. Production of the light tank M3 in the United States had begun in March 1941 and it was the only American tank available to meet these requirements. Responding to a British request in May, President Roosevelt directed that shipments of urgently needed materiel to the Middle East begin at once under the new Lend-Lease program. The deliveries began in June and by the end of July had included 84 M3 light tanks which were later designated by the British as the Stuart.

In Britain, the new tanks were received with some misgiving as indicated by the following excerpt from the War Diary of the 9th Queen's Royal Lancers.

"The General (G.O.C. 1st Armoured Division) was shown over one of the American M3s and its disadvantages were pointed out to him. He told the Colonel to send in a report on these tanks at once, which was done. The chief drawbacks are:

1. No power traverse and the floor of the fighting compartment not revolving with the turret.
2. The high ridge which runs from front to rear (drive shaft tunnel) through the centre of the floor of the fighting compartment so that when the turret is traversed the crew have to step over it.
3. The gunner cannot, except with great difficulty, follow round the floor with his gun on the

Below, British troops are receiving instruction on the new Stuarts at the left and one of the new tanks can be seen at the right. Note that both the riveted and welded turrets are represented.

Above, Stuarts of the 4th Armoured Brigade are dispersed during training in the desert. Note that the sponson machine guns have been eliminated. Other British modifications and stowage can be seen in the photographs at the bottom of the page.

turret being traversed, but has to hand over to another member of the crew.

4. The hand traverse being worked by the loader.

5. No periscope, but a series of shuttered windows at intervals round the turret (with no triplex blocks).

6. The driver cannot close down the front shutter, nor the commander the lid of the turret without help. On the other hand, the engine — a radial one — had the reputation of being most reliable."

The history of the same unit expressed a slightly more favorable opinion of the Stuart:

"However, it must be owned that we did the M3 (or "Honey" as it came to be known) a great injustice. It was old-fashioned and uncomfortable, the splutterings of its engine filled the hearer with apprehension, but the little tank hardly ever broke down and later performed miracles of endurance."

Its 37mm gun was no worse than the Crusader's 2-pounder, though, by German standards, both were inadequate."

The British applied a number of modifications to improve the M3. In details they varied from tank to tank, particularly on the early vehicles. Later a standard stowage chart was developed which showed the various changes. These included a support frame for the cupola hatch cover in the open position. This made it easier for the tank commander to close the cover from inside the hatch. Smoke grenade launchers were mounted on the turret and stowage bins were installed on the right front and both rear fenders. An auxiliary fuel tank was attached on the rear hull to extend the tank's cruising range and sandshields were installed for desert operations. Racks for track grousers (also referred to as spuds) were fitted on the outside of the hull. The interior stowage also was modified to British standards including the installation of the Number 19 radio set.

The Stuart I appears on this page showing the various British modifications to the light tank M3 with the welded, face-hardened turret. The external stowage is identified in the charts below. Later stowage charts eliminated the center spud (grouser) leaving 16 per side.

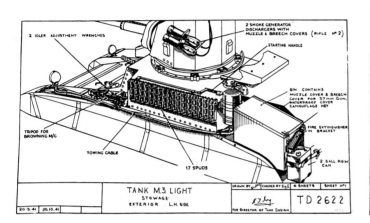
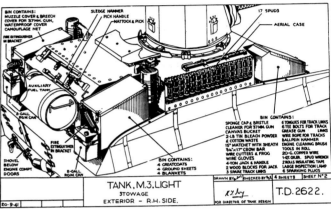
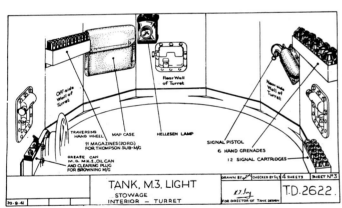
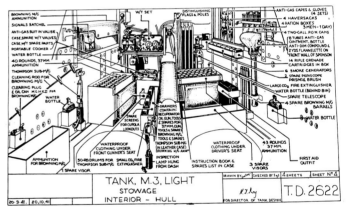

With the sponson machine guns eliminated, a stowage box was installed on the right front fender. Note the support frame for the cupola hatch cover when open. The internal stowage of the British modified vehicle appears in the charts above.

Above and at the left, the 8th King's Royal Irish Hussars of the 4th Armoured Brigade are training with their new Stuarts. These tanks have not been fitted with the frame to support the open cupola hatch.

Although classified by the United States Army as a light tank, the armor on the Stuart was comparable to that of the British cruiser tanks and, as mentioned before, the performance of its 37mm gun was similar to that of the 2 pounder installed in the British vehicles. In fact, with its capped armor piercing projectiles, the 37mm weapon was superior to the 2 pounder for use against the face-hardened armor on some of the German tanks. The Stuart quickly gained a reputation for reliability and usually was referred to as the "Honey" by the British tank crews. Its high speed and rugged suspension were particularly appreciated. The short cruising range and cramped crew space were its major limitations.

As the Stuart became available, it was used to reequip the 4th Armoured Brigade of the British 7th Armoured Division. Despite the numerous modifications required to adapt the Stuart for British service, the 4th Armoured Brigade received its full complement of the new tanks by the end of September 1941. Training of the Brigade with the Stuart was delayed by the rapid initial wear of the rubber block tracks during the trip forward from the railhead. However, it was determined that, after a rapid start, the wear rate stabilized and the tracks remained serviceable.

About 300 Stuarts had arrived in the Middle East by the end of October 1941. On the eve of the Crusader battles in November, the 4th Armoured Brigade was equipped with 165 Stuart tanks. An additional eight were assigned to the headquarters of 30 Corps. Other Stuarts were in the forward reserve and in the base shops.

At the right, Stuart and Grant tanks of the 7th Armoured Division are loaded on railway cars for movement to the front. The two Stuarts have the rounded homogeneous armor turret. The second tank has vision slots in the cupola, but the front one does not. Both vehicles have been fitted with the British smoke launcher.

The first action for the Stuart came late on the second day of the Crusader offensive, 19 November 1941. Operating as part of the 7th Armoured Division, the 4th Armoured Brigade, commanded by Brigadier A. H. Gatehouse, moved toward Gabr Saleh. At about four in the afternoon, they were engaged by Battle Group Stephan from the 5th Panzer Regiment of the 21st Panzer Division. The fight lasted until shortly before dark with 23 Stuarts being put out of action. German records indicate that their losses were two tanks destroyed and six damaged. Despite this inauspicious beginning, the Stuarts provided valuable service through the remainder of the Crusader operation, the German counterattacks, and the lull that followed. By the Spring of 1942, more powerful tanks were arriving in the Middle East. These included the new Grant medium tank armed with the 75mm gun. The Stuart was then returned to its proper role as a fast reconnaisance vehicle. As such, it continued to serve throughout the remainder of the campaign in North Africa.

Above at the left, the M2A2 light tanks of the 192nd Tank Battalion emerge from a smoke screen during the Second Army maneuvers in September 1941, prior to their departure for the Philippines. At the top right, the crew of an M3 on Luzon watches a unit of the 26th Cavalry (Philippine Scouts) operating in the same area.

EARLY OPERATIONS AGAINST THE JAPANESE

The first American manned tanks to fight in World War II were engaged in the defense of the Philippines in December 1941. During that Fall, a major effort was underway to reinforce General Douglas MacArthur's command in the islands. The Army Chief of Staff, General George C. Marshall, directed that the United States Army in the Philippines have the highest priority for the new equipment beginning to come off the production lines. On 8 September, the 194th Tank Battalion embarked from San Francisco arriving in Manila on 26 September. It was followed by the 192nd Tank Battalion which arrived in November. The two battalions were equipped with a combined total of 108 new M3 light tanks and were based at Fort Stotsenburg on Luzon north of Manila. In addition to its 54 tanks, each battalion was provided with 23 half-track vehicles. On 21 November, the two battalions were combined with the 17th Ordnance Company (Armored) to form the Provisional Tank Group under the command of Colonel (later Brigadier General) James R. N. Weaver.

After the attack on Pearl Harbor and the subsequent Japanese landings on Luzon, the Provisional Tank Group moved north to support the United States and Philippine troops and to cover their retreat to the Bataan peninsula. On 21 December, Major (later Lieutenant Colonel) Theodore F. Wickord, commanding the 192nd Tank Battalion, received orders to move the battalion north and to send B Company on ahead for a special mission. During the movement, Captain Donald Hanes, commanding B Company, expected to refuel his tanks at Gerona and again at Bauang. However, fuel was not provided at Gerona and the enemy was rapidly approaching Bauang. The 26th Cavalry (Philippine Scouts) was operating in the area and they had already been under attack by enemy aircraft. When

reports reached General Wainwright that an enemy motorized force was approaching Damortis, he directed Captain Hanes to engage them. Since the company was almost out of gasoline, the available fuel supply was combined to provide enough to fill up a single five tank platoon. Once again, the short cruising range of the light tank M3 was a major disadvantage. Led by Lieutenant Ben R. Morin, the five tanks moved north out of Damortis toward Agoo. Here they ran into elements of the Japanese 4th Tank Regiment becoming the first American troops to engage in tank versus tank action in World War II. The lead M3 left the road to maneuver, but it was hit and set on fire. Lieutenant Morin was wounded and captured along with his crew. The remaining four tanks also were hit by 47mm fire, but they were able to withdraw. Later they were destroyed by enemy aircraft. Despite this tragic start, the 192nd fought skillfully during the remainder of the withdrawal toward Bataan.

The Provisional Tank Group headquarters and the 194th Tank Battalion, commanded by Lieutenant Colonel Ernest B. Miller, had moved north on Christmas Day. The 194th operated to the west of highway 3 with the 192nd to the east. Both battalions fought a series of rearguard actions and were the last troops into the Bataan peninsula. The 192nd crossed the bridge over the Culis river into Bataan during the night of 6-7 January 1942 as the last unit before the bridge was blown.

The losses during the retreat required some reorganization of the battalions. Each company was reduced to ten tanks with three tanks per platoon and one in the company headquarters. During the remainder of the fighting on Bataan, the tank battalions defended the beaches and airfields as well as providing support for the infantry. At about 1830 hours on 8 April 1942, the battalion commanders

At the right is a line of M3 light tanks in Japanese service after the surrender of Bataan. Above, one of the M3s has been recaptured in Manila after the invasion of Luzon in January 1945. The guns have been removed, but it retains the rising sun insignia.

received orders to be prepared to destroy their equipment when they received the code word CRASH. This occurred a few hours later and the Army on Bataan surrendered at 0700 on 9 April 1942.

Some of the captured M3s were taken into service by the Japanese. A few of these were still in use when American forces returned to Luzon in 1945.

Following the Pearl Harbor raid, urgent measures were taken to strengthen the forces in the Pacific. As part of this effort, the 193rd Tank Battalion at Fort Benning, Georgia was reequipped with M3 light tanks and, as described in the Foreword of this book, rushed to Hawaii. Stationed at Schofield Barracks, they reinforced the 11th Tank Company which was the only armor unit in the islands at that time.

At the right is the 2nd Platoon, C Company, 193rd Tank Battalion with their M3 light tanks at Schofield Barracks, Hawaii in early 1942. The soldier at the far left in the photograph is Staff Sergeant (later Colonel) James H. Leach.

At the same time as their attack on the Philippines, the Japanese launched an invasion of Malaya and drove south toward Singapore. Despite the jungle terrain, they made effective use of their tanks to speed the advance. To counter this attack, the British 7th Armoured Brigade in Egypt was equipped with Stuart tanks and embarked for Singapore. The Brigade consisted of the 7th Hussars and the 2nd Royal Tank Regiment. Some evidence indicates that their complement of light tanks included some M2A4s among the M3s. Before the brigade reached its destination, Singapore fell to the Japanese and they were diverted

to Rangoon. With Burma also being overrun by the victorious Japanese, the two regiments fought a series of rearguard battles during the retreat north to India. By early May, the army had reached the Chindwin river and was crossing into India. The 7th Hussars managed to ferry a single tank across the river on a raft, but it was impossible to save any of the remainder. After a final action on 10 May 1942, all of the Stuarts were destroyed to prevent their use by the enemy. The single M3 that crossed into India served later as a command vehicle after its turret was removed.

Above at the left are the Stuarts of the 7th Hussars destroyed and abandoned when they could not cross the Chindwin River. The single M3 that did cross is at the top right after its conversion into the command vehicle "Curse of Scotland".

While the troops held out on Bataan, the Japanese advance expanded rapidly to the south. Rabaul on New Britain was captured on 23 January 1942 and immediately developed into a heavily fortified base. The Netherlands East Indies were lost with the surrender of Java on 9 March. Also in March, the first landings had been made in the Solomon Islands and fighter plane strips were being constructed on Bougainville. On 3 May, a Japanese amphibious force seized Tulagi and established a seaplane base. The Japanese commander at Tulagi then constructed an airfield on Guadalcanal approximately 20 miles away. All of these advances threatened the supply line to the Southwest Pacific.

The policy of the British and American Combined Chiefs of Staff was to defeat Germany first and the major portion of the military resources available were allocated

to that effort. However, Japan was to be contained and Australia and New Zealand were to be protected from invasion. The execution of this policy in the Pacific was assigned to the United States Joint Chiefs of Staff. With the Japanese advance approaching the lines of communication to the Southwest Pacific, the Joint Chiefs of Staff directed on 2 July 1942 that a limited offensive be launched to halt this threat. The objective finally selected for this offensive centered on the Japanese installations on Tulagi and Guadalcanal. The assault force was made up of the 1st Marine Division with reinforcements attached. This included elements of the 1st Marine Tank Battalion equipped with a mixture of M2A4 and M3 light tanks. The

At the right, two M2A4 light tanks are accompanied by one M3 during operations on Guadalcanal. Below, another Marine Corps M2A4 is operating on Guadalcanal during September 1942.

landings began on 7 August at 0800 on Tulagi and 0910 on the north coast of Guadalcanal. The occupation of Tulagi and the nearby islets of Gavutu-Tanambogo was completed by nightfall on 8 August after fierce fighting. However, the battle for Guadalcanal was just beginning. The light tanks supported the infantry after the landings and during the initial operations to expand the bridgehead. On 21 August, a force of Japanese infantrymen attacked the positions of the 2nd Battalion, 1st Marines along the Ilu river. The enemy troops were part of the Ichiki Force which had reached Guadalcanal on 18 August. The Marines held their positions and counterattacked to surround the enemy and drive them back across the river. Just before dark, a platoon of the light tanks crossed the sand bar at the river mouth and destroyed the remainder of the Japanese force.

The light tanks continued to support the Marine infantry, as well as the Army divisions which arrived later, until Guadalcanal was fully secured on 9 February 1943. During this same period, other M3 light tanks, manned by Australian crews, were serving in Papua supporting both Australian and United States forces. Operations in the thick jungle made the tanks vulnerable to ambush and they required close support by the infantry. The thin armor on the light tanks was easily penetrated by the Japanese anti-tank weapons and it was recommended that medium tanks be used in future such operations.

These photographs show the Stuart tanks of the Australian 2/6 Armoured Regiment during the fighting on New Guinea in late December 1942 and early January 1943. The tanks have been fitted with British stowage boxes on the right front and rear fenders. Both welded, face-hardened armor turrets and homogeneous armor turrets can be seen.

398

Below, this Australian Stuart supports the infantry during an attack on Japanese positions at Giropa Point, New Guinea in January 1943. At the right, an Australian Stuart with a round homogeneous armor turret is fording a stream in New Guinea on 19 May 1943.

Guadalcanal also saw the first use in action of the landing vehicle, tracked, LVT. This was the early unarmored LVT(1). However, it was successful beyond all expectations and, as a result, greatly increased emphasis was placed on its future development and production.

At the right, LVT(1)s and an M3A1 (Diesel) light tank are being prepared for use by the 1st Marine Division in the invasion of Guadalcanal. Below, early LVT(1)s are in the water during training exercises.

The light tank M3 at the left above is near Maknassy, Tunisia on 8 April 1943. This tank has the late homogeneous armor turret with vision slots in the cupola. The light tank M3A1 at the top right is being inspected by its German captors. Both tanks belonged to the 1st Armored Division.

NORTH AFRICA, SICILY, AND ITALY

With the landings in North Africa in November 1942, a major role was played once again by the light tanks. The shortage of suitable tank lighters made it difficult to land the larger medium tanks. At Oran, three shallow draft oilers previously used on Lake Maracaibo in Venezuela were modified for use as tank landing ships (LSTs) by installing doors and a landing ramp in the bow. Unfortunately, the exit in the bow of these prototype LSTs was too low to accommodate the M3 medium tank which equipped the medium tank battalions of the 1st and 13th Armored Regiments in the 1st Armored Division. As a result, the light tanks were assigned the task of accompanying the assault troops until port facilities were available to unload the heavier vehicles. The 1st Armored Division was still equipped with the tanks that it had taken to Northern Ireland in early 1942. Thus the light battalions of the 1st and 13th Armored Regiments landed with their M3 and M3A1 light tanks. The 2nd Armored Division and the separate tank battalions that arrived direct from the United States had replaced the earlier vehicles with the new M5 light tanks. Both types performed well during the invasion and easily defeated the obsolete French tanks that tried to oppose them.

As units of the 1st Armored Division moved east toward Tunis, they soon encountered German armor that had been rapidly shifted to North Africa. On 26 November 1942, the 1st Battalion, 1st Armored Regiment, commanded by Lieutenant Colonel John K. Waters, was in position near Chouigui Pass when an enemy force approached from the north. This force included a company from the 190th Panzer Battalion with several Panzerkampfwagen IVs (PzKw IV) armed with the long barreled

7.5cm Kampfwagen Kanone 40 (KwK 40). In addition, there were three or more PzKw IIIs mounting the high powered 5cm KwK 39. Both of these German tanks far outmatched the M3 light tank with its 37mm gun. Company A of the 1st Tank Battalion, commanded by Major Carl Siglin, advanced to engage the enemy force from the southwest in what was to be the first clash between American and German armor in World War II. As the German tanks drove toward Major Siglin's company, they passed by B company, commanded by Major William R. Tuck, which was concealed in hull defilade positions on the reverse slope of a ridge. The impression the powerfully armed German tanks made on the American tank crews is described in the following paragraphs from the book "Armor Command" by Brigadier General Paul Robinett who was then commanding Combat Command B of the 1st Armored Division. This excerpt also quotes several passages from "The Battle of Happy Valley" written by Captain Freeland A. Daubin, Jr. at the Armored School in 1948. The PzKw III and IV were referred to in the American reports as the Mark III and IV.

" The Germans reacted more violently on 26 November, sending a tank force down the Chouigui Pass-Mateur road which Companies A and B were covering. Company B, commanded by Major Tuck, was on the reverse slope covering the road from a distance of 50-100 yards, while Company A was posted on the slope of a hill south of the road. All eyes turned on the new threat while Lieutenant Ray C. Wacker took the tank force under fire with his 75mm assault gun section. He laid a concentration on the target without effect for he had no hollow-charge or special high explosive antitank ammunition. Wacker was taken under fire and ordered back to prevent his destruction. The Germans continued their advance, leading with Mark IV tanks, the first met by American troops in World War II. Major Siglin decided to attack at once and close on the enemy's flank. Company B was to fire on the rear and left of the enemy column. Lieutenant Daubin destroyed an Italian tank as he moved out, but several of Company A's tanks met the same fate as the enemy 'swung their long wicked rifles' around and opened fire. Daubin faced those guns and was shot out of his tank but survived to describe the fight:

'The 37mm gun of the M3 light tank popped and snapped like an angry cap pistol. This frightful engine of destruction had just scuttled into . . . partial defilade . . . The American banged away at the German tank it had singled out as its very own in a column of Mark IV Specials . . . Questing about with his incredibly long, bell snouted, 'souped up' 75mm KwK 40 rifle, the German commander soon spotted his heckler . . . and leisurely commenced closing the 140 yard gap between himself and the light tank, but keeping his thicker, sloping frontal plates turned squarely to the hail of 37mm fire. The crew of the M3 redoubled the serving of their piece. . . . Tracer-tailed armor piercing bolts streaked out of the American's muzzle and bounced like a mashie shot . . . from the plates of the Mark IV. The German shed sparks like a power driven grindstone. In a frenzy of desperation and fading faith in the highly-touted weapon, the M3 crew pumped more than eighteen rounds at the Jerry tank while it came in. Through the scope sight the tracer could be seen to hit and glance straight up. Popcorn balls thrown by Little Bo Peep would have been just as effective. . . . The Mark IV continued to close . . . but a few yards further pulled right and mounted a small hummock completely destroying the slight defilade advantage of the American tank now some thirty yards away. [Daubin decided that] a rapid retrograde movement . . . was in order . . . climbed up for another snoop out of the open

turret hatch as the driver jockeyed his gears. . . . Death, unexplainedly deferred these many seconds, struck as the light tank backed out. . . . The slug . . . struck the vertical surface of the heavy armored driver's door and literally caved in the front of the M3. With its driver instantly dead, the bow gunner blind, stunned, and bleeding, the loader cut down by machine gun fire as he sought cover, . . . the little tank, though sheathed in flame, backed on through the battle until stopped by friendly hands. Bursts of German machine gun fire accelerated [Daubin's] . . . progress toward the wadi he had just left in his tank. Safely in the ditch his thoughts were on two things; how long would it be before the German tanks swept past him and finished him off; and how was the loss of faith in their chief weapon, the 37mm cannon, going to affect the future battle performance of his platoon, company, and battalion?'

But Daubin was not to be polished off. In turning on Company A, the 13 Mark IVs had exposed their sides and rear to Company B. Nine of them were 'riddled through their engine doors and decks.' With the enemy tanks disposed of or withdrawn, Companies A and B hunted down the accompanying infantry and turned a nearby house into a death trap for those who sought shelter there. The survivors withdrew during the following night. But gallant Siglin was instantly killed when his turret was holed by an armor piercing shell."

Subsequent investigation concluded that six PzKw IVs and one PzKw III were destroyed in this action. American losses were six M3 light tanks. Unfortunately, this was not the last time that the light tanks had to engage more powerful adversaries in tank versus tank action, although the availability of medium tanks reduced such occurrences.

The light tank M3A1 at the right has been knocked out by a direct hit of an armor piercing round on its left front armor. The machine guns have been removed from the tank.

401

The 70th Tank Battalion parades its M5 light tanks in Morocco at the top left in a review for President Roosevelt in January 1943. At the top right, an M3A1 light tank leads a truck convoy in the El Guettar sector on 8 April 1943. Below at the left, a light tank M5 from A Company, 899th Tank Destroyer Battalion is near Maknassy, Tunisia on 8 April 1943. At the right below, a British Stuart crew watches a group of German prisoners in Tunisia.

In Sicily, most of the combat elements of the 70th Tank Battalion (Light) came ashore at Gela on 15-16 July, 1943. The waterproofing material was stripped from their M5 light tanks and the battalion moved forward to support the 26th Infantry Regiment in seizing the high ground northeast of Barrafranca. The attack went forward at 0745, but it was soon halted and the troops were forced to withdraw by intense enemy artillery fire. The Germans now counterattacked with 16 PzKw IVs even though intelligence information indicated that none were in the area. The M5s took up positions above each side of the road along which the German tanks advanced. Heavy fire from both tank guns and the supporting artillery stopped the enemy thrust with a total of nine PzKw IVs destroyed.

For the remainder of the Sicilian campaign, the light tanks of the separate battalions as well as those of the 2nd Armored Division supported the infantry during the advance over extremely rough terrain. They were invaluable in knocking out machine gun nests and reducing other enemy strong points.

After the campaign in North Africa, the 1st Armored Division returned to Morocco to be reequipped and to train replacement personnel. The obsolete M3 light and medium

The two views at the right show a light tank M5 in the Ordnance Depot at Oran, Algeria on 5 April 1943.

tanks that were still usable were turned over to the French for training purposes. On 8 June 1943, the status of combat vehicles in the division showed a total of 56 M5 series light tanks, 102 short of the authorized strength of 158. However, additional new tanks soon arrived and the 75mm howitzer motor carriage M8 on the M5 chassis was introduced as a replacement for the 75mm howitzer motor carriage T30 based on the half-track. By the time that the training and reequipment was complete, the Italian campaign had begun and the division moved to Italy in October. The mountainous terrain limited armor operations in most cases to infantry support during the long drive up the Italian peninsula. The smaller size and lighter weight of the light tanks made them valuable during this advance, but their thin armor and inadequate firepower limited their effectiveness. However, the light tank M5A1 continued to serve in the American Fifth Army and the British Eighth Army until the war ended in May 1945.

Below, a 75mm howitzer motor carriage M8 is being maneuvered into position.

Above, M8 75mm howitzer motor carriages of the 1st Armored Regiment bypass a destroyed bridge near Veiano, Italy on 8 June 1944. Each motor carriage is towing its ammunition trailer. Below, the M8s of the 758th Light Tank Battalion are supporting the 442nd Infantry near Seravezza, Italy on 8 April 1945.

Above, a 1st Armored Division M5A1 light tank crosses a road block of rubble during the drive to Rome on 4 June 1944. The snow covered M5A1 from the 13th Tank Battalion, 1st Armored Division is in northern Italy in the Winter of 1944-45. Below, other M5A1s from D Company, 13th Tank Battalion are near Bambiano, Italy on 12 October 1944.

Above at the left, a new light tank M24 is in the Ordnance Base Shop in Leghorn, Italy. At the top right, M24s of D Company, 13th Tank Battalion are refueling in Italy during the Winter of 1944-45.

The Spring of 1944 saw the arrival in Italy of the first M18 tank destroyers armed with the 76mm gun. These highly mobile gun motor carriages provided a lightweight vehicle with firepower equal to the latest American medium tank, but their thin armor and open top turret prevented their use as a light tank. The new light tank M24 also improved the firepower situation, but like the M5A1, it was armored only against heavy machine gun fire. In the latter part of the war, some of the light tanks had their turrets removed and were modified for use as prime movers and command or reconnaissance vehicles. Some photographs also show the light tank M3A3 converted into an armored ambulance to permit the safe evacuation of casualties under fire.

Below, this 76mm gun motor carriage M18 is on the Anzio beachhead in Italy on 7 May 1944. The was the first use in action of the new tank destroyer.

Above, these M18 gun motor carriages and M5A1 light tanks are in the Revere area of Italy near the Po River on 25 April 1945. At the right, an M5A1 is stuck trying to cross a ditch at the 1st Armored Division Training School in the Prato area of Italy on 18 March 1945. Below, these M5A1s from the 91st Division are in the railway station at Verona, Italy on 26 April 1945.

Above, M5 light tanks from the 102nd Cavalry are training in England during 1943. Note the difference between the early and late production M5 in the right photograph. The late vehicle is fitted with the roof ventilator between the drivers' hatches and the other is not.

NORTHWEST EUROPE AND AID TO THE SOVIET UNION

In September 1943, the armored division in the U. S. Army was reorganized eliminating the armored and infantry regiments and decreasing the number of tanks. The old "heavy" armored division had two armored regiments, each consisting of one light and two medium tank battalions. The new division had three tank battalions, each of which had three medium tank companies and one light tank com-pany. At this same time, the separate tank battalions were reorganized to be identical with those in the new armored divisions. The 1st Armored Division was not converted to the new table of organization until after the fall of Rome in the Summer of 1944 and the 2nd and 3rd Armored Divisions retained the old "heavy" organization until the end of World War II. Thus, except for those in the 2nd and

Other light tanks training prior to D-day can be seen below. These M5Als are on the Seaford Range, Sussex, England on 17 May 1944.

Above, this light tank M5A1 of the 34th Cavalry Reconnaissance Squadron has its 37mm gun cleaned during a firing problem at the Seaford Range in England on 17 March 1944. At the top right, training is over and this M5A1 is moving through the rubble of a town in Normandy.

Above is the hedgerow cutter invented by Sergeant Curtis Culin. It was fabricated from the German beach obstacles. Above at the right, the Sergeant himself emerges from the driver's hatch of an M5A1. These photographs were dated late July 1944. Below, a light tank M5A1 overlooks vehicles assembled near Buchet, France on 31 August 1944.

At the right, the crew of a light tank M5A1 takes a break. Note the stowage on the rear of the tank.

3rd Armored Divisions, all of the U. S. tank battalions operating in Northwest Europe after D-day contained one company of light tanks. These units were equipped with the light tank M5A1 until the introduction of the new light tank M24 beginning in December 1944.

The role of the light tank companies in the new battalions was to provide a fast highly mobile element for reconnaissance and to act as a covering force for the battalion. They also would be used to exploit any success of the medium tank companies which formed the main striking power of the battalion. An example of the cooperation between the light and medium tanks during the drive across France is provided by the action described in the following excerpt from ''The Fourth Armored Division from the Beach to Bavaria'' by Captain Kenneth Koyen.

"The liaison planes scouted out Nazi positions immediately ahead of the division's columns as they slugged forward. The enemy had many guns and many defensive positions in Lorraine. He lost some of them November 13 at Marthille. In 30 minutes, an armored advance guard commanded by Major (later Lieutenant Colonel) Albin F. Irzyk, Salem, Massachusetts, wiped out 21 German antitank guns — 10 of them 88s and 11 high velocity 75s — six mortars, seven half-tracks, three trucks, killed 100 enemy, took 50 prisoners and chased 200 more toward the Sarre."

"The advance guard of Shermans, light tanks, and tank destroyers was scouting ahead of a CC B task force under Major Tom Churchill, Cohasett, Massachusetts, then commanding the 8th [Tank Battalion]. Major Irzyk's tanks neared the village of Marthille, northeast of Chateau Salins. Rather than follow the road to the next objective, the hamlet of Destry, the advance guard swung off to climb a muddy slope.

Light tanks led to feel out the enemy. In the first light tank to reach the crest of the hill was S/Sergeant Ellsworth Ranson, Watertown, New York. No sooner did the snout of his M5 poke over the hill than two antitank guns let go at him.

'I saw the flash of the muzzle blast in the bushes about 1000 yards away,' the tank commander said. 'They missed me and we fired our machine guns at the positions to keep the crews busy.' An amazing sight spread before the tankers. From Marthille ran more than 200 German soldiers, part of the crews of the antitank guns.

'They were probably relief crews for the guns and were taking some time off in town,' Major Irzyk guessed. 'In any case, they didn't do much good. Those who reached the guns before they were mowed down were so exhausted from running in the mud that they couldn't fight.'

Some gunners were at the guns, but they could do little against the 8th's flank attack. Cleverly concealed in bushes and hedges, the German weapons were fixed with their fields of fire over the road that the tanks didn't take. Medium tanks moved into the fray with the lights. The smaller tanks shot their 37mm tracers into the antitank positions to point them out to the Shermans, which then blasted the guns with high explosive 75s.

Everything within a radius of half a mile that could hide a man or gun was hit by the tankers. Rocked by the shelling, the Germans broke and fled. They ran with two Panther tanks which fired nervously and ineffectively at the Shermans. The onrushing mediums and lights found bodies at the antitank guns, ammunition ready to be thrown into the breeches. Behind one row of bushes 20 Germans lay crumpled by the tanks' sweeping machine guns. Only one Sherman was damaged and that when it hit a mine.''

At the left, a column of British Stuart VI light tanks is moving along a road. The unit identification markings have been obliterated by the wartime censor.

Above is a lineup of new British Stuart VI light tanks ready for issue to the tank units. Below, a Stuart V is on a road in Normandy.

Above are two views of the British Stuart V light tank. Full armament is installed on this tank.

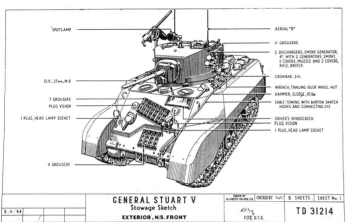
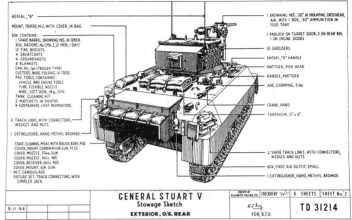

The external (above) and internal (below) stowage for the British Stuart V light tank appears on these charts.

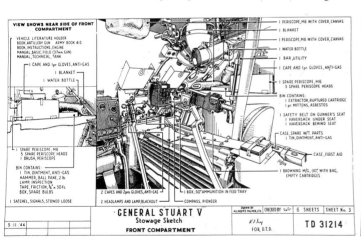
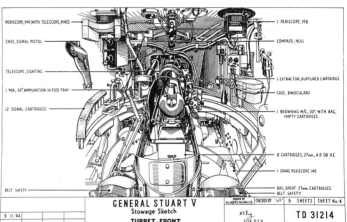

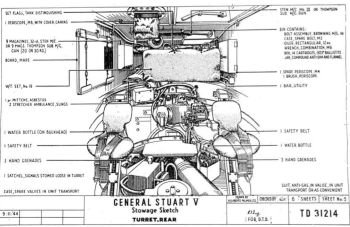
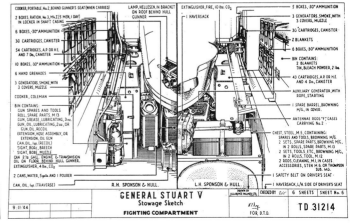

Above, a light tank M5A1, still fitted with the Culin hedgerow cutter, passes through St. Amand, France on 2 September 1944. Below, M5A1s of the 709th Tank Battalion are in Germany on 24 December 1944. Note the deep water fording stack installed on one tank.

The light tank M5A1 above has been painted white for camouflage in the snow and the crew has added logs to the front armor to improve the protection. Below, the crew is painting their light tank M5 to reduce its visibility against the snow covered terrain. Despite the availability of the newer M5A1, some M5s continued to serve until the end of the war.

Note the different configuration of the Culin device on the M5A1 above. This tank, from the 17 Cavalry, was photographed on 22 January 1945. Below, a tanker from D Company, 34th Tank Battalion, 5th Armored Division fires at an enemy aircraft in Vierson, Germany on 2 March 1945.

The light tank M5A1 above from the 5th Armored Division is fitted with a loudspeaker to transmit instructions to civilians in the captured town of Peine, Germany on 10 April 1945. At the right is an M5A1 from the 15th Cavalry Reconnaissance Squadron. Note the track shoes added to the front armor for increased protection.

Above at the left is another light tank M5 that continued to serve late in the war. This tank, photographed in Germany during March 1945, was covered with sand bags to provide some protection against the German panzerfaust. Below, a 3rd Armored Division M5A1 fires at snipers in the woods near Dessau, Germany on 17 April 1945.

Above is a lineup of M24 light tanks near Kornelimunster, Germany on 26 December 1944. The crews are learning the details of their new vehicles.

Although the light tank M5A1 was the standard combat vehicle for the light tank companies throughout most of the campaign in Northwest Europe, one company had the experience of using three different light combat vehicles at the same time. This unit was D Company of the 740th Tank Battalion which had arrived in Belgium shortly before the 16 December 1944 German offensive in the Ardennes. The 740th had been one of the battalions trained to use the highly secret Canal Defense Light (CDL) tanks for night warfare. However, the CDL equipment had been placed in storage and the 740th was converted to a standard tank battalion, but as yet, they had not received any tanks.

As the tactical situation grew worse with the German advance, the 740th moved to the Ordnance Vehicle Depot at Sprimont, Belgium to draw whatever combat vehicles were available. The selection turned out to be extremely limited. As the medium tank companies worked all night to put some of the miscellaneous collection of Shermans,

At the right, the crew of a new light tank M24 scans the area for enemy activity on 14 January 1945.

416

Above are two views of a light tank M24 from D Company, 740th Tank Battalion in Nonceveux, Belgium on 19 January 1945. At this time, the 740th was attached to the 82nd Airborne Division.

tank destroyers, and assault guns into operating condition, the light tank company made a surprising discovery. Two brand new M24 light tanks were in the depot by mistake. Part of the original shipment of 20 M24s to Europe, two had ended up at Sprimont through a shipping error. They were quickly acquired by D Company along with seven reconditioned M5A1 light tanks. The remainder of D Company was brought up to strength with M8 75mm howitzer motor carriages. Thus the light tank company of the 740th went into battle with three types of combat vehicles, many

of which they retained until the end of the war. The M24 light tanks were particularly popular despite their low slung appearance that caused some recognition problems with the accompanying infantry. On several occasions they were stalked by bazooka teams from the 30th Infantry Division and the 82nd Airborne Division who mistook them for German Panther tanks. As a result, the two little tanks were nicknamed "Panther Pups" by the battalion. Additional M24s continued to arrive in Europe during the Spring of 1945 and served alongside the M5A1s until the war ended.

Below, a light tank M24 from the 43rd Cavalry Reconnaissance Squadron crosses a ponton bridge over the Saar River between Saarburg and Trier, Germany on 13 March 1945.

Above, M24 light tanks are being ferried across the Rhine in landing craft. Below, the earlier light tanks also continued to serve and this British Stuart is crossing a Bailey bridge at Antwerp.

Above, the British Locust light airborne tank appears at the left with its carrier, the Hamilcar glider. Note the shortened barrel on the 37mm gun which has been modified to permit the installation of the Littlejohn device. The right photograph shows the tank with the Littlejohn device installed.

As mentioned previously, the M22 light airborne tank was used by the British 6th Airborne Division during the crossing of the Rhine River on 24 March 1945. Named the Locust, 12 of these light tanks, manned by the 6th Airborne Armoured Reconnaissance Regiment, were carried over the river in Hamilcar gliders. The floor of one glider ruptured during the flight and the tank plunged with its crew to their deaths in the mud of the river bank. Half of the Locusts were lost during the landing, but the remainder provided valuable support to the paratroops until they were relieved. The Regiment then exchanged their Locusts for Cromwell tanks for the remainder of the campaign.

During World War II, the Soviet Union received 1683 light tanks from the United States under the Lend-Lease program. They consisted of 1336 M3s, 340 M3A1s, 5 M5A1s, and 2 M24s. All of these tanks were powered by gasoline engines.

Little is known in the West about the employment of these Soviet manned American tanks. However, some Stuarts were used along with M3 medium tanks in the ill-fated Soviet amphibious assault at Ozereyka Bay in the Black Sea during early February 1943. Many of the light tanks were lost when they were launched in water too deep for operation without being prepared for deep water fording.

Below, the Soviet M3A1 light tanks at the left were lost at Ozereyka Bay during the landing in February 1943. At the bottom right, these Soviet M3A1s are operating on the Taman Peninsula during 1943.

Above, a 75mm howitzer motor carriage M8 moves through a battered village enroute to Marigny, France on 26 July 1944. Below, the 75mm howitzer in this M8 is being cleaned near Barenton, France on 9 August 1944. The Culin hedgerow cutter provides a useful platform.

Above, the M8 75mm howitzer motor carriages from Troop C, 15th Cavalry near Blain, France await orders to open fire in support of a reconnaissance patrol. This photograph was dated 23 December 1944. Below, this M8 from Troop E, 106th Cavalry Reconnaissance Group is shelling enemy positions in Geislautern, Germany on 8 February 1945.

These photographs show a 76mm gun motor carriage M18 from the 827th Tank Destroyer Battalion in the Saareburg area of France on 13 December 1944. Note the spare road wheel stowed on the front armor.

Above, a 76mm gun motor carriage M18 moves past the burning town of Irsch, Germany on 27 February 1945. Below, another M18 tank destroyer of the 4th Armored Division crosses the Moselle River in Germany on 15 March 1945.

Above, Brigadier General George Read of the 6th Armored Division is in his command vehicle converted from an M8 motor carriage. The turret and 75mm howitzer have been removed and replaced by an open top superstructure with a .50 caliber machine gun.

Above are British carriers converted from M3 (left) and M5A1 (right) light tanks. The latter is serving as a prime mover for a towed antitank gun. Below are two British carriers converted from the M3A3 light tank. Note the folding canvas cover on the vehicle at the left.

Above, the crew of this Marine Corps M3A1 light tank checks their machine guns after returning from three days of action on the Liana Beachhead near Munda on New Georgia in July 1943.

PACIFIC OFFENSIVE

Although the 37mm gun on the M3 and M5 light tanks was obsolete for operations in Europe, it was still effective against Japanese armor. The use of tanks in the jungle fighting in New Guinea and on Guadalcanal during the latter part of 1942 had shown that, although the heavier armor and firepower of the medium tanks were preferable, it was frequently much easier to employ the smaller light tanks in such terrain.

In January 1943, the Japanese had been defeated on Guadalcanal and in New Guinea and planning was underway for operations against the enemy stronghold of Rabaul. The original intention was to seize Rabaul by a two pronged offensive. One attack would move through New Georgia and Bougainville in the northern Solomons and the other would advance from New Guinea into New Britain converging on Rabaul. However, by the Summer of 1943, the

decision had been made to isolate Rabaul rather than to attack it directly. This was to be achieved by establishing bases from which Allied airpower could dominate the area.

The invasion of New Georgia began on the morning of 21 June 1943 with the landing of the 4th Marine Raider Battalion at Segi Point. The campaign was to last over four months and involve elements of four American Divisions. Once again, M3A1 light tanks supported the infantry

At the right, ammunition is being brought ashore for the Marine Corps light tanks on New Georgia.

Above, Marine Corps M3A1 light tanks are advancing on Munda airfield around the base of Biblio Hill. This photograph on New Georgia was dated 6 August 1943.

throughout the battle. During this same period, General MacArthur's forces in New Guinea advanced through the Markham Valley and on 2 October seized Finschhafen gaining access to the Vitiaz Strait across which lay New Britain. The Australian manned M3 light tanks were active all through this campaign. On 1 November, the other prong

of the offensive landed troops on Bougainville. Thus the advance continued along the two axes in the effort to isolate Rabaul.

While the operations were underway in New Guinea and the Solomons, an island hopping offensive was launched in the Central Pacific. On 20 November 1943, simultaneous landings were made on the Makin and Tarawa Atolls in the Gilbert Islands. The fighting on Butaritari Island in the Makin Atoll ended on 23 November. Supported by both M3 medium tanks and M3A1 light tanks, troops of the 27th Infantry Division killed or captured the entire Japanese force consisting of approximately 300 combat troops and 500 laborers.

The Marine Corps LVT(1) at the left is on Bougainville on 11 February 1944. Note the close front window spacing on this late production LVT(1).

These M3A1 light tanks are operating in support of the 27th Infantry Division on Butaritari Island in the Makin Atoll on 20 November 1943. Above, the crew is considering how to extract the bogged tank. The M3A1 below still has part of the deep water fording stack on its rear deck.

Above is a view of an LVT(2) and an LVT(1) that reached the shore at Tarawa during the November assault. Note the steel plates covering the windows on both vehicles. Below, this Marine Corps M5A1 light tank is participating in training exercises on 10 July 1943 in the South Pacific.

Above, these M3A1 light tanks on Kwajalein Island are supporting the 7th Infantry Division on 6 February 1944. Below is an LVT(A)(1) of the 708th Amphibian Tank Battalion. Note the extra vision slots added for the driver and radio operator.

The situation on Betio Island in the Tarawa Atoll was far different. Here, the assault force from the 2nd Marine Division faced about 3000 well trained combat troops in heavily fortified positions. Although the light tanks of the 2nd Marine Tank Battalion operated on the outlying islands of the atoll, the support for the infantry on Betio was provided by the Sherman tanks of C Company, I Marine Amphibious Corps which had been attached to the 2nd Marine Division for the invasion.

After Tarawa, the action moved west to the Marshall Islands with the seizure of Kwajalein Atoll in February 1944. Elements of the 4th Marine Division landed on Roi Island in the northern part of the atoll. This action saw the first use of the M5A1 light tank in the Pacific. In addition to the medium and light tanks of the 4th Marine Tank Battalion, flame throwing light tanks and LVT(A)(1) amphibian tanks were employed. In Marine terminology, the latter were armored amphibian tractors.

Kwajalein Island in the southern part of the atoll was attacked by units of the Army 7th Infantry Division. They were supported by both medium and light tanks as well as the LVT(A)(1)s of the 708th Amphibian Tank Battalion. As in other theaters of operation, the medium tank had now become the central element of the armored force.

Above is a light tank M5A1 which supported the 27th Infantry Division on Saipan during July 1944. The fighting must be over as the machine guns have been removed from this tank.

The M5A1 was the standard light tank, although some of the earlier M3 series were retained, particularly as flame thrower tanks.

As the fighting moved westward through the Marianas and later in the Philippines, the need for heavier armor and greater firepower increased. On Saipan, the LVT(A)(4) armed with the 75mm howitzer was introduced partially replacing the earlier LVT(A)(1) with the 37mm gun. With this change, the role of the LVT(A)s shifted from that of amphibian tanks to close support artillery. This was the pattern of use for these vehicles in the later battles in the Philippines and on Okinawa.

At the left is a light tank M5A1 which was struck on top of the turret by a high explosive shell during the fighting on Saipan. Note the rupture in the top armor.

Above, LVT(4)s are on the beach at Peleliu on D-day, 15 September 1944. At the right, an LVT(A)(4) has rammed an enemy gun position to silence it on the same day.

Below, a late production LVT(A)(1) is in action on Moratai on 15 September 1944. Note the late type louvers on the rear deck.

At the top left is an LVT(A)(1) from the 1st Marine Amphibian Tractor Battalion in the Marshall Islands during the Summer of 1944. Above, the 37mm gun from a P39 fighter aircraft has been installed on an improvised mount on this LVT(A)(2). The vehicle was operating in the Netherlands East Indies during 1944. The Marine Corps LVT(A)(4) at the left is on the beach at Peleliu on 15 September 1944. Below, an LVT(A)(4), an LVT(2), and an LVT(4) are operating on Iwo Jima. Note the extra armor added to the LVT(2).

Above, the LVTs are crossing the Line of Departure for the assault on Iwo Jima on D-day, 19 February 1945. Below, this LVT(A)(2) is bringing supplies into Iwo Jima on the third day of the invasion. The armor installed to protect the machine gunner is clearly visible in this photograph.

Above, LVT(4)s occupy Yontan airfield on Okinawa. At the top right, a line of Marine Corps LVT(A)(4)s is moving inland on Okinawa. At the right, two late production LVT(A)(1)s are in action on Okinawa. The late type rear deck louvers can be seen on both vehicles. Below, a 75mm gun motor carriage M18 of the 306th Antitank Company, 77th Division fires into enemy positions at Shuri, Okinawa on 11 May 1945.

434

Above are Stuart light tanks of the Indian 7th Light Cavalry during the offensive against the Japanese in Burma.

CHINA-BURMA-INDIA

In India, the troops which had ended their long retreat from Burma in 1942 were slowly reequiped and reinforced. The 7th Light Cavalry of the Indian Army was armed with M3A1, Stuart III, light tanks which they were to use with great effect for the remainder of the war. They also inherited the single M3 that survived the 1942 retreat. As mentioned earlier, it was converted into a command vehicle by removing the turret. A screen was installed over the center compartment and it was dubbed "The Curse of Scotland".

The Stuarts of the Indian 7th Light Cavalry fought with great distinction at Imphal and finally in the pursuit of the defeated Japanese forces toward Rangoon. In addition to the usual British stowage changes, their M3A1s were modified by removing the turret baskets to provide easier access to and from the driving compartment.

At the right is a Stuart of the Indian 7th Light Cavalry during the drive to Rangoon.

435

Above, Stuarts are on maneuvers in western Australia on 25 February 1943. Many of the tanks shipped to Australia and New Zealand were late production M3s with the M3A1 turret, but without the turret basket or power traverse. Some details of these Stuart Hybrids can be seen in the photographs below.

Above, these newly arrived M3A3 light tanks in India are being put into operating condition for use by the Chinese-American 1st Provisional Tank Group. This photograph was dated 12 April 1944.

While the British and Indian troops were fighting in central and southern Burma, another armored unit was operating in the north. This was the Chinese-American 1st Provisional Tank Group commanded by Colonel Rothwell H. Brown, USA. Equipped with Shermans and M3A3 light tanks, they supported the Chinese divisions under the overall command of Lieutenant General Joseph Stilwell.

At the right and below, the M3A3s are on the Ledo Road in Burma manned by their Chinese-American crews. The lower photograph was dated 8 December 1944.

At the top left, an M24 light tank from the 31st Regimental Combat Team participates in training exercises in late March 1950, prior to the outbreak of war in Korea. At the top right, another M24 moves through a crowded Tokyo street.

KOREA

After the end of World War II, the M5A1 light tank rapidly disappeared from the United States Army. The M24 replaced the earlier vehicle as the standard light tank. In Japan, the occupation forces were equipped only with the M24, even though some units were designated as heavy tank battalions. The light tanks were adequate for occupation duties and they caused far less damage to the roads and light bridges.

When North Korea invaded the south in late June 1950, only the M24 light tanks were immediately available in Japan. These tanks were rushed to Korea in an effort to counter the Soviet built T34/85 tanks spearheading the enemy assault. Their first encounter with the North Korean armor occurred on the morning of 10 July 1950 near Chonui. The M24s of A Company 78th Heavy Tank Battalion (note the heavy designation) were supporting the 21st

Below, an M24 light tank moves along a Korean road toward the front on 8 July 1950.

Above, the commander of this M24 light tank scans the sky for enemy aircraft and, at the right, a lonely M24 advances along a Korean road. Both photographs were dated 8 July 1950. Below, this M24 is in a defensive position protecting its thin hull armor on 9 July 1950. Note that the tank is backed into position permitting a rapid withdrawal.

These photographs show the light tank M24 "Rebels Roost" after action on 10 July 1950. As the markings indicate, this vehicle was from the tank platoon of the 24th Reconnaissance Company which, like A Company, 78th Heavy Tank Battalion, was supporting the 21st Infantry.

Infantry, 24th Division. As might be expected, the light tanks were poorly matched against the heavily armored Soviet built tank and its 85mm gun. Signal Corps photographs dated 10 July 1950 show an M24 named "Rebels Roost" and the captions indicate it to be the first American tank to see action in Korea. On the afternoon of the 10th, the M24s participated in a counterattack with the 3rd Battalion, 21st Infantry. During this action, an enemy T34 was disabled, however, the days losses included two M24s. Even worse was to come as five of the lightly armored M24s were knocked out on 11 July by enemy artillery fire and infantry attacks. The obvious answer to the T34 was

Above and at the right below are additional views of the M24 light tank during the action in Korea on 10 July 1950.

the medium tank and large numbers of M4 Shermans and M26 Pershings were rushed to Korea. With the arrival of the medium tanks, the M24s reverted to the normal light tank role of reconnaissance, infantry support, and acting as a flank covering force.

Below, an M24 light tank is in position at the Kum River dike observing enemy positions across the river.

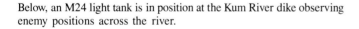

Above at the left, "Rebels Roost" is loading ammunition on 19 July 1950 and, at the top right, the tank commander of this M24 is directing artillery fire onto enemy troops. Below, another M24 is partially concealed in a bush on 24 July. Note that each crew member keeps his steel helmet handy near his crew position.

Above, a light tank M24 from the 25th Reconnaissance Company is concealed under a tree. Below, the crew of another M24 is on the lookout for the enemy. Both photographs were dated 24 July 1950.

Above, a light tank M24 with the 25th Infantry Division is in position to guard a river crossing on 24 July 1950. Below, an M24 from the 25th Reconnaissance Company is moving up to the front on 26 July 1950.

The M24 light tank above is firing at enemy machine gun positions near Chondong-ni, Korea on 8 August 1950. Below, an M24 from the 25th Reconnaissance Company receives a supply of ammunition seven miles north of Masan, Korea on 10 August 1950.

These M19 twin 40mm gun motor carriages are in action here supporting ground troops. Note the .50 caliber machine gun mounted on the front armor in the view above along the Naktong River on 6 September 1950.

Other combat vehicles based on the M24 light tank chassis which were produced too late for World War II saw action for the first time in Korea. These included the 40mm gun motor carriages M19 and M19A1, the 105mm howitzer motor carriage M37, and the 155mm howitzer motor carriage M41. Although there was little opportunity for the M19 and M19A1 to operate in their intended antiaircraft role, they proved to be extremely effective as infantry support weapons. Operations with the M37 and M41 self-propelled howitzers indicated the need for armor on the latter and overhead protection for both vehicles.

Above, a twin 40mm gun motor carriage M19 of the 3rd Antiaircraft Artillery Battalion provides fire support for the 7th Regimental Combat Team on 27 May 1951. Note the extra machine gun on the front of this vehicle. Below, a member of the 187th Regimental Combat Team observes enemy movements from an M19 on 6 June 1951.

These 105mm howitzer motor carriages M37 of the 58th Field Artillery Battalion are in action firing at the enemy across the Imjin River in Korea on 12 April 1951.

Above, the 92nd Field Artillery Battalion prepares to put its M41 155mm howitzer motor carriages into action north of Kamhung, Korea supporting the 32nd Infantry on 2 December 1950. Below, an M41 of Battery B, 999th Armored Field Artillery fires on enemy positions in Korea on 23 February 1952.

Above, these M39 armored utility vehicles are operating as personnel and supply carriers. At the left below, an M39 is evacuating wounded of the 31st Regimental Combat Team on 14 October 1952. At the lower right, an M39 is utilized as an 81mm mortar carrier.

The M39 armored utility vehicle, based on the M18 tank destroyer, also was widely used in Korea in a variety of roles. These included a personnel or supply carrier, a reconnaissance vehicle, a prime mover, and in at least one case a carrier for the 81mm mortar.

The LVT(3) and the LVT(A)(4) were used by the Marine Corps during the Inchon landing and during the Han River crossing. These vehicles, as well as the LVT(3)(C), continued to support the Marine Corps infantry throughout the war in Korea.

The photographs at the left show the troop compartment covers on the LVT(3)C open and closed. These vehicles from the Marine 1st Armored Amphibian Tractor Battalion are practicing landings in the Imjin River in the upper view and breaking ice around a bridge in the lower photograph. Below, this LVT(A)(5) has a heavy layer of sand bags to provide top protection. Note the open escape hatch in the ponton.

Above, a light tank M24 is in the 80th Ordnance Base Depot at Tan Son Nhut, Vietnam on 10 January 1967. Earlier views of the M24 in Vietnam can be seen at the bottom of the page. At the bottom left, a French manned M24 is operating prior to the fall of Dien Ben Phu. At the lower right, an M24 is serving with the security forces at Tan Son Nhut Airbase.

VIETNAM

When the French forces returned to Indochina after World War II, they were equipped with a wide variety of American weapons originally obtained through the Lend-Lease program. These included M3 and M5 series light tanks as well as some M8 75mm howitzer motor carriages. All of these were used by the French in their battle against the Viet Minh. A number of LVT(4)s and LVT(A)(4)s also were obtained. The 75mm howitzers of the LVT(A)(4)s were used to provide fire support for the French infantry. Some LVT(4)s were modified to carry 40mm guns or recoilless rifles so that they could participate in the fire support role.

In late 1950, the French received the first of over 1200 M24 light tanks supplied as military aid from the United States. They replaced many of the old M5A1s as well as some Shermans in the French armored units. At Dien Ben Phu, ten M24s were disassembled and air lifted into the valley. After reassembly, they provided mobile fire support for the garrison until the French surrendered in May 1954. At that time, six of the light tanks were still operational and two others were serving as pillboxes.

With the departure of the French in 1955, the M24s were turned over to the new Army of the Republic of Vietnam (ARVN). Later, additional M24s were supplied by the United States. Some of these were still operational during the invasion from the north which was defeated in 1972. Some of them may have continued to serve until the fall of South Vietnam in 1975.

Above, the Brazilian X1A converted from the light tank M3 appears at the left and the French installation of the low pressure 90mm gun in the M24 can be seen at the right.

FOREIGN MODIFICATIONS

Many of the light tanks furnished to other nations during World War II remained in service long into the postwar period. Some of these have been modernized to the point that they hardly resemble their original configuration. An extreme example of such modification was that applied to the M3A1 light tanks in Brazil. In the early 1970s, two M3A1s were rebuilt with new sloped armor above the tracks and were fitted with a new turret mounting a French low pressure 90mm gun. A new fire control system also was installed. The modified tanks were powered by a 280 horsepower Saab-Scania diesel engine and the original suspension was replaced by a new volute spring design. After tests of the two prototypes, 80 additional M3A1s were rebuilt to the new standard and redesignated as the X1A light tank. The last of these were completed in 1978 and issued to the Cavalry regiments. Experiments also were carried out with a lengthened version of the X1A designated as the X1A1. This vehicle was fitted with an additional suspension bogie and track support roller on each side as well as a new track tension idler.

In Paraguay, other M3 series light tanks received much less drastic modifications. They were fitted with improved power packs and suspensions, but retained the original turret and armament.

During 1967, the French installed a low pressure 90mm gun in the light tank M24. This weapon consisted of a new barrel with a muzzle brake and the original breech assembly after modification. The original recoil mechanism was retained. The new weapon fired 90mm, fin stabilized, high explosive and shaped charge ammunition at a muzzle velocity of 2460 feet/second (750 m/sec). In another experiment, the French also installed the turret and armament from the AMX 13 light tank on an M24 Chassis. Although the conversion was successful, this remained only an experiment and it was not produced in quantity.

The most successful attempt to upgrade the M24 light tank occurred in Norway. By the early 1950s, Norway had acquired 72 M24s from the United States under the Military Assistance Program. They were used by the Norwegian Army for approximately 20 years before a modernization program was considered necessary. In the early 1970s, Thune-Eureka A/S of Oslo, Norway modified an M24 as the prototype for an improved light tank. After evaluation by the Norwegian Army, Thune-Eureka A/S received a contract to retrofit the M24 fleet. Between January 1975 and October 1976, they delivered 54 of the upgraded tanks now designated as the NM-116.

The NM-116 was armed with the French D/925 low pressure 90mm gun in the original recoil mechanism, but without the stabilizer. As mentioned earlier, this weapon was fitted with a muzzle brake and fired HE and HEAT ammunition at a muzzle velocity of 2460 feet/second (750 m/sec). Canister and smoke rounds also were made available. A basket was installed in the turret and the stowage was rearranged to accommodate 41 rounds of 90mm ammunition. Twenty of these were in the right front hull in the space formerly occupied by the bow gunner. The bow machine gun was eliminated and the mount was welded shut. The .30 caliber coaxial machine gun on the M24 was replaced by a .50 caliber weapon in the NM-116. Another .50 caliber machine gun was carried on the turret antiaircraft mount and an additional pedestal mount for this weapon was located on the forward turret roof. Normal stowage included 500 rounds of .50 caliber ammunition.

These photographs show the modernized Norwegian M24 with the French low pressure 90mm gun. At the bottom right is the NM-116 fitted with the laser range finder in Norwegian service.

Four smoke dischargers were located on each side of the turret and provision was made for the installation of the Simrad LV3 laser range finder on top of the 90mm gun mount.

In the NM-116, the M24's twin Cadillac engines were replaced by a single 250 horsepower, supercharged, diesel engine, model 6V-53T, manufactured by the Detroit Diesel Division of the General Motors Corporation. The Hydramatic transmissions in the M24 were superseded by an Allison MT-653 transmission with five speeds forward and one

reverse. The new power plant provided a maximum level road speed of 30 miles/hour (48 km/hr) with a cruising range of about 180 miles (300 km). The original torsion bar suspension and T85E1 tracks were retained, but the German Diehl and the Swedish Hagglund tracks also could be installed. The cold Norwegian weather resulted in an improved heating system and the batteries were relocated into the crew compartment where they could be warmed by the heater. Napco International, Inc. of Hopkins, Minnesota was licensed to convert M24s to this configuration.

453

Above, An American Renault FT17 of the 327/345th Tank Battalion advances with the 42nd Division during the St. Mihiel offensive in 1918.

CONCLUSION

In the period between the introduction of the six-ton M1917 during World War I and the entry of the United States into World War II, the role of the light tank changed drastically. The doctrine developed for the use of the light tank during World War I envisioned it strictly as an infantry support weapon. This continued into the postwar period with the assignment of the tanks to the Infantry. To quote the General Staff directive of April 1922 "The primary mission of the tank is to facilitate the uninterrupted advance of the rifleman in the attack." The six-ton M1917 was well suited to its task and it was referred to as an accompanying tank. This was in contrast to the leading role assigned at that time to the heavy tanks which were intended to precede the infantry. At maximum speeds of five to six miles/hour and a very limited range, neither type strayed too far from the infantry they were intended to support.

The early postwar development of light tanks followed the wartime formula, but with slightly increased speeds and greatly improved reliability. The introduction of the convertible tanks which could operate on either tracks or wheels provided a vehicle with the long range strategic mobility required by the Cavalry. Later improvements in tracks and suspensions rendered the convertible vehicle obsolete and the cavalry mission could be performed by a full-track light tank. The improved running gear coupled with a high power to weight ratio increased the maximum speed of the light tanks to about 40 miles/hour prior to World War II. When the first armored divisions were organized in the Summer of 1940, the light tanks were considered to be its major striking force supported by the heavier medium tanks. Later, it became obvious that the medium tanks were required for the main role and this was confirmed by the early battles in North Africa. By the end of World War II, the light tank was viewed as a fast armored reconnaissance vehicle which could also be used to provide infantry support or a covering force for the flanks of the armored columns. The final American light tank of the war, the M24, was well adapted for this role with its high speed and 75mm gun. Compared to the six-ton M1917, the M24 had increased its weight by more than three times and its maximum speed by about six times. The 75mm medium velocity gun in the M24 completely outclassed the low velocity 37mm gun in the M1917. The armor thickness had approximately doubled providing the M24 protection against .50 caliber machine gun fire compared to rifle caliber protection for the six-ton M1917. Despite the great progress in development, the general configuration remained the same for both tanks with the driver in the front hull, the engine in the rear, and the turret mounted armament in the center with 360 degree traverse. In 1918, the light tank depended upon its armor for survival. By the time of World War II, the main protection of the light tank was provided by its speed and mobility and it was no longer suited for a role in which these features could not be utilized.

At the right, a light tank M24 fires its .50 caliber machine gun on the range. This weapon alone could easily destroy the World War I FT17.

PART V

REFERENCE DATA

Light tank M5A1, late production

Light tank M3A1 during training exercises

Above, a twin turret "Mae West" light tank is fording a stream during training. None of the armament is installed. Below, a Marmon-Herrington T16 light tank of the Provisional Tank Company, 138th Infantry is at Fort Glenn, Alaska in 1942.

Above, the 24th Cavalry puts on a demonstration with their new M5 light tanks. Below, this M5 is firing its 37mm gun. Note the dust from the muzzle blast.

These photographs show the early production versions of the LVT(A)(1) (above) and the LVT(A)(4) (below).

Above, an M24 light tank of the 81st Reconnaissance Squadron, 1st Armored Division passes through the ruins of a town south of Bologna, Italy in the Spring of 1945. Below, the crew of this light tank M24 guards a road junction in Korea during the Summer of 1950.

Above, a light tank M24 moves along a Korean road in the Summer of 1950. Below, this M24 soldiers on serving as a guard post behind its wall of sand bags in Vietnam.

ACCEPTANCES OF LIGHT TANKS AND RELATED VEHICLES
FROM U.S. PRODUCTION DURING THE PERIOD 1940-1945

Vehicle	Total Acceptances	First Acceptances	Final Acceptances
Light Tank M2A4	375	May 1940	April 1942
Light Tank M3	4526	March 1941	October 1942
Light Tank M3 (diesel)	1285	June 1941	January 1943
Light Tank M3A1	4410	May 1942	January 1943
Light Tank M3A1 (diesel)	211	August 1942	October 1942
Light Tank M3A3	3427	September 1942	September 1943
Light Tank M5	2074	April 1942	December 1942
Light Tank M5A1	6810	November 1942	June 1944
Light Tank M22	830	April 1943	February 1944
Light Tank M24	4731	April 1944	August 1945
Medium Tank M7 (Lt. Tk. T7E5)	7	December 1942	February 1943
Light Tank M3A3, Reman.*	166	March 1945	May 1945
Light Tank M5, Reman.*	2	January 1944	May 1944
Light Tank M5A1, Reman.*	775	November 1944	June 1945
40mm GMC M19	300	April 1945	August 1945
75mm HMC M8	1778	September 1942	January 1944
76mm GMC M18	2507	July 1943	October 1944
105mm HMC M37	150	September 1945	October 1945
155mm HMC M41	85	June 1945	September 1945
Armored Utility Vehicle M39*	640	October 1944	March 1945

*Remanufactured or converted

DISTRIBUTION OF LIGHT TANKS AND RELATED VEHICLES TO INTERNATIONAL AID
UNDER THE LEND-LEASE PROGRAM AS OF 1 SEPTEMBER 1945*

Vehicle	Vehicles Assigned To:			Total International Aid
	United Kingdom	Soviet Union	Other	
Light Tank M2A4	36	0	0	36
Light Tank M3	1784	1336	10	3130
Light Tank M3 (diesel)	50	0	120	170
Light Tank M3A1	1594	340	499	2433
Light Tank M3A1 (diesel)	0	0	20	20
Light Tank M3A3	2045	0	1277	3322
Light Tank M5A1	1431	5	226	1662
Light Tank M22	260	0	0	260
Light Tank M24	289	2	0	291
75mm HMC M8	0	0	174	174
76mm GMC M18	2	5	0	7
155mm HMC M41	1	0	0	1

*Transfers in theaters of operation and minor shipments after 1 September 1945 are not included

Data sheets are provided in this section for all of the production light tanks which served in the United States Army during World War II. In addition, sheets are included for the World War I six-ton M1917 and the Ford three-ton M1918 light tanks as well as several later experimental tanks and vehicles based upon the light tank chassis.

The data were obtained from a wide variety of sources which frequently did not agree. The vehicle dimensions were taken from the production drawings if they could be located. Some dimensions, such as the height and ground clearance, obviously varied with the spring compression under changes in vehicle load. If the drawings were not available, test reports from Aberdeen Proving Ground and Fort Knox provided a source of information. Weights taken from such sources often varied widely reflecting modifications and changes in the vehicle stowage. When possible, the weights selected were appropriate for the vehicle during its period of greatest service. For single experimental vehicles, the exact weight is quoted if it is available. In some cases, only estimated weights could be obtained. For production vehicles, the weight is usually rounded off to the nearest 1000 pounds. The combat weights listed included the crew and a full load of fuel and ammunition.

Most of the terms in the data sheets are self-explanatory, but some may need clarification. For example, the fire height is the distance from the ground to the center line of the main weapon bore at zero elevation. Unless otherwise specified, the ground contact length at zero penetration is the distance between the centers of the front and rear road wheels. This value is used to calculate the ground pressure of the vehicle using the combat weight. The tread is the distance between the track center lines. The terms left and right are in reference to someone sitting in the vehicle driver's seat. When available, the engine power and torque are reported as gross and net values. The gross horsepower and torque are those developed by the engine with only the accessories essential to operation. It does not include the effect of such items as generators, air cleaners, and cooling fans. The net horsepower and torque are the values obtained with the engine installed in the vehicle with all of its accessories. All power to weight ratios were calculated using the combat weight of the vehicle.

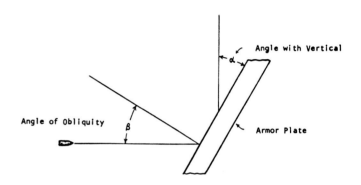

The armor is specified as to type, thickness, and the angle with the vertical. Early vehicles were protected by rolled, face-hardened steel armor and were assembled by riveting or bolting. During World War II, this type of construction was superseded by rolled or cast, homogeneous steel armor and welded assembly. The angle quoted is the angle between a vertical plane and the armor plate surface as indicated by the angle alpha in the sketch. Also note that in this two dimensional sketch, alpha is equal to the angle of obliquity shown by the angle beta. The latter is defined as the angle between a line perpendicular to the plate surface and the path of a projectile impacting the armor. This angle is used to specify the armor penetration performance for various types of projectiles.

SIX-TON TANK M1917 (SIX-TON SPECIAL TRACTOR)

GENERAL DATA

Crew:		2 men
Length: Without tailpiece		166 inches
Length: With tailpiece		197 inches
Width: Over tracks		70 inches
Height:		91 inches
Tread:		57 inches
Ground Clearance:		16.2 inches
Fire Height:		70 inches
Turret Ring Diameter: (inside)		36 inches
Weight, Combat Loaded:		14,500 pounds
Weight, Unstowed:		13,400 pounds
Power to Weight Ratio: Gross		5.8 hp/ton
Ground Pressure: Zero penetration		6.9 psi
	6 inch penetration	4.9 psi
	10 inch penetration	4.1 psi

ARMOR
Type: Rolled face-hardened steel; Bolted and riveted assembly

Hull Thickness:

	Actual	Angle w/Vertical
Front, Driver's Cupola	0.60 inches (15mm)	17 degrees
Driver's Doors	0.31 inches (8mm)	70 degrees
Upper	0.60 inches (15mm)	30 degrees
Lower	0.60 inches (15mm)	30 degrees
Sides	0.60 inches (15mm)	0 degrees
Rear	0.60 inches (15mm)	0 degrees
Top, Front	0.31 inches (8mm)	90 degrees
Rear	0.31 inches (8mm)	65 to 90 degrees
Floor	0.25 inches (6mm)	90 degrees

Turret Thickness:

Gun Shield	0.60 inches (15mm)	0 degrees
Front	0.60 inches (15mm)	12 degrees
Sides	0.60 inches (15mm)	12 degrees
Rear	0.60 inches (15mm)	12 degrees
Top	0.31 inches (8mm)	73 to 90 degrees

ARMAMENT
(1) 37mm Gun M1916 in turret ball mount
Movement of 11 7/8 inch ball mount
   Vertical 56 degrees, horizontal 30 degrees
   or
(1) .30 caliber MG M1919 in turret ball mount (originally Marlin tank MG)
Movement of 9.1 inch ball mount
   Vertical 48 degrees, horizontal 30 degrees

Turret Traverse: Manual, either mount	360 degrees

AMMUNITION
238 rounds 37mm
   or
4200 rounds .30 caliber

SIGHTING AND VISION DEVICES
Driver: Hatch and vision slots (5)
Gunner: Telescopic sight M1918 for 37mm gun
   or
   Open sights for MG (rear, tubular; front, blade)
   Hatch, vision slots (3), and pistol ports (loop holes) (2)
Total Vision Slots: Hull (5), Turret (3) in cupola
Total Pistol Ports: Hull (0), Turret (2) (loopholes)

ENGINE

Make and Model: Buda HU modified	
Type: 4 cylinder, 4 cycle, vertical L-head	
Cooling System: Liquid Ignition: Magneto	
Displacement:	312.1 cubic inches
Bore and Stroke:	4.25 x 5.5 inches
Gross Horsepower:	42 at 1460 rpm
Fuel: Gasoline	30 gallons

POWER TRAIN
Master Clutch: Inverted cone
Transmission: Selective sliding gear, 4 speeds forward, 1 reverse

Gear Ratios:	1st 3.13:1	4th	0.61:1
	2nd 1.54:1	reverse	3.13:1
	3rd 0.94:1		

Steering: Clutch-brake
Brakes: Mechanical, external contracting
Final Drive: Spur gear   Gear Ratio: 30.56:1
Drive Sprocket: At rear of vehicle with 15 teeth
   Diameter: 25.5 inches (outside)

RUNNING GEAR
Suspension: Coil and leaf springs
   10 lower track rollers in 2 bogies (1/track)
   8 lower track rollers in 2 bogies (1/track)
   Lower Roller Diameter: 7 inches
   12 upper track support rollers (6/track)
   Upper Roller Diameter: 4.75 inches
   Adjustable idler at front of each track
   Idler Size: 33.1 inches

Tracks:
   Type: Single pin, 13.375 inch width, cast steel with integral grouser
   Pitch: 9.842 inches
   Shoes per Vehicle: 64 (32/track)
   Ground Contact Length: 79 inches, zero penetration
      110 inches, 6 inch penetration
      131 inches, 10 inch penetration

COMMUNICATIONS
Flag set

FIRE PROTECTION
(2) 1 quart Pyrene fire extinguishers

PERFORMANCE

Maximum Speed: 1st and reverse gears		1.1 miles/hour
2nd gear		2.2 miles/hour
3rd gear		3.5 miles/hour
4th gear		5.5 miles/hour
Maximum Drawbar Pull:		12,600 pounds
Maximum Grade:		70 per cent
Maximum Trench:		7 feet
Maximum Vertical Wall:		36 inches
Maximum Fording Depth:		24 inches
Minimum Turning Circle: (diameter) w/tailpiece		20 feet
Cruising Range: Roads		approx. 30 miles

FORD THREE-TON SPECIAL TRACTOR

GENERAL DATA

Crew:	2	men
Length: Without tailpiece	129	inches
Length: With tailpiece	160	inches
Width:	64	inches
Height:	64	inches
Tread:	57	inches
Ground Clearance:	14	inches
Fire Height:	approx. 42	inches
Weight, Combat Loaded:	7200	pounds
Weight, Unstowed:	6200	pounds
Power to Weight Ratio: Gross	9.4	hp/ton
Ground Pressure: Zero penetration	9.2	psi

ARMOR

Rolled face-hardened steel; Riveted assembly

Hull Thickness:	Actual	Angle w/Vertical
Front, Upper left	0.5 inches (13mm)	0 degrees
Upper right	0.5 inches (13mm)	38 degrees
Lower	0.375 inches (10mm)	60 degrees
Sides, Front	0.5 inches (13mm)	0 degrees
Rear	0.25 inches (6mm)	22 degrees
Rear, Upper	0.375 inches (10mm)	37 degrees
Lower	0.25 inches (6mm)	35 degrees
Top, Front	0.375 inches (10mm)	90 degrees
Rear	0.25 inches (6mm)	60 degrees
Floor	0.25 inches (6mm)	90 degrees

ARMAMENT

(1) .30 caliber Browning or Marlin tank MG in front hull

Traverse Range:	22	degrees
Elevation Range:	38	degrees

AMMUNITION

2000 rounds .30 caliber (estimated)

SIGHTING AND VISION DEVICES

Driver   Front flap, vision slots in cupola (6), tilted cupola, pistol port (1)

Gunner   MG sight, pistol ports (2) 1 front, 1 rear

Total Vision Slots: (6) in cupola

Total Pistol Ports: (3) (loopholes)

ENGINE

Make and Model: Ford dual Model T

Type: 8 cylinder (4/engine), 4 cycle, vertical L-head

Cooling System: Liquid   Ignition: Magneto

Displacement:	353.4 cubic inches
Bore and Stroke:	3.75 x 4.0 inches
Compression Ratio:	3.98:1
Gross Horsepower:	34 hp at 1700 rpm
Fuel: Gasoline	17 gallons
Engine Oil:	8 quarts

POWER TRAIN

Clutch: Multiple disc (2)

Transmission: Ford planetary, 2 speeds forward, 1 reverse

Steering: Clutch-brake

Brakes: Mechanical

Final Drive: Worm gear   Gear Ratio: 7.25:1

Drive Sprocket: At rear of vehicle with 10 double teeth

    Diameter: 22.5 inches

RUNNING GEAR

Suspension: Leaf spring

    12 wheels in 4 bogies (2 bogies/track)

    Wheel Size: 8 x 3.5 inches

    4 track return rollers (2/track)

    Idler at front of each track

    Idler Size: 34 x 3.5 inches

Tracks:

Type: Single pin, 7 inch width, cast steel w/integral grouser

    Pitch: 7 inches

    Shoes per vehicle: 80 (40/track)

    Ground Contact Length: 56 inches, zero penetration

ELECTRICAL SYSTEM

Nominal Voltage: 6 volts DC

Generator: (1) 6 volts

Battery: (1) 6 volts

COMMUNICATIONS

Flag set

FIRE PROTECTION

(2) 1 quart Pyrene fire extinguishers

PERFORMANCE

Maximum Speed:	8	miles/hour
Maximum Drawbar Pull:	3650	pounds
Maximum Grade:	50	per cent
Maximum Trench:	5	feet
Maximum Vertical Wall:	20	inches
Maximum Fording Depth:	21	inches
Minimum Turning Circle: (diameter)	27	feet
Cruising Range:	approx. 34	miles

LIGHT TANK T1E1 (M1)

GENERAL DATA

Crew:	2 men
Length: Over tracks	152.2 inches
Width:	70.5 inches
Height:	85.6 inches
Tread:	58.3 inches
Ground Clearance:	14 inches
Fire Height:	73 inches
Turret Ring Diameter: (inside)	approx. 40 inches
Weight, Combat Loaded:	15,671 pounds
Weight, Unstowed:	approx. 14,500 pounds
Power to Weight Ratio: Gross	14.0 hp/ton
Ground Pressure: Grouser penetration only	8.9 psi
5 inch penetration	5.0 psi

ARMOR

Type: Turret, rolled face-hardened steel; Hull, rolled face-hardened steel; Riveted assembly

Hull Thickness:	Actual	Angle w/Vertical
Front, Driver's hood	0.375 inches (10mm)	13 degrees
Middle	0.25 inches (6mm)	85 degrees
Lower	0.375 inches (10mm)	0 to 30 degrees
Sides	0.375 inches (10mm)	0 degrees
Rear	0.375 inches (10mm)	0 degrees
Top	0.25 inches (6mm)	90 degrees
Floor	0.25 inches (6mm)	90 degrees
Turret Thickness:		
Front	0.375 inches (10mm)	0 degrees
Sides	0.375 inches (10mm)	0 degrees
Rear	0.375 inches (10mm)	0 degrees
Top	0.25 inches (6mm)	75 to 90 degrees

ARMAMENT

(1) 37mm gun M1916 in combination mount T1 in turret
(1) .30 caliber MG M1919 in combination mount T1 in turret
Turret Traverse: Manual, 360 degrees

AMMUNITION

80 rounds 37mm
3000 rounds .30 caliber

FIRE CONTROL AND VISION EQUIPMENT

Telescopic sight M1918 in combination gun mount T1
Vision Devices:
Driver   Front flaps, vision slots (3)
Gunner   Hatch, pistol ports (3), vision slots (3)
Total Vision Slots: Hull (3), Turret (3)
Total Pistol Ports: Hull (0), Turret (3)

ENGINE

Make and Model: Cunningham	
Type: 8 cylinder, 4 cycle, vee	
Cooling System: Liquid Ignition: Delco, battery type	
Displacement:	441.8 cubic inches
Bore and Stroke:	3.75 x 5.0 inches
Gross Horsepower: (max)	110 hp at 2700 rpm
Gross Torque: (max)	303 ft-lb at 1200 rpm
Fuel: Gasoline	50 gallons

POWER TRAIN

Master Clutch: Single disc
Transmission: Cotta sliding gear, 3 speeds forward, 1 reverse

Gear Ratios:	1st 4.56:1	3rd 0.662:1
	2nd 1.0:1	reverse 4.175:1

Steering: Clutch-brake
Brakes: Mechanical
Final Drive: Spur gear
Drive Sprocket: At rear of vehicle with 31 double teeth
Pitch Diameter: 32 inches

RUNNING GEAR

Suspension: Unsprung, link type
16 wheels in 8 bogies (4 bogies/track)
Wheel Size: 8.8 inch diameter over flanges
4 track return rollers (2 rollers/track)
Adjustable idler at front of each track
Idler Size: 30 inch diameter
Tracks:
Type: Single pin, 12 inch width, open shoe cast steel with integral grouser
Pitch: 6.5 inches
Shoes per Vehicle: 102 (51/track)
Ground Contact Length: Grouser penetration only, 72 inches
5 inch penetration, 130 inches

ELECTRICAL SYSTEM

Nominal Voltage: 12 volts DC
Generator: (1) 12 volts
Battery: (1) 12 volts

COMMUNICATION

Flag set

FIRE PROTECTION

(2) 1 quart Pyrene fire extinguishers

PERFORMANCE

Maximum Speed: Level road	18 miles/hour
Maximum Grade:	70 per cent
Maximum Trench:	6 feet
Maximum Vertical Wall:	20 inches
Maximum Fording Depth:	20 inches
Minimum Turning Circle: (diameter)	20 feet
Cruising Range: Roads	approx. 75 miles

GENERAL DATA

Crew:	4 men
Length:	163 inches
Width: Over side stowage	94 inches
Height: Over cupola roof	92 inches
Tread:	72 inches
Ground Clearance:	15 inches
Fire Height:	72 inches
Turret Ring Diameter: (inside)	44.1 inches
Weight, Combat Loaded:	18,790 pounds
Weight, Unstowed:	approx. 17,000 pounds
Power to Weight Ratio: Net	26.6 hp/ton
Gross	27.9 hp/ton
Ground Pressure: Zero penetration	9.4 psi

ARMOR

Type: Turret, rolled face-hardened steel; Hull, rolled face-hardened steel; Riveted assembly

Hull Thickness:

		Actual	Angle w/Vertical
Front, Upper		0.625 inches (16mm)	17 degrees
	Middle	0.625 inches (16mm)	69 degrees
	Lower	0.625 inches (16mm)	21 degrees
Sides		0.5 inches (13mm)	0 degrees
Rear		0.25 inches (6mm)	0 degrees
Top		0.25 inches (6mm)	90 degrees
Floor		0.25 inches (6mm)	90 degrees

Turret Thickness:

	Actual	Angle w/Vertical
Front	0.625 inches (16mm)	0 degrees
Sides	0.625 inches (16mm)	0 degrees
Rear	0.625 inches (16mm)	0 degrees
Top	0.25 inches (6mm)	90 degrees

ARMAMENT

(1) .50 caliber MG HB M2 fixed in combination gun mount M7 in turret
(1) .30 caliber MG HB M2 fixed in combination gun mount M7 in turret
(1) .30 caliber MG HB M2 flexible in ball mount M8 in bow

Turret Traverse: Manual, 360 degrees

AMMUNITION

1800 rounds .50 caliber
4700 rounds .30 caliber

FIRE CONTROL AND VISION EQUIPMENT

Telescopic sight M5 or M1918A2 in combination mount M7
Vision Devices:

Driver	Hatch, vision slots (2)
Asst. Driver	Hatch, vision slots (2)
Commander	Hatch, pistol ports (2), vision slots (6)
Gunner	Pistol port (1), vision slot (1)

Total Vision Slots: Hull (4), Turret (7)
Total Pistol Ports: Hull (0), Turret (3)

ENGINE

Make and Model: Continental R-670-3, -3C, -5 or W-670-7, -8
Type: 7 cylinder, 4 cycle, radial
Cooling System: Air   Ignition: Magneto

Displacement:	668 cubic inches
Bore and Stroke:	5.125 x 4.625 inches
Compression Ratio: R-670-3, R-670-5 or W-670-7	6.1:1
R-670-3C or W-670-8	5.4:1
Net Horsepower: R-670-3, R-670-5 or W-670-7	250 hp at 2400 rpm
R-670-3C or W-670-8	235 hp at 2400 rpm
Gross Horsepower: R-670-3, R-670-5 or W-670-7	262 hp at 2400 rpm
R-670-3C or W-670-8	248 hp at 2400 rpm
Net Torque: (max) R-670-3, R-670-5 or W-670-7	584 ft-lb at 1800 rpm
Gross Torque: (max) R-670-3, R-670-5 or W-670-7	590 ft-lb at 1700 rpm
Weight:	565 pounds, dry
Fuel: High comp. 82 octane gasoline minimum	50 gallons
Low comp. 75 octane gasoline minimum	
Engine Oil:	32 quarts

POWER TRAIN

Clutch: Dry disc, 2 plate
Transmission: Sliding, constant mesh*, 5 speeds forward, 1 reverse

Gear Ratios:	1st	5.37:1	4th	1.09:1
	2nd	2.82:1	5th	0.738:1
	3rd	1.72:1	reverse	6.19:1

Steering: Controlled differential
Bevel Gear Ratio: 2.62:1   Steering Ratio: 1.845:1
Brakes: Mechanical, external contracting
Final Drive: Herringbone gear   Gear Ratio: 2:1
Drive Sprocket: At front of vehicle with 14 teeth
Pitch Diameter: 24.56 inches

RUNNING GEAR

Suspension: Vertical volute spring
8 wheels in 4 bogies (2 bogies/track)
Tire Size: 20 x 6 inches
4 track return rollers (2 rollers/track)
Adjustable idler at rear of each track
Idler Size: 24 x 6 inches
Tracks: Outside guide, rubber bushed; T16 series
Type: (T16E1) Double pin, 11.6 inch width, rubber, reversible
(T16E2) Double pin, 11.6 inch width, rubber, non-reversible
Pitch: 5.5 inches
Shoes per Vehicle: 124 (62/track)
Ground Contact Length: 86 inches

ELECTRICAL SYSTEM

Nominal Voltage: 12 volts DC
Main Generator: (1) 12 volts, 50 amperes, driven by main engine
Auxiliary Generator: None
Battery: (1) 12 volts

COMMUNICATIONS

Radio: SCR 193, SCR 209, or SCR 210 in rear of fighting compartment
Interphone: None

FIRE PROTECTION

(1) 7½ pound carbon dioxide, fixed
(1) 4 pound carbon dioxide, portable

PERFORMANCE

Maximum Speed: Level road	45 miles/hour
Maximum Grade:	60 per cent
Maximum Trench:	4 feet
Maximum Vertical Wall:	24 inches
Maximum Fording Depth:	43 inches
Minimum Turning Circle: (diameter)	42 feet
Cruising Range: Roads	approx. 120 miles

*Later replaced by a synchromesh transmission

GENERAL DATA

Crew:	4	men
Length:	163	inches
Width: Over side stowage	94	inches
Height: Over cupola roof	92	inches
Tread:	72	inches
Ground Clearance:	15	inches
Fire Height: (.50 caliber)	74	inches
Turret Ring Diameter: (inside 36 inch turret)	35.3	inches
(inside 30 inch turret)	29.5	inches
Weight, Combat Loaded:	19,100	pounds
Weight, Unstowed	approx. 17,300	pounds
Power to Weight Ratio: Net	26.0	hp/ton
Gross	27.3	hp/ton
Ground Pressure: Zero penetration	9.6	psi

ARMOR

Type: Turret, rolled face-hardened steel; Hull, rolled face-hardened steel;
Riveted assembly

Hull Thickness:

	Actual	Angle w/Vertical
Front, Upper	0.625 inches (16mm)	17 degrees
Middle	0.625 inches (16mm)	69 degrees
Lower	0.625 inches (16mm)	21 degrees
Sides	0.5 inches (13mm)	0 degrees
Rear	0.25 inches (6mm)	0 degrees
Top	0.25 inches (6mm)	90 degrees
Floor	0.25 inches (6mm)	90 degrees

Turret Thickness:

Front	0.625 inches (16mm)	0 degrees
Sides	0.625 inches (16mm)	0 degrees
Rear	0.625 inches (16mm)	0 degrees
Top	0.25 inches (6mm)	90 degrees

ARMAMENT

(1) .50 caliber MG HB M2 fixed in mount M9 in left turret
or
(1) .30 caliber MG M1919A4 flexible in mount M9A1 in left turret
(1) .30 caliber MG HB M2 flexible in ball mount M14 in right turret
or
(1) .30 caliber MG M1919A4 flexible in ball mount M12 in right turret
(1) .30 caliber MG HB M2 flexible in ball mount M8 in bow
or
(1) .30 caliber MG M1919A4 flexible in ball mount M10 in bow
or
(1) .30 caliber MG M1919A4 flexible in ball mount M13 in bow

Turret Traverse: Manual, each limited by stops to approximately 180 degrees

AMMUNITION
1625 rounds .50 caliber
4700 rounds .30 caliber

FIRE CONTROL AND VISION EQUIPMENT

Telescopic sight M5 or M1918A2 in left turret
Telescopic sight M5 or M1918A2 in right turret

Vision Devices:

Driver	Hatch, vision slots (2)
Asst. Driver	Hatch, vision slots (2)
Commander	Hatch, pistol ports (3), vision slots (7) in left turret
Gunner	Hatch, pistol ports (3), vision slots (6) in right turret

Total Vision Slots: Hull (4), Turret (13)
Total Pistol Ports: Hull (0), Turret (6)

ENGINE

Make and Model: Continental R-670-3, -3C, -5 or W-670-7, -8
Type: 7 cylinder, 4 cycle, radial
Cooling System: Air   Ignition: Magneto

Displacement:	668 cubic inches
Bore and Stroke:	5.125 x 4.625 inches
Compression Ratio: R-670-3, R-670-5 or W-670-7	6.1:1
R-670-3C or W-670-8	5.4:1
Net Horsepower: R-670-3, R-670-5 or W-670-7	250 horsepower at 2400 rpm
R-670-3C or W-670-8	235 horsepower at 2400 rpm
Gross Horsepower: R-670-3, R-670-5 or W-670-7	262 horsepower at 2400 rpm
R-670-3C or W-670-8	248 horsepower at 2400 rpm
Net Torque: (max) R-670-3, R-670-5 or W-670-7	584 ft-lb at 1800 rpm
Gross Torque: (max) R-670-3, R-670-5 or W-670-7	590 ft-lb at 1700 rpm
Weight:	565 pounds, dry
Fuel: High comp. 82 octane gasoline minimum	50 gallons
Low comp. 75 octane gasoline minimum	
Engine Oil:	32 quarts

POWER TRAIN

Clutch: Dry disc, 2 plate
Transmission: Sliding, constant mesh*, 5 speeds forward, 1 reverse

Gear Ratios:	1st	5.37:1	4th	1.09:1
	2nd	2.82:1	5th	0.738:1
	3rd	1.72:1	reverse	6.19:1

Steering: Controlled differential
Bevel Gear Ratio: 2.62:1   Steering Ratio: 1.845:1
Brakes: Mechanical, external contracting
Final Drive: Herringbone gear   Gear Ratio: 2:1
Drive Sprocket: At front of vehicle with 14 teeth
Pitch Diameter: 24.56 inches

RUNNING GEAR

Suspension: Vertical volute spring
8 wheels in 4 bogies (2 bogies/track)
Tire Size: 20 x 6 inches
4 track return rollers (2 rollers/track)
Adjustable idler at rear of each track
Idler Size: 24 x 6 inches
Tracks: Outside guide, rubber bushed; T16 series
Type: (T16E1) Double pin, 11.6 inch width, rubber, reversible
(T16E2) Double pin, 11.6 inch width, rubber, non-reversible
Pitch: 5.5 inches
Shoes per Vehicle: 124 (62/track)
Ground Contact Length: 86 inches

ELECTRICAL SYSTEM

Nominal Voltage: 12 volts DC
Main Generator: (1) 12 volts, 50 amperes, driven by main engine
Auxiliary Generator: None
Battery: (1) 12 volts

COMMUNICATIONS

Radio: SCR 193, SCR 209, or SCR 210 in rear of fighting compartment
Interphone: None

FIRE PROTECTION

(1) 7½ pound carbon dioxide, fixed
(1) 4 pound carbon dioxide, portable

PERFORMANCE

Maximum Speed: Level road	45 miles/hour
Maximum Grade:	60 per cent
Maximum Trench:	4 feet
Maximum Vertical Wall:	24 inches
Maximum Fording Depth:	43 inches
Minimum Turning Circle: (diameter)	42 feet
Cruising Range: Roads	approx. 120 miles

*Later replaced by a synchromesh transmission

LIGHT TANK M2A3

GENERAL DATA

Crew:	4 men
Length:	174.5 inches
Width: Over stowage guard rails	98 inches
Height: Over cupola roof	92 inches
Tread:	72.3 inches
Ground Clearance:	14.5 inches
Fire Height: (.50 caliber)	74 inches
Turret Ring Diameter: (inside 36 inch turret)	33.2 inches
(inside 30 inch turret)	27.3 inches
Weight, Combat Loaded:	21,000 pounds
Weight, Unstowed:	approx. 19,000 pounds
Power to Weight Ratio: Net	23.8 hp/ton
Gross	25.0 hp/ton
Ground Pressure: Zero penetration	9.3 psi

ARMOR

Type: Turret, rolled face-hardened steel; Hull, rolled face-hardened steel; Riveted assembly

Hull Thickness:

	Actual	Angle w/Vertical
Front, Upper	0.875 inches (22mm)	17 degrees
Middle	0.625 inches (16mm)	69 degrees
Lower	0.875 inches (22mm)	21 degrees
Sides	0.625 inches (16mm)	0 degrees
Rear, Upper	0.625 inches (16mm)	0 degrees
Lower	0.625 inches (16mm)	19 degrees
Top	0.375 inches (10mm)	90 degrees
Floor, Front	0.5 inches (13mm)	90 degrees
Rear	0.25 inches (6mm)	90 degrees

Turret Thickness:

Front	0.875 inches (22mm)	0 degrees
Sides	0.625 inches (16mm)	0 degrees
Rear	0.625 inches (16mm)	0 degrees
Top	0.25 inches (6mm)	90 degrees

ARMAMENT

(1) .50 caliber MG HB M2 fixed in mount M9 in left turret
(1) .30 caliber MG M1919A4 flexible in ball mount M13 in right turret
(1) .30 caliber MG M1919A4 flexible in ball mount M12 in bow
Turret Traverse: Manual, each limited by stops to approximately 180 degrees

AMMUNITION

1579 rounds .50 caliber
2370 rounds .30 caliber (4050 w/ SCR 245 or 6210 w/SCR 210A)

FIRE CONTROL AND VISION EQUIPMENT

Telescopic sight M5 or M1918A2 in left turret
Telescopic sight M5 or M1918A2 in right turret
Vision Devices:

Driver	Hatch, vision slots (2)
Asst. Driver	Hatch, vision slots (2)
Commander	Hatch, pistol ports (3), vision slots (7) in left turret
Gunner	Hatch, pistol ports (3), vision slots (4) in right turret

Total Vision Slots: Hull (4), Turret (11)
Total Pistol Ports: Hull (0), Turret (6)

ENGINE

Make and Model: Continental W-670-9	
Type: 7 cylinder, 4 cycle, radial	
Cooling System: Air Ignition: Magneto	
Displacement:	668 cubic inches
Bore and Stroke:	5.125 x 4.625 inches
Compression Ratio:	6.1:1
Net Horsepower: (max)	250 hp at 2400 rpm
Gross Horsepower: (max)	262 hp at 2400 rpm
Net Torque: (max)	584 ft-lb at 1800 rpm
Gross Torque: (max)	590 ft-lb at 1700 rpm
Weight:	565 pounds, dry
Fuel: 80 octane gasoline	54 gallons
Engine Oil:	32 quarts

POWER TRAIN

Clutch: Dry disc, 2 plate
Transmission: Constant mesh*, 5 speeds forward, 1 reverse

Gear Ratios:	1st 5.37:1	4th 1.09:1
	2nd 2.82:1	5th 0.738:1
	3rd 1.72:1	reverse 6.19:1

Steering: Controlled differential
Bevel Gear Ratio: 2.62:1   Steering Ratio: 1.845:1
Brakes: Mechanical, external contracting
Final Drive: Herringbone gear   Gear Ratio: 2.41:1
Drive Sprocket: At front of vehicle with 14 teeth
Pitch Diameter: 24.56 inches

RUNNING GEAR

Suspension: Vertical volute spring
8 wheels in 4 bogies (2 bogies/track)
Tire Size: 20 x 6 inches
4 track return rollers (2 rollers/track)
Adjustable idler at rear of each track
Idler Size: 24 x 6 inches
Tracks: Outside guide, rubber bushed; T16 series
Type: (T16E1) Double pin, 11.6 inch width, rubber, reversible
(T16E2) Double pin, 11.6 inch width, rubber, non-reversible
Pitch: 5.5 inches
Shoes per Vehicle: 134 (67/track)
Ground Contact Length: 97 inches

ELECTRICAL SYSTEM

Nominal Voltage: 12 volts DC
Main Generator: (1) 12 volts, 50 amperes, belt driven by main engine
Auxiliary Generator: None
Battery: (1) 12 volts

COMMUNICATIONS

Radio: SCR 193A, SCR 210A, or SCR 245B in rear of fighting compartment
Interphone: None

FIRE PROTECTION

(1) 7½ pound carbon dioxide, fixed
(1) 4 pound carbon dioxide, portable

PERFORMANCE

Maximum Speed: Level road	36 miles/hour
Maximum Grade:	60 per cent
Maximum Trench:	5 feet
Maximum Vertical Wall:	24 inches
Maximum Fording Depth:	43 inches
Minimum Turning Circle: (diameter)	42 feet
Cruising Range: Roads	approx. 100 miles

*Later replaced by a synchromesh transmission

COMBAT CAR M1 (LIGHT TANK M1A2)

GENERAL DATA

Crew:	4 men
Length:	163 inches
Width: Over side stowage	94 inches
Height: Over MG mount w/o MG	89 inches
Tread:	72 inches
Ground Clearance:	15 inches
Fire Height:	73 inches
Turret Ring Diameter: (inside)	47.5 inches
Weight, Combat Loaded:	18,790 pounds
Weight, Unstowed:	approx. 17,000 pounds
Power to Weight Ratio: Net	26.6 hp/ton
Gross	27.9 hp/ton
Ground Pressure: Zero penetration	9.4 psi

ARMOR

Type: Turret, rolled face-hardened steel; Hull, rolled face-hardened steel; Riveted assembly

Hull Thickness:	Actual	Angle w/Vertical
Front, Upper	0.625 inches (16mm)	17 degrees
Middle	0.625 inches (16mm)	69 degrees
Lower	0.625 inches (16mm)	21 degrees
Sides	0.5 inches (13mm)	0 degrees
Rear	0.25 inches (6mm)	0 degrees
Top	0.25 inches (6mm)	90 degrees
Floor	0.25 inches (6mm)	90 degrees

Turret Thickness:		
Front	0.625 inches (16mm)	30 degrees
Sides	0.625 inches (16mm)	0 degrees
Rear	0.625 inches (16mm)	0 degrees
Top	0.25 inches (6mm)	90 degrees

ARMAMENT

(1) .50 caliber MG HB M2 flexible in mount M15 in left side of turret
or
(1) .30 caliber MG HB M2 flexible in mount M15 in left side of turret
(1) .30 caliber MG HB M2 flexible in mount M16 in right side of turret
or
(1) .30 caliber MG HB M2 flexible in mount M18 in right side of turret
(1) .30 caliber MG HB M2 flexible in ball mount M8 in bow
or
(1) .30 caliber MG M1919A4 flexible in ball mount M10 in bow
or
(1) .30 caliber MG M1919A4 flexible in ball mount M13 in bow
(1) .30 caliber MG HB M2 flexible on AA bracket mount M17 on turret
or
(1) .30 caliber MG M1919A4 flexible on AA bracket mount M19 on turret
or
(1) .30 caliber MG M1919A4 flexible on AA bracket mount M20 on turret
Provision for (1) .45 caliber SMG M1928A1
Turret Traverse: Manual, 360 degrees

AMMUNITION

1100 rounds .50 caliber
6700 rounds .30 caliber
500 rounds .45 caliber

FIRE CONTROL AND VISION EQUIPMENT

Telescopic sight M5 or M1918A2 in mount M15, M16, or M18

Vision Devices:	
Driver	Hatch, vision slots (2)
Asst. Driver	Hatch, vision slots (2)
Commander	Hatch, pistol ports (3), vision slots (0)
Gunner	Hatch, pistol ports (2), vision slots (0)

Total Vision Slots: Hull (4), Turret (0)
Total Pistol Ports: Hull (0), Turret (5)

ENGINE

Make and Model: Continental R-670-3, -3C, -5 or W-670-7, -8
Type: 7 cylinder, 4 cycle, radial
Cooling System: Air   Ignition: Magneto

Displacement:	668 cubic inches
Bore and Stroke:	5.125 x 4.625 inches
Compression Ratio: R-670-3, R-670-5 or W-670-7	6.1:1
R-670-3C or W-670-8	5.4:1
Net Horsepower: R-670-3, R-670-5 or W-670-7	250 hp at 2400 rpm
R-670-3C or W-670-8	235 hp at 2400 rpm
Gross Horsepower: R-670-3, R-670-5 or W-670-7	262 hp at 2400 rpm
R-670-3C or W-670-8	248 hp at 2400 rpm
Net Torque: (max) R-670-3, R-670-5 or W-670-7	584 ft-lb at 1800 rpm
Gross Torque (max) R-670-3, R-670-5 or W-670-7	590 ft-lb at 1700 rpm
Weight:	565 pounds, dry
Fuel: High comp. 82 octane gasoline minimum	50 gallons
Low comp. 75 octane gasoline minimum	
Engine Oil:	32 quarts

POWER TRAIN

Clutch: Dry disc, 2 plate
Transmission: Sliding, constant mesh*, 5 speeds forward, 1 reverse

Gear Ratios:	1st 5.37:1	4th 1.09:1
	2nd 2.82:1	5th 0.738:1
	3rd 1.72:1	reverse 6.19:1

Steering: Controlled differential
Bevel Gear Ratio: 2.62:1   Steering Ratio: 1.845:1
Brakes: Mechanical, external contracting
Final Drive: Herringbone gear   Gear Ratio: 2:1
Drive Sprocket: At front of vehicle with 14 teeth
Pitch Diameter: 24.56 inches

RUNNING GEAR

Suspension: Vertical volute spring
8 wheels in 4 bogies (2 bogies/track)
Tire Size: 20 x 6 inches
4 track return rollers (2 rollers/track)
Adjustable idler at rear of each track
Idler Size: 24 x 6 inches
Tracks: Outside guide, rubber bushed; T16 series
Type: (T16E1) Double pin, 11.6 inch width, rubber, reversible
(T16E2) Double pin, 11.6 inch width, rubber, non-reversible
Pitch: 5.5 inches
Shoes per Vehicle: 124 (62/track)
Ground Contact Length: 86 inches

ELECTRICAL SYSTEM

Nominal Voltage: 12 volts DC
Main Generator: (1) 12 volts, 50 amperes, driven by main engine
Auxiliary Generator: None
Battery: (1) 12 volts

COMMUNICATIONS

Radio: SCR 193, SCR 209, or SCR 210 in rear of fighting compartment
Interphone: None

FIRE PROTECTION

(1) 7½ pound carbon dioxide, fixed
(1) 4 pound carbon dioxide, portable

PERFORMANCE

Maximum Speed: Level road	45 miles/hour
Maximum Grade:	60 per cent
Maximum Trench:	4 feet
Maximum Vertical Wall:	24 inches
Maximum Fording Depth:	43 inches
Minimum Turning Circle: (diameter)	42 feet
Cruising Range: Roads	approx. 120 miles

*Later replaced by a synchromesh transmission

COMBAT CAR M1A1 (LIGHT TANK M1A2)

GENERAL DATA

Crew:	4 men
Length:	174.5 inches
Width: Over side stowage	94 inches
Height: Over MG mount w/o MG	89 inches
Tread:	72 inches
Ground Clearance:	15 inches
Fire Height:	73 inches
Turret Ring Diameter: (inside)	47.5 inches
Weight, Combat Loaded:	approx. 19,000 pounds
Weight, Unstowed:	approx. 17,000 pounds
Power to Weight Ratio: Net	26.3 hp/ton
Gross	27.6 hp/ton
Ground Pressure: Zero penetration	8.4 psi

ARMOR

Type: Turret, rolled face-hardened steel; Hull, rolled face-hardened steel;
Riveted assembly

Hull Thickness:	Actual	Angle w/Vertical
Front, Upper	0.625 inches (16mm)	17 degrees
Middle	0.625 inches (16mm)	69 degrees
Lower	0.625 inches (16mm)	21 degrees
Sides	0.5 inches (13mm)	0 degrees
Rear, Upper	0.375 inches (10mm)	0 degrees
Lower	0.375 inches (10mm)	19 degrees
Top	0.25 inches (6mm)	90 degrees
Floor	0.25 inches (6mm)	90 degrees

Turret Thickness:		
Front	0.625 inches (16mm)	30 degrees
Sides	0.625 inches (16mm)	0 degrees
Rear	0.625 inches (16mm)	0 degrees
Top	0.25 inches (6mm)	90 degrees

ARMAMENT

(1) .50 caliber MG HB M2 flexible in mount M15 in left side of turret
or
(1) .30 caliber MG HB M2 flexible in mount M15 in left side of turret
(1) .30 caliber MG HB M2 flexible in mount M18 in right side of turret
(1) .30 caliber MG M1919A4 flexible in ball mount M13 in bow
(1) .30 caliber MG M1919A4 flexible on AA bracket mount M20 on turret
Provision for (1) .45 caliber SMG M1928A1
Turret Traverse: Manual, 360 degrees

AMMUNITION

1364 rounds .50 caliber
9470 rounds .30 caliber (11,150 rounds w/SCR 245A radio)
500 rounds .45 caliber

FIRE CONTROL AND VISION EQUIPMENT

Telescopic sight M5 or M1918A2 in mount M15 or M18
Vision Devices:

Driver	Hatch, vision slots (2)
Asst. Driver	Hatch, vision slots (2)
Commander	Hatch, pistol ports (3), vision slots (2 in folding roof)
Gunner	Hatch, pistol ports (2), vision slots (0)

Total Vision Slots: Hull (4), Turret (2 in folding roof)
Total Pistol Ports: Hull (0), Turret (5)

ENGINE

Make and Model: Continental W-670-7	
Type: 7 cylinder, 4 cycle, radial	
Cooling System: Air Ignition: Magneto	
Displacement:	668 cubic inches
Bore and Stroke:	5.125 x 4.625 inches
Compression Ratio:	6.1:1
Net Horsepower: (max)	250 hp at 2400 rpm
Gross Horsepower: (max)	262 hp at 2400 rpm
Net Torque: (max)	584 ft-lb at 1800 rpm
Gross Torque: (max)	590 ft-lb at 1700 rpm
Weight:	565 pounds, dry
Fuel: 80 octane gasoline	60 gallons
Engine Oil:	32 quarts

POWER TRAIN

Clutch: Dry disc, 2 plate
Transmission: Constant mesh*, 5 speeds forward, 1 reverse

Gear Ratios:	1st 5.37:1	4th	1.09:1
	2nd 2.82:1	5th	0.738:1
	3rd 1.72:1	reverse	6.19:1

Steering: Controlled differential
Bevel Gear Ratio: 2.62:1   Steering Ratio: 1.845:1
Brakes: Mechanical, external contracting
Final Drive: Herringbone gear   Gear Ratio: 2.41:1
Drive Sprocket: At front of vehicle with 14 teeth
Pitch Diameter: 24.56 inches

RUNNING GEAR

Suspension: Vertical volute spring
8 wheels in 4 bogies (2 bogies/track)
Tire Size: 20 x 6 inches
4 track return rollers (2 rollers/track)
Adjustable idler at rear of each track
Idler Size: 24 x 6 inches
Tracks: Outside guide, rubber bushed; T16 series
Type: (T16E1) Double pin, 11.6 inch width, rubber, reversible
(T16E2) Double pin, 11.6 inch width, rubber, non-reversible
Pitch: 5.5 inches
Shoes per Vehicle: 134 (67/track)
Ground Contact Length: 97 inches

ELECTRICAL SYSTEM

Nominal Voltage: 12 volts DC
Main Generator: (1) 12 volts, 50 amperes, driven by main engine
Auxiliary Generator: None
Battery: (1) 12 volts

COMMUNICATIONS

Radio: SCR 193C, SCR 209C, or SCR 245A in rear of fighting compartment
Interphone: None

FIRE PROTECTION

(1) 7½ pound carbon dioxide, fixed
(1) 4 pound carbon dioxide, portable

PERFORMANCE

Maximum Speed: Level road	36 miles/hour
Maximum Grade:	60 per cent
Maximum Trench:	5 feet
Maximum Vertical Wall:	24 inches
Maximum Fording Depth:	43 inches
Minimum Turning Circle: (diameter)	42 feet
Cruising Range: Roads	approx. 110 miles

* Later replaced by a synchromesh transmission

COMBAT CAR M2 (LIGHT TANK M1A1)

GENERAL DATA

Crew:	4 men
Length:	172 inches
Width: Over idler brackets	90.6 inches
Height: Over MG mount w/o MG	95 inches
Tread:	72 inches
Ground Clearance:	14.5 inches
Fire Height:	75 inches
Turret Ring Diameter: (inside)	47.5 inches
Weight, Combat Loaded:	25,500 pounds
Weight, Unstowed:	approx. 23,000 pounds
Power to Weight Ratio: Net	17.3 hp/ton
Gross	19.2 hp/ton
Ground Pressure: Zero penetration	9.4 psi

ARMOR

Type: Turret, rolled face-hardened steel; Hull, rolled face-hardened steel; Riveted assembly

Hull Thickness:

		Actual	Angle w/Vertical
Front,	Upper	0.625 inches (16mm)	17 degrees
	Middle	0.625 inches (16mm)	69 degrees
	Lower	0.625 inches (16mm)	21 degrees
Sides		0.5 inches (13mm)	0 degrees
Rear,	Upper	0.375 inches (10mm)	0 degrees
	Lower	0.375 inches (10mm)	19 degrees
Top		0.375 inches (10mm)	90 degrees
Floor		0.25 inches (6mm)	90 degrees

Turret Thickness:

	Actual	Angle w/Vertical
Front	0.625 inches (16mm)	30 degrees
Sides	0.625 inches (16mm)	0 degrees
Rear	0.625 inches (16mm)	0 degrees
Top	0.25 inches (6mm)	90 degrees

ARMAMENT

(1) .50 caliber MG HB M2 flexible in mount M15 in left side of turret
(1) .30 caliber MG HB M2 flexible in mount M18 in right side of turret
(1) .30 caliber MG M1919A4 flexible in ball mount M13 in bow
(1) .30 caliber MG M1919A4 flexible on AA bracket mount M20 on turret
Provision for (1) .45 caliber SMG M1928A1
Turret Traverse: Manual, 360 degrees

AMMUNITION

1364 rounds .50 caliber
9470 rounds .30 caliber (11,150 rounds w/SCR 245A radio)
500 rounds .45 caliber

FIRE CONTROL AND VISION EQUIPMENT

Telescopic sight M5 or M1918A2 in mount M15 or M18
Vision Devices:

Driver	Hatch, vision slots (2)
Asst. Driver	Hatch, vision slots (2)
Commander	Hatch, pistol ports (2), vision slots (0)
Gunner	Hatch, pistol ports (2), vision slots (0)

Total Vision Slots: Hull (4), Turret (0)
Total Pistol Ports: Hull (0), Turret (4)

ENGINE

Make and Model: Guiberson T-1020-4	
Type: 9 cylinder, 4 cycle, radial	
Cooling System: Air Ignition: Compression	
Displacement:	1021 cubic inches
Bore and Stroke:	5.125 x 5.5 inches
Compression Ratio:	14.5:1
Net Horsepower: (max)	220 hp at 2200 rpm
Gross Horsepower: (max)	245 hp at 2200 rpm
Net Torque: (max)	580 ft-lb at 1400 rpm
Gross Torque: (max)	645 ft-lb at 1300 rpm
Weight:	730 pounds, dry
Fuel: 40 cetane diesel oil	60 gallons
Engine Oil:	32 quarts

POWER TRAIN

Clutch: Dry disc, 2 plate
Transmission: Synchromesh, 5 speeds forward, 1 reverse

Gear Ratios:	1st	5.37:1	4th	1.09:1
	2nd	2.82:1	5th	0.738:1
	3rd	1.72:1	reverse	6.19:1

Steering: Controlled differential
Bevel Gear Ratio: 2.62:1   Steering Ratio: 1.845:1
Brakes: Mechanical, external contracting
Final Drive: Herringbone gear   Gear Ratio: 2.41:1
Drive Sprocket: At front of vehicle with 14 teeth
Pitch Diameter: 24.56 inches

RUNNING GEAR

Suspension: Vertical volute spring
8 wheels in 4 bogies (2 bogies/track)
Tire Size: 20 x 6 inches
6 track return rollers (3 rollers/track)
Trailing adjustable idler w/volute spring at rear of each track
Idler Size: 30 x 6 inches
Tracks: Outside guide, rubber bushed; T16 series
Type: (T16E1) Double pin, 11.6 inch width, rubber, reversible
(T16E2) Double pin, 11.6 inch width, rubber, non-reversible
Pitch: 5.5 inches
Shoes per Vehicle: 132 (66/track)
Ground Contact Length: 117 inches

ELECTRICAL SYSTEM

Nominal Voltage: 12 volts DC
Main Generator: (1) 12 volts, 50 amperes, belt driven by main engine
Auxiliary Generator: None
Battery: (1) 12 volts

COMMUNICATIONS

Radio: SCR 193C, SCR 209C, or SCR 245A in rear of fighting compartment
Interphone: None

FIRE PROTECTION

(1) 7½ pound carbon dioxide, fixed
(1) 4 pound carbon dioxide, portable

PERFORMANCE

Maximum Speed: Level road, governed	36 miles/hour
Maximum Grade:	60 per cent
Maximum Trench:	6 feet
Maximum Fording Depth:	52 inches
Minimum Turning Circle: (diameter)	42 feet
Cruising Range: Roads	approx. 200 miles

GENERAL DATA

Crew:	4	men
Length:	174.5	inches
Width:	97.25	inches
Height:Over MG mount	104	inches
Tread:	73.0	inches
Ground Clearance:	16.5	inches
Fire Height:	76	inches
Turret Ring Diameter: (inside)	46.75	inches
Weight, Combat Loaded:	25,600	pounds
Weight, Unstowed:	23,500	pounds
Power to Weight Ratio: Net	19.5	hp/ton
Gross	20.5	hp/ton
Ground Pressure: Zero penetration	11.4	psi

ARMOR

Type: Turret, rolled face-hardened steel; Hull, rolled face-hardened steel; Riveted assembly

Hull Thickness:

		Actual	Angle w/Vertical
Front,	Upper	1.0 inches (25mm)	17 degrees
	Middle	0.625 inches (16mm)	69 degrees
	Lower	1.0 inches (25mm)	19 degrees
Sides		1.0 inches (25mm)	0 degrees
Rear,	Upper	1.0 inches (25mm)	0 degrees
	Lower	1.0 inches (25mm)	20 degrees
Top		0.25 inches (6mm)	90 degrees
Floor,	Front	0.5 inches (13mm)	90 degrees
	Rear	0.25 inches (6mm)	90 degrees

Turret Thickness:

	Actual	Angle w/Vertical
Gun Shield	1.0 inches (25mm)	0 to 14 degrees
Front	1.0 inches (25mm)	10 degrees
Sides	1.0 inches (25mm)	0 degrees
Rear	1.0 inches (25mm)	0 degrees
Top	0.25 inches (6mm)	75 to 90 degrees

ARMAMENT

Primary: 37mm Gun M5 in Mount M20 (T12) in turret

Traverse: Manual, 20 degrees in mount	360 degrees
Elevation: Manual	+19 to −6 degrees
Firing Rate: (max)	30 rounds/minute
Loading System:	Manual
Stabilizer System:	None

Secondary:
(1) .30 caliber MG M1919A4 flexible M20 AA mount on turret
(1) .30 caliber MG M1919A4 coaxial w/37mm gun in turret
(1) .30 caliber MG M1919A4 in bow mount
(2) .30 caliber MG M1919A4 fixed, one in each sponson
Provision for (1) .45 caliber SMG M1928A1

AMMUNITION
103 rounds 37mm
500 rounds .45 caliber
8470 rounds .30 caliber

FIRE CONTROL AND VISION EQUIPMENT

Primary Weapon: Telescope M5A1
Vision Devices:

Driver	Hatch, vision slots (2)
Asst. Driver	Hatch, vision slots (2)
Commander	Hatch, pistol ports (5), vision slots (6)
Gunner	Pistol ports (2)

Total Vision Slots: Hull (4), Turret (6) in cupola
Total Pistol Ports: Hull (0), Turret (7)

ENGINE

Make and Model: Continental W-670-9A	
Type: 7 cylinder, 4 cycle, radial	
Cooling System: Air Ignition: Magneto	
Displacement:	668 cubic inches
Bore and Stroke:	5.125 x 4.625 inches
Compression Ratio:	6.1:1
Net Horsepower: (max)	250 hp at 2400 rpm
Gross Horsepower: (max)	262 hp at 2400 rpm
Net Torque: (max)	584 ft-lb at 1800 rpm
Gross Torque: (max)	590 ft-lb at 1700 rpm
Weight:	565 pounds, dry
Fuel: 80 octane gasoline	54 gallons
Engine Oil:	32 quarts

POWER TRAIN

Clutch: Dry disc, 2 plate
Transmission: Synchromesh, 5 speeds forward, 1 reverse

Gear Ratios:	1st	5.37:1	4th	1.09:1
	2nd	2.82:1	5th	0.738:1
	3rd	1.72:1	reverse	6.19:1

Steering: Controlled differential
Bevel Gear Ratio: 2.62:1   Steering Ratio: 1.845:1
Brakes: Mechanical, external contracting
Final Drive: Herringbone gear   Gear Ratio: 2.41:1
Drive Sprocket: At front of vehicle with 14 teeth
Pitch Diameter: 24.56 inches

RUNNING GEAR

Suspension: Vertical volute spring
8 wheels in 4 bogies (2 bogies/track)
Tire Size: 20 x 6 inches
4 track return rollers (2 rollers/track)
Adjustable idler at rear of each track
Idler Size: 24 x 6 inches
Tracks: Outside guide, rubber bushed; T16 series
Type: (T16E1) Double pin, 11.6 inch width, rubber, reversible
(T16E2) Double pin, 11.6 inch width, rubber, non-reversible
Pitch: 5.5 inches
Shoes per Vehicle: 134 (67/track)
Ground Contact Length: 97 inches

ELECTRICAL SYSTEM

Nominal Voltage: 12 volts DC
Main Generator: (1) 12 volts, 50 amperes, belt driven by main engine
Auxiliary Generator: None
Battery: (1) 12 volts

COMMUNICATIONS

Radio: SCR 210 in right sponson;
SCR 245* (command tanks only) in left sponson
Interphone: RC61, 4 stations
*Early vehicles may be equipped with the SCR 193

FIRE PROTECTION

(1) 7½ pound carbon dioxide, fixed
(1) 4 pound carbon dioxide, portable

PERFORMANCE

Maximum Speed: Level road, governed	36 miles/hour
Maximum Grade:	60 per cent
Maximum Trench:	5 feet
Maximum Vertical Wall:	24 inches
Maximum Fording Depth:	36 inches
Minimum Turning Circle: (diameter)	42 feet
Cruising Range: Roads	approx. 70 miles

LIGHT TANK M3 (early production)

GENERAL DATA

Crew:	4 men
Length:	178.4 inches
Width:	88.0 inches
Height: Over MG mount	104 inches
Tread:	73.0 inches
Ground Clearance:	16.5 inches
Fire Height:	76 inches
Turret Ring Diameter: (inside)	46.75 inches
Weight, Combat Loaded:	28,000 pounds
Weight, Unstowed:	25,600 pounds
Power to Weight Ratio: Net	17.9 hp/ton
Gross	18.7 hp/ton
Ground Pressure: Zero penetration	10.3 psi

ARMOR

Type: Turret, rolled face-hardened steel; Hull, rolled face-hardened steel; Riveted and welded assembly

Hull Thickness:

	Actual	Angle w/Vertical
Front, Upper	1.5 inches (38mm)	17 degrees
Middle	0.625 inches (16mm)	69 degrees
Lower (cast)	1.75 inches (44mm)	23 degrees
Sides	1.0 inches (25mm)	0 degrees
Rear, Upper	1.0 inches (25mm)	59 degrees
Middle	1.0 inches (25mm)	0 degrees
Lower	1.0 inches (25mm)	20 degrees
Top	0.5 inches (13mm)	90 degrees
Floor, Front	0.5 inches (13mm)	90 degrees
Rear	0.375 inches (10mm)	90 degrees

Turret Thickness:

Gun Shield	1.5 inches (38mm)	0 to 14 degrees
Front	1.5 inches (38mm)	10 degrees
Sides	1.0 inches (25mm)	0 degrees
Rear	1.0 inches (25mm)	0 degrees
Top	0.5 inches (13mm)	75 to 90 degrees

ARMAMENT

Primary: 37mm Gun M5 in Mount M22 in turret

Traverse: Manual, 20 degrees in mount	360 degrees
Elevation: Manual	+20 to −10 degrees
Firing Rate: (max)	30 rounds/minute
Loading System:	Manual
Stabilizer System:	Elevation only

Secondary:
(1) .30 caliber MG M1919A4 flexible M20 AA mount on turret
(1) .30 caliber MG M1919A4 coaxial w/37mm gun in turret
(1) .30 caliber MG M1919A4 in bow mount
(2) .30 caliber MG M1919A4 fixed, one in each sponson
Provision for (1) .45 caliber SMG M1928A1

AMMUNITION

103 rounds 37mm   12 hand grenades
500 rounds .45 caliber
8270 rounds .30 caliber

FIRE CONTROL AND VISION EQUIPMENT

Primary Weapon: Telescope M5A1
Vision Devices:

Driver	Hatch, vision slots (2)
Asst. Driver	Hatch, vision slots (2)
Commander	Hatch, pistol ports (2), vision slots (6)
Gunner	Pistol port (1)

Total Vision Slots: Hull (4), Turret (6) in cupola
Total Pistol Ports: Hull (0), Turret (3)

ENGINE

Make and Model: Continental W-670-9A	
Type: 7 cylinder, 4 cycle, radial	
Cooling System: Air Ignition: Magneto	
Displacement:	668 cubic inches
Bore and Stroke:	5.125 x 4.625 inches
Compression Ratio:	6.1:1
Net Horsepower: (max)	250 hp at 2400 rpm
Gross Horsepower: (max)	262 hp at 2400 rpm
Net Torque: (max)	584 ft-lb at 1800 rpm
Gross Torque: (max)	590 ft-lb at 1700 rpm
Weight:	565 pounds, dry
Fuel: 80 octane gasoline	54 gallons
Engine Oil:	32 quarts

POWER TRAIN

Clutch: Dry disc, 2 plate
Transmission: Synchromesh, 5 speeds forward, 1 reverse

Gear Ratios:	1st	5.37:1	4th	1.09:1
	2nd	2.82:1	5th	0.738:1
	3rd	1.72:1	reverse	6.19:1

Steering: Controlled differential
Bevel Gear Ratio: 2.62:1   Steering Ratio: 1.845:1
Brakes: Mechanical, external contracting
Final Drive: Herringbone gear   Gear Ratio: 2.41:1
Drive Sprocket: At front of vehicle with 14 teeth
Pitch Diameter: 24.56 inches

RUNNING GEAR

Suspension: Vertical volute spring
8 wheels in 4 bogies (2 bogies/track)
Tire Size: 20 x 6 inches
6 track return rollers (3 rollers/track)
Trailing adjustable idler w/volute spring at rear of each track
Idler Size: 30 x 6 inches
Tracks: Outside guide, rubber bushed, T16 series
Type: (T16E1) Double pin, 11.6 inch width, rubber, reversible
(T16E2) Double pin, 11.6 inch width, rubber non-reversible
Pitch: 5.5 inches
Shoes per Vehicle: 132 (66/track)
Ground Contact Length: 117 inches

ELECTRICAL SYSTEM

Nominal Voltage: 12 volts DC
Main Generator: (1) 12 volts, 50 amperes, belt driven by main engine
Auxiliary Generator: None
Battery: (1) 12 volts

COMMUNICATIONS

Radio: SCR 210 in right sponson; SCR 245* (command tanks only) in left sponson
Interphone: RC61, 4 stations
*Early vehicles may be equipped with the SCR 193

FIRE PROTECTION

(1) 7½ pound carbon dioxide, fixed
(1) 4 pound carbon dioxide, portable

PERFORMANCE

Maximum Speed: Level road, governed	36 miles/hour
Maximum Grade:	60 per cent
Maximum Trench:	6 feet
Maximum Vertical Wall:	24 inches
Maximum Fording Depth:	36 inches
Minimum Turning Circle: (diameter)	42 feet
Cruising Range: Roads	approx. 70 miles

LIGHT TANK M3, Diesel (mid-production)

GENERAL DATA

Crew:	4 men
Length:	178.4 inches
Width:	88.0 inches
Height: Over MG mount	104 inches
Tread:	73.0 inches
Ground Clearance:	16.5 inches
Fire Height:	76 inches
Turret Ring Diameter: (inside)	46.75 inches
Weight, Combat Loaded:	28,000 pounds
Weight, Unstowed:	25,600 pounds
Power to Weight Ratio: Net	15.7 hp/ton
Gross	17.5 hp/ton
Ground Pressure: Zero penetration	10.3 psi

ARMOR

Type: Turret, rolled homogeneous steel; Hull, rolled face-hardened steel;
Riveted and welded assembly

Hull Thickness:	Actual	Angle w/Vertical
Front, Upper	1.5 inches (38mm)	17 degrees
Middle	0.625 inches (16mm)	69 degrees
Lower (cast)	1.75 inches (44mm)	23 degrees
Sides	1.0 inches (25mm)	0 degrees
Rear, Upper	1.0 inches (25mm)	59 degrees
Middle	1.0 inches (25mm)	0 degrees
Lower	1.0 inches (25mm)	20 degrees
Top	0.5 inches (13mm)	90 degrees
Floor, Front	0.5 inches (13mm)	90 degrees
Rear	0.375 inches (10mm)	90 degrees

Turret Thickness:		
Gun Shield	2.0 inches (51mm)	0 to 14 degrees
Front	1.5 inches (38mm)	10 degrees
Sides	1.25 inches (32mm)	0 degrees
Rear	1.25 inches (32mm)	0 degrees
Top	0.5 inches (13mm)	75 to 90 degrees

ARMAMENT

Primary: 37mm Gun M6 in Mount M23 in turret

Traverse: Manual, 20 degrees in mount	360 degrees
Elevation: Manual	+20 to −10 degrees
Firing Rate: (max)	30 rounds/minute
Loading System:	Manual
Stabilizer System:	Elevation only

Secondary:
(1) .30 caliber MG M1919A4 flexible M20 AA mount on turret
(1) .30 caliber MG M1919A4 coaxial w/37mm gun in turret
(1) .30 caliber MG M1919A4 in bow mount
(2) .30 caliber MG M1919A4 fixed, one in each sponson
Provision for (1) .45 caliber SMG M1928A1

AMMUNITION

103 rounds 37mm   12 hand grenades
500 rounds .45 caliber
8270 rounds .30 caliber

FIRE CONTROL AND VISION EQUIPMENT

Primary Weapon: Telescope M5A1

Vision Devices:	Direct	Indirect
Driver	Hatch, vision slots (2)	Protectoscope (1)
Asst. Driver	Hatch, vision slots (2)	Protectoscope (1)
Commander	Hatch, pistol ports (2), vision slots (4) in cupola	Protectoscopes (2)
Gunner	Pistol port (1)	Protectoscope (1)

Total Protectoscopes: Hull (2), Turret (3)
Total Vision Slots: Hull (4), Turret (4) in cupola
Total Pistol Ports: Hull (0), Turret (3)

ENGINE

Make and Model: Guiberson T-1020-4	
Type: 9 cylinder, 4 cycle, radial	
Cooling System: Air Ignition: Compression	
Displacement:	1021 cubic inches
Bore and Stroke:	5.125 x 5.5 inches
Compression Ratio:	14.5:1
Net Horsepower (max):	220 hp at 2200 rpm
Gross Horsepower (max):	245 hp at 2200 rpm
Net Torque (max):	580 ft-lb at 1400 rpm
Gross Torque (max):	645 ft-lb at 1300 rpm
Weight:	730 pounds, dry
Fuel: 40 cetane diesel oil	54 gallons
Engine Oil:	32 quarts

POWER TRAIN

Clutch: Dry disc, 2 plate
Transmission: Synchromesh, 5 speeds forward, 1 reverse

Gear Ratios:	1st	5.37:1	4th	1.09:1
	2nd	2.82:1	5th	0.738:1
	3rd	1.72:1	reverse	6.19:1

Steering: Controlled differential
Bevel Gear Ratio: 2.62:1   Steering Ratio: 1.845:1
Brakes: Mechanical, external contracting
Final Drive: Herringbone gear   Gear Ratio: 2.41:1
Drive Sprocket: At front of vehicle with 14 teeth
Pitch Diameter: 24.56 inches

RUNNING GEAR

Suspension: Vertical volute spring
8 wheels in 4 bogies (2 bogies/track)
Tire Size: 20 x 6 inches
6 track return rollers (3/track)
Trailing adjustable idler w/volute spring at rear of each track
Idler Size: 30 x 6 inches
Tracks: Outside guide, rubber bushed; T16 series
Type: (T16E1) Double pin, 11.6 inch width, rubber, reversible
(T16E2) Double pin, 11.6 inch width, rubber, non-reversible
Pitch: 5.5 inches
Shoes per Vehicle: 132 (66/track)
Ground Contact Length: 117 inches

ELECTRICAL SYSTEM

Nominal Voltage: 12 volts DC
Main Generator: (1) 12 volts, 50 amperes, belt driven by main engine
Auxiliary Generator: None
Battery: (1) 12 volts

COMMUNICATIONS

Radio: SCR 210 in right sponson; SCR 245* (command tanks only) in left sponson
Interphone: RC61, 4 stations
*Early vehicles may be equipped with the SCR 193

FIRE PROTECTION

(1) 7½ pound carbon dioxide, fixed
(1) 4 pound carbon dioxide, portable

PERFORMANCE

Maximum Speed: Level road, governed	36 miles/hour
Maximum Grade:	60 per cent
Maximum Trench:	6 feet
Maximum Vertical Wall:	24 inches
Maximum Fording Depth:	36 inches
Minimum Turning Circle: (diameter)	42 feet
Cruising Range: Roads	approx. 90 miles

LIGHT TANK M3 (late production)

GENERAL DATA

Crew:	4 men
Length:	178.4 inches
Width:	88.0 inches
Height: Over MG mount*	94 inches
Tread:	73.0 inches
Ground Clearance:	16.5 inches
Fire Height:	76 inches
Turret Ring Diameter: (inside)	46.75 inches
Weight, Combat Loaded:	28,000 pounds
Weight, Unstowed:	25,600 pounds
Power to Weight Ratio: Net	17.9 hp/ton
Gross	18.7 hp/ton
Ground Pressure: Zero penetration	10.3 psi

ARMOR

Type: Turret, rolled homogeneous steel; Hull, rolled face-hardened steel; Welded and riveted assembly

Hull Thickness:

		Actual	Angle w/Vertical
Front,	Upper	1.5 inches (38mm)	17 degrees
	Middle	0.625 inches (16mm)	69 degrees
	Lower (cast)	1.75 inches (44mm)	23 degrees
Sides		1.0 inches (25mm)	0 degrees
Rear,	Upper	1.0 inches (25mm)	59 degrees
	Middle	1.0 inches (25mm)	0 degrees
	Lower	1.0 inches (25mm)	20 degrees
Top		0.5 inches (13mm)	90 degrees
Floor,	Front	0.5 inches (13mm)	90 degrees
	Rear	0.375 inches (10mm)	90 degrees

Turret Thickness:

Gun Shield	2.0 inches (51mm)	0 to 14 degrees
Front	1.5 inches (38mm)	10 degrees
Sides	1.25 inches (32mm)	0 degrees
Rear	1.25 inches (32mm)	0 degrees
Top	0.5 inches (13mm)	75 to 90 degrees

ARMAMENT

Primary: 37mm Gun M6 in Mount M23 in turret*

Traverse: Manual, 20 degrees in mount	360 degrees
Elevation: Manual	+20 to −10 degrees
Firing Rate: (max)	30 rounds/minute
Loading System:	Manual
Stabilizer System:	Elevation only

Secondary:
- (1) .30 caliber MG M1919A4 flexible M20 AA mount on turret
- (1) .30 caliber MG M1919A4 coaxial w/37mm gun in turret
- (1) .30 caliber MG M1919A4 in bow mount
- (2) .30 caliber MG M1919A4 fixed, one in each sponson
- Provision for (1) .45 caliber SMG M1928A1

AMMUNITION

103 rounds 37mm	12 hand grenades
500 rounds .45 caliber	
8270 rounds .30 caliber	

FIRE CONTROL AND VISION EQUIPMENT

Primary Weapon: Periscope M4 with Telescope M40

Vision Devices:	Direct	Indirect
Driver	Hatch, vision slots (2)	Protectoscope (1)
Asst. Driver	Hatch, vision slots (2)	Protectoscope (1)
Commander	Hatch, pistol ports (2)	Periscopes M6 (1)
		Protectoscopes (2)
Gunner	Pistol Port (1)	Periscope M4 (1)
		Protectoscope (1)

Total Periscopes: Hull (0), Turret M4 (1), M6 (1)
Total Protectoscopes: Hull (2), Turret (3)
Total Vision Slots: Hull (4), Turret (0)
Total Pistol Ports: Hull (0), Turret (3)

*Fitted w/M3A1 turret w/o basket and w/o the power traverse.

ENGINE

Make and Model: Continental W-670-9A	
Type: 7 cylinder, 4 cycle, radial	
Cooling System: Air Ignition: Magneto	
Displacement:	668 cubic inches
Bore and Stroke:	5.125 x 4.625 inches
Compression Ratio:	6.1:1
Net Horsepower: (max)	250 hp at 2400 rpm
Gross Horsepower: (max)	262 hp at 2400 rpm
Net Torque: (max)	584 ft-lb at 1800 rpm
Gross Torque: (max)	590 ft-lb at 1700 rpm
Weight:	565 pounds, dry
Fuel: 80 octane gasoline	54 gallons
With two 25 gallon jettison tanks	104 gallons
Engine Oil:	32 quarts

POWER TRAIN

Clutch: Dry disc, 2 plate
Transmission: Synchromesh, 5 speeds forward, 1 reverse

Gear Ratios:	1st 5.37:1	4th 1.09:1
	2nd 2.82:1	5th 0.738:1
	3rd 1.72:1	reverse 6.19:1

Steering: Controlled differential
Bevel Gear Ratio: 2.62:1   Steering Ratio: 1.845:1
Brakes: Mechanical, external contracting
Final Drive: Herringbone gear   Gear Ratio: 2.41:1
Drive Sprocket: At front of vehicle with 14 teeth
Pitch Diameter: 24.56 inches

RUNNING GEAR

Suspension: Vertical volute spring
- 8 wheels in 4 bogies (2 bogies/track)
- Tire Size: 20 x 6 inches
- 6 track return rollers (3 rollers/track)
- Trailing adjustable idler w/volute spring at rear of each track
- Idler Size: 30 x 6 inches
- Tracks: Outside guide, rubber bushed; T16 series, T36E6, and T55E1
  - Type: (T16E1) Double pin, 11.6 inch width, rubber, reversible
  - (T16E2) Double pin, 11.6 inch width, rubber, non-reversible
  - (T36E6) Double pin, 11.6 inch width, steel, parallel grouser
  - (T55E1) Double pin, 11.6 inch width, steel, chevron
  - Pitch: 5.5 inches
  - Shoes per Vehicle: 132 (66/track)
  - Ground Contact Length: 117 inches

ELECTRICAL SYSTEM

Nominal Voltage: 12 volts DC
Main Generator: (1) 12 volts, 50 amperes, belt driven by main engine
Auxiliary Generator: None
Battery: (1) 12 volts

COMMUNICATIONS

Radio: SCR 210 in right sponson; SCR 245 (command tanks only) in left sponson
Interphone: RC61, 4 stations

FIRE PROTECTION

- (1) 7½ pound carbon dioxide, fixed
- (1) 4 pound carbon dioxide, portable

PERFORMANCE

Maximum Speed: Level road, governed	36 miles/hour
Maximum Grade:	60 per cent
Maximum Trench:	6 feet
Maximum Vertical Wall:	24 inches
Maximum Fording Depth:	36 inches
Minimum Turning Circle: (diameter)	42 feet
Cruising Range: Roads	approx. 70 miles
w/two 25 gallon jettison tanks	approx. 135 miles

LIGHT TANK M3A1

GENERAL DATA

Crew:	4 men
Length:	178.4 inches
Width:	88.0 inches
Height: Over MG mount	94 inches
Tread:	73.0 inches
Ground Clearance:	16.5 inches
Fire Height:	76 inches
Turret Ring Diameter: (inside)	46.75 inches
Weight, Combat Loaded:	28,500 pounds
Weight, Unstowed:	26,000 pounds
Power to Weight Ratio: Net	17.5 hp/ton
Gross	18.4 hp/ton
Ground Pressure: Zero penetration	10.5 psi

ARMOR

Type: Turret, rolled homogeneous steel; Hull, rolled face-hardened and homogeneous steel; Riveted and welded assembly

Hull Thickness:	Actual	Angle w/Vertical
Front, Upper	1.5 inches (38mm)	17 degrees
Middle	0.625 inches (16mm)	69 degrees
Lower (cast)	1.75 inches (44mm)	23 degrees
Sides	1.0 inches (25mm)	0 degrees
Rear, Upper	1.0 inches (25mm)	59 degrees
Middle	1.0 inches (25mm)	0 degrees
Lower	1.0 inches (25mm)	20 degrees
Top	0.5 inches (13mm)	90 degrees
Floor, Front	0.5 inches (13mm)	90 degrees
Rear	0.375 inches (10mm)	90 degrees

Turret Thickness:		
Gun Shield (cast)	2.0 inches (51mm)	0 to 14 degrees
Front	1.5 inches (38mm)	10 degrees
Sides	1.25 inches (32mm)	0 degrees
Rear	1.25 inches (32mm)	0 degrees
Top	0.5 inches (13mm)	75 to 90 degrees

ARMAMENT

Primary: 37mm Gun M6 in Mount M23 in turret

Traverse: Hydraulic and manual	360 degrees
Traverse Rate: (max)	15 seconds/360 degrees
Elevation: Manual	+20 to −10 degrees
Firing Rate: (max)	30 rounds/minute
Loading System:	Manual
Stabilizer System:	Elevation only

Secondary:
(1) .30 caliber MG M1919A4 flexible AA mount on turret
(1) .30 caliber MG M1919A5 coaxial w/37mm gun in turret
(1) .30 caliber MG M1919A4 in bow mount
Provision for (1) .45 caliber SMG M1928A1

AMMUNITION

106 rounds 37mm	12 hand grenades
350 rounds .45 caliber	
7220 rounds .30 caliber	

FIRE CONTROL AND VISION EQUIPMENT

Primary Weapon: Periscope M4 with Telescope M40

Vision Devices:	Direct	Indirect
Driver	Hatch, vision slots (2)	Protectoscopes (1)
Asst. Driver	Hatch, vision slots (2)	Protectoscopes (1)
Commander	Hatch, pistol ports (2)	Periscopes M6 (1), Protectoscopes (2)
Gunner	Pistol Port (1)	Periscope M4 (1) Protectoscope (1)

Total Periscopes: M4 (1), M6 (1)
Total Protectoscopes: Hull (2), Turret (3)
Total Vision Slots: Hull (4), Turret (0)
Total Pistol Ports: Hull (0), Turret (3)

ENGINE

Make and Model: Continental W-670-9A	
Type: 7 cylinder, 4 cycle, radial	
Cooling System: Air Ignition: Magneto	
Displacement:	668 cubic inches
Bore and Stroke:	5.125 x 4.625 inches
Compression Ratio:	6.1:1
Net Horsepower: (max)	250 hp at 2400 rpm
Gross Horsepower: (max)	262 hp at 2400 rpm
Net Torque: (max)	584 ft-lb at 1800 rpm
Gross Torque: (max)	590 ft-lb at 1700 rpm
Weight:	565 pounds, dry
Fuel: 80 octane gasoline	54 gallons
With two 25 gallon jettison tanks	104 gallons
Engine Oil:	32 quarts

POWER TRAIN

Clutch: Dry disc, 2 plate
Transmission: Synchromesh, 5 speeds forward, 1 reverse

Gear Ratios:	1st	5.37:1	4th	1.09:1
	2nd	2.82:1	5th	0.738:1
	3rd	1.72:1	reverse	6.19:1

Steering: Controlled differential
Bevel Gear Ratio: 2.62:1   Steering Ratio: 1.845:1
Brakes: Mechanical, external contracting
Final Drive: Herringbone gear   Gear Ratio: 2.41:1
Drive Sprocket: At front of vehicle with 14 teeth
Pitch Diameter: 24.56 inches

RUNNING GEAR

Suspension: Vertical volute spring
8 wheels in 4 bogies (2 bogies/track)
Tire Size: 20 x 6 inches
6 track return rollers (3 rollers/track)
Trailing adjustable idler w/volute spring at rear of each track
Idler Size: 30 x 6 inches
Tracks: Outside guide, rubber bushed; T16 series, T36E6, and T55E1
Type: (T16E1) Double pin, 11.6 inch width, rubber reversible
(T16E2) Double pin, 11.6 inch width, rubber, non-reversible
(T36E6) Double pin, 11.6 inch width, steel, parallel grouser
(T55E1) Double pin, 11.6 inch width, steel, chevron
Pitch: 5.5 inches
Shoes per Vehicle: 132 (66/track)
Ground Contact Length: 117 inches

ELECTRICAL SYSTEM

Nominal Voltage: 12 volts DC
Main Generator: (1) 12 volts, 50 amperes, belt driven by main engine
Auxiliary Generator: (1) 12 volts, 50 amperes, driven by the auxiliary engine
Battery: (1) 12 volts

COMMUNICATIONS

Radio: SCR 508 in left sponson; SCR 506 (command tanks only) in right sponson
Interphone: (part of radio) 4 stations

FIRE PROTECTION

(1) 10 pound carbon dioxide, fixed
(1) 4 pound carbon dioxide, portable

PERFORMANCE

Maximum Speed: Level road, governed		36 miles/hour
Maximum Grade:		60 per cent
Maximum Trench:		6 feet
Maximum Vertical Wall:		24 inches
Maximum Fording Depth:		36 inches
Minimum Turning Circle: (diameter)		42 feet
Cruising Range: Roads	approx.	70 miles
w/two 25 gallon jettison tanks	approx.	135 miles

GENERAL DATA

Crew:	4 men
Length: With rear stowage box	197.9 inches
Width: Over sandshields	99.4 inches
Height: Over MG mount	101 inches
Tread:	73.0 inches
Ground Clearance:	16.5 inches
Fire Height:	76 inches
Turret Ring Diameter: (inside)	46.75 inches
Weight, Combat Loaded:	32,400 pounds
Weight, Unstowed:	28,000 pounds
Power to Weight Ratio: Net	15.4 hp/ton
Gross	16.2 hp/ton
Ground Pressure: Zero penetration	11.9 psi

ARMOR

Type: Turret, rolled homogeneous steel; Hull, rolled homogeneous steel; Welded assembly

Hull Thickness:

	Actual	Angle w/Vertical
Front, Upper	1.0 inches (25mm)	48 degrees
Lower (cast)	1.75 inches (44mm)	23 degrees
Sides, Upper	1.0 inches (25mm)	20 degrees
Lower	1.0 inches (25mm)	0 degrees
Rear, Upper	1.0 inches (25mm)	59 degrees
Middle	1.0 inches (25mm)	0 degrees
Lower	1.0 inches (25mm)	20 degrees
Top	0.5 inches (13mm)	90 degrees
Floor, Front	0.5 inches (13mm)	90 degrees
Rear	0.375 inches (10mm)	90 degrees

Turret Thickness:

Gun Shield (cast)	2.0 inches (51mm)	0 to 14 degrees
Front	1.5 inches (38mm)	10 degrees
Sides	1.25 inches (32mm)	0 degrees
Rear	1.25 inches (32mm)	0 degrees
Top	0.5 inches (13mm)	75 to 90 degrees

ARMAMENT

Primary: 37mm Gun M6 in Mount M44 in turret

Traverse: Hydraulic and manual	360 degrees
Traverse Rate: (max)	15 seconds/360 degrees
Elevation: Manual	+20 to −10 degrees
Firing Rate: (max)	30 rounds/minute
Loading System:	Manual
Stabilizer System:	Elevation only

Secondary:
(1) .30 caliber MG M1919A4 flexible AA mount on turret
(1) .30 caliber MG M1919A5 coaxial w/37mm gun in turret
(1) .30 caliber MG M1919A4 in bow mount
Provision for (1) .45 caliber SMG M1928A1

AMMUNITION

174 rounds 37mm*	12 hand grenades
540 rounds .45 caliber	
7500 rounds .30 caliber	

*144 37mm rounds in command tanks

FIRE CONTROL AND VISION EQUIPMENT

Primary Weapon: Telescope M54
Periscope M4 with Telescope M40

Vision Devices:	Direct	Indirect
Driver	Hatch, peephole (1)	Periscope M6 (1)
Asst. Driver	Hatch, peephole (1)	Periscope M6 (1)
Commander	Hatch	Periscope M6 (2)
Gunner	Hatch	Periscope M4 (1)

Total Periscopes: M4 (1), M6 (4)

ENGINE

Make and Model: Continental W-670-9A	
Type: 7 cylinder, 4 cycle, radial	
Cooling System: Air Ignition: Magneto	
Displacement:	668 cubic inches
Bore and Stroke:	5.125 x 4.625 inches
Compression Ratio:	6.1:1
Net Horsepower: (max)	250 hp at 2400 rpm
Gross Horsepower: (max)	262 hp at 2400 rpm
Net Torque: (max)	584 ft-lb at 1800 rpm
Gross Torque: (max)	590 ft-lb at 1700 rpm
Weight:	565 pounds, dry
Fuel: 80 octane gasoline	110 gallons
Engine Oil:	32 quarts

POWER TRAIN

Clutch: Dry disc, 2 plate
Transmission: Synchromesh, 5 speeds forward, 1 reverse

Gear Ratios:	1st 5.37:1	4th 1.09:1
	2nd 2.82:1	5th 0.738:1
	3rd 1.72:1	reverse 6.19:1

Steering: Controlled differential
Bevel Gear Ratio: 2.62:1   Steering Ratio: 1.845:1
Brakes: Mechanical, external contracting
Final Drive: Herringbone gear   Gear Ratio: 2.57:1
Drive Sprocket: At front of vehicle with 14 teeth
Pitch Diameter: 24.56 inches

RUNNING GEAR

Suspension: Vertical volute spring
8 wheels in 4 bogies (2 bogies/track)
Tire Size: 20 x 6 inches
6 track return rollers (3 rollers/track)
Trailing adjustable idler w/volute spring at rear of each track
Idler Size: 30 x 6 inches
Tracks: Outside guide, rubber bushed; T16 series, T36E6, and T55E1
Type: (T16E1) Double pin, 11.6 inch width, rubber, reversible
(T16E2) Double pin, 11.6 inch width, rubber, non-reversible
(T36E6) Double pin, 11.6 inch width, steel, parallel grouser
(T55E1) Double pin, 11.6 inch width, steel, chevron
Pitch: 5.5 inches
Shoes per Vehicle: 132 (66/track)
Ground Contact Length: 117 inches

ELECTRICAL SYSTEM

Nominal Voltage: 12 volts DC
Main Generator: (1) 12 volts, 50 amperes, belt driven by main engine
Auxiliary Generator: (1) 12 volts, 50 amperes, driven by the auxiliary engine
Battery: (1) 12 volts

COMMUNICATIONS

Radio: SCR 508, 528, or 538 in rear of turret; SCR 506 in right sponson (command tanks only)
Interphone: (part of radio) 4 stations
Flag Set M238, spotlight, siren
Flares: 3 each M17 and M18, (command tanks only)
Ground Signals Projector M4 (command tanks only)

FIRE AND GAS PROTECTION

(1) 10 pound carbon dioxide, fixed
(1) 4 pound carbon dioxide, portable
(1) 1½ quart decontaminating apparatus

PERFORMANCE

Maximum Speed: Level road, governed	31 miles/hour
Maximum Grade:	60 per cent
Maximum Trench:	6 feet
Maximum Vertical Wall:	24 inches
Maximum Fording Depth:	36 inches
Minimum Turning Circle: (diameter)	42 feet
Cruising Range: Roads	approx. 135 miles

LIGHT TANK M5

GENERAL DATA

Crew:	4 men
Length: Gun forward, w/o sandshields	174.8 inches
Length: Gun to rear, w/o sandshields	170.8 inches
Length: w/o gun, w/o sandshields	170.8 inches
Gun Overhang: Gun forward, w/o sandshields	4.0 inches
Width: w/o sandshields	88.3 inches
Height: Over MG mount	102 inches
Tread:	88.3 inches
Ground Clearance:	16.5 inches
Fire Height:	77.4 inches
Turret Ring Diameter: (inside)	46.75 inches
Weight, Combat Loaded: w/T16E1 tracks	33,100 pounds
Weight, Unstowed: w/T16E1 tracks	30,800 pounds
Power to Weight Ratio: Net	13.3 hp/ton
Gross	17.9 hp/ton
Ground Pressure: Zero penetration	12.2 psi

ARMOR

Type: Turret, rolled homogeneous steel; Hull, rolled homogeneous steel; Welded assembly

Hull Thickness:

	Actual	Angle w/Vertical
Front, Upper	1.125 inches (29mm)	48 degrees
Lower (cast)	1.75 inches (44mm)	23 degrees
Sides	1.0 inches (25mm)	0 degrees
Rear, Upper	1.0 inches (25mm)	60 degrees
Middle	1.0 inches (25mm)	0 degrees
Lower	1.0 inches (25mm)	17 degrees
Top	0.5 inches (13mm)	90 degrees
Floor, Front	0.5 inches (13mm)	90 degrees
Rear	0.375 inches (10mm)	90 degrees

Turret Thickness:

Gun Shield (cast)	2.0 inches (51mm)	0 to 14 degrees
Front	1.5 inches (38mm)	10 degrees
Sides	1.25 inches (32mm)	0 degrees
Rear	1.25 inches (32mm)	0 degrees
Top	0.5 inches (13mm)	75 to 90 degrees

ARMAMENT

Primary: 37mm Gun M6 in Mount M23 in turret

Traverse: Hydraulic and manual	360 degrees
Traverse Rate: (max)	15 seconds/360 degrees
Elevation: Manual	+20 to −10 degrees
Firing Rate: (max)	30 rounds/minute
Loading System:	Manual
Stabilizer System:	Elevation only

Secondary:
(1) .30 caliber MG M1919A4 flexible AA mount on turret
(1) .30 caliber MG M1919A5 coaxial w/37mm gun in turret
(1) .30 caliber MG M1919A4 in bow mount
Provision for (1) .45 caliber SMG M1928A1

AMMUNITION

123 rounds 37mm	12 hand grenades
420 rounds .45 caliber	
6250 rounds .30 caliber	

FIRE CONTROL AND VISION EQUIPMENT

Primary Weapon: Periscope M4 with Telescope M40

Vision Devices:

	Direct	Indirect
Driver	Hatch, peephole (1)	Periscope M6 (1)
Asst. Driver	Hatch, peephole (1)	Periscope M6 (1)
Commander	Hatch, pistol ports (2)	Periscope M6 (1)
		Protectoscopes (2)
Gunner	Hatch, pistol port (1)	Periscope M4 (1)
		Protectoscope (1)

Total Periscopes: M4 (1), M6 (3)
Total Protectoscopes: (3)
Total Pistol Ports: Hull (0), Turret (3)

ENGINE

Make and Model: Twin Cadillac, Series 42
Type: 16 cylinder (8/engine), 4 cycle, 90 degree vee
Cooling System: Liquid   Ignition: Delco

Displacement:	692 cubic inches (346 cubic inches/engine)
Bore and Stroke:	3.5 x 4.5 inches
Compression Ratio:	7.06:1
Net Horsepower: (max)	220 hp at 3400 rpm (110 hp/engine)
Gross Horsepower: (max)	296 hp at 3200 rpm (148 hp/engine)
Net Torque : (max)	488 ft-lb at 1200 rpm (244 ft-lb/engine)
Gross Torque: (max)	560 ft-lb at 1200 rpm (280 ft-lb/engine)
Weight:	1168 pounds, dry (584 pounds/engine)
Fuel: 80 octane gasoline	89 gallons
Engine Oil:	16 quarts (8 quarts/engine)

POWER TRAIN

Transmission: Hydramatic (2), 4 speeds forward, 1 reverse

Gear Ratios:	1st	3.26:1	4th	1.00:1
	2nd	2.26:1	reverse	3.81:1
	3rd	1.44:1		

Transfer Unit: Hydraulic, 2 speeds
Gear Ratios: 2.37:1 and 1.00:1
Steering: Controlled differential
Bevel Gear Ratio: 2.62:1   Steering Ratio: 1.845:1
Brakes: Mechanical, external contracting
Final Drive: Herringbone gear   Gear Ratio: 2.41:1
Drive Sprocket: At front of vehicle with 14 teeth
Pitch Diameter: 24.56 inches

RUNNING GEAR

Suspension: Vertical volute spring
8 wheels in 4 bogies (2 bogies/track)
Tire Size: 20 x 6 inches
6 track return rollers (3 rollers/track)
Trailing adjustable idler w/volute spring at rear of each track
Idler Size: 30 x 6 inches
Tracks: Outside guide, rubber bushed; T16 series, T36E6, and T55E1
Type: (T16E1) Double pin, 11.6 inch width, rubber, reversible
(T16E2) Double pin, 11.6 inch width, rubber, non-reversible
(T36E6) Double pin, 11.6 inch width, steel, parallel grouser
(T55E1) Double pin, 11.6 inch width, steel, chevron
Pitch: 5.5 inches
Shoes per Vehicle: 132 (66/track)
Ground Contact Length: 117 inches

ELECTRICAL SYSTEM

Nominal Voltage: 12 volts DC
Main Generator: (2, 1/engine) 12 volts, 50 amperes (25 amperes/generator), belt driven by each engine
Auxiliary Generator: 12 volts, 50 amperes, driven by the auxiliary engine
Battery: (1) 12 volts

COMMUNICATIONS

Radio: SCR 508, 528, or 538 in left sponson; SCR 506 in right sponson (command tanks only)
Interphone: (part of radio) 4 stations
Flag Set M238, spotlight, siren
Flares: 3 each M17 and M18 (command tanks only)
Ground Signals Projector M4 (command tanks only)

FIRE AND GAS PROTECTION

(1) 10 pound carbon dioxide, fixed
(1) 4 pound carbon dioxide, portable
(1) 1½ quart decontaminating apparatus

PERFORMANCE

Maximum Speed: Level road	36 miles/hour
Maximum Grade:	60 per cent
Maximum Trench:	5.3 feet
Maximum Vertical Wall:	18 inches
Maximum Fording Depth:	36 inches
Minimum Turning Circle: (diameter)	42 feet
Cruising Range: Roads	approx. 100 miles

GENERAL DATA

Crew:	4 men
Length: Gun forward, w/sandshields & stowage box	190.5 inches
Length: Gun to rear, w/sandshields & stowage box	190.5 inches
Length: w/o gun, w/sandshields & stowage box	190.5 inches
Gun Overhang: w/sandshields & stowage box	0 inches
Width: Over sandshields	90 inches
Height: Over MG mount	101 inches
Tread:	73.3 inches
Ground Clearance:	16.5 inches
Fire Height:	77.4 inches
Turret Ring Diameter: (inside)	46.75 inches
Weight, Combat Loaded: w/rubber tracks	33,500 pounds
w/steel tracks	34,700 pounds
Weight, Unstowed: w/rubber tracks	31,100 pounds
w/steel tracks	32,300 pounds
Power to Weight Ratio: Net, w/rubber tracks	13.1 hp/ton
w/steel tracks	12.7 hp/ton
Gross, w/rubber tracks	17.7 hp/ton
w/steel tracks	17.1 hp/ton
Ground Pressure: Zero penetration, w/rubber tracks	12.3 psi
w/steel tracks	12.8 psi

ARMOR

Type: Turret, rolled homogeneous steel; Hull, rolled homogeneous steel; Welded assembly

Hull Thickness:	Actual	Angle w/Vertical
Front, Upper	1.125 inches (29mm)	48 degrees
Lower (cast)	1.5-2.5 inches (38-64mm)	0 to 23 degrees
Sides, Front	1.125 inches (29mm)	0 degrees
Rear	1.0 inches (15mm)	0 degrees
Rear, Upper	1.0 inches (25mm)	49 degrees
Middle	1.0 inches (25mm)	0 degrees
Lower	1.0 inches (25mm)	17 degrees
Top	0.5 inches (13mm)	90 degrees
Floor, Front	0.5 inches (13mm)	90 degrees
Rear	0.375 inches (10mm)	90 degrees

Turret Thickness:		
Gun Shield (cast)	2.0 inches (51mm)	0 to 14 degrees
Front	1.75 inches (44mm)	10 degrees
Sides	1.25 inches (32mm)	0 degrees
Rear	1.25 inches (32mm)	0 degrees
Top	0.5 inches (13mm)	75 to 90 degrees

ARMAMENT

Primary: 37mm Gun M6 in Mount M44 in turret

Traverse: Hydraulic and manual	360 degrees
Traverse Rate: (max)	15 seconds/360 degrees
Elevation: Manual	+20 to −12 degrees
Firing Rate: (max)	30 rounds/minute
Loading System:	Manual
Stabilizer System:	Elevation only

Secondary:
(1) .30 caliber MG M1919A4 flexible AA mount on turret
(1) .30 caliber MG M1919A5 coaxial w/37mm gun in turret
(1) .30 caliber MG M1919A4 in bow mount
Provision for (4) .45 caliber SMG M3

AMMUNITION

147 rounds 37mm
720 rounds .45 caliber
6750 rounds .30 caliber
12 hand grenades

FIRE CONTROL AND VISION EQUIPMENT

Primary Weapon: Telescope M70D
Periscope M4A1 with Telescope M40

Vision Devices:	Direct	Indirect
Driver	Hatch, peephole (1)	Periscope M6 (1)
Asst. Driver	Hatch, peephole (1)	Periscope M6 (1)
Commander	Hatch	Periscope M6 (2)
Gunner	Hatch	Periscope M4A1 (1)

Total Periscopes: M4A1 (1), M6 (4)

ENGINE

Make and Model: Twin Cadillac, Series 42	
Type: 16 cylinder (8/engine), 4 cycle, 90 degree vee	
Cooling System: Liquid Ignition: Delco	
Displacement:	692 cubic inches (346 cubic inches/engine)
Bore and Stroke:	3.5 x 4.5 inches
Compression Ratio:	7.06:1
Net Horsepower: (max)	220 hp at 3400 rpm (110 hp/engine)
Gross Horsepower: (max)	296 hp at 3200 rpm (148 hp/engine)
Net Torque: (max)	488 ft-lb at 1200 rpm (244 ft-lb/engine)
Gross Torque: (max)	560 ft-lb at 1200 rpm (280 ft-lb/engine)
Weight:	1168 pounds, dry (584 pounds/engine)
Fuel: 80 octane gasoline	89 gallons
Engine Oil:	16 quarts (8 quarts/engine)

POWER TRAIN

Transmission: Hydramatic (2), 4 speeds forward, 1 reverse

Gear Ratios:	1st 3.26:1	4th 1.00:1
	2nd 2.26:1	reverse 3.81:1
	3rd 1.44:1	

Transfer Unit: Hydraulic, 2 speeds
Gear Ratios: 2.37:1 and 1.00:1
Steering: Controlled differential
Bevel Gear Ratio: 2.62:1   Steering Ratio: 1.845:1
Brakes: Mechanical, external contracting
Final Drive: Herringbone gear   Gear Ratio: 2.57:1
Drive Sprocket: At front of vehicle with 13 teeth
Pitch Diameter: 22.8 inches

RUNNING GEAR

Suspension: Vertical volute spring
8 wheels in 4 bogies (2 bogies/track)
Tire Size: 20 x 6 inches
6 track return rollers (3 rollers/track)
Trailing adjustable idler w/volute spring at rear of each track
Idler Size: 30 x 6 inches
Tracks: Outside guide, rubber bushed; T16 series, T36E6, and T55E1
Type: (T16E1) Double pin, 11.6 inch width, rubber, reversible
(T16E2) Double pin, 11.6 inch width, rubber, non-reversible
(T36E6) Double pin, 11.6 inch width, steel, parallel grouser
(T55E1) Double pin, 11.6 inch width, steel, chevron
Pitch: 5.5 inches
Shoes per Vehicle: 132 (66/track)
Ground Contact Length: 117 inches

ELECTRICAL SYSTEM

Nominal Voltage: 12 volts DC
Main Generator: (2, 1/engine) 12 volts, 50 amperes (25 amperes/generator), belt driven by each engine
Auxiliary Generator: 12 volts, 50 amperes, driven by the auxiliary engine
Battery: (1) 12 volts

COMMUNICATIONS

Radio: SCR 508, 528, or 538 in rear of turret; SCR 506 in right sponson (command tanks only)
Interphone: (part of radio) 4 stations
Flag Set M238, spotlight, siren
Flares: 3 each M17 and M18 (command tanks only)
Ground Signals Projector M4 (command tanks only)

FIRE AND GAS PROTECTION

(1) 10 pound carbon dioxide, fixed
(1) 4 pound carbon dioxide, portable
(1) 1½ quart decontaminating apparatus

PERFORMANCE

Maximum Speed: Level road	36 miles/hour
Maximum Grade:	60 per cent
Maximum Trench:	5.3 feet
Maximum Vertical Wall:	18 inches
Maximum Fording Depth:	36 inches
Minimum Turning Circle: (diameter)	42 feet
Cruising Range: Roads	approx. 100 miles

LIGHT TANK T7E5 (MEDIUM TANK M7, PILOT)

GENERAL DATA

Crew:	5 men
Length: Gun forward, w/o fenders	210 inches
Length: Gun to rear, w/o fenders	206 inches
Length: w/o gun, w/o fenders	206 inches
Gun Overhang: Gun forward, w/o fenders	4 inches
Width:	112 inches
Height:	93 inches
Tread:	91.5 inches
Ground Clearance:	16 inches
Fire Height:	77 inches
Turret Ring Diameter: (inside)	64 inches
Weight, Combat Loaded:	53,950 pounds
Weight, Unstowed:	50,000 pounds
Power to Weight Ratio: Net	13.0 hp/ton
Gross	14.8 hp/ton
Ground Pressure: Zero penetration	10.7 psi

ARMOR

Type: Turret, cast homogeneous steel; Hull, cast homogeneous steel; Welded assembly

Hull Thickness:

	Actual	Angle w/Vertical
Front, Upper	1.5 inches (38mm)	50 degrees
Lower	1.5 inches (38mm)	0 degrees
Sides, Upper	1.25 inches (32mm)	0 to 50 degrees
Lower	1.25 inches (32mm)	0 degrees
Rear, Upper	1.0 inches (25mm)	0 degrees
Lower	1.0 inches (25mm)	19 degrees
Top	0.75 inches (19mm)	90 degrees
Floor, Front	1.0 inches (25mm)	90 degrees
Rear	0.5 inches (13mm)	90 degrees

Turret Thickness:

	Actual	Angle w/Vertical
Gun Shield (cast)	2.5 inches (64mm)	0 degrees
Front	2.0 inches (51mm)	23 degrees
Sides, Left	1.5 inches (38mm)	21 degrees
Right	1.5 inches (38mm)	24 degrees
Rear	1.5 inches (38mm)	11 degrees
Top	0.75 inches (19mm)	90 degrees

ARMAMENT

Primary: 75mm Gun M3 in Mount M47 in turret

Traverse: Hydraulic and manual	360 degrees
Traverse Rate: (max)	15 seconds/360 degrees
Elevation: Manual	+18 to −8 degrees
Firing Rate: (max)	20 rounds/minute
Loading System:	Manual
Stabilizer System:	Elevation only

Secondary:
- (1) .30 caliber MG M1919A4 flexible AA mount on turret
- (1) .30 caliber MG M1919A5 coaxial w/75mm gun in turret
- (1) .30 caliber MG M1919A4 in bow mount
- Provision for (1) .45 caliber SMG M1928A1

AMMUNITION

71 rounds 75mm	12 hand grenades
480 rounds .45 caliber	
4500 rounds .30 caliber	

FIRE CONTROL AND VISION EQUIPMENT

Primary Weapon:	Direct	Indirect
	Telescope M55	Azimuth Indicator M19
	Periscope M4 with	Gunner's Quadrant M1
	Telescope M38	Elevation Quadrant M9

Vision Devices	Direct	Indirect
Driver	Hatch, vision slot (1)	Periscope M6 (1)
Asst. Driver	Hatch, vision slot (1)	Periscope M6 (1)
Commander	Hatch	Periscope M6 (2)
Gunner	None	Periscope M4 (1)
Loader	Hatch	Periscope M6 (1)

Total Periscopes: M4 (1), M6 (5)
Total Vision Slots: Hull (2), Turret (0)

ENGINE

Make and Model: Continental R-975-C1	
Type: 9 cylinder, 4 cycle, radial	
Cooling System: Air Ignition: Magneto	
Displacement:	973 cubic inches
Bore and Stroke:	5 x 5.5 inches
Compression Ratio:	5.7:1
Net Horsepower: (max)	350 hp at 2400 rpm
Gross Horsepower: (max)	400 hp at 2400 rpm
Net Torque: (max)	800 ft-lb at 1800 rpm
Gross Torque: (max)	890 ft-lb at 1800 rpm
Weight:	1137 pounds, dry
Fuel: 80 octane gasoline	138 gallons
Engine Oil:	36 quarts

POWER TRAIN

Transfer Case: Spicer, fixed ratio
Gear Ratio: 1.05:1

Transmission: Spicer automatic, 3 speeds forward, 1 reverse
Torque Convertor Ratio: 8.35:1 (max)

Gear Ratios:	1st 10.42:1	3rd 1:1
	2nd 2.085:1	

Steering: Controlled differential
Bevel Gear Ratio: 2.1:1
Brakes: Mechanical, external contracting
Final Drive: Herringbone gear   Gear Ratio: 2.685:1
Drive Sprocket: At front of vehicle with 13 teeth
Pitch Diameter: 22.8 inches

RUNNING GEAR

Suspension: Vertical volute spring
- 8 wheels in 4 bogies (2 bogies/track)
- Tire Size: 20 x 9 inches
- 6 track support rollers (3 rollers/track)
- Trailing adjustable idler w/volute spring at rear of each track
- Idler Size: 30 x 9 inches

Tracks: Outside guide, rubber bushed; T48
- Type: Double pin, 16.56 inch width, rubber chevron
- Pitch: 6 inches
- Shoes per Vehicle: 142 (71/track)
- Ground Contact Length: 152.5 inches

ELECTRICAL SYSTEM

Nominal Voltage: 24 volts DC
Main Generator: (1) 24 volts, 50 amperes, driven by power take-off from main engine
Auxiliary Generator: (1) 30 volts, 50 amperes, driven by auxiliary engine
Battery: (2) 12 volts in series

COMMUNICATIONS

Radio: SCR 508, 528, or 538 in rear of turret; SCR 506 (command tanks only) in right sponson
Interphone: (part of radio) 5 stations
Flag Set M238, Panel Set AP50A, spotlight, siren
Flares: 3 each, M17, M18, M19, and M21 (command tanks only)
Ground Signals Projector M4 (command tanks only)

FIRE AND GAS PROTECTION

- (2) 10 pound carbon dioxide, fixed
- (2) 4 pound carbon dioxide, portable
- (2) 1½ quart decontaminating apparatus

PERFORMANCE

Maximum Speed: Level road	30 miles/hour
Maximum Grade:	50 per cent
Maximum Trench:	6.5 feet
Maximum Vertical Wall:	24 inches
Maximum Fording Depth:	36 inches
Minimum Turning Circle: (diameter)	64 feet
Cruising Range: Roads	approx. 100 miles

LIGHT TANK M22 (T9E1)

GENERAL DATA

Crew:	3 men
Length: Gun forward	156 inches
Length: Gun to rear	155 inches
Length: w/o gun	155 inches
Gun Overhang: Gun forward	1 inch
Width:	88.5 inches
Height:	72.5 inches
Tread:	70.3 inches
Ground Clearance:	10 inches
Fire Height:	58 inches
Turret Ring Diameter: (inside)	47.45 inches
Weight, Combat Loaded:	16,400 pounds
Weight, Unstowed:	14,600 pounds
Power to Weight Ratio: Net	19.8 hp/ton
Gross	23.4 hp/ton
Ground Pressure: Zero penetration	7.1 psi

ARMOR

Type: Turret, cast homogeneous steel; Hull, rolled homogeneous steel;
    Welded assembly

Hull Thickness:	Actual	Angle w/Vertical
Front, Upper	0.5 inches (13mm)	65 degrees
Driver head cover	1.0 inches (25mm)	0 degrees
Lower	1.0 inches (25mm)	0 degrees
Sides, Upper	0.375 inches (10mm)	45 degrees
Lower	0.5 inches (13mm)	0 degrees
Rear	0.5 inches (13mm)	9 degrees
Top	0.375 inches (10mm)	90 degrees
Floor	0.5 inches (13mm)	90 degrees
Turret Thickness:		
Gun Shield	1.0 inches (25mm)	50 degrees
Front	1.0 inches (25mm)	30 degrees
Sides	1.0 inches (25mm)	5 degrees
Rear	1.0 inches (25mm)	0 degrees
Top	0.375-0.75 inches (10-19mm)	90 degrees

ARMAMENT

Primary: 37mm Gun M6 in Mount M53 (T55) in turret

Traverse: Manual	360 degrees
Elevation: Manual	+30 to −10 degrees
Firing Rate: (max)	30 rounds/minute
Loading System:	Manual
Stabilizer System:	None

Secondary:
(1) .30 caliber MG M1919A4 coaxial w/37mm gun in turret
Provision for (3) .45 caliber SMG M3

AMMUNITION

50 rounds 37mm	12 hand grenades
450 rounds .45 caliber	
2500 rounds .30 caliber	

FIRE CONTROL AND VISION EQUIPMENT

Primary Weapon: Periscope M8 with Telescope M46

Vision Devices:	Direct	Indirect
Driver	Head cover, peephole (1)	Periscope M6 (1)
Commander	Hatch	Periscope M6 (2)
Gunner	Hatch	Periscope M8 (1)
Total Periscopes: M6 (3), M8 (1)		

ENGINE

Make and Model: Lycoming O-435T
Type: 6 cylinder, 4 cycle, opposed
Cooling System: Air   Ignition: Delco

Displacement:	434.0 cubic inches
Bore and Stroke:	4.875 x 3.875 inches
Compression Ratio:	6.25:1
Net Horsepower: (max)	162 hp at 2800 rpm
Gross Horsepower: (max)	192 hp at 2800 rpm
Net Torque: (max)	332 ft-lb at 2100 rpm
Gross Torque: (max)	360 ft-lb at 2100 rpm
Weight:	1000 pounds, dry
Fuel: 80 octane gasoline	57 gallons
Engine Oil:	12 quarts

POWER TRAIN

Clutch: Dry disc, 2 plate
Transfer Case: Fixed ratio
    Gear Ratio: 2:1
Transmission: manual, 4 speeds forward, 1 reverse (synchromesh 3rd and 4th)

Gear Ratios:	1st 1.857:1	4th 3.043:1
	2nd 1.000:1	reverse 1.667:1
	3rd 4.634:1	

Steering: Controlled differential
    Bevel Gear Ratio: 3.05:1   Steering Ratio: 2.25:1
Brakes: Mechanical, external contracting
Final Drive: Spur gear   Gear Ratio: 2.23:1
Drive Sprocket: At front of vehicle with 22 teeth
    Pitch Diameter: 21.08 inches

RUNNING GEAR

Suspension: Vertical volute spring
    8 wheels in 4 bogies (2 bogies/track)
    Tire Size: 15 x 6 inches
    4 track return rollers (2 rollers/track)
    Trailing adjustable idler w/volute spring at rear of each track
    Idler Size: 28 x 6 inches
Tracks: Outside guide, dry pin; T78
    Type: Single pin, 11.25 inch width, cast malleable iron
    Pitch: 3 inches
    Shoes per Vehicle: 212 (106/track)
    Ground Contact Length: 102.5 inches

ELECTRICAL SYSTEM

Nominal Voltage: 12 volts DC
Main Generator: (1) 12 volts, 50 amperes, belt driven by main engine
Auxiliary Generator: None
Battery: (2) 6 volts in series

COMMUNICATIONS

Radio: SCR 510 in rear of turret
Interphone: RC99, 3 stations
Flag Set M238
Ground Signals Projector M4 (command tanks only)

FIRE AND GAS PROTECTION

(1) 10 pound carbon dioxide, fixed
(1) 4 pound carbon dioxide, portable
(1) 1½ quart decontaminating apparatus

PERFORMANCE

Maximum Speed: Level road	35 miles/hour
Maximum Grade:	50 per cent
Maximum Trench:	5.5 feet
Maximum Vertical Wall:	18 inches
Maximum Fording Depth:	36 inches
Minimum Turning Circle: (diameter)	38 feet
Cruising Range: Roads	approx. 110 miles

LIGHT TANK M24

GENERAL DATA

Crew:	4 or 5 men
Length: Gun forward, w/sandshields	219 inches
Length: Gun to rear, w/sandshields	198 inches
Length: w/o gun, w/sandshields	198 inches
Gun Overhang, Gun forward, w/sandshields	21 inches
Width: Over sandshields	118 inches
Height: Over AA MG	109 inches
Tread:	96 inches
Ground Clearance:	18 inches
Fire Height:	73 inches
Turret Ring Diameter: (inside)	60 inches
Weight, Combat Loaded:	40,500 pounds
Weight, Unstowed:	36,300 pounds
Power to Weight Ratio: Net	10.9 hp/ton
Gross	14.6 hp/ton
Ground Pressure: Zero penetration, T72 tracks	11.3 psi

ARMOR

Type: Turret, rolled homogeneous steel; Hull, rolled homogeneous steel; Welded assembly

Hull Thickness:

	Actual	Angle w/Vertical
Front, Upper	1.0 inches (25mm)	60 degrees
Lower	1.0 inches (25mm)	45 degrees
Sides, Front	1.0 inches (25mm)	12 degrees
Rear	0.75 inches (19mm)	12 degrees
Rear, Upper	0.75 inches (19mm)	0 degrees
Lower	0.75 inches (19mm)	42 degrees
Top	0.5 inches (13mm)	77 to 90 degrees
Floor, Front	0.5 inches (13mm)	90 degrees
Rear	0.375 inches (10mm)	90 degrees

Turret Thickness:

Gun Shield (cast)	1.5 inches (38mm)	0 to 60 degrees
Front (cast)	1.5 inches (38mm)	0 to 60 degrees
Sides, Right	1.0 inches (25mm)	25 degrees
Left	1.0 inches (25mm)	20 degrees
Rear	1.0 inches (25mm)	0 degrees
Top	0.5 inches (13mm)	68 to 90 degrees

ARMAMENT

Primary: 75mm Gun M6 in Mount M64 in turret

Traverse: Hydraulic and manual	360 degrees
Traverse Rate: (max)	15 seconds/360 degrees
Elevation: Manual	+15 to −10 degrees
Firing Rate: (max)	20 rounds/minute
Loading System:	Manual
Stabilizer System:	Elevation only

Secondary:
(1) .50 caliber MG HB M2 flexible AA mount on turret
(1) .30 caliber MG M1919A4 coaxial w/75mm gun in turret
(1) .30 caliber MG M1919A4 in bow mount
(1) 2 inch Mortar M3 (smoke) fixed in turret
Provision for (4) .45 caliber SMG M3

AMMUNITION

48 rounds 75mm	8 hand grenades
440 rounds .50 caliber	14 2-inch smoke bombs
720 rounds .45 caliber	
3750 rounds .30 caliber	

FIRE CONTROL AND VISION EQUIPMENT

Primary Weapon:	Direct	Indirect
	Telescope M71G	Azimuth Indicator M21
	Periscope M4A1 with	Gunners Quadrant M1
	Telescope M38A2	Elevation Qyadrant M9

Vision Devices:	Direct	Indirect
Driver	Hatch	Periscope M6 (1)
Asst. Driver	Hatch	Periscope M6 (1)
Commander	Vision blocks (6)	Periscope M6 (1)
	in cupola, hatch	
Gunner	None	Periscope M4A1 (1)
Loader	Hatch and pistol port	None

Total Periscopes: M4A1 (1), M6 (3)
Total Vision Cupolas: (1) w/6 vision blocks on turret top
Total Pistol Ports: Hull (0), Turret (1)

ENGINE

Make and Model: Twin Cadillac, Series 44T24	
Type: 16 cylinder (8/engine), 4 cycle, 90 degree vee	
Cooling System: Liquid Ignition: Delco	
Displacement:	692 cubic inches
	(346 cubic inches/engine)
Bore and Stroke:	3.5 x 4.5 inches
Compression Ratio:	7.06:1
Net Horsepower: (max)	220 hp at 3400 rpm
	(110 hp/engine)
Gross Horsepower: (max)	296 hp at 3200 rpm
	(148 hp/engine)
Net Torque: (max)	480 ft-lb at 1200 rpm
	(240 ft-lb/engine)
Gross Torque: (max)	560 ft-lb at 1200 rpm
	(280 ft-lb/engine)
Weight:	1168 pounds, dry
	(584 pounds/engine)
Fuel: 80 octane gasoline	110 gallons
Engine Oil:	16 quarts (8 quarts/engine)

POWER TRAIN

Transmission: Hydramatic (2), 4 speeds

Gear Ratios:	1st 3.92:1	3rd 1.55:1
	2nd 2.53:1	4th 1:1

Transfer Unit: Synchromesh, 2 speeds forward, 1 reverse
Gear Ratios: high 2.34:1   reverse 2.44:1
                low 1.03:1

Steering: Controlled differential
Bevel Gear Ratio: 2.62:1   Steering Ratio: 1.33:1
Brakes: Mechanical, external contracting
Final Drive: Herringbone gear   Gear Ratio: 2.55:1
Drive Sprocket: At front of vehicle with 13 teeth
Pitch Diameter: 22.979 inches

RUNNING GEAR

Suspension: Torsion bar
10 individually sprung dual road wheels (5/track)
Tire Size: 25.5 x 4.5 inches
6 dual track return rollers (3/track)
Dual compensating idler at rear of each track
Idler Size: 22.5 x 5 inches
Shock absorbers fitted on first 2 and last 2 road wheels

Tracks: Center guide, rubber bushed; T72, T72E1, and T85E1
Type: (T72) Single pin, 16 inch width, steel, parallel grouser
(T72E1) Single pin, 16 inch width, steel, parallel grouser*
(T85E1) Double pin, 14 inch width, rubber, chevron 16.5 inch
width w/extended end connectors
*Three holes in the T72E1 track shoe permit the attachment of
28 inch grousers
Pitch: 5.5 inches
Shoes per Vehicle: 150 (75/track)
Ground Contact Length: 112.25 inches

ELECTRICAL SYSTEM

Nominal Voltage: 24 volts DC
Main Generator: (2, 1/engine) 24 volts, 50 amperes, belt driven by each engine
Auxiliary Generator: None
Battery: (4) 6 volts in series

COMMUNICATIONS

Radio: SCR 508, 528, or 538 in rear of turret; SCR 506 in front of assistant
driver (command tanks only)
Interphone: (part of radio) 5 stations
Flag Set M238, Panel Set AP50A, spotlight, siren
Flares: 3 each, M17, M18, M19, and M21 (command Tanks only)
Ground Signals Projector M4 (command tanks only)

FIRE AND GAS PROTECTION

(1) 10 pound carbon dioxide, fixed
(1) 4 pound carbon dioxide, portable
(2) 1½ quart decontaminating apparatus

PERFORMANCE

Maximum Speed: Level road	35 miles/hour
Maximum Grade:	60 per cent
Maximum Trench:	8 feet
Maximum Vertical Wall:	36 inches
Maximum Fording Depth:	40 inches
Minimum Turning Circle: (diameter)	46 feet
Cruising Range: Roads	approx. 100 miles

GENERAL DATA

Crew:	4 or 5 men
Length: Gun forward, w/sandshields	218 inches
Length: Gun to rear, w/sandshields	196 inches
Length: w/o gun, w/sandshields	196 inches
Gun Overhang: Gun forward, w/sandshields	22 inches
Width: Over sandshields	118 inches
Height: Over AA MG	112 inches
Tread:	96 inches
Ground Clearance:	18 inches
Fire Height:	73 inches
Turret Ring Diameter: (inside)	60 inches
Weight, Combat Loaded:	40,000 pounds
Weight, Unstowed:	36,000 pounds
Power to Weight Ratio: Net	20.0 hp/ton
Gross	23.0 hp/ton
Ground Pressure: Zero penetration	11.1 psi

ARMOR

Type: Turret, rolled homogeneous steel; Hull, rolled homogeneous steel; Welded assembly

Hull thickness:	Actual	Angle w/Vertical
Front, Upper	1.0 inches (25mm)	60 degrees
Lower	1.0 inches (25mm)	45 degrees
Sides, Front	1.0 inches (25mm)	12 degrees
Rear	0.75 inches (19mm)	12 degrees
Rear, Upper	0.75 inches (19mm)	0 degrees
Lower	0.75 inches (19mm)	45 degrees
Top	0.5 inches (13mm)	77 to 90 degrees
Floor, Front	0.5 inches (13mm)	90 degrees
Rear	0.375 inches (10mm)	90 degrees

Turret Thickness:		
Gun Shield (cast)	1.5 inches (38mm)	0 to 60 degrees
Front (cast)	1.5 inches (38mm)	0 to 60 degrees
Sides, Right	1.0 inches (25mm)	25 degrees
Left	1.0 inches (25mm)	20 degrees
Rear	1.0 inches (25mm)	0 degrees
Top	0.5 inches (13mm)	68 to 90 degrees

ARMAMENT

Primary: 75mm Gun M5 (T13E1) in Mount T90 in turret

Traverse: Hydraulic and Manual	360 degrees
Traverse Rate: (max)	15 seconds/360 degrees
Elevation: Manual	+15 to −10 degrees
Firing Rate: (max)	20 rounds/minute
Loading System:	Manual
Stabilizer System:	Elevation only

Secondary:
- (1) .50 caliber MG HB M2 flexible AA mount on turret
- (1) .30 caliber MG M1919A4 coaxial w/75mm gun in turret
- (1) .30 caliber MG M1919A4 in bow mount
- (1) 2 inch Mortar M3 (smoke) fixed in turret
- Provision for (4) .45 caliber SMG M3

AMMUNITION

50 rounds 75mm	8 hand grenades
600 rounds .50 caliber	15 2-inch smoke bombs
600 rounds .45 caliber	
2500 rounds .30 caliber	

FIRE CONTROL AND VISION EQUIPMENT

Primary Weapon:	Direct	Indirect
	Telescope T92	Azimuth Indicator M19
	Periscope M4 with	Gunner's Quadrant M1
	Telescope M38	Elevation Quadrant M9

Vision Devices:	Direct	Indirect
Driver	Hatch	Periscope M6 (1)
Asst. Driver	Hatch	Periscope M6 (1)
Commander	Hatch	Periscope M6 (2)
Gunner	None	Periscope M4 (1)
Loader	Hatch	None

Total Periscopes: M4 (1), M6 (4)

ENGINE

Make and Model: Continental R-975-C4	
Type: 9 cylinder, 4 cycle, radial	
Cooling System: Air Ignition: Magneto	
Displacement:	973 cubic inches
Bore and Stroke:	5 x 5.5 inches
Compression Ratio:	5.7:1
Net Horsepower: (max)	400 hp at 2400 rpm
Gross Horsepower: (max)	460 hp at 2400 rpm
Net Torque: (max)	940 ft-lb at 1800 rpm
Gross Torque: (max)	1025 ft-lb at 1800 rpm
Weight:	1212 pounds, dry
Fuel: 80 octane gasoline	160 gallons
Engine Oil:	32 quarts

POWER TRAIN

Transmission: Spicer automatic, 3 ranges forward, 1 reverse

Range Ratios:	low	2.2:1	high	0.80:1
	normal	1.0:1	reverse	2.0:1

Torque Convertor Multiplication: 5.25:1
Steering: Controlled differential
Bevel Gear Ratio: 2.53:1   Steering Ratio: 1.845:1
Brakes: Mechanical, external contracting
Final Drive: Herringbone gear   Gear Ratio: 2.37:1
Drive Sprocket: At front of vehicle with 13 teeth
Pitch Diameter: 23.108 inches

RUNNING GEAR

Suspension: Torsion bar
10 individually sprung dual road wheels (5/track)
Tire Size: 25.5 x 4.5 inches
6 dual track return rollers (3/track)
Dual compensating idler at rear of each track
Idler Size: 25.5 x 5 inches
Shock absorbers fitted on first 2 and last 2 road wheels
Tracks: Center guide, rubber bushed: T72
Type: Single pin, 16 inch width, steel, parallel grouser
Pitch: 5.5 inches
Shoes per Vehicle: 150 (75/track)
Ground Contact Length: 112.25 inches

ELECTRICAL SYSTEM

Nominal Voltage: 24 volts DC
Main Generator: (1) 24 volts, 80 amperes, belt driven by the main engine
Auxiliary Generator: (1) 24 volts, 24 amperes, driven by the auxiliary engine
Battery: (4) 6 volts in series

COMMUNICATIONS

Radio: SCR 508, 528, or 538 in rear of turret; SCR 506 in front of assistant driver (command tanks only)
Interphone: (part of radio) 5 stations
Flag Set M238, Panel Set AP50A, spotlight, siren
Flares: 3 each, M17, M18, M19, and M21 (command tanks only)
Ground Signals Projector M4 (command tanks only)

FIRE AND GAS PROTECTION

(1) 10 pound carbon dioxide, fixed
(1) 4 pound carbon dioxide, portable
(2) 1½ quart decontaminating apparatus

PERFORMANCE

Maximum Speed: Level Road	48 miles/hour
Maximum Grade:	60 per cent
Maximum Trench:	6 feet
Maximum Vertical Wall:	36 inches
Maximum Fording Depth:	50 inches
Minimum Turning Circle: (diameter)	46 feet
Cruising Range: Roads	approx. 160 miles

TWIN 40mm GUN MOTOR CARRIAGE M19 AND M19A1

GENERAL DATA

Crew:		6 men
Length: w/sandshields and rear stowage		228.8 inches
Width: w/sandshields		115.4 inches
Height: Over AA MG		116.7 inches
Tread:		96.0 inches
Ground Clearance:		17.8 inches
Fire Height:		78 inches
Weight, Combat Loaded: M19		39,000 pounds
M19A1		41,000 pounds
Weight, Unstowed: M19		34,500 pounds
M19A1		36,500 pounds
Power to Weight Ratio: Net, M19		11.3 hp/ton
M19A1		10.7 hp/ton
Gross, M19		15.2 hp/ton
M19A1		14.4 hp/ton
Ground Pressure: Zero penetration w/T72 tracks, M19		9.8 psi
M19A1		10.3 psi

ARMOR

Type: Rolled homogeneous steel; Welded assembly

Hull Thickness:	Actual	Angle w/Vertical
Front, Upper	0.5 inches (13mm)	60 degrees
Lower	0.5 inches (13mm)	45 degrees
Sides	0.5 inches (13mm)	12 degrees
Rear, Upper	0.5 inches (13mm)	0 degrees
Lower	0.375 inches (10mm)	0 degrees
Top, Front	0.5 inches (13mm)	90 degrees
Rear	Open	
Floor, Front	0.5 inches (13mm)	90 degrees
Rear	0.375 inches (10mm)	90 degrees
Turret Thickness:		
Gun shields, Front	0.5 inches (13mm)	0 to 45 degrees
Sides	0.25 inches (6mm)	0 degrees
Sides	0.31 inches (8mm)	0 degrees
Rear	0.31 inches (8mm)	0 degrees
Top	Open	

ARMAMENT

Primary: 40 mm Dual Automatic Gun M2 in Mount M4 on rear of chassis

Traverse: Hydraulic and manual	360 degrees
Traverse Rate: (max)	9 seconds/360 degrees
Elevation: Hydraulic and manual	+85 to −3 degrees
Elevation Rate: (max)	25 degrees/second
Firing Rate: (max)	240 rounds/minute
	(120 rounds/gun)
Loading System:	Automatic
Stabilizer System:	None

Secondary:
Provision for (2) .45 caliber SMG M3
Provision for (4) .30 caliber Carbine M1 w/(1) Grenade Launcher M8

AMMUNITION

352 rounds 40mm*	12 hand grenades
420 rounds .45 caliber	10 rifle grenades M9A1
430 rounds .30 caliber (carbine)	

*An additional 320 40mm rounds carried in the ammunition trailer

FIRE CONTROL AND VISION EQUIPMENT

Primary Weapon: This same fire control system is used for antiaircraft fire and for direct and indirect fire against ground targets.
Computing Sight M13 or M13A1 w/reflex sights M23 and M24
Local Control System M16 or M16A1
Azimuth Indicator T23

Vision Devices:	Direct	Indirect
Driver	Hatch	Periscope M6 (1)
Asst. Driver	Hatch	Periscope M6 (1)
Commander	Open top	None
Cannoneers	Open top	None

Total Periscopes: M6 (2)

ENGINE

Make and Model: Twin Cadillac, Series 44T4
Type: 16 cylinder (8/engine), 4 cycle, 90 degree vee
Cooling System: Liquid   Ignition: Delco

Displacement:	692 cubic inches
	(346 cubic inches/engine)
Bore and Stroke:	3.5 x 4.5 inches
Compression Ratio:	7.06:1
Net Horsepower: (max)	220 hp at 3400 rpm
	(110 hp/engine)
Gross Horsepower: (max)	296 hp at 3200 rpm
	(148 hp/engine)
Net Torque: (max)	480 ft-lb at 1200 rpm
	(240 ft-lb/engine)
Gross Torque: (max)	560 ft-lb at 1200 rpm
	(280 ft-lb/engine)
Weight:	1168 pounds, dry
	(584 pounds/engine)
Fuel: 80 octane gasoline	110 gallons
Engine Oil:	16 quarts (8 quarts/engine)

POWER TRAIN

Transmission: Hydramatic (2), 4 speeds

Gear Ratios:	1st	3.92:1	3rd	1.55:1
	2nd	2.53:1	4th	1:1

Transfer Unit: Synchromesh, 2 speeds forward, 1 reverse

Gear Ratios:	high	2.34:1	reverse	2.44:1
	low	1.03:1		

Steering: Controlled differential
Bevel Gear Ratio: 2.62:1   Steering Ratio: 1.33:1
Brakes: Mechanical, external contracting
Final Drive: Herringbone gear   Gear Ratio: 2.94:1
Drive Sprocket: At front of vehicle with 13 teeth
Pitch Diameter: w/T72 or T72E1 tracks 22.979 inches
w/T85E1 tracks 22.816 inches

RUNNING GEAR

Suspension: Torsion bar
10 individually sprung dual road wheels (5/track)
Tire Size: 25.5 x 4.5 inches
8 dual track return rollers (4/track)
Dual compensating idler at rear of each track
Idler Size: 22.5 x 5 inches
Shock absorbers on first 2 and last 2 road wheels of each track
Tracks: Center guide, rubber bushed; T72, T72E1, and T85E1
Type: (T72) Single pin, 16 inch width, steel, parallel grouser
(T72E1) Single pin, 16 inch width, steel, parallel grouser*
(T85E1) Double pin, 14 inch width, rubber, chevron 16.5 inch
width w/extended end connectors
*Three holes in the T72E1 track shoe permit the attachment of
28 inch grousers
Pitch: 5.5 inches
Shoes per Vehicle: 160 (80/track)
Ground Contact Length: 124 inches

ELECTRICAL SYSTEM

Nominal Voltage: 24 volts DC
Main Generator: (2, 1/engine) 24 volts, 150 amperes, belt driven
by each engine
Auxiliary Generator: (1, on M19A1 only) 24 volts, 150 amperes, gear driven
by the auxiliary engine
Battery: (4) 12 volts, 2 sets of 2 in series connected in parallel

COMMUNICATIONS

Radio: (M19) SCR 510 or AN/VRC-5 in drivers' compartment
(M19A1) AN/VRC-5 in drivers' compartment with SCR 593 or
AN/GRR-5 in right turret bulge
Interphone: RC99 w/SCR 510, 4 stations
Flag Set M238, Panel Set AP50A
Flares: 3 each, M17, M18, M19, and M21

FIRE AND GAS PROTECTION

(1) 10 pound carbon dioxide, fixed
(2) 4 pound carbon dioxide, portable
(3) 1½ quart decontaminating apparatus

PERFORMANCE

Maximum Speed: Level road	35 miles/hour
Maximum Grade:	60 per cent
Maximum Trench:	9 feet
Maximum Vertical Wall:	40 inches
Maximum Fording Depth:	42 inches
Minimum Turning Circle: (diameter)	46 feet
Cruising Range: Roads	approx. 100 miles

75mm HOWITZER MOTOR CARRIAGE M8

GENERAL DATA

Crew:	4	men
Length: w/sandshields	196	inches
Width: w/sandshields	91.5	inches
Height: Over AA MG	107	inches
Tread:	73.5	inches
Ground Clearance:	14	inches
Fire Height:	76	inches
Turret Ring Diameter: (inside)	54.4	inches
Weight, Combat Loaded:	34,600	pounds
Weight, Unstowed:	31,000	pounds
Power to Weight Ratio: Net	12.7	hp/ton
Gross	17.1	hp/ton
Ground Pressure: Zero penetration	12.5	psi

ARMOR

Type: Turret, rolled homogeneous steel; Hull, rolled homogeneous steel; Welded assembly

Hull Thickness:	Actual	Angle w/Vertical
Front, Upper	1.125 inches (29mm)	45 degrees
Lower	1.75 inches (44mm)	18 degrees
Sides, Front	1.125 inches (29mm)	0 degrees
Rear	1.0 inches (25mm)	0 degrees
Rear, Upper	1.0 inches (25mm)	50 degrees
Middle	1.0 inches (25mm)	0 degrees
Lower	1.0 inches (25mm)	17 degrees
Top	0.5 inches (13mm)	90 degrees
Floor, Front	0.5 inches (13mm)	90 degrees
Rear	0.375 inches (10mm)	90 degrees

Turret Thickness:		
Howitzer Shield (cast)	1.5 inches (38mm)	0 to 60 degrees
Front	1.5 inches (38mm)	0 to 63 degrees
Sides	1.0 inches (25mm)	20 degrees
Rear	1.0 inches (25mm)	20 degrees
Top	open	

ARMAMENT

Primary: 75mm Howitzer M2 or M3 in Mount M7 in turret

Traverse:	Manual 360 degrees
Elevation:	Manual +40 to −20 degrees
Firing Rate: (max)	6 rounds/minute
Loading System:	Manual
Stabilizer System:	None

Secondary:
(1) .50 caliber MG HB M2 flexible, ring mount on turret
Provision for (1) .45 caliber SMG M1928A1
Provision for (3) .30 caliber Carbine M1

AMMUNITION

46 rounds 75mm	8 hand grenades
400 rounds .50 caliber	
600 rounds .45 caliber	
735 rounds .30 caliber (carbine)	

FIRE CONTROL AND VISION EQUIPMENT

Primary Weapon:	Direct	Indirect
	Telescope M70D	Panoramic Telescope M12A5
		Aiming Post M1
		Gunner's Quadrant M1

Vision Devices:	Direct	Indirect
Driver	Vision door	Periscope M9 (2)
Asst. Driver	Vision door	Periscope M9 (2)
Commander	Open top turret	None
Gunner	Open top turret	None

Total Periscopes: M9 (4)

ENGINE

Make and Model: Twin Cadillac, Series 42	
Type: 16 cylinder (8/engine), 4 cycle, 90 degree vee	
Cooling System: Liquid Ignition: Delco	
Displacement:	692 cubic inches
	(346 cubic inches/engine)
Bore and Stroke:	3.5 x 4.5 inches
Compression Ratio:	7.06:1
Net Horsepower: (max)	220 hp at 3400 rpm
	(110 hp/engine)
Gross Horsepower: (max)	295 hp at 3200 rpm
	(148 hp/engine)
Net Torque: (max)	488 ft-lb at 1200 rpm
	(244 ft-lb/engine)
Gross Torque: (max)	560 ft-lb at 1200 rpm
	(280 ft-lb/engine)
Weight:	1168 pounds, dry
	(584 pounds/engine)
Fuel: 80 octane gasoline	89 gallons
Engine Oil:	16 quarts (8 quarts/engine)

POWER TRAIN

Transmission: Hydramatic, (2) 4 speeds forward, 1 reverse

Gear Ratios:	1st	3.26:1	4th	1.00:1
	2nd	2.26:1	reverse	3.81:1
	3rd	1.44:1		

Transfer Unit: Hydraulic, 2 speeds
Gear Ratios: 2.37:1 and 1.00:1
Steering: Controlled differential
Bevel Gear Ratio: 2.62:1   Steering Ratio: 1.845:1
Brakes: Mechanical, external contracting
Final Drive: Herringbone gear   Gear Ratio: 2.57:1
Drive Sprocket: At front of vehicle with 13 teeth
Pitch Diameter: 22.8 inches

RUNNING GEAR

Suspension: Vertical volute spring
8 wheels in 4 bogies (2 bogies/track)
Tire Size: 20 x 6 inches
6 track return rollers (3 rollers/track)
Trailing adjustable idler w/volute spring at rear of each track
Idler Size: 30 x 6 inches
Tracks: Outside guide, rubber bushed; T16 series, T36E6, and T55E1
Type: (T16E1) Double pin, 11.6 inch width, rubber, reversible
(T16E2) Double pin, 11.6 inch width, rubber, non-reversible
(T36E6) Double pin, 11.6 inch width, steel, parallel grouser
(T55E1) Double pin, 11.6 inch width, steel, chevron
Pitch: 5.5 inches
Shoes per Vehicle: 132 (66/track)
Ground Contact Length: 119 inches

ELECTRICAL SYSTEM

Nominal Voltage: 12 volts DC
Main Generator: (2, 1/engine), 12 volts, 50 amperes
(25 amperes/generator), belt driven by each engine
Auxiliary Generator: (1) 12 volts, 50 amperes, driven by the auxiliary engine
Battery: (1) 12 volts

COMMUNICATIONS

Radio: SCR 510 in right sponson
Interphone: RC99, 3 stations
Flares: 3 each, M17 and M18
Panel Set AP50A
Ground Signals Projector M4

FIRE AND GAS PROTECTION

(1) 10 pound carbon dioxide, fixed
(1) 4 pound carbon dioxide, portable
(3) 1½ quart decontaminating apparatus

PERFORMANCE

Maximum Speed: Level road	36 miles/hour
Maximum Grade:	60 per cent
Maximum Trench:	5.3 feet
Maximum Vertical Wall:	18 inches
Maximum Fording Depth:	36 inches
Minimum Turning Circle: (diameter)	42 feet
Cruising Range: Roads	approx. 100 miles

GENERAL DATA

Crew:	5 men
Length: Gun forward	262 inches
Length: w/o gun	208 inches
Gun Overhang: Gun forward	54 inches
Width: Over track guards	113 inches
Height: Over AA MG	101 inches
Tread:	94.63 inches
Ground Clearance:	14.3 inches
Fire Height:	73.8 inches
Turret Ring Diameter: (inside)	69 inches
Weight, Combat Loaded:	39,000 pounds
Weight, Unstowed:	35,500 pounds
Power to Weight Ratio: Net	20.5 hp/ton
Gross	23.6 hp/ton
Ground Pressure: Based on a 3116 square inch contact area	12.6 psi

ARMOR

Type: Turret, rolled and cast homogeneous steel; Hull, rolled homogeneous steel; Welded assembly

Hull Thickness:	Actual	Angle w/Vertical
Front, Upper	0.5 inches (13mm)	64 degrees
Upper middle	0.5 inches (13mm)	38 degrees
Lower middle	0.5 inches (13mm)	24 degrees
Lower	0.5 inches (13mm)	53 degrees
Sides, Upper	0.5 inches (13mm)	23 degrees
Lower	0.5 inches (13mm)	0 degrees
Rear, Upper	0.5 inches (13mm)	13 degrees
Lower	0.5 inches (13mm)	35 degrees
Top	0.31 inches (8mm)	90 degrees
Floor	0.19 inches (5mm)	90 degrees

Turret Thickness:		
Gun Shield	0.75 inches (19mm)	0 to 60 degrees
Front (cast)	1.0 inches (25mm)	23 degrees
Sides	0.5 inches (13mm)	20 degrees
Rear	0.5 inches (13mm)	9 degrees
Top	Open	

ARMAMENT

Primary: 76mm Gun M1A1, M1A1C, or M1A2 in Mount M1 in turret

Traverse: Hydraulic and manual	360 degrees
Traverse Rate: (max)	15 seconds/360 degrees
Elevation: Manual	+20 to −10 degrees
Firing Rate: (max)	20 rounds/minute
Loading System:	Manual
Stabilizer System:	None

Secondary:
(1) .50 caliber MG HB M2 flexible, ring mount on turret
Provision for (5) .30 caliber Carbine M1

AMMUNITION

45 rounds 76mm	12 hand grenades
800 rounds .50 caliber	4 smoke pots M1 HC
450 rounds .30 caliber (carbine)	

FIRE CONTROL AND VISION EQUIPMENT

Primary Weapon:	Direct	Indirect
	Telescope M76C or T93	Azimuth Indicator M18
	Periscope M4A1 with	Elevation Quadrant M9
	Telescope M47A2	Gunner's Quadrant M1
Vision Devices:	Direct	Indirect
Driver	Hatch	Periscope M6 (1)
Asst. Driver	Hatch	Periscope M6 (1)
Commander	Open top turret	None
Gunner	Open top turret	Periscope M4A1 (1)
Loader	Open top turret	None

Total Periscopes: M4A1 (1), M6 (2)

ENGINE

Make and Model: Continental R-975-C4	
Type: 9 cylinder, 4 cycle, radial	
Cooling System: Air Ignition: Magneto	
Displacement:	973 cubic inches
Bore and Stroke:	5 x 5.5 inches
Compression Ratio:	5.7:1
Net Horsepower: (max)	400 hp at 2400 rpm
Gross Horsepower: (max)	460 hp at 2400 rpm
Net Torque: (max)	940 ft-lb at 1700 rpm
Gross Torque: (max)	1025 ft-lb at 1800 rpm
Weight:	1212 pounds, dry
Fuel: 80 octane gasoline	165 gallons
Engine Oil:	36 quarts

POWER TRAIN

Rear Transfer Case: Spur gear
  Gear Ratio: 1:1
Front Transfer Case: Spur gear
  Gear Ratio: 1.29:1
Transmission: Torqmatic, 3 speeds forward, 1 reverse
  Gear Ratios: 1st   1.000:1   3rd   0.244:1
              2nd   0.421:1   reverse 0.756:1
Torque Convertor: Detroit Transmission 900T
  Ratio: (max) 4.5:1
Steering: Controlled differential
  Bevel Gear Ratio: 3.133:1   Steering Ratio: 1.600:1
Brakes: Mechanical, external contracting
Final Drive: Spur gear   Gear Ratio: 2.176:1
Drive Sprocket: At front of vehicle with 31 teeth (alternate engaged)
  The sprocket and final drive unit is pivoted and fitted with compensating linkage to maintain track tension
  Pitch Diameter: 25.234 inches

RUNNING GEAR

Suspension: Torsion bar
  10 individually sprung dual road wheels (5/track)
  Tire Size: 26 x 4.5 inches
  8 dual track return rollers (4/track)
  Dual adjustable idler at rear of each track
  Idler Size: 23.5 x 4.5 inches
  Shock absorbers on first 2 and last 2 road wheels of each track
Tracks: Center guide, rubber bushed; T69
  Type: Single pin, 12 inch width, steel, parallel grouser
    The 14 3/8 inch long track pins increase the projected ground contact area to 3116 square inches
  Pitch: 5.09 inches
  Shoes per Vehicle: 166 (83/track)
  Ground Contact Length: 116.5 inches

ELECTRICAL SYSTEM

Nominal Voltage: 24 volts DC
Main Generator: (1) 24 volts, 50 amperes, driven by main engine
Auxiliary Generator: (1) 24 volts, 50 amperes, driven by the auxiliary engine
Battery: (2) 12 volts in series

COMMUNICATIONS

Radio: SCR 610 in rear of turret
Interphone: RC99, 5 stations
Flag Set M238
Pistol Pyrotechnic M2

FIRE AND GAS PROTECTION

(2) 10 pound carbon dioxide, fixed
(1) 4 pound carbon dioxide, portable
(2) 1½ quart decontaminating apparatus

PERFORMANCE

Maximum Speed: Level Road	50 miles/hour
Maximum Grade:	60 per cent
Maximum Trench:	6.1 feet
Maximum Vertical Wall:	36 inches
Maximum Fording Depth:	48 inches
Minimum Turning Circle: (diameter)	66 feet
Cruising Range: Roads	approx. 100 miles

105mm HOWITZER MOTOR CARRIAGE T82

GENERAL DATA

Crew:	4 men
Length:	175 inches
Width: Over side rails	95.5 inches
Height: Over MG mount	90.5 inches
Tread:	77.0 inches
Ground Clearance:	17 inches
Fire Height:	67 inches
Weight, Combat Loaded:	32,000 pounds
Weight, Unstowed:	28,000 pounds
Power to Weight Ratio: Net	13.8 hp/ton
Gross	18.5 hp/ton
Ground Pressure: Zero penetration	8.3 psi

ARMOR

Type: Rolled homogeneous steel; Welded assembly

Hull Thickness:	Actual	Angle w/Vertical
Front, Fighting Compartment	0.5 inches (13mm)	28 degrees
Upper Hull	1.125 inches (29mm)	48 degrees
Lower Hull (cast)	1.5 to 2.5 inches (38−64mm)	0 to 23 degrees
Sides, Fighting Compartment	0.25 inches (6mm)	0 degrees
Lower Front	1.125 inches (29mm)	0 degrees
Lower Rear	1.0 inches (25mm)	0 degrees
Rear, Fighting Compartment	0.25 inches (6mm)	0 degrees
Upper Hull	1.0 inches (25mm)	49 degrees
Middle Hull	1.0 inches (25mm)	0 degrees
Lower Hull	1.0 inches (25mm)	17 degrees
Top, Fighting Compartment	Open	
Floor, Front	0.5 inches (13mm)	90 degrees
Rear	0.375 inches (10mm)	90 degrees

ARMAMENT

Primary: 105mm Howitzer M3 in modified Mount M3A1 in front hull

Traverse: Manual	40 degrees (18 left, 22 right)
Elevation: Manual	+35 to −5 degrees
Firing Rate: (max)	8 rounds/minute
Loading System:	Manual
Stabilizer System:	None

Secondary:

(1) .50 caliber MG HB M2 on pedestal mount over howitzer or right front

Provision for (4) .30 caliber Carbine M1

AMMUNITION

58 rounds 105mm	12 hand grenades
500 rounds .50 caliber	
500 rounds .30 caliber (carbine)	

FIRE CONTROL AND VISION EQUIPMENT

Primary Weapon:	Direct	Indirect
	Telescope T117E4 (2)	Panoramic sight M1
		Range Quadrant T15
		Gunner's Quadrant M1

Vision Devices:	Direct	Indirect
Driver	Vision door	Protectoscope (1)
Commander	Open top	None
Cannoneers	Open top	None

Total Protectoscopes: (1) in driver's vision door

ENGINE

Make and Model: Twin Cadillac, Series 42
Type: 16 cylinder (8/engine), 4 cycle, 90 degree vee
Cooling System: Liquid   Ignition: Delco

Displacement:	692 cubic inches (346 cubic inches/engine)
Bore and Stroke:	3.5 x 4.5 inches
Compression Ratio:	7.06:1
Net Horsepower: (max)	220 hp at 3400 rpm (110 hp/engine)
Gross Horsepower: (max)	296 hp at 3200 rpm (148 hp/engine)
Net Torque: (max)	488 ft-lb at 1200 rpm (244 ft-lb/engine)
Gross Torque: (max)	560 ft-lb at 1200 rpm (280 ft-lb/engine)
Weight:	1168 pounds, dry (584 pounds/engine)
Fuel: 80 octane gasoline	89 gallons
Engine Oil:	16 quarts (8 quarts/engine)

POWER TRAIN

Transmission: Hydramatic (2), 4 speeds forward, 1 reverse

Gear Ratios:	1st	3.26:1	4th	1.00:1
	2nd	2.26:1	reverse	3.81:1
	3rd	1.44:1		

Transfer Unit: Hydraulic, 2 speeds
Gear Ratios: 2.37:1 and 1.00:1
Steering: Controlled differential
Bevel Gear Ratio: 2.62:1   Steering Ratio: 1.845:1
Brakes: Mechanical, external contracting
Final Drive: Herringbone gear   Gear Ratio: 2.57:1
Drive Sprocket: At front of vehicle with 13 teeth
Pitch Diameter: 22.8 inches

RUNNING GEAR

Suspension: Vertical volute spring
8 wheels in 4 bogies (2 bogies/track)
Tire Size: 20 x 6 inches
6 track return rollers (3 rollers/track)
Trailing adjustable idler w/volute spring at rear of each track
Idler Size: 30 x 6 inches
Tracks: Outside guide, rubber bushed; T55E1 w/extended end connectors
Type: Double pin, 16 inch width, steel, chevron
Pitch: 5.5 inches
Shoes per Vehicle: 132 (66/track)
Ground Contact Length: 121 inches

ELECTRICAL SYSTEM

Nominal Voltage: 12 volts DC
Main Generator: (2, 1/engine) 12 volts, 50 amperes, (25 amperes/generator), belt driven by each engine
Auxiliary Generator: None
Battery: (1) 12 volts

COMMUNICATIONS

Radio: SCR 510 in left sponson
Interphone: None
Flag Set M238, Panel Set AP50A
Flares: 3 each M17, M18, M19, and M21

FIRE AND GAS PROTECTION

(1) 10 pound carbon dioxide, fixed
(1) 4 pound carbon dioxide, portable
(1) 1½ quart decontaminating apparatus

PERFORMANCE

Maximum Speed: Level road	36 miles/hour
Maximum Grade:	60 per cent
Maximum Trench:	5.3 feet
Maximum Vertical Wall:	18 inches
Maximum Fording Depth:	36 inches
Minimum Turning Circle: (diameter)	42 feet
Cruising Range: Roads	approx. 100 miles

105mm HOWITZER MOTOR CARRIAGE M37

GENERAL DATA
Crew:	7 men
Length: w/rear stowage	216 inches
Width:	118 inches
Height: Over AA MG	112 inches
Tread:	96 inches
Ground Clearance:	18 inches
Fire Height:	66 inches
Weight, Combat Loaded:	46,000 pounds
Weight, Unstowed:	38,000 pounds
Power to Weight Ratio: Net	9.7 hp/ton
Gross	12.9 hp/ton
Ground Pressure: Zero penetration w/T72 tracks	11.6 psi

ARMOR
Type: Rolled homogeneous steel; Welded assembly

Hull Thickness:	Actual	Angle w/Vertical
Front, Upper	0.5 inches (13mm)	60 degrees
Lower	0.5 inches (13mm)	45 degrees
Fighting Compartment	0.5 inches (13mm)	0 degrees
Sides, Front	0.5 inches (13mm)	12 degrees
Fighting Compartment	0.5 inches (13mm)	0 degrees
Rear, Upper	0.5 inches (13mm)	0 degrees
Lower	0.5 inches (13mm)	45 degrees
Top, Front	0.5 inches (13mm)	90 degrees
Fighting Compartment	Open	
Floor, Front	0.5 inches (13mm)	90 degrees
Rear	0.375 inches (10mm)	90 degrees
Howitzer Shield:	0.5 inches (13mm)	0 to 38 degrees

ARMAMENT
Primary: 105mm Howitzer M4 in Mount M5 (T14) in front hull

Traverse: Manual	51.7 degrees
	(25.4 left, 26.3 right)
Elevation: Manual	+42.8 to −10.5 degrees
Firing Rate: (max)	8 rounds/minute
Loading System:	Manual
Stabilizer System:	None

Secondary:
- (1) .50 caliber MG HB M2 on ring mount at right front of hull
- Provision for (1) .45 caliber SMG M3
- Provision for (6) .30 caliber Carbine M2

AMMUNITION
126 rounds 105mm	8 hand grenades
990 rounds .50 caliber	
750 rounds .45 caliber	
960 rounds .30 caliber (carbine)	

FIRE CONTROL AND VISION EQUIPMENT
Primary Weapon:	Direct	Indirect
	Telescope M76G	Panoramic Telescope M12A2
		Range Quadrant T14
		Gunner's Quadrant M1

Vision Devices:	Direct	Indirect
Driver	Hatch	Periscope M6 (1)
Commander	Open top	None
Cannoneers	Open top	None

Total Periscopes: M6 (1)

ENGINE
Make and Model: Twin Cadillac, Series 44T4	
Type: 16 cylinder, (8/engine), 4 cycle, 90 degree vee	
Cooling System: Liquid Ignition: Delco	
Displacement:	692 cubic inches
	(346 cubic inches/engine)
Bore and Stroke:	3.5 x 4.5 inches
Compression Ratio:	7.06:1
Net Horsepower: (max)	220 hp at 3400 rpm
	(110 hp/engine)
Gross Horsepower: (max)	296 hp at 3200 rpm
	(148 hp/engine)
Net Torque: (max)	480 ft-lb at 1200 rpm
	(240 ft-lb/engine)
Gross Torque: (max)	560 ft-lb at 1200 rpm
	(280 ft-lb/engine)
Weight:	1168 pounds, dry
	(584 pounds/engine)
Fuel: 80 octane gasoline	110 gallons
Engine Oil:	16 quarts (8 quarts/engine)

POWER TRAIN
Transmission: Hydramatic (2), 4 speeds

Gear Ratios:	1st 3.92:1	3rd 1.55:1
	2nd 2.53:1	4th 1:1

Transfer Unit: Synchromesh, 2 speeds forward, 1 reverse

Gear Ratios:	high 2.34:1	reverse 2.44:1
	low 1.03:1	

Steering: Controlled differential
Bevel Gear Ratio: 2.62:1   Steering Ratio: 1.33:1
Brakes: Mechanical, external contracting
Final Drive: Herringbone gear   Gear Ratio: 2.973:1
Drive Sprocket: At front of vehicle with 13 teeth
   Pitch Diameter: w/T72 or T72E1 tracks 22.979 inches
                   w/T85E1 tracks 22.816 inches

RUNNING GEAR
Suspension: Torsion bar
   10 individually sprung dual road wheels (5/track)
   Tire Size: 25.5 x 4.5 inches
   8 dual track return rollers (4/track)
   Dual compensating idler at rear of each track
   Idler Size: 22.5 x 5 inches
   Shock absorbers on first 2 and last 2 road wheels of each track
Tracks: Center guide, rubber bushed; T72, T72E1, and T85E1
   Type: (T72) Single pin, 16 inch width, steel, parallel grouser
         (T72E1) Single pin, 16 inch width, steel parallel grouser*
         (T85E1) Double pin, 14 inch width, rubber, chevron 16.5 inch
                 width w/extended end connectors
   *Three holes in the T72E1 track shoe permit the attachment of
    28 inch grousers
   Pitch: 5.5 inches
   Shoes per Vehicle: 160 (80/track)
   Ground Contact Length: 124 inches

ELECTRICAL SYSTEM
Nominal Voltage: 24 volts DC
Main Generator: (2, 1/engine) 24 volts, 50 amperes, belt driven by each engine
Auxiliary Generator: None
Battery: (4) 6 volts in series

COMMUNICATIONS
Radio: None
Interphone: RC99, 3 stations
Flag Set M238, Panel Set AP50A
Flares: 3 each, M17, M18, M19, and M21

FIRE PROTECTION
   (1) 10 pound carbon dioxide, fixed
   (1) 4 pound carbon dioxide, portable

PERFORMANCE
Maximum Speed: Level road	35 miles/hour
Maximum Grade:	60 per cent
Maximum Trench:	9 feet
Maximum Vertical Wall:	36 inches
Maximum Fording Depth:	42 inches
Minimum Turning Circle: (diameter)	46 feet
Cruising Range: Roads	approx. 100 miles

155mm HOWITZER MOTOR CARRIAGE M41

GENERAL DATA
Crew: 5 men
Length: 230 inches
Width: 112 inches
Height: 94 inches
Tread: 96 inches
Ground Clearance: 17 inches
Fire Height: 77 inches
Weight, Combat Loaded: 42,500 pounds
Weight, Unstowed: 38,500 pounds
Power to Weight Ratio: Net 10.4 hp/ton
    Gross 13.9 hp/ton
Ground Pressure: Zero penetration, T72 tracks 0.7 psi

ARMOR
Type: Rolled homogeneous steel; Welded assembly

Hull Thickness:	Actual	Angle w/Vertical
Front, Upper	0.5 inches (13mm)	60 degrees
Lower	0.5 inches (13mm)	45 degrees
Sides	0.5 inches (13mm)	12 degrees
Rear	0.5 inches (13mm)	0 degrees
Tailgate	0.25 inches (6mm)	0 degrees (raised)
Top, Front	0.5 inches (13mm)	90 degrees
Rear	open	
Crew Shields	0.25 inches (6mm)	0 degrees
Floor, Front	0.5 inches (13mm)	90 degrees
Rear	0.375 inches (10mm)	90 degrees

ARMAMENT
Primary: 155mm Howitzer M1 in Mount M14 (T19) on rear of chassis
Traverse: Manual 37.5 degrees
    (20.5 left, 17 right)
Elevation: Electric and manual +45 to −5 degrees
Firing Rate: (max) 4 rounds/minute
Loading System: Manual
Stabilizer System: None
Secondary:
    Provision for (2) .45 caliber SMG M3
    Provision for (3) .30 caliber Carbine M1

AMMUNITION
22 rounds 155mm
420 rounds .45 caliber
480 rounds .30 caliber (carbine)
12 hand grenades

FIRE CONTROL AND VISION EQUIPMENT

Primary Weapon:	Direct	Indirect
	Telescope M69D*	Panoramic Telescope M12*
		Gunner's Quadrant M1

*Later, the Telescope M69D was eliminated and the Panoramic Telescope M12A6 was used for both direct and indirect fire

Vision Devices:	Direct	Indirect
Driver	Hatch	Periscope M6 (1)
Asst. Driver	Hatch	Periscope M6 (1)
Commander	Open top	None
Cannoneers	Open top	None

Total Periscopes: M6 (2)

ENGINE
Make and Model: Twin Cadillac, Series 44T4
Type: 16 cylinder (8/engine), 4 cycle, 90 degree vee
Cooling System: Liquid   Ignition: Delco
Displacement: 692 cubic inches
    (346 cubic inches/engine)
Bore and Stroke: 3.5 x 4.5 inches
Compression Ratio: 7.06:1
Net Horsepower: (max) 220 hp at 3400 rpm
    (110 hp/engine)
Gross Horsepower: (max) 296 hp at 3200 rpm
    (148 hp/engine)
Net Torque: (max) 480 ft-lb at 1200 rpm
    (240 ft-lb/engine)
Gross Torque: (max) 560 ft-lb at 1200 rpm
    (280 ft-lb/engine)
Weight: 1168 pounds, dry
    (584 pounds/engine)
Fuel: 80 octane gasoline 110 gallons
Engine Oil: 16 quarts (8 quarts/engine)

POWER TRAIN
Transmission: Hydramatic (2), 4 speeds

Gear Ratios:	1st 3.92:1	3rd 1.55:1
	2nd 2.53:1	4th 1:1

Transfer Unit: Synchromesh, 2 speeds forward, 1 reverse
    Gear Ratios: high 2.34:1   reverse 2.44:1
                    low 1.03:1
Steering: Controlled differential
    Bevel Gear Ratio: 2.62:1   Steering Ratio: 1.33:1
Brakes: Mechanical, external contracting
Final Drive: Herringbone gear   Gear Ratio: 2.94:1
Drive Sprocket: At front of vehicle with 13 teeth
    Pitch Diameter: 22.979 inches

RUNNING GEAR
Suspension: Torsion bar
    10 individually sprung dual road wheels (5/track)
    Tire Size: 25.5 x 4.5 inches
    8 dual track return rollers (4/track)
    Dual compensating idler at rear of each track
    Idler Size: 22.5 x 5 inches
    Shock absorbers on first 2 and last 2 road wheels of each track
Tracks: Center guide, rubber bushed; T72, T72E1, and T85E1
    Type: (T72) Single pin, 16 inch width, steel, parallel grouser
         (T72E1) Single pin, 16 inch width, steel, parallel grouser*
         (T85E1) Double pin, 14 inch width, rubber, chevron
         16.5 inch width w/extended end connectors
    *Three holes in the T72E1 track shoe permit the attachment of
       28 inch grousers
    Pitch: 5.5 inches
    Shoes per Vehicle: 160 (80/track)
    Ground Contact Length: 124 inches

ELECTRICAL SYSTEM
Nominal Voltage: 24 volts DC
Main Generator: (2, 1/engine) 24 volts, 50 amperes, belt driven by each engine
Auxiliary Generator: None
Battery: (4) 6 volts in series

COMMUNICATIONS
Radio: SCR 510, 610, or 619 in drivers' compartment
Interphone: RC99, 3 stations
Flag Set M238, Panel Set AP50A
Flares: 3 each, M17, M18, M19, and M21

FIRE PROTECTION
    (1) 10 pound carbon dioxide, fixed
    (2) 4 pound carbon dioxide, portable

PERFORMANCE
Maximum Speed: Level road 35 miles/hour
Maximum Grade: 60 per cent
Maximum Trench: 9 feet
Maximum Vertical Wall: 40 inches
Maximum Fording Depth: 42 inches
Minimum Turning Circle: (diameter) 46 feet
Cruising Range: Roads approx. 100 miles

LANDING VEHICLE TRACKED (ARMORED) MARK 1

GENERAL DATA

Crew:	6 men
Length:	313 inches
Width:	128 inches
Height:	121 inches
Tread:	113.5 inches
Ground Clearance: Hard surface	18 inches
Fire Height:	107 inches
Draft: Loaded	50 inches
Turret Ring Diameter: (inside)	46.75 inches
Weight, Combat Loaded:	32,800 pounds
Power to Weight Ratio: Net	15.2 hp/ton
Gross	16.0 hp/ton
Ground Pressure: Zero penetration	9.1 psi

ARMOR

Type: Turret, rolled homogeneous steel; Hull, rolled homogeneous steel; Welded assembly

Hull Thickness:

	Actual	Angle w/Vertical
Front, Upper (cab)	0.5 inches (13mm)	30 degrees
Middle	0.25 inches (6mm)	83 degrees
Lower	0.25 inches (6mm)	35 to 90 degrees
Sides	0.25 inches (6mm)	0 degrees
Pontoons	12 gauge mild steel	0 degrees
Rear, Upper	0.25 inches (6mm)	0 degrees
Lower	0.25 inches (6mm)	60 degrees
Top	0.25 inches (6mm)	90 degrees
Floor	10 gauge mild steel	90 degrees

Turret Thickness:

Gun Shield (cast)	2.0 inches (51mm)	0 to 14 degrees
Front	0.5 inches (13mm)	10 degrees
Sides	0.5 inches (13mm)	0 degrees
Rear	0.5 inches (13mm)	0 degrees
Top	0.25 inches (6mm)	75 to 90 degrees

ARMAMENT

Primary: 37mm Gun M6 in Mount M44 in turret

Traverse: Hydraulic and manual	360 degrees
Traverse Rate: (max)	15 seconds/360 degrees
Elevation: Manual	+25 to −10 degrees
Firing Rate: (max)	30 rounds/minute
Loading System:	Manual
Stabilizer System:	Elevation only

Secondary:
(1) .30 caliber MG M1919A5 coaxial w/37mm gun in turret
(2) .30 caliber MG M1919A4 on Mark 21 Scarff mounts behind turret

AMMUNITION

104 rounds 37mm
6000 rounds .30 caliber

FIRE CONTROL AND VISION EQUIPMENT

Primary Weapon: Telescope M54
Periscope M4 with Telescope M40

Vision Devices:	Direct	Indirect
Driver	Hatch and front window	Periscope M6 (1)
Asst. Driver	Hatch	Periscope M6 (1)
Commander	Hatch	Periscope M6 (2)
Gunner	Hatch	Periscope M4 (1)
Machine Gunners	Open Mount	None

Total Periscopes: M4 (1), M6 (4)

ENGINE

Make and Model: Continental W-670-9A	
Type: 7 cylinder, 4 cycle, radial	
Cooling System: Air Ignition: Magneto	
Displacement:	668 cubic inches
Bore and Stroke:	5.125 x 4.625 inches
Compression Ratio:	6.1:1
Net Horsepower: (max)	250 hp at 2400 rpm
Gross Horsepower: (max)	262 hp at 2400 rpm
Net Torque: (max)	584 ft-lb at 1800 rpm
Gross Torque: (max)	590 ft-lb at 1700 rpm
Weight:	565 pounds, dry
Fuel: 80 octane gasoline	106 gallons
Engine Oil:	32 quarts

POWER TRAIN

Clutch: Dry disc, 2 plate
Transmission: Synchromesh, 5 speeds forward, 1 reverse

Gear Ratios:	1st	5.37:1	4th	1.09:1
	2nd	2.82:1	5th	0.738:1
	3rd	1.72:1	reverse	6.19:1

Steering: Controlled differential
Bevel Gear Ratio: 2.62:1   Steering Ratio: 1.845:1
Brakes: Mechanical, external contracting
Final Drive: Herringbone gear   Gear Ratio: 3.150:1
Drive Sprocket: At front of vehicle with 37 teeth (alternate engaged)
Pitch Diameter: 23.49 inches

RUNNING GEAR

Suspension: Torsilastic
22 road wheels (11/track)
Tire Size: 12 x 7.25 inches
4 track return rollers (2/track)
Adjustable idler sprocket w/33 teeth at rear of each track
Idler Sprocket Pitch Diameter: 20.95 inches
Tracks: Outside guide, dry pin
Type: Steel link, 14.25 inch width, extruded grousers
Pitch: 8 inches (4 inches each for inside and outside links)
Shoes per Vehicle: 146 (73/track)
Ground Contact Length: 126.5 inches

ELECTRICAL SYSTEM

Nominal Voltage: 12 volts DC
Main Generator: (1) 12 volts, 50 amperes, belt driven by main engine
Auxiliary Generator: (1) 12 volts, 50 amperes, driven by the auxiliary engine
Battery: (1) 12 volts

COMMUNICATIONS

Radio: TCS (Navy) in right side of driving compartment
Interphone: 6 stations

FIRE PROTECTION

(2) 10 pound carbon dioxide, fixed
(1) 15 pound carbon dioxide, portable

PERFORMANCE

Maximum Speed: Level road	25 miles/hour
In water	7 miles/hour
Maximum Grade:	60 per cent
Maximum Trench:	5 feet
Angle of Approach:	35 degrees
Angle of Departure:	30 degrees
Maximum Vertical Wall:	36 inches
Maximum Fording Depth:	Floats
Minimum Turning Circle: (diameter) Land	30 feet
Water	48 feet
Cruising Range: Roads	approx. 125 miles
Water	approx. 75 miles

LANDING VEHICLE TRACKED (ARMORED) MARK 4 AND 5

GENERAL DATA

Crew:	6 men
Length:	313 inches
Width:	128 inches
Height:	122.5 inches
Tread:	113.5 inches
Ground Clearance: Hard surface	18 inches
Fire Height:	109 inches
Draft: Loaded, front	22 inches
rear	38 inches
Turret Ring Diameter: (inside)	54.4 inches
Weight, Combat Loaded:	approx. 40,000 pounds
Power to Weight Ratio: Net	12.5 hp/ton
Gross	13.1 hp/ton
Ground Pressure: Zero penetration	11.1 psi

ARMOR

Type: Turret, rolled homogeneous steel; Hull, rolled homogeneous steel; Welded assembly

Hull Thickness:

	Actual	Angle w/Vertical
Front, Upper (cab)	0.5 inches (13mm)	30 degrees
Middle	0.25 inches (6mm)	83 degrees
Lower	0.25 inches (6mm)	35 to 90 degrees
Sides	0.25 inches (6mm)	0 degrees
Pontoons	12 gauge mild steel	0 degrees
Rear, Upper	0.25 inches (6mm)	0 degrees
Lower	0.25 inches (6mm)	60 degrees
Top	0.25 inches (6mm)	90 degrees
Floor	10 gauge mild steel	90 degrees

Turret Thickness:

Gun Shield (cast)	1.5 inches (51mm)	0 to 60 degrees
Front	1.0 inches (25mm)	0 to 63 degrees
Sides	1.0 inches (25mm)	20 degrees
Rear	1.0 inches (25mm)	0 degrees
Top	Open	

ARMAMENT

Primary: 75mm Howitzer M3 in Mount M7 [LVT(A)(4)] or M12 [LVT(A)(5)] in turret

Traverse: LVT(A)(4) Manual	360 degrees
LVT(A)(5) Hydraulic and manual	360 degrees
Traverse Rate: (max) LVT(A)(5)	15 seconds/360 degrees
Elevation: Manual	+40 to −20 degrees
Firing Rate: (max)	6 rounds/minute
Loading System:	Manual
Stabilizer System: LVT(A)(4)	None
LVT(A)(5)	Elevation only

Secondary:

LVT(A)(4) early: (1) .50 caliber MG HB M2, ring mount on turret

LVT(A)(4) late and LVT(A)(5): (2) .30 caliber MG M1919A4, one on each side of turret

LVT(A)(4) late and LVT(A)(5): (1) .30 caliber MG M1919A4 in cab bow mount

AMMUNITION

100 rounds 75mm

400 rounds .50 caliber [early LVT(A)(4) only]

2000 rounds .30 caliber [early LVT(A)(4) only]

6000 rounds .30 caliber [late LVT(A)(4) and LVT(A)(5)]

FIRE CONTROL AND VISION EQUIPMENT

Primary Weapon:	Direct	Indirect
	Telescope M70C LVT(A)(4)	Panoramic Telescope M12A5
	Telescope M70R LVT(A)(5)	Gunner's Quadrant M1
		Fuze Setter M14 or M27

Vision Devices:	Direct	Indirect
Driver, LVT(A)(4) early	Hatch and front window	Periscope M6 (1)
LVT(A)(4) late and LVT(A)(5)	Hatch and (2) vision blocks	None
Asst. Driver, LVT(A)(4) early	Hatch	Periscope M6 (1)
LVT(A)(4) late and LVT(A)(5)	Hatch and (2) vision blocks	Periscope M6 or Periscope M12 (1)
Commander	Open turret and (1) vision block*	None
Gunner	Open turret and (1) vision block*	None
Loader	Open turret and (1) vision block*	None
Cannoneer	Open turret	None

*Late model turrets only

Total Periscopes: LVT(A)(4) early, M6 (2)

LVT (A)(4) late and LVT(A)(5), M6 or M12 (1)

Total Vision Blocks: LVT(A)(4) late and LVT(A)(5) (7)

ENGINE

Make and Model: Continental W-670-9A	
Type: 7 cylinder, 4 cycle, radial	
Cooling System: Air Ignition: Magneto	
Displacement:	668 cubic inches
Bore and Stroke:	5.125 x 4.625 inches
Compression Ratio:	6.1:1
Net Horsepower: (max)	250 hp at 2400 rpm
Gross Horsepower: (max)	262 hp at 2400 rpm
Net Torque: (max)	584 ft-lb at 1800 rpm
Gross Torque: (max)	590 ft-lb at 1700 rpm
Weight:	565 pounds, dry
Fuel: 80 octane gasoline	106 gallons
Engine Oil:	32 quarts

POWER TRAIN

Transmission: Synchromesh, 5 speeds forward, 1 reverse

Gear Ratios:	1st	5.37:1	4th	1.09:1
	2nd	2.82:1	5th	0.738:1
	3rd	1.72:1	reverse	6.19:1

Steering: Controlled differential

Bevel Gear Ratio: 2.62:1   Steering Ratio: 1.845:1

Brakes: Mechanical, external contracting

Final Drive: Herringbone gear   Gear Ratio: 3.150:1

Drive Sprocket: At front of vehicle with 37 teeth (alternate engaged)

Pitch Diameter: 23.49 inches

RUNNING GEAR

Suspension: Torsilastic

22 road wheels (11/track)

Tire Size: 12 x 7.25 inches

4 track return rollers (2/track)

Adjustable idler sprocket w/33 teeth at rear of each track

Idler Sprocket Pitch Diameter: 20.95 inches

Tracks: Outside guide, dry pin

Type: Steel link, 14.25 inch width, extruded grousers

Pitch: 8 inches (4 inches each for inside and outside links)

Shoes per Vehicle: 146 (73/track)

Ground Contact Length: 126.5 inches

ELECTRICAL SYSTEM

Nominal Voltage: 12 volts DC

Main Generator: (1) 12 volts, 50 amperes, belt driven by main engine

Auxiliary Generator: LVT(A)(4), (1) 12 volts, 50 amperes, driven by the auxiliary engine

LVT(A)(5), (2) 12 volts, 50 amperes, driven by the auxiliary engines

Battery: (2) 12 volts in series

COMMUNICATIONS

Radio: SCR 508 or 528 in right side of driving compartment

Late LVT(A)(4) and LVT(A)(5) have AN/VRC-3 in left rear of turret

AN/GRC-9 (command vehicles only) in hull behind cab

Interphone: (part of radio) 6 stations

FIRE PROTECTION

(2) 10 pound carbon dioxide, fixed

(1) 15 pound carbon dioxide, portable

PERFORMANCE

Maximum Speed: Level road	25 miles/hour
In water	7 miles/hour
Maximum Grade:	60 per cent
Maximum Trench:	5 feet
Angle of Approach:	35 degrees
Angle of Departure:	30 degrees
Maximum Vertical Wall:	36 inches
Maximum Fording Depth:	Floats
Minimum Turning Circle: (diameter) Land	30 feet
Water	48 feet
Cruising Range: Roads	approx. 125 miles
Water	approx. 75 miles

Armament for the light tanks described in this volume ranged from the 37mm gun M1916 in the six-ton tank M1917 to the lightweight 75mm gun M6 in the light tank M24. The latter was identical in ballistic performance to the 75mm gun M3 which armed the major portion of the Sherman medium tanks. The light tank chassis also served as a motor carriage for weapons as heavy as the 155mm howitzer M1. Data describing the characteristics of the various weapons installed on these chassis are tabulated on the following pages. The dimensions used are defined in the sketches below.

CANNON WITH SLIDING WEDGE BREECHBLOCK

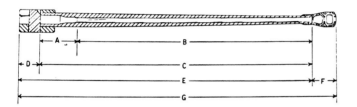

A. Length of Chamber (to rifling)
B. Length of Rifling
C. Length of Bore
D. Depth of Breech Recess
E. Length, Muzzle to Rear Face of Breech
F. Additional Length, Muzzle Brake, Etc.
G. Overall Length
H. Length, Breechblock and Firing Lock

CANNON WITH INTERRUPTED SCREW BREECHBLOCK

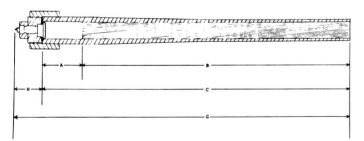

The official nomenclature for each type of ammunition is that used during its period of greatest service. However, since this was frequently changed during the service life, a standard nomenclature is added in parentheses to prevent confusion. These standard terms, which are used separately and in combination, are defined as follows.

AP	Armor piercing, uncapped
APBC	Armor piercing with ballistic cap
APCBC	Armor piercing with armor piercing cap and ballistic cap
APCR	Armor piercing, composite rigid
HE	High explosive
HEAT	High explosive antitank, shaped charge
CP	Concrete piercing
–T	Tracer

Penetration performance data for the various types of armor piercing ammunition are quoted for 30 degree angles of obliquity as this was the common practice during World War II. It should be noted that the relative performance between different types of projectiles at 30 degrees is not necessarily maintained at other angles of obliquity. For example, the AP monoblock shot may be more effective than APCR at high angles of obliquity, but the reverse is true at low angles. The simplified sketch in the introduction to the vehicle data sheets defined the angle of obliquity as the angle between a line perpendicular to the armor plate and the projectile path. However, in three dimensions, the calculation of the true angle is a little more complicated as indicated in these sketches. Here, the angle of obliquity is shown to be the angle whose cosine equals the product of the cosines for the vertical and lateral attack angles.

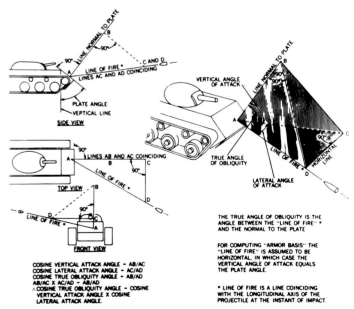

37mm GUNS M5 AND M6

Carriage and Mount	Light Tanks M2A4 in Mount M20 (M5 gun)
	Light Tanks M3 in Mount M22 (M5 Gun)
	Light Tanks M3A1 and M5 in Mount M23 (M6 Gun)
	Light Tanks M3A3 and M5A1 in Mount M44 (M6 Gun)
	LVT(A)(1) in Mount M44 (M6 Gun)
Length of Chamber (to rifling)	9.55 inches
Length of Rifling	63.35 inches (M5 Gun), 68.45 inches (M6 Gun)
Length of Chamber (to projectile base)	8.1 inches (square base projectiles)
Travel of Projectile in Bore	64.8 inches (M5 Gun), 69.9 inches (M6 Gun)
Length of Bore	72.9 inches, 50.0 calibers (M5 Gun)
	78.0 inches, 53.5 calibers (M6 Gun)
Depth of Breech Recess	4.5 inches
Length, Muzzle to Rear Face of Breech	77.4 inches, 53.1 calibers (M5 Gun)
	82.5 inches, 56.6 calibers (M6 Gun)
Additional Length, Muzzle Brake, etc.	None
Overall Length	77.4 inches (M5 Gun), 82.5 inches (M6 Gun)
Diameter of Bore	1.457 inches (37mm)
Chamber Capacity	19.35 cubic inches (APC M51), 19.19 cubic inches (HE M63)
Weight, Tube	138 pounds (M6 Gun)
Total Weight	185 pounds (M6 Gun)
Type of Breechblock	Manually operated vertical sliding wedge (M5 Gun)
	Semiautomatic vertical sliding wedge (M6 Gun)
Rifling	12 grooves, uniform right-hand twist, one turn in 25 calibers
Ammunition	Fixed
Primer	Percussion

Weight, Complete Round	APC M51 Shot (APCBC-T)	3.48 pounds
	AP M74 Shot (AP-T)	3.34 pounds
	HE M63 Shell (HE)	3.13 pounds
	Canister M2	3.49 pounds
Weight, Projectile	APC M51 Shot (APCBC-T)	1.92 pounds
	AP M74 Shot (AP-T)	1.92 pounds
	HE M63 Shell (HE)	1.61 pounds
	Canister M2 (122 steel balls)	1.94 pounds
Maximum Powder Pressure	50,000 psi	
Maximum Rate of Fire	30 rounds/minute	

		M5	M6
Muzzle Velocity	APC M51 Shot (APCBC-T)	2855 ft/sec	2900 ft/sec
	AP M74 Shot (AP-T)	2855 ft/sec	2900 ft/sec
	HE M63 Shell (HE)	2565 ft/sec	2600 ft/sec
	Canister M2	2470 ft/sec	2500 ft/sec
Muzzle Energy of Projectile, KE=$\frac{1}{2}MV^2$	APC M51 Shot (APCBC-T)	108 ft-tons	112 ft-tons
Rotational energy is neglected and	AP M74 Shot (AP-T)	108 ft-tons	112 ft-tons
values are based on long tons	HE M63 Shell (HE)	73 ft-tons	75 ft-tons
(2240 pounds)	Canister M2	82 ft-tons	84 ft-tons
Maximum Range (independent of mount)	APC M51 Shot (APCBC-T)	12,725 yards	12,850 yards
	AP M74 Shot (AP-T)	8,625 yards	8,725 yards
	HE M63 Shell (HE)	9,425 yards	9,500 yards
	Canister M2	(M5 and M6) approx. 150 to 200 yards	

Penetration Performance, M6 Gun*

Homogeneous steel armor at 30 degrees obliquity

Range	500 yards	1000 yards	1500 yards	2000 yards
APC M51 Shot (APCBC-T)	2.1 inches (53mm)	1.8 inches (46mm)	1.6 inches (40mm)	1.4 inches (35mm)

Face-hardened steel armor at 30 degrees obliquity

Range	500 yards	1000 yards	1500 yards	2000 yards
APC M51 Shot (APCBC-T)	1.8 inches (46mm)	1.6 inches (40mm)	1.5 inches (38mm)	1.3 inches (33mm)

*The lower velocity of the M5 gun reduced the penetration by approximately 0.1 inches (3mm) at all ranges

40MM DUAL AUTOMATIC GUN M2

Carriage and Mount	Motor Carriages M19 and M19A1 in Mount M4
Length of Chamber (to rifling)	12.73 inches
Length of Rifling	75.85 inches
Length of Chamber (to projectile base)	11.2 inches (square base shot AP-T M81A1)
	9.8 inches (boat-tailed shell HE-T Mk II)
Travel of Projectile in Bore	77.4 inches (square base shot AP-T M81A1)
	78.8 inches (boat-tailed shell HE-T Mk II)
Length of Bore	88.58 inches, 56.3 calibers
Depth of Breech Recess	5.9 inches, approx.
Length, Muzzle to Rear Face of Breech	95 inches, approx.
Length of Flash Hider	10 inches, approx.
Length of Automatic Loader Assembly	39 inches, approx.
Overall Length	144 inches, approx.
Diameter of Bore	1.573 inches (40mm)
Chamber Capacity	29.9 cubic inches
Weight of Barrel Assembly (each)	296 pounds
Total Weight	2000 pounds, approx.
Type of Breechblock	Semiautomatic, vertical sliding wedge
Rifling	16 grooves, increasing twist, one turn in 45 to 30 calibers
Automatic Loader	Each w/7 round magazine loaded from 4 round clips
Ammunition	Fixed
Primer	Percussion
Weight, Complete Round	AP-T M81A1 Shot (AP-T) 4.57 pounds
	HE-T Mk II Shell (HE-T) 4.70 pounds
Weight, Projectile	AP-T M81A1 Shot (AP-T) 1.96 pounds
	HE-T Mk II Shell (HE-T) 1.93 pounds
Maximum Rate of Fire	240 rounds/minute (120 rounds/gun)
Muzzle Velocity	AP-T M81A1 Shot (AP-T) 2870 ft/sec
	HE-T Mk II Shell (HE-T) 2870 ft/sec
Muzzle Energy of Projectile KE=½MV²	AP-T M81A1 Shot (AP-T) 112 ft-tons
Rotational energy is neglected and values are based on long tons (2240 pounds)	HE-T Mk II Shell (HE-T) 110 ft-tons
Maximum Range (independent of mount)	AP-T M81A1 Shot (AP-T) 9,475 yards
	HE-T Mk II Shell (HE-T) 10,850 yards*

Penetration Performance   Homogeneous steel armor at 30 degrees obliquity

Range	500 yards	1000 yards	1500 yards	2000 yards
AP-T M81A1 Shot (AP-T)	1.9 inches (48mm)	1.6 inches (41mm)	1.2 inches (30mm)	1.0 inches (25mm)

Face-hardened steel armor at 30 degrees obliquity

Range	500 yards	1000 yards	1500 yards	2000 yards
AP-T M81A1 Shot (AP-T)	1.8 inches (46mm)	1.5 inches (38mm)	1.2 inches (30mm)	1.0 inches (25mm)

*Actual range limited by shell destroying tracer to approximately 5200 yards horizontal and 5100 yards vertical

Carriage and Mount	Light Tank T7E2 in turret combination mount
Length of Chamber (to rifling)	18.02 inches
Length of Rifling	78.18 inches
Length of Chamber (to projectile base)	16.2 inches
Travel of Projectile in Bore	80.0 inches
Length of Bore	96.2 inches, 42.9 calibers
Depth of Breech Recess	4.75 inches
Length, Muzzle to Rear Face of Breech	100.95 inches, 45.0 calibers
Additional Length, Muzzle Brake, etc.	None
Overall Length	100.95 inches
Diameter of Bore	2.244 inches (57mm)
Chamber Capacity	100.05 cubic inches (AP M70), 98.87 cubic inches (APC M86)
Total Weight	761 pounds
Type of Breechblock	Semiautomatic, vertical sliding wedge
Rifling	24 grooves, uniform right-hand twist, one turn in 30 calibers
Ammunition	Fixed
Primer	Percussion

Weight, Complete Round	APC M86 Projectile (APCBC/HE-T)	13.88 pounds
	AP M70 Shot (AP-T)	12.92 pounds
Weight, Projectile	APC M86 Projectile (APCBC/HE-T)	7.27 pounds
	AP M70 Shot (AP-T)	6.28 pounds
Maximum Powder Pressure	46,000 psi	
Maximum Rate of Fire	30 rounds/minute	
Muzzle Velocity	APC M86 Projectile (APCBC/HE-T)	2580 ft/sec
	AP M70 Shot (AP-T)	2830 ft/sec
Muzzle Energy of Projectile, KE=½MV²	APC M86 Projectile (APCBC/HE-T)	335 ft-tons
Rotational energy is neglected and values are based on long tons (2240 pounds)	AP M70 Shot (AP-T)	349 ft-tons
Maximum Range (independent of mount)	APC M86 Projectile (APCBC/HE-T)	approx. 13,000 yards
	AP M70 Shot (AP-T)	approx. 8,900 yards

Penetration Performance

Homogeneous steel armor at 30 degrees obliquity

Range	500 yards	1000 yards	1500 yards	2000 yards
APC M86 Projectile (APCBC/HE-T)	3.0 inches (76mm)	2.7 inches (69mm)	2.3 inches (58mm)	2.0 inches (51mm)

Face-hardened steel armor at 30 degrees obliquity

Range	500 yards	1000 yards	1500 yards	2000 yards
APC M86 Projectile (APCBC/HE-T)	2.8 inches (71mm)	2.7 inches (69mm)	2.5 inches (64mm)	2.4 inches (61mm)

Carriage and Mount	Motor Carriage M8 in Mount M7	
	LVT(A)(4) in Mount M7, LVT(A)(5) in Mount M12	
Length of Chamber (to rifling)	11.12 inches	
Length of Rifling	35.91 inches	
Length of Chamber (to projectile base)	7.7 inches (boat-tailed projectiles)	
Travel of Projectile in Bore	39.3 inches (boat-tailed projectiles)	
Length of Bore	47.03 inches, 15.9 calibers	
Depth of Breech Recess	7.15 inches	
Length, Muzzle to Rear Face of Breech	54.18 inches, 18.4 calibers	
Additional Length, Muzzle Brake, etc.	None	
Overall Length	54.18 inches	
Diameter of Bore	2.950 inches (75mm)	
Chamber Capacity	59.08 cubic inches (HE M48)	
Total Weight	318 pounds (M2 Howitzer), 421 pounds (M3 Howitzer)	
Type of Breechblock	Manually operated, horizontal sliding wedge	
Rifling	28 grooves, uniform right-hand twist, one turn in 20 calibers	
Ammunition	Semifixed and Fixed (HC BI M89 and HEAT M66)	
Primer	Percussion	
Weight, Complete Round	HE M48 Shell (HE)	18.24 pounds
	HE M41A1 Shell (HE)	17.40 pounds
	HEAT M66 Shell (HEAT-T)	16.30 pounds
	WP M64 Shell, Smoke	18.89 pounds
Weight, Projectile	HE M48 Shell (HE)	14.60 pounds
	HE M41A1 Shell (HE)	13.76 pounds
	HEAT M66 Shell (HEAT-T)	13.10 pounds
	WP M64 Shell, Smoke	15.25 pounds
Maximum Powder Pressure	29,000 psi	
Maximum Rate of Fire	8 rounds/minute	
Muzzle Velocity	HE M48 Shell (HE) Charge 4	1250 ft/sec
	HE M41A1 Shell (HE) Charge 4	1250 ft/sec
	HEAT M66 Shell (HEAT-T)	1000 ft/sec
	WP M64 Shell, Smoke, Charge 4	1250 ft/sec
Muzzle Energy of Projectile, KE=½MV²	HE M48 Shell (HE) Charge 4	158 ft-tons
Rotational energy is neglected and	HE M41A1 Shell (HE) Charge 4	149 ft-tons
values are based on long tons	HEAT M66 Shell (HEAT-T)	91 ft-tons
(2240 pounds)	WP M64 Shell, Smoke, Charge 4	165 ft-tons
Maximum Range (independent of mount)	HE M48 Shell (HE) Charge 4	9620 yards
	HE M41A1 Shell (HE) Charge 4	9650 yards
	HEAT M66 Shell (HEAT-T)	7900 yards
	WP M64 Shell, Smoke, Charge 4	9620 yards
Penetration Performance	Homogeneous steel armor at 0 degrees obliquity	
HEAT M66 Shell (HEAT-T)	3.6 inches at any range	

Muzzle Energy of Projectile, $KE = \frac{1}{2}MV^2$

Carriage and Mount	Medium Tank M7 in Mount M47 (M3 Gun)
	Light Tank M24 in Mount M64 (M6 and M17 Guns)
Length of Chamber (to rifling)	14.4 inches
Length of Rifling	96.2 inches
Length of Chamber (to projectile base)	12.96 inches (APC M61), 11.5 inches (HE M48)
Travel of Projectile in Bore	97.67 inches (APC M61), 99.1 inches (HE M48)
Length of Bore	110.63 inches, 37.5 calibers
Depth of Breech Recess	7.75 inches (M3 Gun), 5.75 inches (M6 and M17 Guns)
Length, Muzzle to Rear Face of Breech	
M3 Gun	118.38 inches, 40.1 calibers
M6 Gun	116.38 inches, 39.4 calibers
M17 Gun	116.4 inches, 39.4 calibers
Additional Length, Muzzle Brake, etc.	None (M3 and M6 Guns), approx. 5 inches (M17 Gun) w/Muzzle Brake M5
Overall Length	118.38 inches (M3 Gun), 116.38 inches (M6 Gun), approx. 121 inches (M17 Gun)
Diameter of Bore	2.950 inches (75mm)
Chamber Capacity	88.05 cubic inches (APC M61), 80.57 cubic inches (HE M48)
Total Weight	893 pounds (M3 Gun), 410 pounds (M6 Gun), 457 pounds (M17 Gun w/Muzzle Brake)
Type of Breechblock	Semiautomatic sliding wedge, gun mounted so breechblock slides at 45 degrees in Mount M47 and horizontally in Mount M64
Rifling	24 grooves, uniform right-hand twist, one turn in 25.59 calibers
Ammunition	Fixed
Primer	Percussion
Weight, Complete Round	APC M61 Projectile (APCBC/HE-T)	19.92 pounds
	HVAP T45 Shot (APCR-T)*	13.60 pounds
	AP M72 Shot (AP-T)	18.80 pounds
	HE M48 Shell (HE), Supercharge	19.56 pounds
	HE M48 Shell (HE), Normal	18.80 pounds
	HC BI M89 Shell, Smoke	9.83 pounds
	WP M64 Shell, Smoke	20.26 pounds
Weight, Projectile	APC M61 Projectile (APCBC/HE-T)	14.96 pounds
	HVAP T45 Shot (APCR-T)*	8.40 pounds
	AP M72 Shot (AP-T)	13.94 pounds
	HE M48 Shell (HE)	14.70 pounds
	HC BI M89 Shell, Smoke	6.61 pounds
	WP M64 Shell, Smoke	15.25 pounds
Maximum Powder Pressure	38,000 psi
Maximum Rate of Fire	20 rounds/minute
Muzzle Velocity	APC M61 Projectile (APCBC/HE-T)	2030 ft/sec
	HVAP T45 Shot (APCR-T)*	2850 ft/sec
	AP M72 Shot (AP-T)	2030 ft/sec
	HE M48 Shell (HE), Supercharge	1980 ft/sec
	HE M48 Shell (HE), Normal	1520 ft/sec
	HC BI M89 Shell, Smoke	850 ft/sec
	WP M64 Shell Smoke	1980 ft/sec
Muzzle Energy of Projectile, KE=½MV²	APC M61 Projectile (APCBC/HE-T)	427 ft-tons
Rotational energy is neglected and	HVAP T45 Shot (APCR-T)	473 ft-tons
values are based on long tons	AP M72 Shot (AP-T)	398 ft-tons
(2240 pounds)	HE M48 Shell (HE), Supercharge	400 ft-tons
	HE M48 Shell (HE), Normal	235 ft-tons
	HC BI M89 Shell, Smoke	33 ft-tons
	WP M64 Shell, Smoke	414 ft-tons
Maximum Range (independent of mount)	APC M61 Projectile (APCBC/HE-T)	14,000 yards
	AP M72 Shot (AP-T)	10,650 yards
	HE M48 Shell (HE), Supercharge	14,000 yards
	HE M48 Shell (HE), Normal	11,400 yards
	HC BI M89 Shell, Smoke (at 12 degrees elevation)	1,500 yards
	WP M64 Shell, Smoke	13,860 yards

Penetration Performance

Homogeneous steel armor at 30 degrees obliquity

Range	500 yards	1000 yards	1500 yards	2000 yards
APC M61 Projectile (APCBC/HE-T)	2.6 inches (66mm)	2.4 inches (60mm)	2.2 inches (55mm)	2.0 inches (50mm)
HVAP T45* (APCR-T)	4.6 inches (117mm)	3.8 inches (97mm)	3.1 inches (79mm)	2.5 inches (64mm)
AP M72 Shot (AP-T)	3.0 inches (76mm)	2.5 inches (63mm)	2.0 inches (51mm)	1.7 inches (43mm)

Face-hardened steel armor at 30 degrees obliquity

Range	500 yards	1000 yards	1500 yards	2000 yards
APC M61 Projectile (APCBC/HE-T)	2.9 inches (74mm)	2.6 inches (67mm)	2.4 inches (60mm)	2.1 inches (54mm)
AP M72 Shot (AP-T)	2.6 inches (66mm)	2.1 inches (53mm)	1.6 inches (41mm)	1.3 inches (33mm)

*Experimental only

Carriage and Mount	Motor Carriages T56 and T57 on a pedestal mount
Length of Chamber (to rifling)	23.15 inches
Length of Rifling	126.85 inches
Length of Chamber (to projectile base)	21.5 inches (square base projectiles)
Travel of Projectile in Bore	128.5 inches (square base projectiles)
Length of Bore	150.0 inches, 50.0 calibers
Depth of Breech Recess	8.1 inches
Length, Muzzle to Rear Face of Breech	158.1 inches, 52.7 calibers
Additional Length, Muzzle Brake, etc.	None
Overall Length	158.1 inches
Diameter of Bore	3.000 inches
Chamber Capacity	205.585 cubic inches (APC M62), 203.50 cubic inches (HE M42A1)
Total Weight	1990 pounds
Type of Breechblock	Semiautomatic, vertical sliding wedge
Rifling	28 grooves, uniform right-hand twist, one turn in 40 calibers
Ammunition	Fixed
Primer	Percussion

Weight, Complete Round		
	APC M62 Projectile (APCBC/HE-T)	27.24 pounds
	HVAP M93 Shot (APCR-T)	20.77 pounds
	AP M79 Shot (AP-T)	26.56 pounds
	HE M42A1 Shell (HE)	24.91 pounds
	HC BI M88 Shell, Smoke	15.40 pounds

Weight, Projectile		
	APC M62 Projectile (APCBC/HE-T)	15.44 pounds
	HVAP M93 Shot (APCR-T)	9.40 pounds
	AP M79 Shot (AP-T)	15.00 pounds
	HE M42A1 Shell (HE)	12.87 pounds
	HC BI M88 Shell, Smoke	7.38 pounds

Maximum Powder Pressure	38,000 psi
Maximum Rate of Fire	15 rounds/minute

Muzzle Velocity		
	APC M62 Projectile (APCBC/HE-T)	2600 ft/sec
	HVAP M93 Shot (APCR-T)	3400 ft/sec
	AP M79 Shot (AP-T)	2600 ft/sec
	HE M42A1 Shell (HE)	2800 ft/sec
	HC BI M88 Shell, Smoke	900 ft/sec

Muzzle Energy of Projectile, KE=$\frac{1}{2}MV^2$ Rotational energy is neglected and values are based on long tons (2240 pounds)		
	APC M62 Projectile (APCBC/HE-T)	724 ft-tons
	HVAP M93 Shot (APCR-T)	753 ft-tons
	AP M79 Shot (AP-T)	703 ft-tons
	HE M42A1 Shell (HE)	699 ft-tons
	HC BI M88 Shell, Smoke	41 ft-tons

Maximum Range (independent of mount)		
	APC M62 Projectile (APCBC/HE-T)	16,100 yards
	HVAP M93 Shot (APCR-T)	13,100 yards
	AP M79 Shot (AP-T)	12,770 yards
	HE M42A1 Shell (HE)	14,780 yards
	HC BI M88 Shell, Smoke (at 12 degrees elevation)	2,000 yards

Penetration Performance — Homogeneous steel armor at 30 degrees obliquity

Range	500 yards	1000 yards	1500 yards	2000 yards
APC M62 Projectile (APCBC/HE-T)	3.7 inches (93mm)	3.5 inches (88mm)	3.2 inches (82mm)	3.0 inches (75mm)
HVAP M93 Shot (APCR-T)	6.2 inches (157mm)	5.3 inches (135mm)	4.6 inches (116mm)	3.9 inches (98mm)
AP M79 (AP-T)	4.3 inches (109mm)	3.6 inches (92mm)	3.0 inches (76mm)	2.5 inches (64mm)

76mm GUNS M1A1, M1A1C AND M1A2

Carriage and Mount	Motor Carriages M18, T86, and T86E1 in Mount M1
Length of Chamber (to rifling)	22.46 inches
Length of Rifling	133.54 inches
Length of Chamber (to projectile base)	20.7 inches (square base projectiles)
Travel of Projectile in Bore	135.3 inches (square base projectiles)
Length of Bore	156.00 inches, 52.0 calibers
Depth of Breech Recess	7.75 inches
Length, Muzzle to Rear Face of Breech	163.75 inches, 54.6 calibers
Additional Length, Muzzle Brake, etc.	11.6 inches, Muzzle Brake M2 on M1A1C and M1A2 only
Overall Length	163.75 inches (M1A1), 175.4 inches (M1A1C and M1A2)
Diameter of Bore	3.000 inches
Chamber Capacity	142.6 cubic inches (APC M62), 140.50 cubic inches (HE M42A1)
Weight, Tube (w/o muzzle brake)	940 pounds (M1A1)
Weight, Complete (w/o muzzle brake)	1206 pounds (M1A1C), 1231 pounds (M1A2)
Weight, Muzzle Brake M2	62 pounds
Total Weight	1268 pounds (M1A1C), 1293 pounds (M1A2)
Type of Breechblock	Semiautomatic sliding wedge. Gun mounted so breechblock sides at 45 degrees in Mount M1
Rifling	28 grooves, uniform right-hand twist, one turn in 40 calibers (M1A1 and M1A1C) or 32 calibers (M1A2)
Ammunition	Fixed
Primer	Percussion
Weight, Complete Round	APC M62 Projectile (APCBC/HE-T) 24.80 pounds
	HVAP M93 Shot (APCR-T) 18.91 pounds
	AP M79 Shot (AP-T) 24.24 pounds
	HE M42A1 Shell (HE) 22.23 pounds
	HC BI M88 Shell, Smoke 13.43 pounds
Weight, Projectile	APC M62 Projectile (APCBC/HE-T) 15.44 pounds
	HVAP M93 Shot (APCR-T) 9.40 pounds
	AP M79 Shot (AP-T) 15.00 pounds
	HE M42A1 Shell (HE) 12.87 pounds
	HC BI M88 Shell, Smoke 7.38 pounds
Maximum Powder Pressure	43,000 psi
Maximum Rate of Fire	20 rounds/minute
Muzzle Velocity	APC M62 Projectile (APCBC/HE-T) 2600 ft/sec
	HVAP M93 Shot (APCR-T) 3400 ft/sec
	AP M79 Shot (AP-T) 2600 ft/sec
	HE M42A1 Shell (HE) 2700 ft/sec
	HC BI M88 Shell, Smoke 900 ft/sec
Muzzle Energy of Projectile, $KE=\frac{1}{2}MV^2$ Rotational energy is neglected and values are based on long tons (2240 pounds)	APC M62 Projectile (APCBC/HE-T) 724 ft-tons
	HVAP M93 Shot (APCR-T) 753 ft-tons
	AP M79 Shot (AP-T) 703 ft-tons
	HE M42A1 Shell (HE) 650 ft-tons
	HC BI M88 Shell, Smoke 41 ft-tons
Maximum Range (independent of mount)	APC M62 Projectile (APCBC/HE-T) 16,100 yards
	HVAP M93 Shot (APCR-T) 13,100 yards
	AP M79 Shot (AP-T) 12,770 yards
	HE M42A1 Shell (HE) 14,200 yards
	HC BI M88 Shell, Smoke (at 12 degrees elevation) 2,000 yards
Penetration Performance*	Homogeneous steel armor at 30 degrees obliquity

Range	500 yards	1000 yards	1500 yards	2000 yards
APC M62 Projectile (APCBC/HE-T)	3.7 inches (93mm)	3.5 inches (88mm)	3.2 inches (82mm)	3.0 inches (76mm)
HVAP M93 Shot (APCR-T)	6.2 inches (157mm)	5.3 inches (135mm)	4.6 inches (116mm)	3.9 inches (98mm)
AP M79 Shot (AP-T)	4.3 inches (109mm)	3.6 inches (92mm)	3.0 inches (76mm)	2.5 inches (64mm)

* Penetration values are for the M1A1 gun. A slight increase for APC was obtained with the M1A2 gun at the longer ranges.

502

90mm GUN M3

Carriage and Mount	Installed experimentally on Motor Carriage M18 in the M36 turret
	Proposed for use on the Motor Carriage T78
Length of Chamber (to rifling)	24.8 inches
Length of Rifling	152.4 inches
Length of Chamber (to projectile base)	20.8 inches (boat-tailed projectiles)
Travel of Projectile in Bore	156.4 inches (boat-tailed projectiles)
Length of Bore	177.15 inches, 50.0 calibers
Depth of Breech Recess	9.00 inches
Length, Muzzle to Rear Face of Breech	186.15 inches, 52.5 calibers
Additional Length, Muzzle Brake, etc.	16.0 inches, Muzzle Brake M3 on late production guns
Overall Length	202.2 inches with Muzzle Brake M3
Diameter of Bore	3.543 inches (90mm)
Chamber Capacity	300 cubic inches
Weight, Complete (w/o muzzle brake)	2300 pounds
Weight, Muzzle Brake M3	149.5 pounds
Total Weight	2450 pounds
Type of Breechblock	Semiautomatic vertical sliding wedge
Rifling	32 grooves, uniform right-hand twist, one turn in 32 calibers
Ammunition	Fixed
Primer	Percussion

Weight, Complete Round	APC M82 Projectile (APCBC/HE-T) early	42.75 pounds
	APC M82 Projectile (APCBC/HE-T) late	43.87 pounds
	HVAP M304 (T30E16) Shot (APCR-T)	37.13 pounds
	AP T33 Shot (APBC-T)	43.82 pounds
	HE M71 Shell (HE)	41.93 pounds
	WP M313 Shell, Smoke	41.93 pounds
Weight, Projectile	APC M82 Projectile (APCBC/HE-T)	24.11 pounds
	HVAP M304 (T30E16) Shot (APCR-T)	16.80 pounds
	AP T33 Shot (APBC-T)	24.06 pounds
	HE M71 Shell (HE)	23.29 pounds
	WP M313 Shell, Smoke	23.29 pounds
Maximum Powder Pressure	38,000 psi	
Maximum Rate of Fire	8 rounds/minute	
Muzzle Velocity	APC M82 Projectile (APCBC/HE-T) early	2650 ft/sec
	APC M82 Projectile (APCBC/HE-T) late	2800 ft/sec
	HVAP M304 (T30E16) Shot (APCR-T)	3350 ft/sec
	AP T33 Shot (APBC-T)	2800 ft/sec
	HE M71 Shell (HE)	2700 ft/sec
	WP M313 Shell, Smoke	2700 ft/sec
Muzzle Energy of Projectile, KE=½MV²	APC M82 Projectile (APCBC/HE-T) early	1174 ft-tons
Rotational energy is neglected and	APC M82 Projectile (APCBC/HE-T) late	1310 ft-tons
values are based on long tons	HVAP M304 (T30E16) Shot (APCR-T)	1307 ft-tons
(2240 pounds)	AP T33 Shot (APBC-T)	1310 ft-tons
	HE M71 Shell (HE)	1177 ft-tons
	WP M313 Shell, Smoke	1177 ft-tons
Maximum Range (independent of mount)	APC M82 Projectile (APCBC/HE-T) early	20,400 yards
	APC M82 Projectile (APCBC/HE-T) late	21,400 yards
	HVAP M304 (T30E16) Shot (APCR-T)	15,700 yards
	AP T33 Shot (APBC-T)	21,000 yards
	HE M71 Shell (HE)	19,560 yards
	WP M313 Shell, Smoke	19,560 yards

Penetration Performance — Homogeneous steel armor at 30 degrees obliquity

Range	500 yards	1000 yards	1500 yards	2000 yards
APC M82 Projectile (APCBC/HE-T) early	4.7 inches (120mm)	4.4 inches (112mm)	4.1 inches (104mm)	3.8 inches (96mm)
APC M82 Projectile (APCBC/HE-T) late	5.1 inches (129mm)	4.8 inches (122mm)	4.5 inches (114mm)	4.2 inches (106mm)
HVAP M304 (T30E16) Shot (APCR-T)	8.7 inches (221mm)	7.9 inches (200mm)	7.0 inches (178mm)	6.1 inches (156mm)
AP T33 Shot (APBC-T)	4.7 inches (119mm)	4.6 inches (117mm)	4.5 inches (114mm)	4.3 inches (109mm)

105mm HOWITZER M3

Carriage and Mount	Motor Carriage T82 in modified Mount M3A1
Length of Chamber (to rifling)	15.0 inches
Length of Rifling	51.0 inches
Length of Chamber (to projectile base)	11.4 inches (boat-tailed projectiles)
Travel of Projectile in Bore	54.6 inches (boat-tailed projectiles)
Length of Bore	66.0 inches, 16.0 calibers
Depth of Breech Recess	8.3 inches
Length, Muzzle to Rear Face of Breech	74.3 inches, 17.9 calibers
Additional Length, Muzzle Brake, etc.	None
Overall Length	74.3 inches
Diameter of Bore	4.134 inches (105mm)
Chamber Capacity	153.80 cubic inches
Total Weight	955 pounds
Type of Breechblock	Manually operated, horizontal sliding wedge
Rifling	36 grooves, uniform right-hand twist, one turn in 20 calibers
Ammunition	Semifixed, variable charge except for HEAT M67
Primer	Percussion

Weight, Complete Round	HE M1 Shell (HE), Charge 5	40.46 pounds
	HEAT M67 Shell (HEAT-T)	36.65 pounds
	HC BE M84 Shell, Smoke, Charge 5	40.32 pounds
	WP M60 Shell, Smoke, Charge 5	41.83 pounds
Weight, Projectile	HE M1 Shell (HE)	33.00 pounds
	HEAT M67 Shell (HEAT-T)	29.22 pounds
	HC BE M84 Shell, Smoke	32.87 pounds
	WP M60 Shell, Smoke	34.31 pounds
Maximum Powder Pressure	28,000 psi	
Maximum Rate of Fire	8 rounds/minute	
Muzzle Velocity	HE M1 Shell (HE), Charge 5	1020 ft/sec
	HEAT M67 Shell (HEAT-T)	1020 ft/sec
	HC BE M84 Shell, Smoke, Charge 5	1020 ft/sec
	WP M60 Shell, Smoke, Charge 5	1020 ft/sec
Muzzle Energy of Projectile, $KE = \frac{1}{2}MV^2$	HE M1 Shell (HE), Charge 5	238 ft-tons
Rotational energy is neglected and	HEAT M67 Shell (HEAT-T)	211 ft-tons
values are based on long tons	HC BE M84 Shell, Smoke, Charge 5	237 ft-tons
(2240 pounds)	WP M60 Shell, Smoke, Charge 5	247 ft-tons
Maximum Range (independent of mount)	HE M1 Shell (HE), Charge	5 8295 yards
	HEAT M67 Shell (HEAT-T)	8490 yards
	HC BE M84 Shell, Smoke, Charge 5	8295 yards
	WP M60 Shell, Smoke, Charge 5	8295 yards

Penetration Performance
   HEAT M67 Shell (HEAT-T)

Homogeneous steel armor at 0 degrees obliquity
    4.0 inches at any range

Concrete at 0 degrees obliquity

	Range	0 yards	500 yards	1000 yards	2000 yards
HE M1 Shell, Charge 5, w/Concrete Piercing Fuze M78 (T105)		1.0 feet	0.9 feet	0.8 feet	0.7 feet

Carriage and Mount	Motor Carriage M37 in Mount M5
Length of Chamber (to rifling)	15.03 inches
Length of Rifling	78.02 inches
Length of Chamber (to projectile base)	11.38 inches (boat-tailed projectiles)
Travel of Projectile in Bore	81.67 inches (boat-tailed projectiles)
Length of Bore	93.05 inches, 22.5 calibers
Depth of Breech Recess	8.25 inches
Length, Muzzle to Rear Face of Breech	101.30 inches, 24.5 calibers
Additional Length, Muzzle Brake, etc.	None
Overall Length	101.30 inches
Diameter of Bore	4.134 inches (105mm)
Chamber Capacity	153.80 cubic inches
Total Weight	1140 pounds
Type of Breechblock	Manually operated, horizontal sliding wedge
Rifling	36 grooves, uniform right-hand twist, one turn in 20 calibers
Ammunition	Semifixed, variable charge except for HEAT M67
Primer	Percussion

Weight, Complete Round		
	HE M1 Shell (HE), Charge 7	42.07 pounds
	HEAT M67 Shell (HEAT-T)	36.85 pounds
	HC BE M84 Shell, Smoke, Charge 7	41.94 pounds
	WP M60 Shell, Smoke, Charge 7	43.77 pounds
Weight, Projectile	HE M1 Shell (HE)	33.00 pounds
	HEAT M67 Shell (HEAT-T)	29.22 pounds
	HC BE M84 Shell, Smoke	32.97 pounds
	WP M60 Shell, Smoke	34.31 pounds
Maximum Powder Pressure	28,000 psi	
Maximum Rate of Fire	8 rounds/minute	
Muzzle Velocity	HE M1 Shell (HE), Charge 7	1550 ft/sec
	HEAT M67 Shell (HEAT-T)	1250 ft/sec
	HC BE M84 Shell, Smoke, Charge 7	1550 ft/sec
	WP M60 Shell, Smoke, Charge 7	1550 ft/sec
Muzzle Energy of Projectile, KE=½MV²	HE M1 Shell (HE), Charge 7	550 ft-tons
Rotational energy is neglected and	HEAT M67 Shell (HEAT-T)	317 ft-tons
values are based on long tons	HC BE M84 Shell, Smoke, Charge 7	547 ft-tons
(2240 pounds)	WP M60 Shell, Smoke, Charge 7	571 ft-tons
Maximum Range (independent of mount)	HE M1 Shell (HE), Charge 7	12,205 yards
	HEAT M67 Shell (HEAT-T)	8,590 yards
	HC BE M84 Shell, Smoke, Charge 7	12,205 yards
	WP M60 Shell, Smoke, Charge 7	12,150 yards

Penetration Performance
    HEAT M67   Homogeneous steel armor at 0 degrees obliquity
        4.0 inches at any range
    Concrete at 0 degrees obliquity

Range	0 yards	500 yards	1000 yards	2000 yards
HE M1 Shell, Charge 7 w/Concrete Piercing Fuze M78 (T105)	1.5 feet	1.4 feet	1.3 feet	1.1 feet

4.5 inch GUN M1

Carriage and Mount	Motor Carriage T16 in Mount M1
Length of Chamber (to rifling)	30.41 inches
Length of Rifling	156.83 inches
Length of Chamber (to projectile base)	25.08 inches
Travel of Projectile in Bore	162.16 inches
Length of Bore	187.24 inches, 41.6 calibers
Depth of Breech Recess	6.40 inches
Length, Muzzle to Rear Face of Breech	193.64 inches, 43.0 calibers
Additional Length, Breech Mechanism	7 inches approx.
Overall Length	201 inches approx.
Diameter of Bore	4.50 inches
Chamber Capacity	531 cubic inches
Total Weight	4075 pounds
Type of Breechblock	Stepped thread, interrupted screw, horizontal swing
Rifling	32 grooves, uniform right-hand twist, one turn in 25 calibers
Ammunition	Separate loading
Primer	Percussion

Weight, Complete Round	HE M65 Shell (HE)	61.963 pounds
	HE M65 Shell (HE) Supercharge	66.315 pounds
Weight, Projectile	HE M65 Shell (HE)	54.90 pounds
Maximum Powder Pressure	40,000 psi	
Maximum Rate of Fire	4 rounds/minute	
Muzzle Velocity	HE M65 Shell (HE)	1820 ft/sec
	HE M65 Shell (HE) Supercharge	2275 ft/sec
Muzzle Energy of Projectile, KE=½MV²	HE M65 Shell (HE)	1261 ft-tons
Rotational energy is neglected and values are based on long tons (2240 pounds)	HE M65 Shell (HE) Supercharge	1970 ft-tons
Maximum Range (independent of mount)	HE M65 Shell (HE)	16,650 yards
	HE M65 Shell (HE) Supercharge	21,125 yards

Penetration Performance
Concrete at 0 degrees obliquity

Range	0 yards	1000 yards	5000 yards	10,000 yards
HE M65 Shell (HE) w/Concrete Piercing Fuze M78 (T105)	3.8 feet	3.5 feet	2.1 feet	1.2 feet

155mm HOWITZER M1

Carriage and Mount	Motor Carriage M41 (T64E1) in Mount M14 (T19)
Length of Chamber (to rifling)	27.2 inches
Length of Rifling	113.10 inches
Length of Chamber (to projectile base)	19.6 inches (boat-tailed projectiles)
Travel of Projectile in Bore	120.68 inches (boat-tailed projectiles)
Length of Bore	140.3 inches, 23.0 calibers
Depth of Breech Recess	8.9 inches
Length, Muzzle to Rear Face of Breech	149.2 inches, 24.5 calibers
Additional Length, Breech Mechanism	5 inches approx.
Overall Length	154 inches approx.
Diameter of Bore	6.102 inches (155mm)
Chamber Capacity	725 cubic inches
Total Weight	3825 pounds
Type of Breechblock	Stepped thread, interrupted screw, horizontal swing
Rifling	48 grooves, uniform right-hand twist, one turn in 25 calibers
Ammunition	Separate loading
Primer	Percussion

Weight, Complete Round	HE M107 Shell (HE), Charge M4A1	108.91 pounds
	HC BE M116 Shell, Smoke, Charge M4A1	109.01 pounds
	H M110 Shell, Chemical, Charge M4A1	109.11 pounds
Weight, Projectile	HE M107 Shell (HE)	95.00 pounds
	HC BE M116 Shell, Smoke	95.10 pounds
	H M110 Shell, Chemical	95.20 pounds
Maximum Powder Pressure	32,000 psi	
Maximum Rate of Fire	4 rounds/minute	
Muzzle Velocity	HE M107 Shell (HE), Charge M4A1	1850 ft/sec
	HC BE M116 Shell, Smoke, Charge M4A1	1850 ft/sec
	H M110 Shell, Chemical, Charge M4A1	1850 ft/sec
Muzzle Energy of Projectile, $KE=\frac{1}{2}MV^2$	HE M107 Shell (HE), Charge M4A1	2254 ft-tons
Rotational energy is neglected and	HC BE M116 Shell, Smoke, Charge M4A1	2256 ft-tons
values are based on long tons	H M110 Shell, Chemical, Charge M4A1	2259 ft-tons
(2240 pounds)		
Maximum Range (independent of mount)	HE M107 Shell (HE), Charge M4A1	16,355 yards
	HC BE M116 Shell, Smoke, Charge M4A1	16,355 yards
	H M110 Shell, Chemical, Charge M4A1	16,374 yards

Penetration Performance		Concrete at 0 degrees obliquity			
	Range	0 yards	1000 yards	3000 yards	5000 yards
HE M107 Shell (HE) w/Concrete Piercing Fuze M78 (T105)		2.9 feet	2.6 feet	2.0 feet	1.6 feet

REFERENCES AND SELECTED BIBLIOGRAPHY

Books and Manuscripts

Appleman, Roy E., "South to the Naktong, North to the Yalu", The U.S. Army in the Korean War, Office of the Chief of Military History, Washington, D.C., 1961

Barnes, Lieutenant Colonel Gladeon M., "Tank Development Program for the U.S. Army", Army War College, 15 April 1938

Chase, Daniel, "A History of Combat Vehicle Development", unpublished manuscript

Jones, Major Ralph E., Rarey, Captain George H., Icks, First Lieutenant Robert J., "The Fighting Tanks Since 1916", The National Service Publishing Company, Washington, D.C., June 1933

Koyen, Captain Kenneth, "The Fourth Armored Division from the Beach to Bavaria", published 1946

Perkins, Major Norris H. and Rogers, Michael E., "Roll Again Second Armored, The Prelude to Fame 1940-1943", Produced and published for the authors by Kristall Productions Ltd, Surbiton, Surrey, England, 1988

Robinett, Brigadier General Paul McDonald, "Armor Command", published 1948

Rubel, Colonel George Kenneth, "Daredevil Tankers, The Story of the 740th Tank Battalion", published 19 September 1945

Wagner, William, "Continental, Its Motors and its People", Armed Forces Journal International with Aero Publishers, Inc., Fallbrook, California, 1983

Whiting, Theodore E., Crawford, Richard H., and Cook, Lindsley F., "Statistics: Procurement", The U.S. Army in World War II, Office of the Chief of Military History, Washington, D.C., 9 April 1952

Whiting, Theodore E., Todd, Carrel I., Craft, Anne P., "Statistics: Lend-Lease", The U.S. Army in World War II, Office of the Chief of Military History, Washington, D.C., 15 December 1952

Wilson, Dale E., "Treat 'Em Rough, The Birth of American Armor, 1917-1920", Presidio Press, Novato, California, 1989

Reports and Offical Documents

"Catalogue of Standard Ordnance Items—Tanks and Automotive Vehicles", Office of the Chief of Ordnance, Washington, D.C., Revised to June 1945

"The Design, Development, and Production of Tanks in World War II", Office of the Chief of Ordnance, Washington, D.C., 15 August 1944

"The Employment of Armor in Korea, Volume I", The Armor School, Fort Knox, Kentucky, 1952

"Fire Warfare", Office of Scientific Research and Development, National Defense Research Committee, Washington, D.C., 1946

"A Handbook of Ordnance Automotive Engineering—Combat and Tracklaying Vehicles", Aberdeen Proving Ground, Maryland, 1 May 1945

"Handbook of the Six-ton Special Tractor Model 1917", War Department, Washington, D.C., July 15, 1918

"New Ordnance Materiel", Office of the Chief of Ordnance, Washington, D.C., January 1945

"Notes on Materiel, Light Tank T24E1", American Car & Foundry Company, Berwick, Pennsylvania, 28 December 1944

"Notes on the Medium Tank M7", Rock Island Arsenal, Illinois, February 1943

"Pacific Area Materiel" Office of the Chief of Ordnance, Washington, D.C., July 1945

"Record of Army Ordnance Research and Development—Tanks", Office of the Chief of Ordnance, Washington, D.C., undated

"Report of the Fiscal Year 1944-1945, Research and Development Service", Office of the Chief of Ordnance, Washington, D.C., October 1945

"Research, Investigation & Experimentation in the Field of Amphibian Vehicles for the United States Marine Corps", Final Report, Ingersoll Kalamazoo Division, Borg-Warner Corporation, Kalamazoo, Michigan, December 1957

"Summary of Combat Vehicle Development", Office of the Chief of Ordnance, Detroit, Michigan, 1945

"Technical Manual TM9-252, 40mm Automatic Gun M1 (AA) and 40mm Anti-aircraft Gun Carriages M2 and M2A1", War Department, Washington, D.C., 17 January 1944

"Technical Manual TM9-303, 57mm Guns M1 and Mk III (British) and Carriages M1, M1A1, M1A2, M1A3, and M2", War Department, Washington, D.C., 25 April 1944

"Technical Manual TM9-307, 75mm Tank Guns M2 and M3 and Mounts M1, M34, and M34A1", War Department, Washington, D.C., 23 March 1944

"Technical Manual TM9-312, 75mm Gun AN-M5 and Aircraft Mount AN-M9", War Department, Washington, D.C., 16 November 1944

"Technical Manual TM9-313, 75mm Gun M6 and Combination Gun Mount M64", Department of the Army, Washington, D.C., 27 January 1948

"Technical Manual TM9-318, 75mm Howitzers M2 and M3", War Department, Washington, D.C., 14 December 1944

"Technical Manual TM9-324, 105mm Howitzer M4 (Mounted in Combat Vehicles)", Department of the Army, Washington, D.C., August 1950

"Technical Manual TM9-717, 105mm Howitzer Motor Carriage M37", Department of the Army, Washington, D.C., 6 October 1947

"Technical Manual TM9-724, Light Tank T9E1", War Department, Washington, D.C., 17 November 1943

"Technical Manual TM9-725, Light Tanks", War Department, Washington, D.C., May 15, 1941

"Technical Manual TM9-726, Light Tank M3", War Department, Washington, D.C., July 15, 1942

"Technical Manual TM9-727, Light Tanks M3A1 and M3A3", War Department, Washington, D.C., 4 December 1943

"Technical Manual TM9-729, Light Tank T24", War Department, Washington, D.C., 27 June 1944

"Technical Manual TM9-732, Light Tanks M5 and M5A1", War Department, Washington, D.C., 27 November 1943

"Technical Manual TM9-732B, 75mm Howitzer Motor Carriage M8", War Department, Washington, D.C., October 10, 1942

"Technical Manual TM9-744, 155mm Howitzer Motor Carriage M41", War Department, Washington, D.C., 17 September 1947

"Technical Manual TM9-755, 76mm Gun Motor Carriage M18 and Armored Utility Vehicle M39", War Department, Washington, D.C., 25 April 1945

"Technical Manual TM9-757, Twin 40mm Gun Motor Carriage M19", War Department, Washington, D.C., 7 July 1945

"Technical Manual TM9-761, Twin 40mm Gun Motor Carriage M19A1", Department of the Army, Washington, D.C., 3 March 1953

"Technical Manual TM9-775, Tracked Landing Vehicles (Armored) Mk 1 (LVT(A)(1) and Mk2 (LVT(A)(2), Tracked Landing Vehicle Mk 2 (LVT(2)", War Department, Washington, D.C., 5 February 1944

"Technical Manual TM9-775, Tracked Landing Vehicle Mk 4 (LVT(4), Tracked Landing Vehicles (Armored) Mk 4 (LVT(A)(4) and Mk 5 (LVT(A)(5)", Department of the Army, Washington, D.C., June 1951

"Technical Manual TM9-1728, Ordnance Maintenance, Power Train for Light Tanks M3 and M3A1", War Department, Washington, D.C., April 8, 1942

"Technical Manual TM9-1729B, Ordnance Maintenance, Light Tank M24 and Twin 40mm Gun Motor Carriage M19—Transmission, Transfer Unit, Propeller Shaft, Controlled Differential, and Final Drives", War Department, Washington, D.C., 10 February 1945

"Technical Manual TM9-1729C, Ordnance Maintenance, Light Tank M24 and 155mm Howitzer Motor Carriage M41—Tracks, Suspension, Hull, and Turret", War Department, Washington, D.C., 9 September 1947

"Technical Manual TM9-2853, Preparation of Ordnance Materiel for Deep Water Fording", War Department, Washington, D.C., 7 July 1945